D1674101

International Civil Aviation

INTERNATIONAL CIVIL AVIATION

Treaties, Institutions and Programmes

Dick van het Kaar

international publishing

Published, sold and distributed by Eleven International Publishing
P.O. Box 85576
2508 CG The Hague
The Netherlands
Tel.: +31 70 33 070 33
Fax: +31 70 33 070 30
e-mail: sales@elevenpub.nl
www.elevenpub.com

Sold and distributed in USA and Canada
Independent Publishers Group
814 N. Franklin Street
Chicago, IL 60610
USA
Order Placement: (800) 888-4741
Fax: (312) 337-5985
orders@ipgbook.com
www.ipgbook.com

Eleven International Publishing is an imprint of Boom uitgevers Den Haag.

ISBN 978-94-6236-972-6
ISBN 978-94-6274-221-1 (E-book)

© 2019 Dick van het Kaar | Eleven International Publishing

Printed in the Netherlands

Table of Contents

Abbreviations

ACAS	Airborne Collision Avoidance System
ACI	Airports Council International
AFCAC	African Civil Aviation Commission
AFTN	Aeronautical Fixed Telecommunication Network
AFUA	Advanced Flexible Use of Airspace
AIP	Aeronautical Information Publication
AIS	Aeronautical Information Service
AMC	Acceptable Means of Compliance
ANC	Air Navigation Commission
APEC	Asia-Pacific Economic Cooperation
ASAM	ASEAN Single Aviation Market
ASEAN	Association of Southeast Asian Nations
ASIAP	Aviation Safety Implementation Assistance Partnership
ATC	Air Traffic Control
ATM	Air Traffic Management
ATS	Air Traffic Service
CAA	Civil Aviation Authority
CAB	Civil Aeronautics Board
CAEP	Committee on Aviation Environment Protection
CATA	Comprehensive Air Transport Agreement
CITEJA	Comité International Technique d'Experts Juridiques Aériens
CNS/ATM	Communications, Navigation, Surveillance/Air Traffic Management
CORSIA	Carbon Offsetting and Reduction Scheme for International Aviation
COSPAS	Cosmicheskaya Sistema Poiska Avariynyh Sudov
CRS	Computer Reservation System
DGCA	Directors General of Civil Aviation
DME	Distance Measuring Equipment
DOT	US Department of Transportation
EASA	European Aviation Safety Agency
EASTI	European Aviation Security Training Institute
EC	European Community
ECA	European Cockpit Association

ECAA	European Common Aviation Area
ECAC	European Civil Aviation Conference
ECJ	European Court of Justice
EDTO	Extended Diversion Time Operation
EEA	European Express Association
EFPL	Extended Flight Plan
EFTA	European Free Trade Association
ELT	Emergency Locator Transmitter
ETOPS	Extended Twin Operations
ETS	Emissions Trading System
EU	European Union
EUROCONTROL	European Organization for the Safety of Air Navigation
FAA	Federal Aviation Administration of the United States
FIR	Flight Information Region
GADSS	Global Aeronautical Distress and Safety System
GANP	Global Air Navigation Plan
GASP	Global Aviation Safety Plan
GMT	Greenwich Mean Time
GNSS	Global Navigation Satellite System
IASA	International Aviation Safety Assessment Program
IASTA	International Air Services Transit Agreement
IATA	International Air Transport Association
ICAN	International Commission for Air Navigation
ICAO	International Civil Aviation Organization
ICJ	International Court of Justice
IDERA	Irrevocable De-Registration and Export Request Authorization
IETC	International Explosives Technical Commission
IFALPA	International Federation of Air Line Pilots' Associations
IFFAS	International Financial Facility for Aviation Safety
IFR	Instrument Flight Rules
ILS	Instrument Landing System
IMO	International Maritime Organization
IOSA	IATA Operational Safety Audit
ISCS	International Satellite Communication System
ISSG	Industry Safety Strategy Group
ITU	International Telecommunication Union
JAA	Joint Aviation Authorities

JAR	Joint Aviation Requirements
MALIAT	Multilateral Agreement on the Liberalization of International Air Transportation
MEOSAR	Medium-altitude Orbit Satellite System for Search and Rescue
NOTAM	Notice to Airmen
OAA	Open Aviation Area
OCC	Operational Control Centre
OECD	Organization for Economic Cooperation and Development
PANS	Procedures for Air Navigation Services
PEL	Personnel Licensing
PICAO	Provisional International Civil Aviation Organization
RCC	Rescue Coordination Centre
RNAV	Area Navigation
RPAS	Remotely Piloted Aerial System
SAATM	Single African Air Transport Market
SACA	Safety Assessment of Community Aircraft
SADIS	Secure Aviation Data Information Service
SAFA	Safety Assessment of Foreign Aircraft
SAR	Search and Rescue
SARPs	International Standards and Recommended Practices
SARSAT	Search and Rescue Satellite Aided Tracking
SES	Single European Sky
SESAR	Single European Sky ATM Research
SI	International System of Units
SJU	Single European Sky ATM Joint Undertaking
SMS	Safety Management System
SSO	State Safety Oversight
SSP	State Safety Programme
SSR	Secondary Surveillance Radar
STOL	Short Take-off and Landing
SWIM	System-wide Information Management
TFEU	Treaty on the Functioning of the European Union
UK	United Kingdom
ULB	Underwater Locator Beacon
UN	United Nations
US	United States of America
USAP	Universal Security Oversight Audit Programme

USOAP	Universal Safety Oversight Audit Programme
USSR	Union of Soviet Socialist Republics
UTC	Universal Time Coordinated
VFR	Visual Flight Rules
XML	Extensible Markup Language
YD	Yamoussoukro Decision

PREFACE

Codification of international law:

Under Article 15 of the International Law Commission Statute of 1947, the expression 'codification of international law' is used for convenience as meaning the more precise formulation and systematization of rules of international law in fields where there already has been extensive State practice, precedent and doctrine, whereas the expression 'progressive development of international law' is used for convenience as meaning the preparation of draft conventions on subjects which have not yet been regulated by international law or in regard to which the law has not yet been sufficiently developed in the practice of States.

This treatise was made in response to a question of a senior lecturer of the Aviation Academy of the Amsterdam University of Applied Sciences. Air law is an integral part of bachelor's and master's programmes of the Aviation Academy for which the content is obtained from a variety of air law-related books and documents. However, there was a need for a single, more compact reference book.

The answer to the question was a comprehensive treatise, adapted to reflect international aviation treaties, institutions and aviation safety-related programmes. The international courses of study offered by the Aviation Academy mainly focus on operational aviation processes, aircraft design, airworthiness and maintenance, airline network planning, aerodrome and airspace infrastructure and aviation safety and security. These and other related subjects, all have a history of creation up to the amended format of today. The relevant rules and standards are determined by treaties, elaborated and issued by various organizations such as the International Civil Aviation Organization (ICAO), implemented, executed and enforced by States and assessed by aviation safety audit programmes.

This treatise should be viewed as a basic reference source and not as an exhaustive piece of work. It is intended to serve as a study guideline as well as a purely informative book by describing the most significant treaties, institutions and safety programmes in the field of civil aviation in the last 100 years.[1]

In that particular time span, the aviation industry has made tremendous progress. Obviously, this also applies to a diversity of aviation rules and regulations, from elemen-

---

1   Treaty means an international agreement concluded between States in written form and governed by international law, whether embodied in a single instrument or in two or more related instruments and whatever its particular designation (Art. 2. Use of terms, Vienna Convention on the Law of Treaties, done at Vienna on 23 May 1969, entered into force on 27 January 1980). The Vienna Convention applies to treaties between States.

tary regulations to smart regulation principles, modern customized regulations intended for specific aviation target groups.

Due to the international character of civil aviation, comprehensive international legal regulations have been developed. Each and every year, billions of scheduled passengers (about 4.3 billion in 2018) are travelling by air all over the world, which undoubtedly demonstrates the globalizing nature of international air traffic. To regulate this tremendous flow of air traffic, a harmonized and uniform international legal framework is even more essential in the coming years.

Air transport has unique characteristics compared with other industries in the world. Within the next 15 years, air traffic will approximately be doubled, according to the passengers growth forecast of the International Air Transport Association (IATA). As a consequence, more and more areas in the world will have to deal with increasing air traffic in a finite amount of airspace.

Moreover, the introduction of Unmanned Aerial Systems (UAS), in any capacity whatsoever, within non-segregated and seemingly congested and complex airspace, needs adequate rules and regulations, mainly to ensure aviation safety.

In addition to the currently valid basic rules and regulations, new customized rules and modifications to the existing regulations will continue to be required in the future world of aviation. In this ever-expanding international aviation domain, with air carriers connecting a record number of cities across the world, with doubling numbers of unique city-pair connections within 20 years, the challenges to regulate global air traffic are immense, which could not have been imagined in the early years of aviation. Air traffic in those years was rather primitive, albeit rapidly increasing in the aftermath of World War I.

Due to the start of scheduled air services on a more or less regular basis, it was considered necessary to incorporate principal rules, applicable to all States, into conventions.[2] Since there is no actual 'Code of International Air Law', international air law is made mainly on a decentralized basis by the actions of practically all States which together form the international world community. Codification of air law principles appeared to be successful.

Legal regulation of air traffic was studied as early as 1901. Earlier local rules, such as a number of (local) government decrees prohibiting hot air balloons from flying without a special permit over densely populated areas to protect persons and property on the ground, only had limited legal significance. Due to the increase of air traffic following the first successful flights of the Wright brothers, State authorities realized that more stringent national rules regarding air navigation were deemed necessary. But it soon

---

2   On 25 August 1919, the first regular international daily air service in the world started between Hounslow Heath Aerodrome, London and Le Bourget, Paris, operated by the British Aircraft Transport and Travel Ltd. (AT&T). However, the world's first (national) scheduled passenger airline service (by airboat) was started on 1 January 1914 between St. Petersburg and Tampa, Florida, USA.

became clear that not only national rules should be complied with. Crossing of national borders by aircraft especially gave rise to conflicts and was a reason to attempt to regulate the operational issues of flight into and over foreign territory.

In Europe, in 1902, the *Institut de Droit International* met in Brussels and considered a proposed convention on the regulation of aerial navigation. A French jurist, Dr. Paul Auguste Joseph Fauchille, a pioneer of air law, assisted by the Brussels lawyer Ernest Nys, proclaimed his famous doctrine of freedom of the air as an analogy to the freedoms of the seas. This treatise was entitled *Le Domaine Aérien et le Régime Juridique des Aérostats*. Fauchille argued that there should be a freedom of the air meaning unrestricted freedom of flight over the territory of any other State up to a certain altitude. With respect to the legal status of airspace, he emphasized that the air, as free as the seas, cannot be appropriated and occupied.

However, a year later, he differentiated this freedom with regard to public or private airspace use insofar as the State in question should be entitled to impose restrictions upon the free use of airspace for reasons of security, foreign military interference and health. In other words, the air is only subject to the rights of States in the interest of their self-preservation. Sovereignty in international law does not involve the same concept of possession as private law, because it is about control and not physical possession. To outline the concept of sovereignty, a distinction should be made between *terra nullius*, the high seas (*Grotius*) and free flight space, insofar as it relates to the issue of possession.

There is a difference between the three spaces or spatial areas: *terra nullius* can be occupied by individual States, while the high seas and free flight space cannot be occupied. Recognizable similarities are: the spaces are not created under the sovereignty of any State and every State and its nationals have the right to fly in the airspace above its own territory, while in time of peace, no State may exercise jurisdiction over an aircraft flying the flag of another State in these spaces, except by consent or in cases of piracy or self-defence.[3]

13 October 1919 was the date the first international multilateral treaty on civil aviation, the Convention Relating to the Regulation of Aerial Navigation, was concluded in Paris. Considering this Paris Convention as the first international aviation legal framework, it will be the starting point of this treatise, though in this context it is noteworthy that it was preceded by the failed but constructive 1910 Paris International Air Navigation Conference (*Conférence Internationale de Navigation Aérienne, Paris 18 mai-28 juin 1910*), in terms of a determining factor with respect to later aviation treaties.

---

3   Melgar, B.H., *The Transit of Goods in Public International Law,* Leiden: Brill Nijhoff, 2015, p. 88.

During the 1910 Paris Conference, delegations challenged each other through doctrinal debates whether freedom of the air or complete and exclusive sovereignty over the territorial airspace was to become the new official legal standard.[4] Following lengthy theoretical discussions, the Conference evidenced tacit but actual agreement of the delegations of the States there represented, that each State had full sovereignty in airspace over its national lands and waters, as part of its territory, that any division of such territorial airspace into zones is impractical and unnecessary and that no general right of international transit or commerce exists for aircraft of other States through such territorial airspace. However, the Conference failed because of political controversy between the governments represented in it.[5]

Nevertheless, the delegates attempted to formulate the principles of international law relating to civil aviation. They managed to identify and address a number of safety-related issues, regarding the operation of civil aviation, such as nationality and registration of aircraft, airworthiness, cabotage and personnel licensing. The unadopted provisions proved to be essential for the future regulation of international air navigation, and in this respect, certainly influenced the 1919 Convention Relating to the Regulation of Aerial Navigation (Paris Convention) and subsequently, the 1944 Convention on International Civil Aviation (Chicago Convention).

The internationally oriented Paris Convention appeared to settle the undecided diplomatic dispute of the 1910 Paris Conference, and demonstrated that, according to the delegations present in 1910, the only practical method of regulating international flights was by international agreements providing for the grant, therefore not as a matter of natural right or of mere privileges to the aircraft of other States under certain terms and conditions.

Through the years to date, the principle of States' sovereignty over the airspace above its territory has played a major role in numerous civil aviation treaties, of which the comprehensive 1944 Chicago Convention is of significant value in ensuring the safe and orderly growth of international civil aviation throughout the world.

---

4   It is a fundamental principle of international law that each State is possessed of supreme sovereignty over its national domain, and that national domain is defined to include land, territorial waters and superjacent airspace. Each State therefore has complete and exclusive control over the airspace above its territory. The concept of sovereignty permits each State to exercise exclusive jurisdiction within its own territory and thereby control the transit and landing of foreign air transport within its boundaries. Thomas Jr. A.J., International Economic Regulation of Air Transport I, 1950 *Wash. U.L.Q. 324* (1950), pp. 325-326.

5   Cooper, J.C., The International Air Navigation Conference, Paris 1910, *J. Air L. & Com.* 127 (1952), p. 143.

INTRODUCTION

From the First Flight to International Air Regulations

The date of 17 December 1903 marked not only the first flight of the Wright brothers on the beach at Kitty Hawk, North Carolina, United States, but also the birth of international civil aviation. Already in the early years of aviation, people with foresight had realized that the advent of the airplane added a new dimension to transport, which could no longer be contained within strictly national confines.

First, balloons and dirigibles started to cross national borders with increasing frequency, then heavier-than-air vehicles followed, jeopardizing safety and infringing the sovereignty of a State.

The domestic and international activities of even the earliest aviators immediately led to the issue of government edicts and decrees on a regulatory basis, but also to escalating friction between States. Many different considerations have led State authorities, practically all over the world, to control aviation on military and economic grounds as well as for safety reasons.

In consequence of the upcoming international character of air navigation, due to the perseverance of those pioneering aviators, it soon became evident that most of the legal issues could not be solved on a purely national level. International regulation of air navigation was deemed necessary.

Aviation is characterized by two special features: it is of an international nature and it is extremely susceptible to technical progress. Both of these characteristics have had their effects on the present aviation regulatory framework. The early conventions on international civil aviation, such as the 1919 Paris Convention and the Inter-American Convention on Commercial Aviation (1928 Havana Convention, also known as Pan-American Convention) are merely of historic interest nowadays, although most of their provisions are reflected in the Chicago Convention, done at Chicago on 7 December 1944, which still forms the leading legal framework for modern international civil aviation regulation and therefore represents the primary source of public international air law.

International air law is a body of rules governing the use of airspace and its benefits for aviation, the general public and the nations of the world.[1] International air law consists of and is based on the following sources:

1. Treaties between States. Treaties are fast becoming the most important source of international law. They offer States a deliberate method by which to create binding

---

[1] Diederiks-Verschoor, I.H.Ph., Butler, M.A. (Legal adviser), *An Introduction to Air Law*, Eighth Revised Edition, Alphen aan den Rijn: Kluwer Law International, 2006, p. 1.

international law.

In the field of civil aviation, there are multilateral (multipartite) aviation conventions (primary sources) establishing rules expressly recognized by the Contracting States, which are considered law-making treaties, as well as bilateral (bipartite) air services agreements. Furthermore, there are contracts, involving a contractual obligation for the parties concerned, between States and airline companies and mutual contracts between airline companies.[2]

> Unlike ordinary treaties, the conventions on uniform private air law do not primarily create rights and duties as between States, but rather between air carriers, aircraft users, aircraft accident victims, and so on. For this purpose, they have to be transformed into law in every State according to local constitutional practice.[3]

1. International custom, as evidence of general practice accepted as air law, although sometimes difficult to determine. Prerequisites are that there must be widespread and consistent State (including the government, parliament and courts) practice, and there has to be *opinio juris*.
   In particular, State practice may give rise to customary international law when that practice is uniform, coherent and general, and if it is coupled with a belief that the practice is obligatory rather than habitual.
2. General principles of law as recognized by civilized nations, and, as subsidiary means for the determination of rules of international air law. Rules of international air law derived from the general principles of law tend to be interpreted more flexibly than rules derived from a bilateral or multilateral treaty. That can often be traced back to the content and the way in which the rule was created. Some general principles of international law have developed into a generally binding, mandatory law. They belong to *jus cogens*, being peremptory norms from which no derogation is permitted.[4]
3. National, regional law and regulations, in particular European Union legislation, and decisions of judicial and arbitral tribunals, subject to the provisions of Article 59 Statute of the International Court of Justice (ICJ):

---

2 Participation in a treaty under international law is not confined exclusively to sovereign States, but sovereign States are the only entities which have *locus standi* before the International Court of Justice (ICJ) in litigious cases. Similar terms for treaty are: accord, act, agreement, convention, covenant, charter, declaration, exchange of notes, memorandum of understanding, pact, protocol, statute and other less known synonyms.

3 Sand, P.H., The International Unification of Air Law, *Law and Contemporary Problems,* Volume 30, No. 2 (Spring 1965), p. 409.

4 Vienna Convention on the Law of Treaties (with Annex), concluded at Vienna on 23 May 1969, Art. 53. Treaties conflicting with a peremptory norm of general international law (*jus cogens*).

The decision of the Court has no binding force except between the parties and in respect of the particular case.

However, a number of States are reluctant with respect to jurisprudence law due to the fact that decisions made by judges decades ago under different circumstances no longer have a decisive influence on current matters.

Apart from the above-mentioned sources as methods by which the international rules of law are created and the specific rights or obligations they stipulate can be identified, there are norms and resolutions of international organizations such as international standards, regulations, declarations, agreements, recommendations and decisions concerning international aviation. To a greater or lesser extent, those acts may have binding force or unifying effects, in their turn affecting obligations of States. Depending on their general acceptability, they can influence the development of international air law.

In addition, distinguished writings on air law, mostly by highly qualified international publicists, are also considered subsidiary means for the determination of rules of law. However, they do not create air law, but may be used as a persuasive guide to the content of international air law.[5]

The preamble of the Chicago Convention expresses, among other things, that international civil aviation may be developed in a safe and orderly manner and that international air transport services may be established on the basis of equality of opportunity and operated soundly and economically. Especially the Technical Annexes to the Chicago Convention, that contain the international Standards and Recommended Practices (SARPs), which are applied universally and have produced a degree of technical uniformity, have enabled international civil aviation to develop in a safe, orderly and efficient manner.

All Annexes are the responsibility of the International Civil Aviation Organization. Many Annexes cover the positive side of aviation, in particular flight safety, accomplished by minimum standards of training, safety procedures and specifications. Other Annexes, however, cover the pernicious aspects associated with civil aviation like environmental issues and security measures for safeguarding air transport against acts of unlawful interference.

ICAO is not only an organization involved with aviation safety, but it is, in view of all operations, the largest and leading aviation organization in the world that has made a significant contribution to the development of international civil aviation.[6]

Global harmonization and implementation of standards, specifications and practices will mean that practically all States have access to substantial advantages of enhanced safe and reliable air transport.

---

5   *See also* Statute of the International Court of Justice (ICJ), Art. 38.1.
6   MacKenzie, D., *ICAO: A History of the International Civil Aviation Organization*, Toronto: University of Toronto Press, 2010, p. 258.

In 2017, more than four billion people participated in commercial air travel, a significant increase compared to previous years, according to the IATA. All indicators lead to growing demand in the following years. IATA expects that the world needs to prepare for at least a doubling of air travellers within the next 20 years, which means a total of approximately eight billion passengers around 2035. In 2017, air carriers connected a record number of cities worldwide, providing regular services (at least one weekly connecting flight) to more than 20,000 unique city-pairs, a doubling of services since 1995, when there were less than 10,000 city-pair connections globally, according to IATA.

The largest increase is expected in the Asia-Pacific region. In addition to this significant increase, the safety level of international air transport should keep pace, but most importantly for mankind, the protection of the environment must be guaranteed.[7]

The following descriptions of aviation regulations, agreements, organizations and programmes are, as far as practicable, placed in chronological order. Agreements, conventions, protocols, etc. that relate to the same or practically the same subject are for reasons of clarity presented in a cluster.

Furthermore, since a large part of the text consists of instruments of international law, the following treaty article may be of interest.

The Vienna Convention on the Law of Treaties of 23 May 1969 (entered into force on 27 January 1980) stipulates in Article 53 *Treaties conflicting with a peremptory norm of general international law ('jus cogens')* that:

> A treaty is void if, at the time of its conclusion, it conflicts with a peremptory norm of general international law. For the purposes of the present Convention, a peremptory norm of general international law is a norm accepted and recognized by the international community of States as a whole as a norm from which no derogation is permitted and which can be modified only by a subsequent norm of general international law having the same character.

---

7   IATA Annual Review 2018, Industry Story in 2017. IATA-Future of the Airline Industry 2035.

Chapter I: Unification of Aerial Navigation Regulations

1.1 Paris Conference 1910

International Air Navigation Conference

In 1910, the French government convened in Paris a conference on the regulation of air navigation, the 1910 Paris International Air Navigation Conference, which was attended by representatives of 19 European States, including France. The reason to come to this first attempt to create a set of rules and regulations for aviation on an international scale was the fact that repeatedly there were alleged German-French border crossings by German air balloons and thus unauthorized overflying over French territory.[1]

The prime purpose of the international conference, initiated by the French government, was to discuss the operation of flights into and over foreign territory in order to devise regulatory procedures to avoid international confrontations. The overall objective was to complete a draft convention dealing with subjects including aircraft nationality and registration requirements, approval of aircraft certificates of airworthiness, crew licensing, logbooks, customs and freight, transport of explosives, prohibited zones, photographic and radio equipment in aircraft and special provisions dealing with civil aircraft.

When the 1910 Paris Conference occurred, no acceptable coherent policy existed for international flight regulation. The successive putative airspace infringements above French territory especially indicated that regulation of the airspace boundaries must therefore be the subject of studies and consultation.

No customary international law governed any form of transport in the atmosphere above the surface of the Earth. One broad opinion maintained that the atmosphere surrounded the Earth, and that all political entities bordered the atmosphere in the same way that maritime territories bordered the sea. Therefore, the same rules applied to the air as applied to the sea. Since the freedom of the high seas had been established in international law, freedom of the atmosphere was a logical consequence. However, the theory of

---

1   The first international (bilateral) aviation agreement on regulating international air navigation was the convention between Germany and Austria-Hungary on the legal status of military training balloons overflying the frontier, of 8 June to 2 November 1898. Source: Research Project by Sand, P.H., de Sousa Freitas, J., Pratt, G.N., *An Historical Survey of International Air Law before the Second World War*, Institute of Air and Space Law, McGill University, p. 31. *See also* Kean, A. (Ed.), *Essays in Air Law*, The Hague: Martinus Nijhoff Publishers, 1982, p. 313. Noteworthy, however, this military agreement is beyond the scope of this treatise.

freedom of the air was not in favour anymore at the outbreak of World War I (1914-1918), according to the convincing general tendency at that time.[2]

The other approach maintained that since States exercised absolute sovereignty over and beneath the surface of their territories, they were entitled to exercise similar jurisdiction with respect to the atmosphere above their territories. Under this doctrine (the theory of air sovereignty), the owner of the territory was the owner of the whole airspace above it without any limits whatsoever.

Each participating State would admit the flight of aircraft of other participating States within and above its territory, but subject to certain restrictions. This conception, although formulated differently on essential points by supporting States, was a starting point in the discussion which, however, in turn raised delicate questions, especially the issue of the fundamental needs for protection of States.[3]

The German government submitted at the beginning of the Conference an entire multinational air navigation draft convention containing 43 articles and two annexes as part of the German reply to the questionnaire, previously sent by the French government to each participating State. In fact, this prepared document can be considered the first multilateral air navigation draft convention.

This German draft providing a legal topic issue was entitled *Examination of the Principle of Admission of Air Navigation within the Limits of or above Foreign Territory*. This supplementary question, added to the rather narrow and technical conference programme, raised the basic problem concerning the legal status of airspace and the competence scope of the subjacent State authority to regulate flight over its territorial lands and internal waters.

Those attending the Conference were divided between the concept of freedom of the air or freedom of air navigation and the principle of national sovereignty over national airspace. The theory of freedom of the air indicates that aircraft of any kind may fly through the airspace of States at any height without being disturbed. This theory was criticized because it does not appropriately take into account the fundamental needs for the protection of States.

World War I brought advancements at least with regards to the question of national air sovereignty, as both the States involved in the war and the neutral States were of the opinion that the airspace above their national lands and waters was unrestrictedly subject to their national sovereignty, both with respect to space and matter. Those States undoubtedly manifested the principle of air sovereignty.[4]

---

2   Verzijl, J.H.W., *International Law in Historical Perspective*, Volume III, Leyden: Sijthoff, 1970, Part III State Territory, Chapter II, Section 4 The Air Column, pp. 75-77.

3   Giemulla, E.M., Weber, L. (Eds.). *International and EU Aviation Law*, Selected Issues, Alphen aan den Rijn: Kluwer Law International, 2011, pp. 7-8.

4   Honig, J.P., *The Legal Status of Aircraft*, Proefschrift ter verkrijging van de graad van Doctor in de rechtsgeleerdheid aan de Rijksuniversiteit te Leiden (Dissertation to obtain the degree of Doctor at the Leiden University), The Hague: Martinus Nijhoff, 1956, pp. 9-20.

The draft convention of 1910 made no clear pronouncement on the choice between the two principles, sovereignty over national airspace or freedom of the air. As a matter of fact, in view of developing international political tensions and the real prospect of war in Europe, national interests and national security gained momentum.

Generally, armed conflicts reinforce nationalism and will give a defensive character to the respectable principle of State sovereignty. That is precisely why a number of European States passed legislation to close national airspace to all foreign aircraft.

Whereas the majority of attending States first favoured the principle of freedom of the air, a proposal of the Paris Conference legal sub-commission would make airspace subject to the complete and exclusive sovereignty of the subjacent territory. However, the 1910 Paris Conference had not taken a decisive resolution on the issue of sovereignty over the air, the reason why the draft convention was not adopted. It was designated as a diplomatic failure. Only since 1919 did total sovereignty over airspace prevail.

In fact, the 1910 Paris Conference came to a final disagreement on this purely political question as to what restrictions could be applied by the subjacent State to aircraft of other participating States, *casu quo* Contracting States in case of an agreement. The failure was not, as was actually assumed, due to opposed theories of freedom of the air and State sovereignty. Nonetheless, the 1910 Paris Conference can be considered as the first political effort to constitute principles of international air law.[5]

The various positions of the delegates have been of paramount importance with regard to the further development of international air law. In this respect, the draft convention actually formed the basis for subsequent air law conventions. The 1919 Paris Convention actually contains provisions compiled during the 1910 Paris Conference.

Moreover, the 1944 Chicago Convention, in turn, is clearly influenced by the Paris provisions. First of all, the recognition that every State has complete and exclusive sovereignty over the airspace above its territory, and in the second place, the freedom of innocent passage of aircraft of Contracting States over the territory of other Contracting States and the right to make stops for non-traffic purposes at public aerodromes of those States, subject to certain conditions and rights of the State flown over, were laid down in the Chicago Convention.[6]

---

5   Bartsch, R.I.C., *International Air Law : A Practical Guide*, Milton Park, Abingdon, Oxon: Routledge, 2016, National Sovereignty, International Conventions.

6   Cooper, J.C., The International Air Navigation Conference, Paris 1910, 19 *J. Air L. & Com.* 127 (1952).

1.2   PARIS CONVENTION 1919

Convention Relating to the Regulation of Aerial Navigation

The Convention Relating to the Regulation of Aerial Navigation, signed at Paris on 13 October 1919, became the first legal instrument to enter into force in the area of air law.

It was the first international convention to address the political obstacles and complexities involved in international air navigation. Considered from this perspective, as mentioned above, a very first attempt at international regulation of air navigation was already made in 1910 by 19 European States meeting in Paris at the International Air Navigation Conference. At that time a draft convention was discussed, but unanimous agreement on a final text could not be reached. After the outbreak of World War I, international cooperation regarding civil aviation activities, like attempts to elaborate air navigation regulations, immediately ceased.

Military aircraft, as a new weapon in wartime, prevailed. World War I is also considered as the nationalistic war par excellence. Not only in Germany, but also in Great Britain, France, Italy and some other States, nationalist sentiments and war enthusiasm were rampant. However, instead of an anticipated controlled momentary armed conflict, this war became an Armageddon, resulting in unprecedented devastation, millions of almost exclusively military victims as well as millions of civilian refugees and ultimately a rearrangement of the European map.

In the wake of World War I, the idea of international collaboration on air navigation matters was taken up at the opening of the Peace Conference in Versailles. No doubt it was increasingly evident that this new and highly advanced means of transport required international attention. It was obvious that a general convention related to rules for air traffic would be immediately necessary to reduce the confusing diversity of ideologies and regulations which differed by State. Such a universal convention needed to be prepared without delay in order to lay down the guiding principles and provisions to serve as the basis for uniform national regulations in the Contracting States. It was high time to move from nationalism to internationalism, although sovereignty over national airspace remained an issue.

A special Inter-Allied Aeronautical Commission, which had its origin in the Inter-Allied Aviation Committee established in 1916, was formed on 6 March 1919 to advise the Peace Conference on all air navigation matters. The Inter-Allied Aeronautical Commission made preparations for a convention regarding international air navigation in the time of peace. An agreement among the ex-Allied States was at this time rather feasible because the governments realized that aviation in itself, in which so many improvements had been made during the recent war, was going to develop very rapidly.[7]

The Inter-Allied Aeronautical Commission drew up a draft convention for the general regulation of post-war international aviation by using the relevant regulatory framework done at the 1910 Paris Conference. However, the implementation by states of the final agreement, the Paris Convention, took quite some years. It was eventually ratified by 32 States. Ultimately, it has never been adopted by most of the Latin American States and the United States.

The reason why the United States did not ratify the Paris Convention, nor adopted the Versailles Treaty and never joined the League of Nations, was the reserved position of the U.S. Congress despite the visionary work of the presidential team.

A proposal with 14 points, set down by President Thomas Woodrow Wilson, to be used for peace negotiations after World War I and to ensure world peace in the future, was opposed by the U.S. Senate after an unyielding presidential campaign. This far-reaching decision was a clear sign of increasing U.S. isolationist policies of America first, not least with regard to its airspace. To harmonize with the customary international law principle of exclusive sovereignty of States over the use of their airspace, enshrined in Article 1 of the Paris Convention, the United States asserted its sovereignty over the airspace above its territory through the Air Commerce Act of 1926, signed into law by President John Calvin Coolidge Jr.[8]

> 1919 Paris Convention, Article 1: The High Contracting Parties recognize that every Power has complete and exclusive sovereignty over the airspace above its territory.

The 1919 Paris Convention consisted of 43 Articles that dealt with all organizational, technical and operational aspects of international civil aviation and also established the creation of the International Commission for Air Navigation, commonly called by its initials ICAN, enshrined in Article 34 of the Paris Convention.

ICAN or CINA (*Commission Internationale de la Navigation Aérienne*) was given a wide range of supervisory powers in the field of technical matters. ICAN, the first quasi-supranational civil aviation organization, possessed administrative, legislative, executive and judicial powers, and was also an advisory body and a central documentation unit.[9] The work of ICAN, a precursor of ICAO, and its sub-commissions proved to be very

---

7   Northrup, C.C. (Ed.), *Encyclopedia of World Trade: From Ancient Times to the Present,* Volumes 1-4, Milton Park, Abingdon, Oxon: Routledge, 2015, Aviation, The Operation of Aircraft, pp. 84-88.

8   Brady, T. (Ed.), *The American Aviation Experience: A History,* Carbondale and Edwardsville, IL: Southern Illinois University Press, 2000, The Air Commerce Act of 1926.

9   Johnson, D.H.N., *Rights in Air Space,* Manchester: Manchester University Press, 1965, pp. 34-38.

helpful in the drafting of the technical Annexes to the Chicago Convention. In 1947, ICAO took over the ICAN secretariat offices located at Paris.

During the 1919 Paris Conference, the High Contracting Parties recognized that every Power has complete and exclusive sovereignty over the airspace above its territory, and recognized the desirability of the greatest freedom of international air navigation consistent with State sovereignty and security concerns and that every aircraft should possess the nationality of the Contracting State. For the purpose of the Paris Convention, the territory of a State shall be understood as including the national territory, both that of the mother country and of the colonies, and the territorial waters adjacent thereto (Art. 1).

The later concluded Chicago Convention adopted most of the Paris Convention, in particular the all-important statement of airspace sovereignty. Enshrined in Article 1 of both the Paris Convention and the Chicago Convention, the doctrine of airspace sovereignty was the most elementary principle. In fact, it was the customary international law principle of exclusive sovereignty of States over the use of their airspace. Sovereignty over airspace, in earlier times a rather controversial issue, was by this time undoubtedly an established right of international law. The Paris Convention and ICAN entered into force on 11 July 1922. However, no attempt was made to define the meaning of airspace, neither in the Paris Convention nor in the Chicago Convention.

Some technical Annexes (A to H) were added to the Paris Convention to achieve a certain degree of uniformity. Annex A contained the first generally accepted definition of the term 'aircraft':

> An aircraft is any machine that can derive support in the atmosphere from the reactions of the air (*Le mot aéronef désigne tout appareil pouvant se soutenir dans l'atmosphère grâce aux réactions de l'air*).[10]

1.3 MADRID CONVENTION 1926

Ibero-American Convention on Air Navigation

In 1919, Spain, as one of the ex-neutral governments in World War I, declined the invitation to adhere to the 1919 Paris Convention, partially due to Article 34 of this Convention that was related to the uneven equivalency between parties. Another key aspect was that Spain withdrew from the League of Nations in 1926. Its claim for a permanent seat on the League's Council was not granted.

---

10 Diederiks-Verschoor, I.H.Ph., Butler, M.A. (Legal adviser), *An Introduction to Air Law,* Eighth Revised Edition, Alphen aan den Rijn: Kluwer Law International, 2006, p. 5.

Article 34 describes the institution of ICAN, a permanent body placed under the direction of the League of Nations, the duties, the determination of the rules of its own procedure and the place of its permanent seat and the composition and voting rights of representatives of certain Contracting States. Furthermore, Article 34 provides an explanation about the voting method on modifications of the provisions of any one of the Annexes, and the number of representatives per Contracting State, which however was disputed by Spain because it was not offered the same voting power as France or Italy.[11]

Following the growth of commercial air transport activity between the Iberian Peninsula and South America and as a result of the reasoned absence of the United States and most Central and South American States at the Paris Convention, Spain decided to initiate a diplomatic counteraction and invited all Latin American and Caribbean States as well as Portugal to the so-called Ibero-American Conference to be held in Madrid from 25 to 30 October 1926. On 1 November 1926, 21 European and American States of Spanish and Portuguese origins signed the Ibero-American Convention on Air Navigation (*Convineo Ibero-Americano de Navegación Aérea, CIANA*).[12]

This Convention, more commonly known as the 1926 Madrid Convention, was modelled after the Paris Convention and its wording was virtually identical in most of the articles. Only the rather offensive articles of the Paris Convention were significantly amended to assure the equality of States and to eliminate any discriminatory implications concerning the Contracting States.

The voting rights of the Contracting States laid down in the Madrid Convention (in Art. 34) deviated from the Paris Convention in that it differently took account of the principle of equality. In this respect, see also the voting issue and duties of the ICAO Council as laid down in Article 52 of the 1944 Chicago Convention.

Another discrepancy was the fact that the Madrid Convention declared a right for a Contracting State to permit the flight above its territory of an aircraft that did not possess the nationality of a Contracting State (Art. 5), while under the Paris Convention such a flight was not permitted, except by a special and temporary authorization.

The Madrid Convention had only limited impact, mainly due to the low number of seven ratifications it received, but also, when the Havana Convention emerged in 1928, it was said that there was no longer need for a second alternative to the Paris Convention. In fact, the Madrid Convention was largely a reflection of the text and Annexes of the 1919 Paris Convention. In course of time, Spain and Argentina renounced the Madrid Convention and joined ICAN in 1933.

---

11   Art. 34. There shall be instituted, under the name of the International Commission for Air Navigation, a permanent Commission placed under the direction of the League of Nations and composed of: Two representatives of each of the following States: the United States of America, France, Italy and Japan; One representative of Great Britain and one of each of the British Dominions and of India; One representative of each of the other Contracting States (...).

12   Milde, M., *International Air Law and ICAO*, Essential Air and Space Law Volume 4, Series Editor Benkö, M.E., Utrecht: Eleven International Publishing, 2008, p. 12.

The Madrid Convention was never registered with any international body, never came into force and was completely ignored by the Chicago Convention. Article 80 of the Chicago Convention only mentions the fact that the Chicago Convention supersedes the Paris Convention and the Havana Convention. The Madrid Convention, never having had actual international importance, appeared to be no more than the result of the pure political megalomania of Spain trying to assert leadership in Latin America.

Eventually, the Madrid Convention was unsuccessful, principally due to three factors:

1. Aircraft in those times were not sufficiently developed in order to bridge the distance between Iberia and Latin America, let alone to operate scheduled air services.
2. Spain's political environment in the 1930s was quite unsettled, eventually resulting in the devastating Spanish Civil War (1936-1939).
3. A few years after the conclusion of the Madrid Convention, Latin American society and interests focused more and more on North America, away from the colonial empires of Spain and Portugal.[13]

1.4   HAVANA CONVENTION 1928

Pan-American (or Inter-American) Convention on Commercial Aviation

Although U.S. President Thomas Woodrow Wilson played a leading role in the establishment of the League of Nations in the wake of World War I, he was unable to guide the United States into this general society of States. The fact that the International Commission for Air Navigation was linked with the League of Nations was one of the reasons why within the United States there was a strong opposition from the U.S. Senate, together with the disapproval of isolationist politicians, to joining the League of Nations. The need for a separate form of international cooperation on a regional American basis, especially in the Western Hemisphere, was the result of this dissonance.

The Inter-American Commercial Aviation Commission, an inter-American technical commission created by means of a resolution adopted during the Fifth International Conference of American States, which was held at Santiago de Chile from 25 March to 3 May 1923, was instructed by the delegates of 18 American States to consider the policy, laws and regulations relative to commercial aviation. In concrete terms, its task was to prepare a draft of laws and regulations with respect to commercial aviation, the adoption of which had to be recommended to all the American States, the determination of aerial routes, the formulation of special customs procedures for aircraft and the definition of

---

13 Cooper, J.C., Edited by Vlasic, I.A., *Explorations in the Aerospace Law, Selected Essays 1946-1966*, Montreal: McGill University Press, 1968, p. 237. *See also* The Postal History of ICAO, 1926: The Ibero-American Convention www.icao.int/secretariat/PostalHistory/1926_the_Ibero_American_Convention.htm.

standard landing places and recommendations with respect to the points where such landing places shall be established.

Basically, it laid down elementary principles and rules for air traffic, recognizing that every State had complete and exclusive sovereignty over the airspace above its territory, including the adjacent territorial waters. The conclusions of this commission were to be drawn up in the form of a convention or subsequent conventions which were to be submitted to the consideration of the States Members of the Pan-American Union.

The Inter-American Commercial Aviation Commission, which had drawn up a project of an Inter-American convention of aerial navigation, eventually met at Washington, D.C., from 2 to 19 May 1927. The majority of the States represented were the same States which had concluded the 1926 Madrid Convention.[14]

The Inter-American Commercial Aviation Commission, just as the Madrid Conference, took the 1919 Paris Convention as a starting point and copied many of its provisions, although it carried out a lot of important modifications. The resulting document, the Pan-American Convention on Commercial Aviation was finalized at Havana in early 1928 under the auspices of the Sixth Pan-American Conference, held from 16 January to 20 February 1928. This document weakened the international stature of ICAN.

This Conference, completely dominated by the United States, whose fierce foreign policy hardly had any appreciation, adopted a number of resolutions and conventions on different topics including commercial aviation, and marked a crucial turning point in Inter-American relations. A few years later, in 1933, during the Seventh International Conference of American States, the good neighbour policy of President Franklin Delano Roosevelt eased the mistrustful relations.[15]

The Havana Convention was signed by 21 States, including the United States, on 20 February 1928, and entered into force on 13 June 1929. The Convention was a most liberal instrument. Inasmuch as the establishment of airlines was seen as an international right of commercial freedom, it dealt with routes and traffic rights, unlike other known international air navigation agreements, leaving the additional operational aspects of civil aviation like the establishment of international air routes and granting of traffic rights to particular bilateral or multilateral negotiations.

Article 21 of the Havana Convention:

> The aircraft of a Contracting State engaged in international air commerce shall be permitted to discharge passengers and a part of its cargo at one of the airports designated as a port of entry of any other Contracting State, and to proceed to any other airport or airports in such State for the purpose of dischar-

---

14 The Postal History of ICAO, 1928: the Havana Convention. www.icao.int/secretariat/PostalHistory/1928_the_Havana_convention.htm.

15 Leonard, T.M. (Ed.), *Encyclopedia of U.S.-Latin-American Relations,* Volume 1, Los Angeles, CA: CQ Press, 2012, p. 531.

ging the remaining passengers and portions of such cargo and in like manner to take on passengers and load cargo destined for a foreign State or States, provided that they comply with the legal requirements of the country over which they fly, which legal requirements shall be the same for native and foreign aircraft engaged in international traffic and shall be communicated in due course to the Contracting States and to the Pan American Union.

Thus, the principles of the Havana Convention tended to be based on the multilateral granting of international air services, including mutual freedom of air passage and the provision that the aircraft from a Contracting State were entitled to carry passengers and cargo to and from any airport, authorized as port of entry, in any other Contracting State and *vice versa*, considered a theoretical freedoms of the air agreement concept *avant la lettre*.[16]

Unlike the Paris Convention, the Havana Convention made no attempt to develop uniform technical standards, nor was there any provision for periodic discussion on common problems through the agency of a permanent organization like the later ICAO Secretariat. The Convention had no annexes, which means that all rules were contained in the agreement itself. Furthermore, the Havana Convention applied only to private aircraft (government aircraft were not included) and explicitly endeavoured to govern commercial aviation.

Aircraft regulation was done according to the laws of each State, which precluded any form of uniformity. Nevertheless, the Havana Convention as well as the earlier Paris Convention served a useful purpose in laying down rules regarding air navigation. However, both Conventions caused, to some extent, confusion in actual practice as they consisted of two separate sets of rules resulting in uncertainty.

Because of the tremendous wartime development of international air transport, the provisions laid down in the Havana Convention could by no means regulate modern air navigation in the decades following World War II, which itself was a real catalyst for the technical development of the aircraft.[17] Yet, the Havana Convention incorporated aspects of private air law.

In the final phase of the war, it already became obvious that because of the dynamic technological progress and the post-war economic reconstruction, commercial air rights as well as universally applicable technical and navigational regulations should be gov-

---

16 Larsen, P.B., Sweeney, J.C., Gillick, J.E., *Aviation Law, Cases, Laws and Related Sources*, Second Edition, Leiden: Martinus Nijhoff Publishers, 2012, p. 36. *See also* Milde, M., *International Air Law and ICAO*, Utrecht: Eleven International Publishing, 2008, p. 13.

17 Stadlmeier, S., *International Commercial Aviation: From Foreign Policy to Trade in Services*, Forum for Air and Space Law (Edited by Marietta Benkö in cooperation with Willem de Graaff), Volume 5, Paris: Editions Frontières, 1998, pp. 38-41.

erned by international agreements on a global scale. The answer to that visionary point of view was the realization of the Chicago Convention and its technical Annexes.

The 1944 Chicago Convention superseded the provisions of both the 1928 Havana Convention and 1919 Paris Convention. Article 80 of the Chicago Convention:

> Paris and Habana Conventions.
> Each Contracting State undertakes, immediately upon the coming into force of this Convention, to give notice of denunciation of the Convention relating to the Regulation of Aerial Navigation signed at Paris on October 13, 1919 or the Convention on Commercial Aviation signed at Habana on February 20, 1928, if it is a party to either. As between Contracting States, this Convention supersedes the Convention of Paris and Habana previously referred to.

1.5   CHICAGO CONFERENCE 1944

International Civil Aviation Conference

On 11 September 1944, the United States extended an invitation to 53 governments and the ministers of Denmark and Thailand with the rank of ambassadors attending in their personal capacities, residing in Washington, D.C., without the privilege of voting, for an international civil aviation conference to be convened in the United States on 1 November 1944. Following several studies initiated by the United States and various consultations with its major Allies, and the rather favourable course of the war, the invitation came at the right time, although many delegates, in particular those representing occupied States, travelled to Chicago at great personal risk.

The delegations came from the Allied States in wartime and their associated States, and from States that remained neutral during the war. Only Saudi Arabia and the Soviet Union did not participate for various reasons.

On request of President Franklin Delano Roosevelt, the U.S. Department of State announced on 7 October 1944 the selection of the Stevens Hotel in Chicago, Illinois as the site for the International Civil Aviation Conference, to be held from 1 November to 7 December 1944. The main objective of the Conference was to design a blueprint for the worldwide regulation of post-war international civil aviation and to discuss the principles and methods to be followed in the adoption of a new aviation convention. The assignment was to make arrangements for the immediate establishment of provisional air routes and services, to set up an interim council to collect, record and to study data concerning international aviation and to make recommendations for its improvement.

Earlier, in August 1943, at the Anglo-American Conference in Quebec City, FDR and Winston Leonard Spencer-Churchill discussed, with remarkable foresight, post-war aviation policy and plans for a coordinating organization to handle global aspects of international civil aviation. As the year 1944 progressed and as the war took a turn for the better, it became even more apparent that the time was rapidly approaching when some States would want to initiate new international air services on a regular commercial basis, with diverse options.

The option of the United States was complete market access without restrictions, while the United Kingdom proposed tight regulation with an independent international governing body to coordinate air services and to determine and control tariffs, frequencies and capacity. Canada, during the Chicago Conference acting as a mediator due to the fact that it possessed an immense aviation industry with an internationally recognized expertise accompanied by strong links with Europe, put on the agenda the establishment of a multilateral regulatory body, more like the British proposal, allowing limited competition; on the other hand, Australia and New Zealand suggested international ownership and management of all international air services. Eventually, the option of the United Kingdom was preferred.

The Chicago Conference was inaugurated with the reading of a message from the president of the United States. On 7 December 1944, three years to the day after Pearl Harbour, the Conference concluded with a signature of a final act that was a formal and official record summarizing the work. Forty delegations signed on that date their adherence to the new Convention on International Civil Aviation of 1944 (Chicago Convention), a source of public international air law, which sets out as its prime objective the development of international civil aviation in a safe and orderly manner, such that international air transport services would be established on the basis of equality of opportunity and be operated soundly and economically.

One of the main objectives of the drafters of the Chicago Convention was international cooperation and to delegate, as far as was practicable, to States the ability to provide systems and infrastructure and to adopt measures in accordance with standards which may be recommended or established from time to time, pursuant to the Chicago Convention (Art. 28). The Chicago Convention was established to promote cooperation and to create and preserve friendship and understanding among the States and peoples of the world. All in all, the Chicago Conference turned out to be one of the most successful, productive and influential conferences ever held.

For the first time in the history of international civil aviation, a universal authority would facilitate order in airspace and introduce the greatest standardization and harmonization in technical matters possible to unify the methods of exploitation and settle any differences that may occur.

Chapter II: Prevailing Public International Air Law

2.1   Chicago Convention 1944

Convention on International Civil Aviation

The Chicago Convention (ICAO Doc 7300), as an instrument that provided a complete modernization of the basic public international air law, ensures a comprehensive and flexible multilateral framework for creating technical norms and procedural standards with regard to requirements for the operation of international air transport services by commercial air carriers at the global level. In fact, it covers a wide range of topics vital for international civil aviation.

The categories of air transport services covered by the Chicago Convention include: non-scheduled international air services, subject to the provisions of Article 5, scheduled international air services, considered a special permission under Article 6 and cabotage air services, including scheduled and non-scheduled air services, pursuant to Article 7.

The signed document received the requisite 26th ratification on 5 March 1947. Thereafter, on the 30th day after the deposit of the 26th instrument, the Convention entered into force on 4 April 1947.

The authentic language of the text was English. In 1968, French and Spanish were (by Protocol) added with the status of authentic language. In 1977 the same status was assigned to a Russian text (by Protocol), resulting in four languages of equal authenticity. In 1995, the Arabic language was added (by Protocol) and in 1998, the Chinese language was added by the Protocol on the Authentic Six-Language Text of the Convention on International Civil Aviation, signed at Montreal, on 1 October 1998.

The preamble of the Chicago Convention:

> Whereas the future development of international civil aviation can greatly help to create and preserve friendship and understanding among the nations and peoples of the world, yet its abuse can become a threat to the general security; and
> Whereas it is desirable to avoid friction and to promote that cooperation between nations and peoples upon which the peace of the world depends;
> Therefore, the undersigned governments having agreed on certain principles and arrangements in order that international civil aviation may be developed in

a safe and orderly manner and that international air transport services may be established on the basis of equality of opportunity and operated soundly and economically;

Have accordingly concluded this Convention to that end.

The main documents produced by the Chicago Conference, together forming the Chicago Convention system, are the following:

1. The Interim Agreement on International Civil Aviation. Its purpose was that of a bridging mechanism to permit an early beginning of the global effort while awaiting sufficient ratifications to the Convention. Pending the 26th ratification, the Provisional International Civil Aviation Organization (PICAO) was established to serve as a temporary and coordinating body. This organization functioned remarkably well from 6 June 1945 until 4 April 1947, the date the Convention entered into force following the ratification by 26 signatory States, a quorum stipulated in Article 91, Ratification of Convention, under (b).

   Consequently, the provisional aspects of PICAO were no longer relevant, and it officially was converted into the International Civil Aviation Organization (ICAO). From October of the same year, ICAO became a specialized agency of the United Nations Economic and Social Council (ECOSOC).

2. The Convention on International Civil Aviation, opened for signature on 7 December 1944 at Chicago, only in the English text version. The Convention came into force on 4 April 1947, superseding the 1919 Paris Convention and the 1928 Havana Convention (Chicago Convention, Art. 80).

3. The International Air Services Transit Agreement (IASTA) (ICAO Doc 7500), consisting of two freedoms of the air under which the aircraft from Member States may fly over each other's territory and land for non-traffic purposes (Two Freedoms Agreement).

4. The International Air Transport Agreement (IATA) consisting of the two freedoms of IASTA and three additional freedoms concerning commercial transport rights (Five Freedoms Agreement).

5. Extensive Drafts of 12 Technical Annexes, documenting the scope of international consensus and cooperation regarding the technical and operational aspects of international civil aviation such as airworthiness, rules of the air, telecommunications, air traffic control, etc. The Conference achieved significant advances in technical matters to be able to make international air transport considerably safer, more reliable and more uncomplicated than in the *interbellum*.

6. A standard Form of Bilateral Agreements for the exchange of air routes and traffic rights was prepared and recommended by the Conference as part of its final act.[1]

Article 37 of the Chicago Convention requests the following, in implementing the international Standards and Recommended Practices and procedures adopted by ICAO:

> Each Contracting State undertakes to collaborate in securing the highest, practicable degree of uniformity in regulations, standards, procedures, and organization in relation to aircraft, personnel, airways and auxiliary services in all matters in which such uniformity will facilitate and improve air navigation.

To this end the ICAO shall adopt and amend from time to time, as may be necessary, international standards and recommended practices and procedures dealing with:
-   Communications systems and air navigation aids, including ground marking;
-   Characteristics of airports and landing areas;
-   Rules of the air and air traffic control practices;
-   Licensing of operating and mechanical personnel;
-   Airworthiness of aircraft;
-   Registration and identification of aircraft;
-   Collection and exchange of meteorological information;
-   Log books;
-   Aeronautical maps and charts;
-   Customs and immigration procedures;
-   Aircraft in distress and investigation of accidents; and such other matters concerned with the safety, regularity, and efficiency of air navigation as may from time to time appear appropriate.

Article 1 gives a clear statement:

> Sovereignty.
> The Contracting States recognize that every State has complete and exclusive sovereignty over the airspace above its territory.

---

1   Havel, B.F., *Beyond Open Skies: A New Regime for International Aviation*, Alphen aan den Rijn: Kluwer Law International, 2009, p. 100. *See also* Haanappel, P.P.C., *The Law and Policy of Air Space and Outer Space: A Comparative Approach*, The Hague: Kluwer Law International, 2003, p. 43.

Thereafter, Article 2 states:

> Territory.
> For the purpose of this Convention the territory of a State shall be deemed to be the land areas and territorial waters adjacent thereto under the sovereignty, suzerainty, protection or mandate of such State.

Quite similar is the content of Article 1 of the 1919 Paris Convention:

> The High Contracting Parties recognize that every Power has complete and exclusive sovereignty over the airspace above its territory. For the purpose of the present Convention, the territory of a State shall be understood as including the national territory, both that of the mother country and of the colonies, and the territorial waters adjacent thereto.

In this context, the definition of a State is of relevance:

Article 1 of the Montevideo Convention on the Rights and Duties of States, signed at Montevideo on 26 December 1933:

> The State as a person of international law should possess the following qualifications: (a) a permanent population; (b) a defined territory; (c) government; and (d) capacity to enter into relations with the other States.

The aims and objectives of the Chicago Convention and its Organization are enshrined in Article 44:

> Objectives.
> The aims and objectives of the Organization are to develop the principles and techniques of international air navigation and to foster the planning and development of international air transport so as to:
> – Insure the safe and orderly growth of international civil aviation throughout the world;
> – Encourage the arts of aircraft design and operation for peaceful purposes;
> – Encourage the development of airways, airports, and air navigation facilities for international civil aviation;
> – Meet the needs of the peoples of the world for safe, regular, efficient and economical air transport;
> – Prevent economic waste caused by unreasonable competition;

- Insure that the rights of Contracting States are fully respected and that every Contracting State has a fair opportunity to operate international airlines;
- Avoid discrimination between Contracting States;
- Promote safety of flight in international air navigation;
- Promote generally the development of all aspects of international civil aeronautics.

The Chicago Convention has two principal functions: it is a source of international air law, and it describes the constitution of an international organization. The Chicago Convention, the general body of public international air law, covers four parts:
- *Part I, Air Navigation*, including:
    1. Chapter I, General principles and application of the Convention;
    2. Chapter II, Flight over territory of Contracting States;
    3. Chapter III, Nationality of aircraft;
    4. Chapter VI, Measures to facilitate air navigation;
    5. Chapter V, Conditions to be fulfilled with respect to aircraft;
    6. Chapter VI, International Standards and Recommended Practices (SARPs); and
- *Part II, the International Civil Aviation organization*, including:
    1. Chapter VII, The organization;
    2. Chapter VIII, the Assembly;
    3. Chapter IX, the Council;
    4. Chapter X, the Air Navigation Commission;
    5. Chapter XI, Personnel;
    6. Chapter XII, Finance;
    7. Chapter XIII, Other international arrangements; and
- *Part III, International Air Transport*, including:
    1. Chapter XIV, Information and reports;
    2. Chapter XV, Airports and other air navigation facilities;
    3. Chapter XVI, Joint operating organizations and pooled services; and
- *Part IV, Final Provisions*, including:
    1. Chapter XVII, Other aeronautical agreements and arrangements;
    2. Chapter XVIII, Disputes and default;
    3. Chapter XIX, War;

4. Chapter XX, Annexes;
5. Chapter XXI, Ratifications, adherences, amendments, and denunciations; and
6. Chapter XXII, Definitions.

Signature of Convention.[2]
In witness whereof, the undersigned plenipotentiaries, having duly authorized, sign this Convention on behalf of their respective governments on the dates appearing opposite their signatures.

Whereas Article 94 gives the standard rule in public international law that amendments to the Chicago Convention only come into force with respect to the States that have ratified such amendments, over the years several amendments were adopted to the original document of the Chicago Convention, wherein the major ones relate to Article 3 *bis*, a contemporary addition to Article 3, Article 48a, the frequencies of Assemblies, Article 50a, increase in the Council members, Article 56, increase in the members of the Air Navigation Commission (ANC) and Article 83 *bis*, transfer of certain functions and duties, and the authentic text of the Convention, amended by several protocols, the latter of which is the Six-language text as per Protocol, signed at Montreal on 1 October 1998.[3]

There are a number of Protocols relating to an amendment to the Chicago Convention:
1. Protocol Relating to an Amendment to the Convention on International Civil Aviation (Art. 93 *bis*), signed at Montreal, on 27 May 1947 (incorp. in ICAO Doc 7300).
2. Protocol Relating to an Amendment to the Convention on International Civil Aviation (Art. 45), signed at Montreal, on 14 June 1954 (incorp. in ICAO Doc 7300).
3. Protocol Relating to an Amendment to the Convention on International Civil Aviation (Arts. 48 (a), 49 (e) and 61), signed at Montreal, on 14 June 1954 (incorp. in ICAO Doc 7300).
4. Protocol Relating to an Amendment to the Convention on International Civil Aviation (Art. 50 (a)), signed at Montreal, on 21 June 1961 (incorp. in ICAO Doc 7300).
5. Protocol Relating to an Amendment to the Convention on International Civil Aviation (Art. 48 (a)), signed at Rome, on 15 September 1962 (incorp. in ICAO Doc 7300).

---

2   States are categorized by ICAO Membership as follows: A Contracting State of ICAO is a State which has adhered to the Convention on International Civil Aviation, whether or not it is a Member of the United Nations and/or any of its other Agencies, a non-Contracting State of ICAO is a State which has not signed and does not adhere to the Convention on International Civil Aviation, but which is a Member of the United Nations and/or any of its other Agencies, and a third category of States which are not signatories to the Convention on International Civil Aviation and which are not Members of the United Nations nor of any of its Agencies. However, most States in the world fall into the Contracting State category.

3   *See also* Haanappel, P.P.C., *The Law and Policy of Air Space and Outer Space: A Comparative Approach*, The Hague: Kluwer Law International, 2003, pp. 43-50.

6. Protocol on the Authentic Trilingual Text of the Convention on International Civil Aviation, signed at Buenos Aires, on 24 September 1968 (ICAO Doc 7300).

7. Protocol Relating to an Amendment to the Convention on International Civil Aviation (Art. 50 (a), signed at New York, on 12 March 1971 (ICAO Doc 8970, incorp. in ICAO Doc 7300).

8. Protocol Relating to an Amendment to the Convention on International Civil Aviation (Art. 56), signed at Vienna, on 7 July 1971 (ICAO Doc 8971, incorp. in ICAO Doc 7300).

9. Protocol Relating to an Amendment to the Convention on International Civil Aviation (Art. 50 (a)), signed at Montreal, on 16 October 1974 (ICAO Doc 9123, incorp. in ICAO Doc 7300).

10. Protocol Relating to an Amendment to the Convention on International Civil Aviation (Final Paragraph, Russian Text), signed at Montreal, on 30 September 1977 (ICAO Doc 9208, incorp. in ICAO Doc 7300).

11. Protocol on the Authentic Quadrilingual Text of the Convention on International Civil Aviation, signed at Montreal, on 30 September 1977 (ICAO Doc 9217, incorp. in ICAO Doc 7300).

12. Protocol Relating to an Amendment to the Convention on International Civil Aviation (Art. 83 *bis*), signed at Montreal, on 6 October 1980 (ICAO Doc 9318, incorp. in ICAO Doc 7300).

13. Protocol Relating to an Amendment to the Convention on International Civil Aviation (Art. 3 *bis*), signed at Montreal, on 10 May 1984 (ICAO Doc 9436, incorp. in ICAO Doc 7300).

14. Protocol Relating to an Amendment to the Convention on International Civil Aviation (Art. 56), signed at Montreal, on 6 October 1989 (ICAO Doc 9544).

15. Protocol Relating to an Amendment to the Convention on International Civil Aviation (Art. 50 (a)), signed at Montreal, on 26 October 1990 (ICAO Doc 9561).

16. Protocol on the Authentic Quinquelingual Text of the Convention on International Civil Aviation, signed at Montreal, on 29 September 1995 (ICAO Doc 9663)

17. Protocol Relating to an Amendment to the Convention on International Civil Aviation (Final Paragraph, Arabic Text), signed at Montreal, on 29 October 1995 (ICAO Doc 9664).

18. Protocol Relating to an Amendment to the Convention on International Civil Aviation (Final Paragraph, Chinese Text), signed at Montreal, on 1 October 1998 (ICAO Doc 9722).

19. Protocol on the Authentic Six-Language Text of the Convention on International Civil Aviation, signed at Montreal, on 1 October 1998 (ICAO Doc 9721).

20. Protocol Relating to an Amendment to the Convention on International Civil Aviation (Art. 50 (a)), signed at Montreal, on 6 October 2016 (ICAO Doc 10077).

21. Protocol Relating to an Amendment to the Convention on International Civil Aviation (Art. 56), signed at Montreal, on 6 October 2016 (ICAO Doc 10076).[4]

2.2 SUMMARY OF THE ANNEXES TO THE CONVENTION ON INTERNATIONAL CIVIL AVIATION (ICAO ANNEXES)

> When one considers that there is perhaps no other form of human activity endowed with such an international character as civil aviation, it is obvious that the existence of internationally accepted and applied standards and procedures is a first essential for safe and efficient air navigation.[5]

At the Chicago Conference in 1944, drafts of 12 technical annexes were completed to serve as a guide to worldwide practice pending the coming into force of the Chicago Convention, and from that particular date to be formally adopted by the appointed ICAO Council and subsequently accepted by the Contracting States.

The Chicago Conference provided for a provisional organization of a technical and advisory nature for the purpose of collaboration in the field of international civil aviation, PICAO, pursuant to the Interim Agreement on International Civil Aviation, to function in the interim period until 26 governments had ratified the Chicago Convention. When PICAO came into existence, the city of Montreal was selected as its permanent headquarters. The choice of Montreal, as the centre of Canadian civil aviation and infrastructure, a major hub in North America and strategically located, given the limited range of aircraft at that time, was formally proposed by Chile and supported by the United States, the United Kingdom, Peru and Australia.

Much of the work done by PICAO, largely by means of technical divisions, involved the drafting of recommendations concerning standards, practices and procedures (PICAO Recommendations for Standards, Practices and Procedures) to be adopted by Contracting States pending the establishment of international SARPs by the permanent ICAO.

Apart from the draft recommendations, PICAO is to be credited with very effective and useful work, in setting up the procedures and working methods for the Assembly and the Council of the permanent ICAO, organizing the Secretariat, and selecting both the President of the Council and the secretary general, who would become officials of ICAO.

As forerunner of ICAO, ICAN which was established by the 1919 Paris Convention and operational till the end of the PICAO interim period, was the first attempt to accomplish the orderly development of international civil aviation. However, ICAN was dis-

---

4   *See* Current Lists of Parties to Multilateral Air Law Treaties 2016, www.icao.int.
5   Kamminga, M.S., *The Aircraft Commander in Commercial Air Transportation*, The Hague: Martinus Nijhoff, 1953, p. 12.

solved when the Chicago Convention entered into force, and its assets were transferred to ICAO.[6]

The ICAO Council's first official act, at the opening day of its First Session on 28 May 1947, was the election of Dr Edward Warner as its President and the appointment of Dr Albert Roper as Secretary General.

A few weeks earlier, with the creation of ICAO, the status of the SARPs underwent a significant change, as the work of the technical divisions was considered by the ANC, then adopted by the Council and finally submitted to the Contracting States. Adoption of these SARPs, especially the Standards, by the Council gives them the status as Annexes to the Chicago Convention.

SARPs are technical specifications adopted in accordance with Article 37 of the Chicago Convention in order to achieve the highest practicable degree of uniformity in regulations, standards, procedures and organization in relation to aircraft, personnel, airways and auxiliary services in all matters in which such uniformity will facilitate and improve international air navigation. SARPs are published by ICAO in the form of Annexes to the Chicago Convention, but do not have the same legal binding force, let alone compulsory force as the Convention itself, due to the fact that the Annexes are to be no integral part of the Convention, and consequently not considered international treaties, so they are not subject to the law of treaties. However, ICAO Standards are highly authoritative in practice.[7]

If a predetermined, two-third majority of the Contracting States does not register disapproval of these SARPs, they become effective. Subsequently, each Contracting State is bound to bring its own regulations or practices into full accord with any international standard and procedures, or to notify ICAO of any differences between any of its own practices and those established by an international standard (Art. 38).[8]

These deviations are to be reported to the ICAO Council for publication in a supplement to the Annex concerned. The Standards contained in the Annexes are considered to be binding for Contracting States that have not notified ICAO about a national difference. As safety is the principal objective of air navigation, implementation of ICAO SARPs should be carried out in a uniform matter worldwide, because uniformity of those

---

6   *See also* www.icao.int/secretariat/postalhistory/from_picao_to_icao_organizational_similarities.htm.

7   Abeyratne, R.I.R., *Aeronomics and Law: Fixing Anomalies*, Berlin, Heidelberg: Springer-Verlag, 2012, p. 170.

8   ICAO Assembly Resolution A36-13 Consolidated statement of continuing ICAO policies and associated practices related specifically to air navigation, Appendix A, Formulation of Standards and Recommended Practices (SARPs) and Procedures for Air Navigation Services (PANS). Appendix D, Implementation of SARPs and PANS. States should consider the practicability of modifying the internal processes by which they give effect to the provisions of SARPs and PANS, if such modifications expedite or simplify the processes or make them more effective.

standards, especially in the field of safety and security which are fundamental issues, is one of the most important criteria governing the ICAO legislative process.[9]

Once a rule or procedure is adopted by the ICAO Council as a Standard, Member States are obliged to implement that rule or procedure uniformly, unless they find it impracticable to comply as stipulated earlier. Unfortunately, the mode of implementation in national laws varies from State to State, which in turn, makes it rather complicated to enforce compliance. Consecutive non-compliance without any notification by unwilling, nonchalant or reluctant States could have severe consequences with respect to aviation safety.

Deficiencies in documents, licensing, airworthiness of aircraft, etc. could mean safety reasons, and probably disapproval by other States in any form whatsoever, but more importantly, enforcement by ICAO. Safe operation of international air services must be seen as a global activity. Therefore, enforcement of ICAO Standards is especially an essential prerequisite for the highest practical degree of uniformity, and in general to enhance international aviation safety.[10]

However, ICAO only has, apart from quasi-legislative powers and its law-making authority over the high seas, rather insignificant enforcement powers to achieve at most consensus, uniformity and stability. Demanding compliance from delinquent States is a seemingly endless issue, due to the absence of an actual sanction regime as available to the UN Security Council (Charter of the United Nations, Chapter VII, in particular Art. 41). An effective answer to the rather modest enforcement powers of ICAO has led to the establishment of its primary enforcement mechanism, a mandatory oversight audit programme concerning flight safety.[11]

Over the years, the ICAO Council has developed and adopted 19 Annexes to the Chicago Convention, being soft law instruments. Out of the 19 Annexes, 17 are of a technical nature and therefore fall within the responsibilities of the Air Navigation Bureau and its sections. The other two Annexes, Facilitation and Security, are under the purview of the Air Transport Bureau. The Annexes are drafted in uniform patterns.

After World War II, the ANC was to replace the PICAO-created Air Navigation Committee, but with the coming into force of ICAO in 1947, the new ANC was not yet established, as the American argument was that PICAO's existing commission on air

---

9   Huang, J., *Aviation Safety and ICAO*, Proefschrift ter verkrijging van de graad van Doctor aan de Universiteit Leiden (Dissertation to obtain the degree of Doctor at the Leiden University), Montreal: ICAO, 2009, pp. 61-63.

10 *See also* Mendes de Leon, P.M.J., The Legal Force of ICAO SARPs in a Multilevel Jurisdictional Context, *Journaal Luchtrecht* No. 2-3, June 2013, Special Edition, Liber Amicorum in Honour of Roderick D. van Dam, The Hague: Sdu Publishers, pp. 11-17.

11 The Universal Safety Oversight Audit Programme was established during ICAO's 32nd Assembly in 1998, featuring mandatory, systematic and harmonized safety audits to be carried out regularly in all sovereign Member States. It superseded the voluntary ICAO Safety Oversight Programme. In 2002, ICAO launched the Universal Security Audit Programme, providing for the conduct of universal, mandatory and regular audits of the aviation security system in all ICAO Member States.

navigation was working well. Any change, according to the United States, would disrupt the organization's work, and moreover, whereas the existing Committee was under direct control of the Council members, the new ANC would be more independent.

It was not until the Second Session of the Assembly, held in Geneva from 1 to 21 June 1948, that Resolution A2-8 recommended to proceed as may be feasible the implementation of Article 54 (Mandatory functions of Council, sub (e) Establish an Air Navigation Commission, in accordance with the provisions of Chapter X), and Article 56 (Nomination and appointment of Commission) of the Chicago Convention and that the permanent ANC could enter into function in so far as practicable and legally permissible. The ANC came into operation on 7 February 1949. The number of members of the ANC was increased to 19. The text of Article 56 of the Chicago Convention was amended by the 27th Session of the Assembly (Montreal 1989).[12]

The ANC is tasked by the Council to manage the technical work programme of ICAO. In that respect, the ANC considers and recommends SARPs and Procedures for Air Navigation Services (PANS) for the safety and efficiency of international civil aviation, which are adopted or approved by the Council. Since its establishment, the ANC has considered and recommended the development of SARPs in 16 of the 19 Annexes and five PANS by the year 2015.

The Annexes and PANS relate to aspects of international civil aviation including, but not limited to: accident investigation, aerodromes, air routes and ground aids, aeronautical maps and charts, aeronautical telecommunications and radio aids, airworthiness and identification of aircraft, rules of the air, air traffic services and management, aeronautical meteorology, search and rescue (SAR), safety management, systems of dimensional units, dangerous goods and training requirements. Challenges currently faced by the ANC include maintaining and improving aviation safety and air navigation efficiency while integrating increased air traffic into the current aviation infrastructure, introducing advanced systems, as well as proactively identifying risks and devising mitigation measures, in accordance with the Global Aviation Safety Plan (GASP) and the Global Air Navigation Plan (GANP).

The GASP (ICAO Doc 10044) sets out a strategy which supports the prioritization and continuous improvement of civil aviation safety. This plan provides a framework for the development and implementation of regional, subregional and national plans. The overall purpose is to guide the harmonized development of regional and State safety planning. The GANP (ICAO Doc 9750), being evolved to serve as a worldwide reference to evolutionarily transform the air navigation system, is the strategy to achieve a global interoperable air navigation system, for all users during all phases of flight, that meets agreed levels of aviation safety, provides for optimum economic operations, is environmentally sustainable and meets national security requirements.

---

12 www.icao.int/about-icao/AirNavigationCommission.

The international SARPs contained in the Annexes are applied universally and have produced a degree of technical uniformity which has enabled international civil aviation to develop in a safe, orderly and efficient manner. Apart from the Annexes which only make a direct positive contribution to put civil aviation at a higher level, there are some Annexes that must treat the negative side of civil aviation, which means preventive measures and procedures to withstand or mitigate potential threats or impacts in any capacity to or through civil aviation.[13] Considered from this point of view, their provisions will definitely contribute to reducing the negative effects of international aviation on global social life and nature.

Those particular Annexes are: Annex 16-Environmental protection (aircraft noise, pollutants, engine emissions etc.), Annex 17-Security-Safeguarding International Civil Aviation against Acts of Unlawful Interference and Annex 18-The Safe Transport of Dangerous Goods by Air.

In 2014, there were around 12,000 international SARPs reflected in 19 Annexes, all of which have been agreed by consensus through ICAO. It is through these provisions, as well as ICAO's complementary policy, auditing and capacity-building efforts, that the air transport system today is to operate more than 100,000 daily scheduled commercial flights, safely and securely in every region of the world.

ICAO verifies compliance with SARPs through audits, which are official inspections regarding the overall method of State oversight systems by two mandatory, systematic, harmonized and regularly executed programmes: the Universal Safety Oversight Audit Programme (USOAP) and the Universal Security Oversight Programme (USAP), applicable to all Member States. USAP fits in ICAO's strategy for strengthening aviation security worldwide and for achieving commitment from Member States in a collaborative effort to create a global aviation security system.

USOAP audits focus on the capability of a Contracting State to adequately provide safety oversight by assessing whether the State has effectively and consistently implemented the critical elements of a safety oversight system. In other words, USOAP audits are conducted by assessing eight critical elements which are considered essential for a State to establish, implement and maintain an effective safety oversight system. The audits include the following critical elements for safety oversight:
– Primary aviation legislation
– Specific operating regulations
– State's civil aviation system and safety oversight functions
– Technical personnel qualification and training
– Technical guidance, tools and the provision of safety-critical information
– Licensing, certification, authorization and approval obligations

---

13 Globalization, Transport and the Environment, Policy Instruments to Limit Negative Environmental Impacts: International Law, 10.2 International Air Transport, *OECD*, 2000.

- Surveillance obligations
- Resolution of safety concerns[14]

Negative audit results can inflict reputational losses on States and could have serious civil aviation-related consequences with, or even imposed sanctions by, other Contracting States. For example, the Member States of the European Union created a so-called black-list of air carriers declared unsafe, based on random assessments on foreign aircraft at European airport ramps, in accordance with international safety standards, and as such, then not permitted to enter European airspace again or land at European airports.[15]

The reason to launch USOAP was the previously widespread concern about the adequacy of aviation safety oversight by a relatively large number of Contracting States and the lack of reliable information concerning the method of implementation of the critical elements of a safety oversight system.

Article 37 of the Chicago Convention requires each Contracting State to collaborate in securing the highest practicable degree of uniformity in regulations and practices in all matters, including aviation safety and security issues, in which such uniformity will facilitate and improve air navigation.

In 2005, USOAP was expanded to the USOAP Comprehensive Systems Approach (CSA), to include safety-related provisions contained in all safety-related Annexes to the Chicago Convention. The monitoring performance of USOAP will improve by including the application of a new approach based on the concept of continuous monitoring.

In 2010, the ICAO Assembly adopted by means of Resolution A37-5 the new USOAP Continuous Monitoring Approach (CMA), a method that will incorporate the analysis of safety risk factors and be applied on a universal basis in order to assess States' oversight capabilities. It introduced a systematic and more proactive conduct of monitoring activities enabling a more effective and efficient use of ICAO resources and reducing the burden on Contracting States, caused by repetitive audits.

Moreover, aviation safety can be effectively improved only if relevant organizations have access to sufficient resources. USOAP CMA continues to maintain as core elements the key safety provisions contained in Annex 1-Personnel Licensing, Annex 6-Operation of Aircraft, Annex 8-Airworthiness of Aircraft, Annex 11-Air Traffic Services, Annex 13-Aircraft Accident and Incident Investigation and Annex 14-Aerodromes, and provides for the sharing of significant safety concerns (SSCs) with interested stakeholders.[16]

---

14 Schlumberger, C.E., Weisskopf, N, *Ready for take-off?: The Potential for Low Cost Carriers in Developing Countries*. Directions in Development. Washington DC: World Bank, 2014, pp. 74-75. *See also* cfapp.icao.int/fsix/criticalelements.pdf.

15 Schnitker, R.M., van het Kaar, D., *Safety Assessment of Foreign Aircraft Programme: A European Approach to Enhance Global Aviation Safety*, Essential Air and Space Law Volume 11, Series Editor Benkö, M.E., The Hague: Eleven International Publishing, 2013, Chapter 8, EU Blacklist.

16 Guimulla, E.M., Weber, L. (Eds.), *International and EU Aviation Law: Selected Issues*, Alphen aan den Rijn: Kluwer Law International, 2011, p. 104.

USOAP CMA has been fully launched in 2013 as a top priority system and will continue to evolve in order to support Contracting States in their efforts to implement the State Safety Programme (SSP) and safety management.

While certain obligations for Contracting States are laid down in the Chicago Convention, ICAO, as an international organization with largely limited enforcement powers, vested by mutual express consent of its Member States, can only determine State disregard or non-implementation by the instrument of auditing and continuous monitoring in the interest of a safe global air transport system.

To ensure the implementation by Contracting States with respect to ICAO's safety related SARPs, associated procedures and guidance material, USOAP mandatory audits are regularly conducted.

USOAP helps in identifying deficiencies in the implementation of safety-related SARPs in the Contracting States. An important consequence of these observations was the establishment by the ICAO Council of the International Financial Facility for Aviation Safety (IFFAS) in 2002, upon a request from the Assembly by Resolution A33-10 in 2001. IFFAS became operational in 2003 and is working under the ICAO umbrella as a self-financed quasi-independent entity.

The global aviation industry is a cyclical sector. Company profits are alternated with losses as a result of declining revenues caused by a global macroeconomic slowdown, decreasing passenger traffic and reduced demand for air cargo, increasing costs due to skyrocketing fuel prices, inclusion of aviation in emissions trading schemes and tighter security requirements.

This combination inevitably will lead to significant air carrier consolidation, restructuring and bankruptcies. This situation implies declining budgets for States and air carriers, resulting in less money for budgetary items related to aviation safety, especially when priority is given to security. Most of the developing countries and least developed countries (LDCs) attribute more importance to aviation safety, while the developed countries tend to prioritize aviation security. To ensure the safe and orderly growth of civil aviation worldwide, ICAO has a pronounced obligation in assisting Contracting States in financing aviation safety-related projects, identified principally through USOAP.

The primary purpose of the IFFAS is to provide financial assistance to those States that have difficulty in securing the necessary money through existing funding mechanisms and procedures in order to apply corrective measures to the aviation safety gap discovered by the audits. ICAO's IFFAS is to be financed from contributions of Contracting States, regional groups of States as well as international organizations. These, however very limited, voluntary contributions are intended to be used to improve aviation safety through recovery actions. Major beneficiaries would be the less developed States of the world.[17]

---

17 Saba, J., Worldwide Safe Flight: Will the International Financial Facility for Aviation Safety Help It Happen, 68 *J. Air L. & Com.* 537 (2003).

As SARPs were developed, either the subjects of Annexes were split or new Annexes were conceived, and most of the titles were revised. The lettering system of the Annexes was based on the English alphabet, which however might have led to confusion in other languages.

As a result, the nomenclature of the Annexes has been changed to numerals. Since first adoption of the Annexes, many amendments to them were considered in a continuous process of improvement and development, resulting in a total of 19 Annexes, the most recent of which is about the topic of safety management. The aim of most of the Annexes is to promote progress in flight safety, particularly by guaranteeing satisfactory minimum standards of training and safety procedures and by ensuring uniform international practices.

An Annex is made up of the following component parts, not all of which, however, are necessarily found in every Annex; they have the status indicated.

1. Material comprising the Annex proper:
   a. Standards and Recommended Practices adopted by the Council under the provisions of the Chicago Convention. ICAO verifies compliance with SARPs through audits of State oversight systems. Currently there are two audit programmes: the USOAP and USAP. SARPs are defined as follows:

      Standard: any specification for physical characteristics, configuration, material, performance, personnel or procedure, the uniform application of which is recognized as necessary for the safety or regularity of international air navigation, which has been adopted by the Council pursuant to Article 54(1) of the Convention, and to which Contracting States will conform in accordance with the Convention, and in respect of which non-compliance must be notified by Contracting States to the Council in accordance with Article 38.

      Recommended Practice: any specification for physical characteristics, configuration, material, performance, personnel or procedure, the uniform application of which is recognized as desirable in the interest of safety, regularity or efficiency of international air navigation, which has been adopted by the Council pursuant to Article 54(l) to the Convention, and to which Contracting States will endeavour to conform in accordance with the Convention.

   b. Appendices comprising material grouped separately for convenience but forming part of the SARPs adopted by the Council.
   c. Definition of terms used in the SARPs which are not self-explanatory in that they do not have accepted dictionary meanings. A definition does not have an independent status but it is an essential part of each SARP in which the term is used, since a change in the meaning of the term would affect the specification.
   d. Tables and figures which add to or illustrate a Standard or a Recommended Practice and which are referred to therein, form part of the associated Standard or Recommended Practice and have the same status.

2. Material approved by the Council for publication in association with the SARPs:
   a. Forewords comprising historical and explanatory material based on the action of the Council and including an explanation of the obligations of States with regard to the application of the SARPs ensuing from the Convention and the Resolution of Adoption.
   b. Introductions comprising explanatory material introduced at the beginning of parts, chapters or sections of the Annex to assist in the understanding of the application of the text.
   c. Notes included in the text, where appropriate, to give factual information or references bearing on the SARPs in question, but not constituting part of the SARPs.
   d. Attachments comprising material supplementary to the SARPs or included as a guide to their application.

The written text of all Annexes is supposed to be gender-neutral.

The PANS contain material prepared as an amplification of the basic principles in the corresponding SARPs, laid down in various Annexes, which are adopted by the Council in pursuance of Article 37 of the Chicago Convention.

PANS comprise operating practices and material too detailed for SARPs. To qualify for PANS status, the material concerned should be suitable for application, approved by the Council and recommended to Contracting States for worldwide application. As such, they attempt to make air navigation services uniform across the globe. The Council invites Contracting States to publish any differences in their Aeronautical Information Publications (AIPs) when knowledge of the differences is important to the safety of air navigation.

Over the years, PANS-ATC changed from title in Procedures for Air Navigation Services – Rules of the Air and Air Traffic Control (PANS-RAC), to be changed again to Procedures for Air Navigation Services – Air Traffic Management (PANS-ATM). Other PANS are, among other things, related to aircraft operations (PANS-OPS), to abbreviations and codes (PANS-ABC), to aerodromes (PANS-ADR), to meteorology (PANS-MET) and to training (PANS-TRG).[18]

Annex 1 Personnel Licensing

The ICAO technical division on Personnel Licensing (PEL), which was given the responsibility for establishing standards for the licensing of operational and mechanical personnel, held its First Session from 15 to 23 January 1946. The Second Session of the PEL division was held in Montreal from 7 to 25 January 1947. Following this session, SARPs

---

18   https://www.icao.int/Documents/annexes_booklet.pdf.

for PEL were adopted by the Council on 14 April 1948 pursuant to the provisions of Article 37 of the Chicago Convention and designated as Annex 1.

As long as air travel cannot do without aircraft pilots (except for unmanned aircraft systems) and other air and ground personnel, their competence, skills and training will remain the essential guarantee for efficient and safe operations. Adequate personnel training and licensing also endear confidence between States, leading to international recognition and acceptance of personnel qualifications and licences and greater reliance in aviation on the part of the traveller.

As Article 32 of the Chicago Convention only requires the licensing of the members of the operating crew of an aircraft engaged in international air navigation, in modern aviation the need for minimum standards regarding specialized aviation personnel other than crew members is required due to the advancing technology and rapidly modifying environment in which the aviation industry operates.

ICAO Standards, considered as minimum standards for the licensing of flight crew members (pilots, flight engineers), air traffic controllers, aeronautical station operators, maintenance technicians and flight dispatchers, are provided by Annex 1.

Today's aircraft operations are so diverse and complex that protection must be provided against the possibility, however remote, of total system breakdown due to either human error or failure of a system component. The human being is still the vital link in the chain of aircraft operations but is also by nature the most creative, flexible and variable. Proper training is necessary so as to minimize human error and provide able, skilful, proficient and competent personnel.

The Human Factors programme addresses known human capabilities and limitations, providing States with basic information on this vital subject as well as the material necessary to design proper training programmes. ICAO's objective is to improve safety in aviation by making States more aware of, and responsive to, the importance of human factors in civil aviation operations. Licensing is the act of authorizing defined activities which should otherwise be prohibited due to the potentially serious results of such activities being performed improperly.

One of ICAO's main tasks in the field of personnel licensing is to foster the resolution of differences in licensing requirements and to ensure that international licensing standards are kept in line with current practices and probable future developments. This is even more crucial as the flight crew will be exposed to increasing traffic density and airspace congestions, highly complicated terminal area patterns and more sophisticated equipment. To accomplish this task, Annex 1 is regularly amended to reflect the rapidly developing aviation industry.

Annex 2 Rules of the Air

Air travel must be safe, orderly and efficient. This requires, among others, a set of internationally agreed rules of the air. Established by PICAO, the Rules of the Air and Air Traffic Control (RAC) division held its First Session between 15 October and 19 November 1945. The Second Session of the RAC division met from 3 December 1946 to 6 January 1947 and proposed SARPs for the Rules of the Air. The SARPs were adopted by the ICAO Council on 15 April 1948 and became effective on 15 September 1948 as Annex 2 – Rules of the Air.

Subsequently, the Council adopted on 27 November 1951 a completely revised and rearranged text of the Annex, which no longer contained Recommended Practices. Annex 2 (Amendment 1) with the new title of International Standards – Rules of the Air, became effective on 1 April 1952 and applicable on 1 September 1952. The rules of the air represent the basic code of conduct in the air ensuring safe and orderly flight. Of great importance are the rules for collision avoidance and for flights over the high seas. Especially over the high seas, no State can exercise jurisdiction to stipulate the rules of the air in a way that is harmonized for all users.

It should be noted that the Council resolved, in adopting Annex 2 in April 1948 and Amendment 1 to this Annex in November 1951, that the Annex constitutes – Rules Relating to the Flight and Manoeuvre of Aircraft. On 15 November 1972, when adopting Amendment 14 to Annex 2 relating to authority over aircraft operating over the high seas, the Council emphasized that this Amendment was intended solely to enhance safety of flight and to ensure adequate provision of air traffic services over the high seas. The Amendment in no way affects the legal jurisdiction of States of Registry over their aircraft or the responsibility of Contracting States under Article 12 of the Chicago Convention for enforcing the rules of the air.

Article 12:

Rules of the air.
Each Contracting State undertakes to adopt measures to insure that every aircraft flying over or manoeuvring within its territory and that every aircraft carrying its nationality mark, wherever such aircraft may be, shall comply with the rules and regulations, relating to the flight and manoeuver of aircraft there in force. Each Contracting State undertakes to keep its own regulations in these respects uniform, to the greatest possible extent, with those established from time to time under this Convention. Over the high seas, the rules in force shall be those established under this Convention. Each Contracting State undertakes to insure the prosecution of all persons violating the regulations applicable.

The rules developed by ICAO, which consist of general rules, visual flight rules (VFR) and instrument flight rules (IFR) contained in Annex 2, apply without exception over the high seas, and over national territories to the extent that they shall not conflict with the rules of the State being overflown. The Standards in Annex 2 apply over the high seas without exception. In this particular case, Contracting States do not have the right to file differences, on the basis of Article 38, as they do with other SARPs. Consequently, the ICAO Council is the sole legislative body with power to enact the rules of the air over the high seas on behalf of the international community. This Annex includes rules relating to the flight and manoeuvres of aircraft within the meaning of Article 12 of the Chicago Convention.

An aircraft must be flown in accordance with the general rules and either the visual flight rules or the instrument flight rules. Flight in accordance with VFR is permitted if a flight crew is able to remain clear of clouds by a distance of at least 1500 metres horizontally and at least 300 metres (1000 ft) vertically and to maintain a forward visibility of at least 8 kilometres. For flights in some portions of the airspace and at low altitudes, and for helicopters, the requirements are less stringent. An aircraft cannot be flown under VFR at night or above 6100 metres (20,000 ft) except by special permission. Balloons are classified as aircraft, but unmanned free balloons can be flown only under specified conditions detailed in the Annex.

Instrument flight rules must be complied with in weather conditions other than those applicable for VFR. A State may also require that they be applied in designated airspaces regardless of weather conditions, or a pilot may choose to apply them even if the weather is good (which means equal to or better than established VFR minimums, depending on altitude and airspace classification). The pilot-in-command of an aircraft is at all times responsible for compliance with the rules of the air. Most air carriers fly under IFR at all times.

Depending upon the type or classification of airspace, these aircraft are provided with air traffic control service, air traffic advisory service or flight information service, regardless of actual or expected weather conditions. To operate under IFR, an aircraft must be equipped with suitable instruments and navigation equipment appropriate to the route to be flown. When operating under air traffic control, an aircraft must maintain precisely the route and altitude that have been assigned to it and shall keep air traffic control informed about its position.

A flight plan must be filed with air traffic services units for IFR flights, all flights that will cross international borders and for most other flights that are engaged in commercial operations. The flight plan provides information on the aircraft's identity and equipment, the point and time of departure, the route and altitude to be flown, the destination and estimated time of arrival and the alternate airport to be used should landing at destination be impossible. The flight plan must also specify whether the flight will be carried out under visual or instrument flight rules. Moreover, a filed flight plan could be of utmost importance for prompt search and rescue actions in the proper area if necessary.

Regardless of the type of flight plan, the pilots are responsible for avoiding collisions when operating in visual meteorological conditions (VMC), in accordance with the principle of see-and-avoid. However, flights operating under IFR are either kept separated by air traffic control units or provided with collision-hazard information.

Right-of-way rules in the air are similar to those on the surface; however, as aircraft in flight operate in three dimensions, some additional rules are required.

When two aircraft are converging at approximately the same level, the aircraft on the right has the right of way except that aeroplanes must give way to airships, gliders and balloons, and to aircraft which are towing objects. An aircraft which is being overtaken has the right of way and the overtaking aircraft must remain clear by altering heading to the right. When two aircraft are approaching each other head on they must both alter heading to the right.

As interceptions of civil aircraft are, in all cases, potentially hazardous, the Council of ICAO has formulated special recommendations in Annex 2 which States are urged to implement through appropriate regulatory and administrative action. These special recommendations are contained in Attachment A to the Annex.

The adoption and amendments of Annex 2 is and remains a constitutional prerogative of the Council under Articles 37, 54 subparagraphs (l) and (m) and 90 to the Chicago Convention.[19]

Annex 3 Meteorological Services for International Air Navigation

From the early days of aviation, it was realized that meteorological information was vital for flight planning and a constant consideration for the safe conduct of flights. Pilots need to be informed about meteorological conditions along the routes to be flown and at their destination aerodromes.

As early as 1947, the PICAO Council authorized the final report including Recommendations for Standards, Practices and Procedures, prepared during sessions of the Meteorology Division, to Contracting States for comments and amendments to be brought to meteorological codes laid down in an Annex to the Chicago Convention. The new Annex 3 – Meteorological Codes – was first adopted by the ICAO Council on 16 April 1948, providing the codes for the transmission of meteorological information for aeronautical information.

---

19 *See also* Standardized European Rules of the Air (SERA). Commission Implementing Regulation (EU) 2016/1185 of 20 July 2016 amending Implementing Regulation (EU) No. 923/2012 as regards the update and completion of the common rules of the air and operational provisions regarding services and procedures in air navigation (SERA Part C) and repealing Regulation (EC) No. 730/2006. *OJ EU* L 196/3, 21.7.2016.

With the introduction of SARPs governing the obligations of Contracting States relating to the establishment of a meteorological organization in each Contracting State, a change of title of Annex 3, in short – Meteorology, was adopted by the Council in 1955. With a complete revision of Annex 3, incorporating PANS-MET specifications (Procedures for Air Navigation Services – Meteorology), taking into account recently approved operational requirements and up-to-date methods of meeting them, and with the introduction of new SARPs relating to serve for operators and flight crew members, meteorological information for air traffic services and for search and rescue services, together with requirements for communications and their use, the title of Annex 3 was, accordingly, amended to read Meteorological Services for International Air Navigation, adopted by the Council on 26 November 1975.

Modern aviation, as accurate in on-time performance as it can be, requires that optimum use must be made of available meteorological data and that forecasting precision must continue to be improved. State obligations under Annex 3 essentially consist in determining the meteorological service required to meet the needs of international air navigation within their airspace.

Annex 3 governs the meteorological services which covers the forecasting, observation and reporting of weather data. The objective of the meteorological service, outlined in Annex 3, for international air navigation shall be to contribute towards the safety, efficiency and regularity of air navigation. This objective shall be achieved by supplying necessary meteorological information to operators, flight crew members, air traffic services units, SAR units, airport management and others concerned with aviation for the performance of their respective functions. Aeronautical meteorological information is crucial to the safe and efficient conduct of civil aviation. Close communication is essential between those supplying meteorological information and those using it.

At international aerodromes, the meteorological information is normally supplied to aeronautical users by a meteorological office. Suitable telecommunications facilities are made available by States to supply via aerodrome meteorological offices all information needed to air traffic services and search and rescue services.

To assist pilots with their flight planning, most States provide meteorological briefings which are increasingly carried out using automated (digital) systems. Briefings comprise details of en route weather, upper winds and upper-air temperatures, often given in the form of meteorological charts, warnings to hazardous phenomena en route such as volcano eruptions and possible ash contamination, severe icing conditions, suspected turbulence generated by mountains, convective cloud formations, strong surface winds, jet streams and aircraft wake, as well as reports and forecasts for the destination aerodrome and its en route and destination alternates.

Aerodrome reports and forecasts are required by aeronautical users to carry out their functions. Aerodrome reports include surface winds, visibility, runway visual range, present weather, clouds, air and dew-point temperature and atmospheric pressure, and are issued either half-hourly or hourly. These reports are complemented by special reports whenever any parameter changes beyond pre-fixed limits of operational significance. Aerodrome forecasts include surface wind, visibility, weather, clouds and temperature, and are issued every three or six hours for a validity period of 9 to 24 hours. Aerodrome forecasts are under continuous review and amended by the meteorological office concerned, as may be necessary.

Landing forecasts are prepared for international aerodromes to meet requirements of landing aircraft. They are appended to the aerodrome reports and have a validity of two hours. Landing forecasts contain expected conditions over the runway complex with regard to surface wind, visibility, weather and clouds.

To provide aircraft in flight with information about significant changes in weather, meteorological watch offices are maintained. They prepare warnings of hazardous weather conditions, including thunderstorm activities, tropical cyclones, severe squall lines, heavy hail, severe turbulence or clear air turbulence (CAT), severe icing conditions, mountain waves, sandstorms and dust storms and volcanic ash clouds. Moreover, they issue aerodrome weather conditions that could adversely affect aircraft and ground facilities like warnings of expected snowstorms and wind shear during approach, landing and take-off and climb-out.

Furthermore, aircraft in flight are required to report severe weather phenomena encountered en route. These reports are disseminated by air traffic services units to all aircraft concerned on the same routes and areas. On international routes, especially over remote areas and the high seas, routine weather observations are made by aircraft and (automatically) transmitted in flight such as upper winds and temperatures and any significant phenomena. These observations provide data that can be used in the development of forecasts.

Improving the accuracy and quality of all aeronautical meteorological information in an increasingly globalized and capacity-constraint aviation operating environment is a primary objective. As far as route forecasts are concerned, all flights require advance and accurate meteorological information so as to chart a course that will permit them to make use of the most favourable winds and conserve fuel. With rising fuel costs, this has become increasingly important. Therefore, ICAO has implemented the World Area Forecast System (WAFS). This system is based on two world area forecast centres which use the most up-to-date computers and satellite telecommunications (ISCS and SADIS) to prepare and disseminate global forecasts in digital form. It provides States and aviation users with standardized and high-quality forecasts of global upper winds, upper-air temperature and humidity, geopotential altitude of flight levels, flight level and temperature of tropopause, horizontal extent and flight levels of base and top of (tropical) cumulonimbus clouds, icing potential, clear air turbulence potential, in-cloud turbulence potential and significant weather phenomena.[20]

During the past years, a number of incidents have occurred due to unexpected aircraft encounters with volcanic ash clouds following volcanic eruptions. In order to provide for the observation and reporting of volcanic ash clouds and the issuance of warnings to pilots and airline companies, ICAO, with the assistance of other international organizations, has established an International Airways Volcano Watch (IAVW). Nine volcanic ash advisory centres issue advisory information on volcanic ash globally, both to aviation users and meteorological offices concerned.

Automated observing systems are becoming increasingly useful at aerodromes and currently are considered to meet the aeronautical requirements as far as observations of the surface wind, visibility, runway visual range and height of the cloud base, air and dew-point temperature and atmospheric pressure is concerned. In view of the improved performance of automated systems, they may now be used, without any human intervention, during non-operational hours of the aerodrome.

As years ago in-flight weather observation and processing of gathered weather data was done by crew members, today the increasing use of modern flight management computers and the establishment on board aircraft of reliable data links between aircraft and ground stations make it possible to monitor flight progress and update flight plans on the basis of actual weather conditions.

Annex 4 Aeronautical Charts

The world of aviation, which by its very nature knows no geographical or political borders, requires maps that are unlike those used in ground transportation such as the well-known road maps. It started right from the beginning of aviation. Shortly after the Wright brothers made their historic first flights in the early 1900s, the skies began to fill with aircraft. Visibility and visual ground contact were the key navigational tools at that time. Thus, aircraft were limited to rather short flights in clear weather only. Aviators used transportation routes, mostly roads, rivers and railroads, as well as other eye-catching landmarks to navigate.

A pioneer in aerial navigation was Captain Elrey Berber Jeppesen (1907-1996) who recorded and made sketches of all the landing sites, obstacles and other significant features along the routes. He put this collected information into the form of a manual containing a series of charts, later known as the Jeppesen Airway Manual.

In 1934, the International Commission for Air Navigation (ICAN) published the first Sheet of Basic Aeronautical Map intended for the preparation of routes in accordance

---

20   ISCS International Satellite Communication System, SADIS Secure Aviation Data Information Service.

with the provisions laid down in Annexes to the 1919 Paris Convention. It was clear that standardized products and symbols were further needed to support air operations.

In modern times, it is essential for the planning and safe execution of air operations that a current, comprehensive and authoritative source of navigation information should be made available at all times. Aeronautical charts provide for a convenient medium for supplying this information in a manageable, condensed and coordinated manner.

Aeronautical charts not only provide the two-dimensional information common in most maps, but also often portray three-dimensional air traffic service systems. Almost all ICAO Contracting States produce aeronautical charts and most segments of aviation refer to them for planning, air traffic control and navigation purposes. Without the global standardization of aeronautical charts, it would be difficult for pilots and other chart users to effectively find and interpret important navigation information. The safe and efficient flow of air traffic is facilitated by aeronautical charts, either digital or traditional, drawn to accepted ICAO Standards.

The SARPs and explanatory notes in this Annex define the obligations of States to make available certain ICAO aeronautical chart types, and specify chart coverage, format, identification and content including standardized symbolism and colour use. The aim is to satisfy the need for uniformity and consistency in the provision of aeronautical charts that contain appropriate information of a defined quality. When a published aeronautical chart contains 'ICAO' in the title, this indicates that the chart producer has conformed to both general Annex 4 Standards and those pertaining to a particular ICAO chart type.

The vast majority of scheduled flights will take place along routes defined by radio and electronic navigation systems that make visual reference to the ground unnecessary. This type of navigation is conducted under instrument flight rules and the flight is required to comply with air traffic control services procedures. The *Enroute Chart – ICAO* portrays the air traffic service system, radio navigation aids and other aeronautical information essential to en route navigation under IFR.

It is designed for easy handling in the crowded space of an aircraft flight deck, and the presentation of information is such that it can easily be read in varying conditions of natural and artificial light.

Where flights cross extensive oceanic and remote areas, the *Plotting Chart – ICAO* provides a means of maintaining a continuous flight record of aircraft lat-long position and is sometimes produced to complement the more complex en route charts.

For all phases of flight and types of aircraft, ICAO provides a variety of designated aeronautical charts for planning and visual navigation, each with a different scale: *Aeronautical Navigation Chart-ICAO Small Scale, World Aeronautical Chart-ICAO 1:1.000.000, Aeronautical Chart-ICAO 1:500.000*. These charts are suitable for use at low speed, short- or medium-range flights performed at low and intermediate altitudes.

As a flight approaches its destination, more detail is required about the layout of the aerodrome of intended landing, or in case of diversion, the alternate aerodrome. There are different charts available to guide pilots from top of descent to approach and landing. First is the *Area Chart-ICAO* that provides accurate information to facilitate the transition from cruise level flight to the final approach phase, sometimes supplemented by the *Radar Minimum Chart-ICAO,* enabling flight crews to monitor and cross-check altitudes assigned while under radar control, then the *Standard Arrival Chart-Instrument (STAR)-ICAO,* the *Visual Approach Chart-ICAO* illustrating the basic aerodrome chart layout and surrounding features easily recognizable from the air, then the *Instrument Approach Chart-ICAO* providing the pilots with a graphic presentation of the instrument approach and missed approach procedure in case of a go-around. This chart contains both a plan and profile view of the approach with full details of associated radio navigation aids such as the Instrument Landing System (ILS), VHF Omni-directional Radio Range (VOR), Distance Measuring Equipment (DME), Non-directional Radio Beacon (NDB) and ILS Marker Beacons as well as necessary aerodrome and topographical information.[21]

Taxiing at an aerodrome to a designated parking position requires the *Aerodrome Ground Movement Chart-ICAO* and the *Aircraft Parking/Docking Chart-ICAO.* For departure, the *Standard Departure Chart-Instrument (SID)-ICAO* is required. Furthermore, the *Aerodrome Obstacle Charts-ICAO* Type A, B and C, and the *Aerodrome/Heliport Chart-ICAO* are available.

Recent developments associated with so-called glass cockpit technologies, the availability and exchange of electronic aeronautical information, and the increased implementation of navigation systems with high positional accuracies and continuous position fixing, have created an environment well suited to the rapid development of variable electronic charts for display in the cockpit.[22] A fully developed electronic aeronautical chart display has the potential for functionality that extends well beyond paper charts and could offer significant benefits such as continuous plotting of the aircraft's position and customization of the chart display depending on the phase of flight and other operational considerations. Chapter 20, *Electronic Aeronautical Chart Display-ICAO* provides basic requirements aimed at standardizing electronic aeronautical chart display while not unduly limiting the development of this new cartographic technology.

ICAO is constantly monitoring, improving and updating (electronic) aeronautical chart specifications.

---

21 More and more VORs, NDBs and ILS Outer, Middle and Inner Markers are being discontinued to reduce the number of operational navigation aids to a minimum operating network due to the use of Area Navigation (RNAV) by DME/IRU (Inertial Reference Unit), Global Positioning System, and GNSS (Global Navigation Satellite System) Landing System. A RNAV system's suitability is dependent upon availability of ground and/or satellite navigation aids that are needed to meet any route performance criteria that may be prescribed in route specifications to navigate the aircraft along the route to be flown.

22 The term 'glass cockpit' is the primary interface between man and aircraft and generally refers to a LCD display in which the primary instruments are located within a single Primary Flight Display (PFD) or Multi Functional Display (MFD), which comprises of flat, glass-panel displays capable of displaying all of the traditional instruments and a multitude of additional data such as aircraft engines and systems parameters, checklists, weather radar and traffic information.

Annex 5 Units of Measurement to Be Used in Air and Ground Operations

One of the challenges of international air transport is handling different units of measure in different States and regions. Since World War I, aircraft built in continental Europe usually had instruments in metric units, while aircraft manufactured in the United States were equipped with instruments based on the imperial measurement system. Due to the expected growth of intercontinental air transport following World War II, and the purchase of thousands of surplus transport aircraft by emerging air carriers to meet the specific demand, a mix of units of measurement was inescapable, and practically annoying, if not confusing.

Units of measurement, relevant for aircraft and principles of flight fall into six categories: vertical distance, such as height, altitude, elevation and flight level, horizontal distance, such as runway length, visibility and runway visual range, speed, such as wind speed, indicated air speed and vertical speed, mass, temperature, such as dew point and ram air temperature and air pressure.[23]

At the International Civil Aviation Conference held in Chicago in 1944, the importance of a common system of measurement was realized and a resolution was adopted calling on States to make use of the metric system as the primary international standard. By Resolution A1-35, the first ICAO Assembly, held in May 1947, recommended that the Council should adopt the first ICAO Table of Units as an ICAO Standard, as rapidly as practicable, for use in air-ground communications and relevant publications on international air navigation. The Annex 5, named Dimensional Units to be Used in Air-Ground Communications, was first adopted by the ICAO Council on 16 April 1948 and became applicable on 1 January 1949.

The Annex originally contained an ICAO Table of Units based essentially on the metric system, but it also contained four additional interim tables of units for use by those States unable to use the primary table.

The first ICAO Table of Units was based on, amongst others, nautical miles and tens, metres, knots, millibars, degrees centigrade, kilograms and metric tons and the time in 24-hours (the day beginning at midnight Greenwich Mean Time GMT, in 1972 superseded the international civil time standard by Universal Time Coordinated, UTC).

In fact, Annex 5 contains specifications for the use of a standard system of units of measurement in international civil aviation and ground operations. This standard system is based on the International System of Units or *le Système International d'Unités* (SI) and certain non-SI units considered necessary to meet the specialized requirements in inter-

---

23 The imperial system developed from what were first known as British Imperial units, as did the related system of U.S. Customary units. While many units of the U.S. system are essentially similar to their imperial counterparts, there are significant differences between the systems. The metric system (SI) is the dominant language of measurement used today. Its standardization and decimal features make it especially well-suited for the aviation industry.

national civil aviation. The SI, the modern metric system, was promulgated by the General Conference on Weights and Measures (*Conférence Générale des Poids et Mesures*, CGPM) in 1960. The SI defines seven units of measure as a basic set from which all other units are derived. The SI base units and their physical quantities are: metre for length, kilogram for mass, second for time, ampere for electric current, Kelvin for thermodynamic temperature, mole for amount of substance and candela for luminous intensity.

There are some non-SI units which have a special place in aviation and which will have to be retained, at least temporarily. These are the nautical mile, the knot, as well as the foot when it is used in the measurement of altitude, elevation or height only. Some practical problems arise in the termination of the use of these units and it has not yet been possible to plan a termination date.

The metre was one of the first natural measures. The Decimal Metric System (*Système Métrique Décimal*) was introduced in France on 7 April 1795 by the Law on Weights and Measures (*Décret Relatif aux Poids et aux Mesures*), causing a major change in the everyday life of ordinary people.

In the twentieth century, ICAN had already adopted the metric system as a standard for air navigation.

The principal purpose of Annex 5 was to reduce the number of different combinations of units used in air-ground communications and to provide for a progressive elimination of tables until only the ICAO Table is used throughout the world.

Recognizing the possibility that some States would find it impossible to employ these units in all cases, the Assembly further recommended that the Council should incorporate into the Standards suitable alternatives to be adopted by those States obliged to continue using, for example, the pound, foot or statute mile as basic units, in order to reduce the hazards resulting from the absence of uniformity.

Every effort was developed by ICAO to encourage States to move progressively towards the ICAO Table, and further amendments to Annex 5 were adopted in 1951 to actually reduce the number of alternatives to the ICAO Table. This way the long-term policy of achieving the unification of the units of measurements was affirmed. By 1961, the number of tables of units in Annex 5 had been reduced to two.

In order to improve the level of standards, a number of amendments were introduced over the years. The important Amendment 13, adopted in March 1979, extended considerably the scope of ICAO's role in standing units of measurement to cover all aspects of air and ground operations. Provisions of Annex 5 are regularly amended to reflect the changing environment, such as the definition of units or technical improvements towards a safer aviation.[24]

ICAO attempted to agree to a global standard. The ICAO Standards are used in most parts of the world; however, even these are a mixture: height in feet, speed in knots, wind

---

24 *See* ICAO Annex 5 Fifth Edition July 2010.

speed in knots, distance in nautical miles, runway length in metres and feet, weight in kilograms, temperature in degrees Celsius, pressure in hectopascals, visibility in metres and kilometres, volumes in litres and gallons and oil replenishment in pints or U.S. quarts.

While the United States is retaining a modified Imperial system with height in feet, speed in knots, distance in nautical miles, weight in pounds, temperature in degrees Fahrenheit, pressure in inches of mercury, visibility in feet and statute miles and volume in U.S. gallons, Russia and China are using the metric system throughout in aviation: height in metres, speed in kilometres per hour, wind speed in metres per second, distance in kilometres, runway length in metres, weight in kilograms, temperature in degrees Celsius, pressure in millimetres of mercury and volumes in litres.

Aircraft operating within the United States and complying with ICAO Standards have to convert almost every unit to U.S. standards. The same counts for aircraft operating within Russian and Chinese airspace to be committed to operate according to the metric system.

Amendment 13 to Annex 5 represented a major step forward in the difficult process of standardizing units of measurement in international civil aviation. Although complete standardization is an issue that needs to be addressed in the future, the foundation has been laid for resolving a problem which has been recognized by ICAO since its inception.

Because of Amendment 13, a very large degree of standardization has been achieved between civil aviation and other scientific and engineering communities. Amendments 14 and 15 to Annex 5 introduced a new definition of the metre, and references to temporary non-SI units were deleted.

Annex 6 Operation of Aircraft

According to ICAO Annex 6, operational control is the authority over the initiation, continuation or termination of a flight in the interest of aircraft safety and of the regularity and efficiency of the flight. It requires the aircraft operator to have a system in place to ensure monitoring of day-to-day flight safety activities and regularity of its operations. However, it could also have a broader context. In the situation stated above, it is intended for the day-to-day operations of the aircraft operator, although the State also should substantially contribute to creating and maintaining an overall aviation safety culture. Lack of up-to-date aviation rules and regulations, or poor aviation infrastructure and activities such as insufficiently equipped aerodromes, low-profile ATS and communications as well as unsatisfactory aviation security or negligent handling of dangerous goods shall significantly contribute to an unsafe aviation culture. Therefore, both the State, as a regulator and oversight authority, and the aircraft operator have responsibilities for the safe conduct of flight operations.

The SARPs for the Operation of Aircraft – Scheduled International Air Services were first adopted on 10 December 1948, pursuant to the provisions of Article 37 of the Chicago Convention, to become effective on 15 July 1949. The SARPs were based on recommendations of Contracting States that attended the Operations Divisional Meeting held in April 1946, which in turn were further developed at the Second Session in February 1947. These recommendations form the basis of Part I of Annex 6. Further amendments to the Annex were based on recommendations of successive sessions of the Operational Division in 1949 and 1951. At the Fourth Session in 1951, a number of amendments to Annex 6 were recommended, to a great extent dealing with fuel and oil requirements, emergency and survival equipment to be carried on board of aircraft and aircraft navigation lights. In the same year, Annex 6 was renamed Operations of Aircraft – International Commercial Air Transport.

The current Annex 6, Operations of Aircraft, is divided into three Parts or Volumes, namely, Part I: International Commercial Air Transport – Aeroplanes, Part II: International General Aviation – Aeroplanes, dealing exclusively with international general aviation and Part III: International Operations – Helicopters, dealing with all international helicopter operations.

Recognizing the growing importance and tremendous increase of international civil flying other than international air transport for remuneration or hire, it would be unpractical to provide one international set of operational rules and regulations for this wide variety of aircraft. Assembly Resolution A15-15 (Consideration of the needs of international general aviation in relation to the scope of ICAO technical activities) stipulated that appropriate SARPs and related material should be examined to determine their suitability for all international civil aviation. Consequently, the ANC prepared SARPS for operation of aircraft in general aviation (Part II) in 1968, followed later by helicopter operations (Part III), adopted by the ICAO Council on 14 March 1986. Part III originally addressed only helicopter flight recorders, but an amendment completing the coverage of international helicopter operations in the same comprehensive manner as fixed-wing aircraft operations covered in Parts I and II was adopted for applicability in November 1990.

The essence of this composite Annex 6 is that all operations of aircraft engaged in international air transport must be as standardized as possible to ensure the highest levels of safety and efficiency. Over the years a great deal of amendments followed, as well as comprehensive studies, guidance material and requirements of operations with modern, high-performance turbojet airplanes.

Annex 6 Part I contains SARPs adopted by ICAO as minimum standards applicable to the operation of aeroplanes by operators authorized to conduct international commercial air transport operations. These operations include scheduled international air services and non-scheduled international air transport operations for remuneration or hire. The distinction between the two operations lies in the fact that scheduled international air services are especially provided for in the Chicago Convention in contradiction to international air transport operations in general, of which non-scheduled international air transport operations for remuneration or hire were considered most urgently to require the establishment of international SARPs. It is no longer considered necessary to differentiate in the SARPs between scheduled international air services and non-scheduled international air transport operations.[25]

The purpose of Annex 6 Part I is to contribute to the safety of international air navigation by providing criteria of safe operating practice and to contribute to the efficiency and regularity of international air navigation, by encouraging States to facilitate the passage over their territories of aeroplanes in international commercial air transport belonging to other States that operate in conformity with such criteria.

In order to keep pace with a new and vital industry, the original provisions have been and are being constantly reviewed. This applies to all three parts. This subdivision is established because each aircraft has unique handling characteristics relative to its type and, under varying environmental conditions, may have specific operational limitations.

Notwithstanding technological progress throughout aviation, equipment installed in some general aviation aircraft may not meet the same standards as in commercial transport aircraft, and general aviation operations are subject to less rigorous standards and conducted with a greater degree of freedom than is found in commercial transport operations. Because of this, ICAO recognizes that international general aviation pilots and their passengers may not necessarily enjoy the same level of safety as the fare-paying passenger in commercial air transport. That is why Part II was designed specifically to ensure an acceptable level of safety to third parties (persons on the ground and persons in the air in other aircraft). Thus, operations involving commercial and general aviation aircraft in a common environment are required to adhere to the minimum safety standards.

The very international nature of commercial aviation, and of general aviation to a lesser degree, requires operators and pilots to conform to a wide variety of rules and regulations. ICAO Standards do not preclude the development of national standards which may be more stringent than those contained in the Annex. In all phases of aircraft operations, minimum ICAO Standards are the most acceptable compromise as they make commercial and general aviation viable without prejudicing safety.

Those Standards, accepted by all Contracting States, cover such areas as civil aircraft operations, airworthiness, performance, communications and navigation equipment, maintenance, rules limiting the flight time and flight duty periods for flight crew members, flight documents, responsibilities of the operator and flight personnel and the security of the aircraft.

---

25   ICAO Annex 6 Operation of Aircraft Part I International Commercial Air Transport - Aeroplanes, Tenth Edition July 2016, Foreword.

Clearly defined ICAO SARPs exist with respect to operating minima based on the aircraft and the environmental factors found at each aerodrome. Other factors to take into account are, for example, aircraft tracking throughout its area of operations under specific conditions, aircraft operator certificate, aircraft performance criteria, operations manual for each aircraft type and instructions for all operations personnel, minimum flight altitudes and aerodrome operational minima up to Cat IIIC, 3D instrument approach operations, flight instruments, navigation and communication equipment such as flight recorders, data link recorders, weather radar, ground proximity warning systems (GPWS), emergency locator transmitter (ELT), wind shear warning system, electronic flight bags (EFBs), fuel policies, aircraft operating minima based on aircraft characteristics and environmental aspects, requirements for operations with turbine engine-equipped aeroplanes beyond 60 minutes to an en route alternate aerodrome, including extended diversion time operations (EDTO). EDTO may be referred to in some related documents as ETOPS, to ensure safe operations by twin-engine aeroplanes operating over extended areas, often oceanic crossings.[26]

Other subjects are regulatory oversight of aircraft, fatigue management, human factors, a method of supervising flight operations to ensure a continuing level of safety, safety and security training of flight crew members, adequate rest periods to recuperate after a flight or successive flights over a period of time.

The pilot-in-command (aircraft commander) is responsible for flight preparation and is required to certify flight preparation forms when satisfied that the aircraft is airworthy, and that other criteria are met with regard to instruments, maintenance release, mass and balance, passengers manifest, airway bill, securing of the load and operating limitations of the aircraft. Hijacking of civil aircraft has placed an additional burden on the pilot-in-command. The various safety precautions that such acts necessitate, in addition to precautions of a purely technical nature, have been studied by ICAO and made to cover as many emergency situations as possible.

Today, ICAO is actively engaged in efforts to foresee the requirements of future operations such as the acceptance of a new set of procedures which revise obstacle clearance limit requirements and instrument approach procedures for all categories of international civil commercial aviation.

---

26 *See also* www.skybrary.aero/index.php/Extended_Range_Operations. Attachment D to Annex 6 – Guidance for operations by turbine engine aeroplanes beyond 60 minutes to an en-route alternate aerodrome including Extended Diversion Time Operations. This Attachment will be re-designated Attachment B with effect from an amendment to Annex 6 which will be effective from 5 November 2020, but its content will not change.
EDTO has been introduced in place of ETOPS, Extended Range Operations, previously called Extended Range Twin-engine Operations. However, EASA currently continues to use ETOPS as originally defined as well as LROPS, Long Range Operations.

Annex 7 Aircraft Nationality and Registration Marks

Annex 7 contains Standards adopted by ICAO as the minimum international standards for the display of marks to indicate appropriate nationality and registration which have been determined to comply with Article 20 of the Chicago Convention. ICAO Standards for aircraft nationality and registration marks were first adopted by the ICAO Council on 8 February 1949 pursuant to the provisions of Article 37 of the Chicago Convention and designated as Annex 7 to this Convention.

The relevant Articles are:

Article 17:
Nationality of aircraft.
Aircraft have the nationality of the State in which they are registered.

Article 18:
Dual registration.
An aircraft cannot be validly registered in more than one State, but its registration may be changed from one State to another.

Article 19:
National laws governing registrations.
The registration or transfer of registration of aircraft in any Contracting State shall be made in accordance with its laws and regulations.

Article 20:
Display of Marks.
Every aircraft engaged in international air navigation shall bear its appropriate nationality and registration marks.

Article 21:
Reports of registrations.

Each Contracting State undertakes to supply to any other Contracting State or to the International Civil Aviation Organization, on demand, information concerning the registration and ownership of any particular aircraft registered in that State. In addition, each Contracting State shall furnish reports to the International Civil Aviation Organization, under such regulations as the latter may prescribe, giving such pertinent data as can be made available concerning the ownership and control of aircraft registered in that State and habitually engaged in international air navigation. The data thus obtained by the

International Civil Aviation Organization shall be made available by it on request to the other Contracting States.

It was already in October 1922 at the Second Session of ICAN in London, that the French delegation suggested that it would be more practical to adopt the same letters for aircraft nationality marks as those allocated for use as wireless call signs. The aircraft marks identify distinctively a civil aircraft. The markings have been amended and completed over the years, but the status of the Standards prepared at the 1944 Chicago Conference underwent major changes. So, the original Annex H – Aircraft Registration and Identification Marks became Annex 7 – Aircraft Nationality and Registration Marks.

Since Article 77 of the Chicago Convention permits joint operating organizations, Amendment 3 was introduced to define 'Common Mark', 'Common Mark Registering Authority' and 'International Operating Agency', to enable aircraft of internationally operating agencies to be registered on other than a national basis. The determining principle of the related provisions is that each international operating agency must be assigned a distinctive common mark by ICAO, this being selected from a series of symbols included in the radio call sign allocated by the International Telecommunication Union (ITU). The nationality mark shall be notified to ICAO by ITU.

The Annex sets out procedures for selection by ICAO Contracting States of nationality marks from the nationality symbols. It sets ICAO Standards for the use of letters, numbers and other graphic symbols to be used in the nationality and registration marks, and spells out where these characters will be located on different types of airborne vehicles, such as lighter-than-air aircraft and heavier-than-air aircraft. The letters shall be capital letters in Roman characters and the numbers shall be Arabic numbers, both without ornamentation.

The nationality or common mark and registration mark shall consist of a group of characters. The nationality or common mark shall precede the registration mark. When the first character of the registration mark is a letter, it shall be preceded by a hyphen. The nationality mark shall be letters, numbers or a combination of letters and numbers, and shall be that assigned by the State of Registry or common mark registering authority.

When letters are used for the registration mark, combinations shall not be used which might be confused with the five-letter combinations used in the International Code of Signals, Part II, the three-letter combinations beginning with Q used in the Q-Code and with the distress signal SOS or other similar urgent signals, for example XXX, PAN and TTT.[27]

Annex 7 provides a format of the certificate of registration for use by ICAO Contracting States. According to Article 29 of the Convention, the certificate of registration must be carried on board every aircraft engaged in international air navigation, and an identification plate, bearing at least the nationality of the aircraft, or common mark and regis-

---

27 ICAO Annex 7, Sixth Edition July 2012, Chapter 3 Nationality, common and registration marks to be used.

tration mark, must be affixed in a prominent position to the main entrance, or in the case of an unmanned free balloon, affixed conspicuously to the exterior of the payload, or in the case of a remotely piloted aircraft, secured in a prominent position near the main entrance or compartment or affixed conspicuously to the exterior of the aircraft if there is no main entrance or compartment.

The objective is that the classification of aircraft should be as simple as possible, and yet should encompass as many types of flying machines as the human mind can devise.

Annex 8 Airworthiness of Aircraft

Airworthiness is a term used to describe both the legal and mechanical status of an aircraft with regard to its readiness for flight

A State must protect the safety of its nationals, even abroad. It is possible that in an aerostat taking off from one country there will be nationals of another State, or cargo belonging to citizens of one State may be carried by a foreign aerostat, and it is right that the State should know that they are not in danger on board, that they will arrive safely at their destination; the development of international commerce requires that air machines should be guaranteed to be airworthy.

It is not just the safety of persons and goods on board that requires a prior permit, it is also the safety of persons and property in the countries below who are exposed to dangers and damage, particularly at the time of landing; in this regard, foreign countries are just as interested as the country of the aerostat's nationality.[28]

Most aircraft developed are the complex product of a team effort by a large number of aviation experts such as designers, engineers and skilled technicians. In a time of unprecedented pace of technological development, there is very little doubt that a newly designed aircraft will fly. Today, aircraft are not designed any more on practice-based assumptions and simple drawings, but according to known scientific laws, mathematical formulae, empiricism and comprehensive computer-aided research.

In the interest of aviation safety, an aircraft must be designed, constructed, operated and maintained in compliance with the appropriate airworthiness requirements of the State of Registry of the aircraft. The result of all this is an aircraft with handling characteristics and performance similar, equal to or even better than computer calculations and wind tunnel tests. Consequently, the aircraft is issued with a Certificate of Airworthi-

---

28 Dr. Paul Auguste Joseph Fauchille (1858-1926). Fauchille's proposals regarding Certificates of Airworthiness, among other things, were endorsed by the Paris International Air Navigation Conference (1910) with the purpose of drafting a multilateral international treaty to regulate international air navigation.

ness declaring the aircraft is fit to fly. Obviously, continuous airworthiness can only be achieved by thorough maintenance.

SARPs for the airworthiness of aircraft were adopted by the Council on 1 March 1949 pursuant to the provisions of Article 37 of the Chicago Convention and designated as Annex 8 to the Convention. As a result of studies made by the ANC and an international body of airworthiness experts, a revised policy on international airworthiness was developed, and it was approved by the Council in 1956. According to this policy, the principle of certification in an ICAO category was abandoned.

Instead, Annex 8 included broad standards which defined, for application by the competent national authorities, the complete international minimum basis for the recognition by States of Certificates of Airworthiness for the purpose of the flight of aircraft of other States into or over their territories, thereby achieving, among other things, protection of other aircraft, third persons and property.

Article 31 of the Chicago Convention specifies that every aircraft engaged in international navigation shall be provided with a Certificate of Airworthiness issued or rendered valid by the State in which it is registered. Article 33 stipulates that Certificates of Airworthiness, just as certificates of competency and licenses, issued or rendered valid by the Contracting State in which the aircraft is registered, shall be recognized as valid by the other Contracting States, provided that the requirements under which such Certificates of Airworthiness were issued or rendered valid are equal to or above the minimum standards which may be established from time to time pursuant to this Convention.

It was recognized that the ICAO Standards of airworthiness would not replace national regulations and that national codes of airworthiness containing the full scope and extent of detail, considered necessary by individual States, would be required as the basis for the certification of individual aircraft. Each State would establish its own comprehensive and detailed code of airworthiness or would select a comprehensive and detailed code established by another Contracting State. The level of airworthiness required to be maintained by a national code is indicated by the broad ICAO Standards of Annex 8, supplemented, where necessary, by guidance material provided in ICAO's Airworthiness Technical Manual (ICAO Doc 9760).

Present policy on international airworthiness: There was some concern about the slow progress that had been made over the years with respect to developing supplementary airworthiness specifications in the form of Acceptable Means of Compliance (AMC). It was noted that the majority of these AMCs in Annex 6 and 8 had been developed in 1957 and were therefore applicable to only those aeroplane types operating at that time. No effort had been made to update the specifications in these AMCs nor had there been any recommendations from the Airworthiness Committee, established by the Council in 1957, for upgrading of any of the provisional AMCs, which had been developed as potential material for full-fledged AMCs.

The ANC therefore requested the Airworthiness Committee to review the progress made by it since its inception with a careful view to determining whether or not desired results had been achieved and to recommend any changes to improve the development of detailed airworthiness specifications. After a detailed study by the Airworthiness Committee, the principle of AMC was abandoned in favour of an airworthiness technical manual to be prepared and published by ICAO to include guidance material intended to facilitate the development and uniformity of national airworthiness codes by Contracting States.

In 2000, the ANC reviewed the recommendations of the Continuing Airworthiness Panel and the Airworthiness Study Group, in light of the introduction of the type certification process, to introduce the type certificate concept. It came to the conclusion that this internationally used and known certificate was already introduced in the Airworthiness Technical Manual, issued in early 1974, and that its introduction complements its type certification process, making the text of Annex 8 consistent with its international airworthiness use.

It was further noted that the State of Registry, which is in charge of the issuance or validation of Certificates of Airworthiness by virtue of Article 31 of the Convention, and the State of Design may be different States, with separate functions and duties, and two independent responsibilities.

Accordingly, the requirements governing the issuance of type certificates in accordance with applicable provisions of Annex 8 are not part of the minimum standards which govern the issuance or validation of Certificates of Airworthiness, and lead to the recognition of their validity pursuant to Article 33 of the Convention.

A Certificate of Airworthiness shall be issued by a Contracting State on the basis of satisfactory evidence that the aircraft shall comply with the design aspects of the appropriate airworthiness requirements. Certification of airworthiness is initially conferred by a Certificate of Airworthiness from a national aviation authority and is maintained by performing the required maintenance actions. After all, airworthiness is the measure of an aircraft's suitability for safe flight.

The application of airworthiness defines the condition of an aircraft and supplies the basis for judgment of suitability for flight of that aircraft. It must be designed with engineering precision, being meticulously constructed and maintained and expected to operate to approved standards and limitations. This specialized work must be done by competent and approved individuals, who are acting as members of an approved organization and whose work is both certified as correct and accepted on behalf of the State of Manufacture and the State of Registry. The airworthiness of aircraft ranges from the initial approval of a new aircraft design to ensuring an aircraft's ongoing safety standard.

Sufficient data on the performance of the aeroplane shall be determined and scheduled in the flight manual to provide operators with the necessary information for the purpose of determining the total mass of the aeroplane on the basis of the values, particular to the proposed flight, of the relevant operational parameters, in order that the flight may be made with the reasonable assurance that a safe minimum performance for that flight will be achieved. These minimum performance standards are contained in Annex 8.

The performance standards require that the aeroplane shall be capable of accomplishing the minimum performance specified in the Annex at all phases of flight, for example, in the take-off and initial climb phases. In the event of a failure of the critical power unit and the remaining power units (multi-engine aeroplane) are operating within their take-off power limitations, the aircraft must be capable of safely continuing or rejecting its take-off. Continuation of the take-off beyond the V_1 decision speed means that after the initial take-off flight path (the first climb segment ends when the landing gear is fully retracted, the second climb segment is the performance limiting segment, at the end of which the transition is from maximum take-off thrust to maximum continuous thrust for level flight acceleration and final climb segment), the aeroplane must be capable of continuing climb (specified minimum engine out climb gradient for obstacle clearance) up to a height at which the aeroplane can continue safe flight and landing, while the remaining power units are operating within their continuous power limitations. Criteria such as engine out climb gradients and obstacle clearance are both critically important.

The aeroplane must be controllable and stable under all anticipated operating conditions without exceptional skill, alertness or strength on the part of the pilots, even in the event of failure of any power unit. Furthermore, the stall characteristics of the aeroplane must be such as to give the pilots a clear warning, and it should be possible for the pilots to maintain full control of the aeroplane without altering engine power. Special consideration is given to requirements dealing with design features which affect the ability of the flight crew to maintain controlled flight.

The layout of the flight deck must be such as to minimize the possibility of incorrect operation of controls and instruments due to confusion, fatigue or interference. It should allow a sufficiently clear, extensive and undistorted field of vision for the safe operation of the aeroplane. Design features for the safety, health and well-being of occupants are taken into account such as a comfortable cabin environment and the means of a rapid and safe evacuation in case of an on-ground emergency.

Requirements for the certification of engines and accessories are designed to ensure that they function reliably under the anticipated operating conditions by thoroughly testing under extreme conditions.

All standards, including those standards relating to the production process, are of utmost importance in light of facilitating the import and export of aircraft, as well as the exchange of aircraft for lease, charter or interchange purposes and to facilitate operations of aircraft in international air navigation.

Following terrorist acts on board aircraft and aircraft hijacking, special security features have been included in aircraft design to improve the protection of the aircraft. These include special features in aircraft systems, identification of a least-risk bomb location and strengthening of the flight deck door, ceilings and floors of the cabin compartment.

Annex 8 is divided into four parts: Part I includes definitions, Part II deals with procedures for certification and continuing airworthiness of aircraft, Part III includes technical requirements for the certification of new large aircraft design and Part IV deals with helicopters.[29]

Under the provisions related to continuing airworthiness of aircraft, the State of Registry must inform the State of Design when it first enters in its register an aircraft of the type certified by the latter. This procedure is to enable the State of Design to transmit to the State of Registry any generally applicable information it has found necessary for the continuing airworthiness and for the safe operation of the aircraft. The State of Registry must also transmit to the State of Design all continuing airworthiness information originated by it for transmission, as necessary, to other Contracting States known to have on their registers the same type of aircraft.

One of the supporting clauses in the definitions used in the Annex defines the environment in which an aircraft is expected to perform as 'anticipated operating conditions'. These are conditions which are known from experience or which can be reasonably envisaged to occur during the operational life of the aircraft, taking into account the operations for which the aircraft is made eligible.

They also include conditions relative to the weather, terrain surrounding the aerodromes from which the aircraft is expected to operate, functioning of the aircraft, efficiency of personnel and other factors affecting safety in flight. Anticipated operating conditions do not include those extremes which can be effectively avoided by operating procedures and those extremes which occur so infrequently that higher levels of airworthiness to meet them would render aircraft operations impracticable.

Requirements for detailed design and construction provide for a reasonable assurance that all aeroplane parts will function reliably and effectively. While design should minimize the possibility of in-flight fires, cabin depressurization and toxic gases in the aeroplane and protect the aeroplane against lightning and static electricity, innovative methods of fabrication and assembly must produce a consistently sound structure for sustainability.

Aeroplane design features also provide for the safety, health and well-being of occupants by providing an adequate cabin environment during the anticipated flight (next generation aircraft, no bleed architecture, cabin air conditioning and temperature control system, (CACTCS), etc.) and ground and water operating conditions, the means for rapid and safe evacuation in emergency landing situations and the equipment necessary for the survival of the occupants following an emergency landing in the expected external environment for a reasonable time span.

---

29 ICAO Annex 8 Airworthiness of Aircraft, Eleventh Edition July 2010.

Annex 9 Facilitation

Global air traffic is expected to increase significantly in the coming years, creating an unprecedented need to reconcile facilitation and security procedures with passenger flows to be controlled at the borders. This estimation means that current and emerging facilitation risks need to be addressed proactively to ensure that this tremendous capacity expansion is carefully managed and supported through strategic regulatory and infrastructure developments at international airports as well as focused State programmes. Future international air traffic brings into sharp focus the need for travel documents, rules and related systems that are up to the task of tomorrow's facilitation and security challenges.[30]

Airport facilitation consists of the efficient management of the flow of passengers, baggage, cargo and mail through the airport facilities, ensuring that services are delivered in a healthy, safe and secure environment. Facilitation is not just achieved by airport operators in isolation, but requires a high level of interaction and coordination with airport partners and stakeholders that are responsible for the different steps of the end-to-end passenger process, from the time of booking to the time the passengers arrive at their final destination.[31]

ICAO SARPs inevitably take two forms: first a 'negative' form, that States shall not impose more than certain maximum requirements in the way of paperwork, restrictions of freedom of movement, etc., and second a 'positive' form, that States shall provide certain minimum facilities for passenger convenience, for traffic which is merely passing through, etc.[32]

Annex 9 embodies the SARPs and guidance material pertaining specifically to the facilitation of landside formalities for clearance of aircraft and passengers, goods and mail, with respect to the requirements of customs, immigration, public health and agriculture authorities. As such, it provides a frame of reference for planners and managers of international airport operations, describing the obligations of industry as well as the minimum facilities to be provided by governments.

In addition, Contracting States shall adopt appropriate measures for the clearance of aircraft arriving from or departing to another Contracting State and shall implement them in such a manner as to prevent unnecessary delays, at the same time taking into account the application of aviation security and narcotics control measures, where appropriate. In a more compact description, facilitation is the efficient management of border control processes to expedite clearance accompanied by a minimum of inconvenience. It

---

30   ICAO Security and Facilitation. Background of Facilitation Programmes.
31   Airport Facilitation, Airports Council International.
32   ICAO Annex 9 Facilitation, Fifteenth Edition October 2017, Foreword. *See also* Abeyratne, R.I.R., *Law and Regulation of Air Cargo*, Cham: Springer International Publishing, 2018, p. 129.

addresses integrated border management, including the balance between border security and facilitation.

Annex 9 specifies methods and procedures for carrying out clearance operations in such a way as to achieve compliance with the law of States while enabling maximum productivity for the air transport operators, airports and government inspection agencies involved.

The provisions of some Articles of the Convention form the basis of the SARPs regarding facilitation. Articles 22, 23 and 37 have in common that Contracting States are obliged to adopt all practicable measures, through the issuance of special regulations or otherwise, to facilitate and expedite navigation by aircraft between the territories of Contracting States, and to prevent unnecessary delays to aircraft, crews, passengers and cargo, especially in the administration of the laws relating to immigration, quarantine, customs and clearance.

Article 10 (Landing at customs airport) requires all aircraft entering the territory of a Contracting State, if the regulations of that State so require, to land at an airport designated by that State for the purpose of customs and other examination. On departure from the territory of a Contracting State, such aircraft shall depart from a similarly designated customs airport. Particulars of all designated customs airports shall be published by the State and transmitted to ICAO for communication to all other Contracting States.

Article 13 of the Chicago Convention:

> Entry and clearance regulations.
> The laws and regulations of a Contracting State as to the admission to or departure from its territory of passengers, crew or cargo of aircraft, such as regulations relating to entry, clearance, immigration, passports, customs, and quarantine shall be complied with by or on behalf of such passengers, crew or cargo upon entrance into or departure from, or while within the territory of that State.

Article 14 (Prevention of spread of disease) obliges each Contracting State to take effective measures to prevent the spread through air navigation of cholera, typhus (epidemic), smallpox, yellow fever, plague and such other communicable diseases as the Contracting States shall from time to time decide to designate. Therefore, Contracting States will keep in close consultation with the agencies concerned with international regulations relating to sanitary measures applicable to aircraft. In cases where evidence of protection against a quarantine-type disease is required, Contracting States shall accept the International Certificate of Vaccination or Revaccination form, prescribed by the World Health Organization (WHO) in the International Health Regulations. With hundreds of thousands of people embarking on airplanes every day, infectious diseases unfortunately have unprecedented opportunities to spread farther and faster.

Regarding customs duty, Article 24 also deals with facilitation. Fuel, lubricating oils, spare parts, regular equipment and aircraft stores on board an aircraft of a Contracting State, on arrival in the territory of another Contracting State and retained on board on leaving the territory of that State shall be exempt from customs duties, inspection fees or similar national or local duties and charges.

This exemption shall not apply to any quantities or articles unloaded, except in accordance with the customs regulations of the State, which may require that they shall be kept under customs supervision.

Each Contracting State undertakes, as it may find practicable, to establish customs and immigration procedures affecting international air navigation in accordance with the practices which may be established or recommended from time to time, pursuant to the Chicago Convention. Nothing in this Convention shall be construed as preventing the establishment of customs-free airports.[33]

Other articles have been taken into account with respect to the preparation of Annex 9 such as Article 29 – Documents carried in aircraft, and Article 35 – Cargo restrictions.

Annex 9, the first edition of which was adopted in 1949, provides a frame of reference for planners and managers of international airport operations, describing maximum limits on obligations of industry and minimum facilities to be provided by governments. In addition, Annex 9 specifies methods and procedures for carrying out clearance operations in such a manner as to meet the twin objectives of effective compliance with the laws of States and productivity for the operators, airports and government inspection agencies involved.

States' resources for inspection regimes could not keep pace with the recent growth of traffic volumes. The facilitation of landside clearance formalities became a much more complex issue. While Annex 9 previously retained its original strategies of reducing paperwork, standardizing documentation and simplifying procedures, due to traffic accumulation, the focus shifted to inspection techniques based on risk management, with the objectives to increase efficiency, reduce delays and enhance security in the area of controlling abuses such as narcotics trafficking and travel document fraud, which in fact are major issues.

Contracting States shall take all necessary measures to ensure that the time required for the accomplishment of border control in respect of persons and aircraft and for the release or clearance of goods is kept to the minimum, in particular to reduce congestion in airports and generally to support the growth of international trade and travel. A minimum of inconvenience is to be achieved by the application of more effective administrative and control requirements.

---

33   Art. 23 of the Chicago Convention.

The Contracting States must ensure that the exchange of relevant information between Contracting States, operators and airports is fostered and promoted to the greatest extent possible, and optimal levels of security and compliance with the law are attained. Contracting States shall develop effective information technology to increase the efficiency and effectiveness of their procedures at airports.

Enhancing the security of travel documents and tackling illegal migration are among the major changes introduced into Annex 9 through its 12th and succeeding editions. To reflect international realities, a number of chapters are substantially amended.[34]

According to a new Standard in Chapter 3, Contracting States shall regularly update security features in new versions of their travel documents, to guard against their misuse and to facilitate detection of cases where such documents have been unlawfully altered, replicated or issued. They must establish controls on the creation and issuance of travel documents in order to safeguard against the theft of their stocks and the misappropriation of newly issued travel documents.

States are also now obliged to issue separate passports to all persons, regardless of age, and to issue them in machine-readable form, in accordance to ICAO's specifications.[35] States and airlines are required to collaborate in combating travel document fraud. As for crew members, States are obliged to place adequate controls on the issuance of crew member certificates and other official crew identity documents.

Chapter 5 is devoted to the growing problem of inadmissible persons and deportees. SARPS set out in clear terms the obligation of States and airlines for the transport of potentially illegal migrants and similar widespread problem cases that the international air transport industry comes across in ever greater numbers daily. The Contracting State obligation to remove fraudulent travel documents from circulation or genuine documents used fraudulently will greatly help to constrict the flow of illegal migrants the world over.

Chapter 6 deals with airports and the fast-growing problem of unruly passengers in international aviation. Chapter 7 contains procedures with respect to the subject of landing elsewhere than at international airports. Each Contracting State shall take steps to ensure that all possible assistance is rendered by its public authorities to an aircraft, which, for reasons beyond the control of the pilot-in-command, has landed elsewhere than at one of its international airports and, to this end, shall keep control formalities and procedures, in such cases, but above all in case of a short stopover, to a minimum.

Each Contracting State shall ensure that efficient customs, immigration, quarantine and health border clearance services, as required, are provided at international airports that see congestion more often due to mass travel. The answer to this rather complex issue is to reduce obsolete documentation, to simplify procedures, in particular by technically advanced electronic data interchange systems.

---

34   *See* Annex 9 Fifteenth Edition October 2017.
35   Machine Readable Travel Documents (MRTDs).

Other facilitation provisions are facilitation of search, rescue, accident investigation and salvage, implementation of international health regulations and related provisions, communicable disease outbreak national aviation plan, establishment of national facilitation programmes, facilitation of the transport of persons with disabilities and assistance to aircraft accident victims and their families.[36]

Chapter 9 contains provisions related to Advance Passenger Information (API) and Electronic Travel Systems (ETS), to integrate the pre-travel verification system with an interactive API system. Each Contracting State requiring Passenger Name Record (PNR) data shall align its data requirements and its handling of such data with the guidelines on passenger name record data contained in ICAO Doc 9944, and in PNRGOV message implementation guidance materials published and updated by the World Customs Organization (WCO) and endorsed by ICAO and IATA.

Annex 10 Aeronautical Telecommunications

Three of the most complex and essential elements of international air navigation are aeronautical communications, navigation and surveillance.

Annex 10 is divided into five volumes:
– Volume I – Radio navigation aids
– Volume II – Communication procedures including those with PANS status
– Volume III – Communication systems
  1. Part I – Digital data communication systems
  2. Part II – Voice communication systems
– Volume IV – Surveillance Radar and Collision Avoidance Systems
– Volume V – Aeronautical Radio Frequency Spectrum Utilization

The five volumes of this Annex contain SARPs, PANS and guidance material on aeronautical communication, navigation and surveillance systems.

Volume I is a technical document which defines for international aircraft operations the systems, together with essential parameter specifications, necessary to provide radio navigation aids used by aircraft in all phases of flight such as the Global Navigation Satellite System (GNSS), Instrument Landing System (ILS), Microwave Landing System (MLS), Very High Frequency (VHF) Omni-directional Radio Range (VOR), Non-directional Radio Beacons (NDB) and Distance Measuring Equipment (DME), and all aspects for reliable system operation.

Both Volumes II and III cover two general categories of voice and data communications that serve international civil aviation. They are the ground-ground communication between points on the surface and air-ground communication between aircraft and

---

36   Annex 9 Chapter 8.

points on the ground. An important element of ground-ground communication is the Aeronautical Fixed Telecommunications Network (AFTN), a worldwide network organized to meet the specific requirements of international air navigation. It is an integrated system of aeronautical fixed circuits provided as part of the Aeronautical Fixed Service (AFS) for the exchange of communication and/or digital data between the aeronautical stations having the same or compatible communication characteristics.

In Volume II, administrative and operational procedures pertaining to aeronautical fixed and mobile communications are presented.

Volume III contains SARPs and guidance material for various air-ground and ground-ground voice and data communications systems, including Aeronautical Telecommunication Network (ATN) Aeronautical Mobile-Satellite Service (AMSS), Secondary Surveillance Radar (SSR), mode S air-ground data link, Very High Frequency airground Digital Link (VDL), AFTN, aircraft addressing system, High Frequency Data Link (HFDL), aeronautical mobile service, Selective Calling System (SELCAL), aeronautical speech circuits and Emergency Locator Transmitter (ELT).

Volume IV contains SARPS and guidance material for Secondary Surveillance Radar and Airborne Collision Avoidance Systems (ACAS) including SARPs for SSR Mode A, Mode C and Mode S, and the technical characteristics of ACAS.

Volume V includes SARPS and guidance material on the utilization of aeronautical frequencies. The International Telecommunication Union (ITU) has set up a framework in which the demands for radio spectrum from individual States are balanced with the interests of different radio service users to produce a planned radio environment incorporating interference-free, effective and efficient radio spectrum use. Volume V also contains information on the assignment planning of aeronautical, individual radio stations operating or planned to operate in different frequency bands.

Annex 11 Air Traffic Services

Control of air traffic was almost unknown in 1944. Today, air traffic control, flight information and alerting services, which together comprise air traffic services, rank high among the indispensable ground support facilities which ensure the safe and efficient operation of air traffic throughout the world. The world's airspace is divided into a series of contiguous Flight Information Regions (FIRs) within which Air Traffic Services (ATS) are provided. Sometimes the FIRs cover large oceanic areas with relatively low air traffic density, within which only flight information service and alerting service are provided.

A State is obliged to determine, according to the provisions of Annex 11, if air traffic services must be provided in its airspace and at aerodromes in its territory. Subsequently, the responsible State should monitor that these services shall be established and executed according to the set provisions. If a State delegates the provision of air traffic services to another State, this should be done without prejudice to national sovereignty.

Annex 11 pertains to the establishment of airspace, units and services necessary to promote a safe, orderly and expeditious flow of air traffic. A clear distinction is made between air traffic control service, flight information service and alerting service. Its purpose, together with Annex 2, is to ensure that flying on international routes is carried out under uniform conditions designed to improve the safety and efficiency of air operation.

The prime objective of air traffic services, as defined in Annex 11, is to prevent collisions between aircraft, whether taxiing on the manoeuvring area (with or without obstacles), during taking off, landing, en route or in the holding pattern at the destination aerodrome, and furthermore, to expedite and maintain an orderly flow of air traffic, to provide advice and information useful for the safe and efficient conduct of flights, to notify appropriate organizations regarding aircraft in need of search and rescue aid and to assist such organizations as required. The need for the provision of air traffic services shall be determined by consideration of the following:

1. the types of air traffic involved;
2. the density of air traffic;
3. the meteorological conditions;
4. such other factors as may be relevant.

The SARPs in Annex 11 apply in those parts of the airspace under the jurisdiction of a Contracting State wherein air traffic services are provided and also wherever a Contracting State accepts the responsibility of providing air traffic services over the high seas or in airspace of undetermined sovereignty. A Contracting State accepting such responsibility may apply the SARPs in a manner consistent with that adopted for airspace under its jurisdiction. Those portions of the airspace over the high seas or in airspace of undetermined sovereignty where air traffic services will be provided shall be determined on the basis of regional air navigation agreements.

The Contracting States shall determine, in accordance with the provisions of Annex 11 and for the territories over which they have jurisdiction, those portions of the airspace and those aerodromes where air traffic services will be provided. They shall thereafter arrange for such services to be established and provided in accordance with the provisions, except that, by mutual agreement, a State may delegate to another State or a designated organization (e.g. EUROCONTROL) the responsibility for establishing and providing air traffic services in FIRs, Control Areas (CTAs) or Control Zones (CTRs) extending over the territory of the former State.[37]

---

37 Schwenk, W., Schwenk, R., *Aspects of International Co-operation in Air Traffic Management*, Utrecht Studies in Air and Space Law, Volume 17, The Hague: Martinus Nijhoff Publishers, 1998, pp. 41-42.

In the North Atlantic region, several States are offering air navigation services for the purpose of the safe, orderly and expeditious flow of the tremendous amount of air traffic over the high seas that are connecting the continents on each side of the Atlantic. Iceland, Denmark, Canada, Portugal (Azores) and the United States, as well as the United Kingdom have the burden of responsibility for flights crossing the Atlantic Ocean because of their geographical nature.

Especially Iceland and Denmark (Greenland and Faroe Islands) are tasked with operating and maintaining the services without interruption. Navigation facilities and services must also be provided for air routes traversing the high seas and regions of undetermined sovereignty.

To collectively finance and facilitate air navigation services in the North Atlantic region, two agreements were concluded at Geneva on 25 September 1956, the Agreement on the Joint Financing of Certain Air Navigation Services in Iceland (ICAO Doc 9586) and the Agreement on the Joint Financing of Certain Air Navigation Services in Greenland and the Faroe Islands (ICAO Doc 9585). Greenland and the Faroe Islands are autonomous constituent States within the Kingdom of Denmark. Both multilateral agreements, providing for the joint financing of air traffic control, communications and meteorological services, were opened to any State that wishes to participate in the funding of these services for the North Atlantic region. Both agreements entered into force in 1958, and have been amended and updated in 1982 and 2008.

Operators of aircraft crossing the North Atlantic are charged for using these services. Remaining actual costs to maintain the services are agreed to be shared by the States Parties to the agreements, proportionally based on the number of crossings performed by commercial air carriers located in the respective States. Such proportions shall be determined for each State Party in respect of each calendar year by the number of crossings, or between Europe and North America any portion of which lies north of the 45th parallel North between the meridians of 15° West and 50° West performed in that year by its civil aircraft. Partial crossings are for example, Iceland-Europe, North America-Iceland or Greenland-Canada, and all *vice versa*.

Safety is the overriding concern of international air navigation, and air traffic management contributes substantially to safety in civil aviation. Annex 11 contains an important requirement for States to implement systematic and appropriate ATS safety management programmes to ensure that safety is maintained in the provision of these services within airspaces and at aerodromes. Safety systems and programmes will serve as an important contribution with a view to ensuring safety in international civil aviation.[38]

Annex 11 deals with the establishment and operation of air traffic control, flight information and alerting services mainly based on appropriate portions of the Annexes to

---

38 Bartsch, R.I.C., *International Aviation Law: A Practical Guide*, Milton Park, Abingdon, Oxon: Routledge, 2016, p. 271.

the 1919 Paris Convention, especially Annex D, published by the International Commission for Air Navigation.

Annex 11 was first adopted by the Council on 18 May 1950 and recommended for worldwide application. The Annex has been continuously modified, adopted and expanded over the years since the adoption of the First Edition through recommendations issued by divisional meetings, numerous air navigation conferences, the ANC and various technical panels established by the ANC. In order to make it clear that air traffic control service was a part of the services covered by Annex 11, together with flight information service and alerting service, the new title became Air Traffic Services.

The PANS-ATM, Procedures for Air Navigation Services-Air Traffic Management contain material prepared as an amplification of the basic principles contained in the SARPs which are adopted in pursuance of Article 37 of the Chicago Convention. As more aircraft fill the crowded FIR air routes, air traffic control concepts, procedures, equipment and rules will continue to evolve as will the provisions of Annex 11.

Annex 12 Search and Rescue

Search and rescue services are organized to respond to persons apparently in distress and in need of help. At the present stage of technical development, a forced landing or aircraft accident on the sea or outside an aerodrome is a very rare occurrence. As early as 1938, when the Brussels Convention was concluded, an attempt was made to lay down rules on the subject.[39] This Convention was partly a matter of public law, because it contained a statutory obligation to render assistance, and partly private law because it gave rules concerning the remuneration for the services rendered.

ICAO has also drawn up regulations concerning search and rescue. These regulations, which are to be found in Annex 12, are based on different principles and cover a different field from the Brussels Convention. Prompted by the need to rapidly locate and rescue survivors of aircraft accidents, a set of internationally agreed SARPs has been incorporated in Annex 12 – Search and Rescue. Proposals for Annex 12 were originally made in 1946. By 1951, the proposals had been reviewed and revised to meet international civil aviation requirements, and were embodied as SARPs in the First Edition of Annex 12.

Annex 12 is primarily intended to give effect to Article 25, Aircraft in distress, of the Chicago Convention, whereby the Contracting States are obliged to take steps to render assistance to aircraft in distress on their territory, to cooperate in measures of assistance provided by the owners of the missing aircraft or the State in which the missing aircraft

---

39   International Convention for the Unification of Certain Rules Relating to Assistance and Salvage of Aircraft or by Aircraft, at Sea, 1938. The Convention was adopted at Brussels on 28 September 1938 (not yet in force).

was registered and, in general, to collaborate in coordinated measures which may be recommended from time to time pursuant to the Chicago Convention.

In Montreal, an important meeting of the Rules of the Air, Air Traffic Services and Search and Rescue (RAC/SAR) Division was held from 21 October to 14 November 1958. Its recommendations involved fairly extensive amendments to several Annexes, including Annex 12 which required the addition of provisions designed to facilitate the passage of search and rescue units across national borders, the modification of the re-commended practices of the delineation of the boundaries of search and rescue areas to give efficiency priority over observance of the principle that the boundaries of those areas should coincide with the FIR-boundaries, and the revision of the procedures for initiating search and rescue action for an aircraft whose position is unknown, as well as the im-provement of the procedures to be followed by Rescue Coordination Centres (RCCs) in terminating search and rescue operations.

Later, revisions were made to Annex 12 and amendments were based on the recom-mendations made by the ICAO Air Navigation Commission.

The Annex, which is complemented by a three-part Search and Rescue Manual deal-ing with search and rescue organization, management and procedures, sets forth the provisions for the establishment, maintenance and operation of SAR services of ICAO Contracting States in their territories and over the high seas. ICAO is continuously work-ing with the International Maritime Organization (IMO) on numerous subjects of mutual concern, especially on the harmonization of aeronautical and maritime SAR-proce-dures.[40]

Containing five chapters, the Annex details the organization and cooperative princi-ples appropriate to effective SAR operations, outlines required necessary preparatory measures and sets forth proper operating procedures for SAR services in actual emergen-cies. One of the first aspects addressed in the organizational chapter is the requirement for States to provide SAR services within their territories and over those portions of the high seas or areas of undetermined sovereignty as determined in regional air navigation agreements and approved by the Council of ICAO. Annex 12 provides also for mobile SAR units, the means of communication for these units and the designation of other elements of public or private services suitable for search and rescue activity.

Cooperation between the SAR services of neighbouring States is essential to the effi-cient conduct of SAR operations. ICAO Contracting States are required to publish and disseminate all information needed for the expeditious entry into their territories of res-cue units of other States. It is also recommended that persons qualified in the conduct of aircraft accident investigation accompany rescue units in order to facilitate accident in-vestigation.

---

40   See also ICAO/IMO Joint Working Group on SAR. www.international-maritime-rescue.org/news/icao-imo-joint-working-group-on-sar.

Provisions concerning equipment requirements of rescue units reflect the need to give adequate assistance at the scene of accidents, due regard being given to the number of passengers involved, as is stated in Chapter 3.

Preparatory measures contained in Chapter 4 set forth the requirements for collation and publication of information needed by the SAR services. This part of Annex 12 specifies that detailed plans of operation must be prepared for the conduct of SAR operations and indicates the necessary information for inclusion in the plans. Preparatory measures required to be undertaken by rescue units, training requirements and removal of aircraft wreckage are also covered. A search and rescue operation is a dynamic activity requiring uniformly comprehensive operating procedures that are sufficiently flexible to meet extraordinary needs. Chapter 5 details action to be taken for each category of event. Three distinct phases categorize emergency situations. First is the 'uncertainty phase' which is commonly declared when radio contact has been lost with an aircraft and cannot be re-established or when an aircraft fails to arrive at its destination. During this phase the RCC concerned may be activated, which collects and evaluates reports and data pertaining to the subject aircraft.

Depending on the situation, the uncertainty phase may develop into an 'alert phase', at which time the RCC alerts appropriate SAR units and initiates further action. The 'distress phase' is declared when there is reasonable certainty that an aircraft is in distress. In this phase, the RCC is responsible for taking action in order to assist the aircraft and to determine its location as rapidly as possible.

In compliance with a predetermined set of procedures, the aircraft operator, the State of Registry, air traffic services units concerned, adjacent RCCs and appropriate accident investigation authorities are informed. A plan for the conduct of the search and rescue operation is drawn up and its execution is coordinated.

An Appendix to the Annex provides three sets of signals, the first of which are signals for use by aircraft and surface craft during the conduct of a SAR operation. The second and third sets consist of ground-to-air visual signals for use by survivors and ground rescue units.

Annex 13 Aircraft Accident and Incident Investigation

As air traffic continues to grow fast, tremendous efforts are required to keep air transport safe and sustainable. The aviation safety culture should therefore be regarded as a continuous effort to enhance that particular safety where possible. Although civil aviation is considered to be the safest means of transport, it is an activity facing many potential hazards.

If an aviation accident occurs, the consequences are mostly dramatic and the impact on society would absolutely be disastrous and far-reaching. Aviation accidents usually result from a combination of failures, occurring sequentially or on occasion simultaneously in one or more activities. For the most part, numerous factors are involved in aviation accidents.

Aircraft accidents could generally be classified as being caused by technical defects or human error or a combination of both factors. Investigation of technical (mechanical, electronic, etc.) causes of aircraft accidents has become much more precise given the wide spectrum of advanced investigation techniques available nowadays. Human factors in aircraft accidents and incidents are less tangible and detectable than technical defects. Factual determination of the (probable) cause of an accident is of utmost importance. It improves air safety in helping to prevent recurrences of such accidents.

The international character of civil aviation necessitates the development of law that would make sure that any aircraft accident or incident anywhere in the world should be subject to a uniform technical investigation. A prerequisite is to make use of available standardized rules regarding the conduct of accident investigations.

States shall, according to the provisions laid down in Annex 13, first adopted under the name of Aircraft Accident Inquiry by the Council on 11 April 1951, investigate or delegate the investigation of accidents which have occurred in their respective territories.

When an aircraft accident happens involving an international civil aviation flight, Annex 13 sets out the rights on who should conduct the investigation, what exactly are the parties that can be involved, what rights each party has, in what way the investigation should be conducted and the manner in which the final results will be reported. Normally the State of Occurrence, the State of Registry, the State of the Operator, the State of Design and the State of Manufacture participate. Other parties that may be involved are representatives of the Contracting States which rendered assistance on request with respect to the accident.

Annex 13 also re-emphasizes the need for aircraft accident prevention purposes, to separate accident investigation from judicial or legal processes in order to prevent thorough and competent technical investigation from being impeded. In other words, the sole objective of the investigation of an aircraft accident or incident is to prevent future accidents and incidents and that the investigation is not to apportion blame or liability.

It is evident that information contained in the records shall in principle not be made available to other entities such as judicial authorities for purposes other than the safety investigation into these events, unless there are weighty arguments in favour of disclosure, rather than the negative effects that would most probably be caused by this disclosure (Annex 13, Art. 5.12).

In respect of accident investigation, it is of great importance for the general improvement of the safety of air navigation that, to the greatest practicable extent, a Contracting State in which an accident has occurred involving aircraft other than of its manufacture shall as soon as possible communicate to the State of Manufacture any pertinent information which results from the investigation and which may reflect on the airworthiness of the aircraft type or its equipment, or which might be used to effect improvement in safety.[41]

Responsibility for an investigation belongs to the State in which the accident or incident occurred. That State usually conducts the investigation, but it may delegate all or part of the investigation to another State. If the occurrence takes place outside the territory of any State, for example on the high seas or in an area of undetermined sovereignty, the State of Registry of the aircraft concerned has the responsibility to conduct the investigation. However, it may delegate the whole or any part of the investigation to another State by mutual arrangement and consent.[42]

The Chicago Convention is explicitly drawing attention to the subject of aviation accident and incident investigation. Article 26, Investigation of accidents, contains a number of important and decisive elements concerning international aircraft accident investigation, whereas pursuant to the provisions of Article 37, SARPs for aircraft accident inquiries were developed and adopted. Article 37 of the Convention is the controlling article concerning the development of Annex 13, but aircraft accident inquiry or investigation itself is the subject reserved to Article 26 of the Convention.

The Accident Investigation and Prevention Divisional Meeting (AIG/1974) noted that in many States the word 'inquiry' had judicial connotations, which seemed undesirable in Annex 13 or even contrary to its objective. The reason for the difference in meaning is the fact that next to a comprehensive technical investigation, a judicial inquiry will also be conducted, their concurrence quite usually leading to unwanted interference and difficulties in interpretation.

Annex 13 is mainly concerned with technical considerations. The Meeting also noted that the use of the two words 'inquiry' and 'investigation' had in the past caused problems in the formulation and understanding of Annex 13.

Article 26 contains the following provisions:

Investigation of accidents.
In the event of an accident to an aircraft of a Contracting State occurring in the territory of another Contracting State, and involving death or serious injury, or indicating serious technical defect in the aircraft or air navigation facilities, the State in which the accident occurs will institute an inquiry into the circumstances of the accident, in accordance, as far as its laws permit, with the procedure which may be recommended by the International Civil Aviation Organization. The State in which the aircraft is registered shall be given the opportunity to appoint observers (Accredited Representatives and Technical

---

41 Assembly Resolution A14-27, Appendix P. Assembly Resolution A15-8, Appendix P, adopted at the Fifteenth Session (Montreal, June-July 1965) consolidated and superseded Resolution A14-27, Appendix P.
42 Annex 13, Arts. 5.3 and 5.4.

Advisors) to be present at the inquiry and the State holding the inquiry shall communicate the report and findings in the matter to that State.

An interesting provision of Article 26 is that the Contracting State which is investigating the accident will conduct the investigation in conformity with the procedures recommended by ICAO, so far as its national laws permit. National legislation prevails in this particular case, rather than the ICAO established procedures.

Remarkably, Article 26 does not give any indication concerning a number of problems and questions referring directly to accident investigation, such as: what is the purpose of the investigation, what is the relationship with other investigation types such as a criminal inquiry, which format should the investigation have and what will be the status of the results, the findings of the investigation?

Annex 13 gives partial attention to these subjects, but the legal status of the SARPs in this Annex differ fundamentally from the other provisions laid down in the relevant articles of the Chicago Convention.

The provisions of Annex 13 are for any part of a procedural nature. These provisions focus on the obligations and rights of States which will arise following an aircraft accident in the territory of a Contracting State, as well as accidents in non-Contracting States or on the high seas. The term high seas means all parts of the sea that are not included in the territorial sea or in the internal waters of a State. The high seas being open to all nations, no State may validly purport to subject any part of them to its sovereignty.[43]

The investigation process includes the gathering, recording and analysis of all relevant information; the determination of the causes; formulating appropriate safety recommendations and the completion of the Final Report.

A major aircraft accident is always a significant event that may challenge the competency of the State investigating authority. The credibility of the State investigating authority, its investigation and its Final Report and recommendations will hinge on the independence of its investigation and on its ability to communicate investigation information in timely fashion to those entities having an interest in the investigation, including entities external to the investigation such as survivors, families of victims and the media. No information should be released without the express approval of the State responsible for the investigation.

Annex 13 provides for accident data reporting which consists of a detailed Final Report prepared by the State instituting the investigation and distributed with maximum dispatch to Contracting States together with any safety recommendations, as the entire aviation industry has a crucial interest in the results of any aircraft accident investigation anywhere in the world. Computerized databases greatly facilitate the storage and analysis of information on aircraft accidents and incidents. The sharing of such technical safety

---

43   Arts. 1 and 2 of the Convention on the High Seas, Geneva, 29 April 1958.

information is regarded crucial in preventing aviation accidents. ICAO operates a computerized database known as the Accident/Incident Data Reporting (ADREP), a system which facilitates the exchange of aviation safety information among Contracting States.

The SARPs outlined in Annex 13 are complemented by ICAO Doc 9756 – Manual of Aircraft Accident and Incident Investigation (Part I Organization and Planning, Part II Procedures and Checklists, Part III Investigation, Part IV Reporting) and ICAO Doc 9156 – Accident/Incident Reporting Manual.

Annex 13 defines that the Contracting States will commit themselves to collaborate in securing the highest practicable degree of uniformity by implementing the SARPs in their national legislations.

Article 2.1 concerning the applicability of the Annex, stated in the 7th edition of 22 May 1988: "Unless otherwise stated, the specifications in this Annex apply to activities following accidents and incidents occurring in the territory of a Contracting State to aircraft registered in another Contracting State."

In the 8th edition of 25 July 1994, the provision concerning the applicability of Annex 13 has been changed considerably. It just states: "Unless otherwise stated, the specifications in this Annex apply to activities following accidents and incidents, wherever they occurred."[44]

The decision to change Article 2.1 in this way has given rise to some commotion within the ICAO staff, because of the fact that the scope of applicability will not be restricted anymore to international accidents and incidents only. This remarkable change will put national accidents and incidents under the effective operation of Annex 13 as well.

The scope will be extended to promote international cooperation in the investigation of domestic accidents and incidents. This is quite an improvement from the point of view of harmonization of accident investigation worldwide. However, a large number of Contracting States are already not making any distinction between international and domestic accidents in their respective relevant national legislations. But the underlying legal problem is whether the Convention shall permit such modification with regard to the provisions of Article 26.

Annex 13 has the following starting points:
–   An investigation into the cause of an aircraft accident has to be conducted independently by the investigation authority (Art. 5.4). Article 5.4 states:

> The accident investigation authority shall have independence in the conduct of the investigation and have unrestricted authority over its conduct, consistent with the provisions of this Annex. The investigation shall normally include:

---

44   *See also* Eleventh Edition, July 2016, Art. 2.1.

1. the gathering, recording and analysis of all available information on that accident or incident;
2. the protection of certain accident and incident investigation records in accordance with 5.12;
3. if appropriate, the issuance of safety recommendations;
4. if possible, the determination of the causes and/or contributing factors; and
5. the completion of the Final Report.

When feasible, the scene of the accident shall be visited, the wreckage examined and statements taken from witnesses. The extent of the investigation and the procedure to be followed in carrying out such an investigation shall be determined by the accident investigation authority, depending on the lessons it expects to draw from the investigation for the improvement of safety.

– The investigation should be indifferent, transparent with respect to the question of guilt (Art. 3.1). Fear for guilt and consequent punishment shall withhold people who are involved in an aircraft accident or serious incident to give any statement or opinion concerning that event.[45]
– Information that could adversely affect the situation as it would be a matter of focusing on establishing the question of guilt, should however be limited to be used for the safety (technical) investigation.

In Article 5.12 (non-disclosure of records) it is defined that, if disclosure will have a negative effect on the availability of records for the investigation or any future investigations, these records only are to be used for that specific investigation. The background reason for Article 5.12 is the avoidance of investigations which suffer from an absence of statements made by witnesses because of fear of being convicted in a criminal case (self-incrimination). Article 5.12:

The State conducting the investigation of an accident or incident shall not make the following records available for purposes other than accident and incident investigation, unless the competent authority designated by that State determines, in accordance with national laws and subject to Appendix 2 and 5.12.5, that their disclosure or use outweighs the likely adverse domestic and international impact such action may have on that or any future investigations:
1. Cockpit voice recordings and airborne image recordings and any transcripts from such recordings; and

---

45 Art. 3.1 The sole objective of the investigation of an accident or incident shall be the prevention of accidents and incidents. It is not the purpose of this activity to apportion blame or liability.

2. Records in the custody or control of the accident investigation authority being:

    a. all statements taken from persons by the accident involved authority in the course of their investigation;

    b. all communications between persons having been involved in the operation of the aircraft;

    c. medical or private information regarding persons involved in the accident or incident;

    d. recordings and transcripts of recordings from air traffic control units;

    e. analysis of the opinions about information, including flight recorder information, made by the accident involved authority and accredited representatives in relation to the accident or incident; and

    f. the draft Final Report of an accident or incident investigation.

5.12.2 The records listed in 5.12 shall be included in the Final Report or its appendices only when pertinent to the analysis of the accident or incident. Parts of the records not relevant to the analysis shall not be disclosed.

While Annex 13 has been adopted pursuant to the provisions of Article 37 of the Convention, Aircraft Accident Inquiry is itself the subject of Article 26 of the Convention. Article 26 imposes an obligation on the State in which the aircraft accident occurs to institute an inquiry in certain circumstances and, as far as its laws permit, to conduct the inquiry in accordance with the ICAO procedure. However, Article 26 does not preclude the taking of further action in the field of aircraft accident investigation. The procedures set forth in Annex 13 are not limited solely to an inquiry instituted under the requirements of Article 26; however, under prescribed circumstances these procedures apply in the event of an inquiry into any aircraft accident within the terms of the definition herein. In order to maintain the correct relationship between the provisions of Article 26 and those of Annex 13, the following principles have been observed:

a) Article 37 of the Convention is the controlling article in the development of an Aircraft Accident Inquiry Annex, but nothing in the Annex must contravene the express terms of Article 26, or any other article of the Convention, nor should it contain any provision which would do violence to the spirit and intent of the Convention.

b) Subject to a) the Annex may deal with any relevant matter whether or not expressly dealt with by Article 26 or by any other article of the Convention. For instance it is not a contravention of the Convention for the Annex to deal with the rights or obligations of States other than the State of Registry and the State in which the accident occurred (State of Occurrence); similarly, the Annex may deal with the privileges to be accorded to observers entitled by Article 26 to be present at the inquiry. These are matters upon which Article 26 is silent. The Annex may also deal with accidents of a kind which do not fall within the provisions of Article 26.

Article 37 contains the following provisions:

> Adoption of international standards and procedures.
> Each Contracting State undertakes to collaborate in securing the highest, practicable degree of uniformity in regulations, standards, procedures, and organization in relation to aircraft, personnel, airways and auxiliary services in all matters in which such uniformity will facilitate and improve air navigation.
> To this end the International Civil Aviation Organization shall adopt and amend from time to time, as may be necessary, international standards and recommended practices and procedures dealing with: [...]
> k. Aircraft in distress and investigation of accidents; and such other matters concerned with the safety, regularity, and efficiency of air navigation as may from time to time appear appropriate.

The 11th edition of Annex 13 consists of eight chapters, two appendices and five attachments.

The first three chapters cover definitions, applicability and general information. Chapter 1 covers relevant definitions, Chapter 2 includes applicability and the following applicability rule:

> In this Annex the specifications concerning the State of the Operator apply only when the aircraft is leased, chartered or interchanged and when that State is not the State of Registry and if it discharges, in respect of this Annex, in part or in whole, the functions and obligations of the State of Registry (Art. 2.2).

Chapter 3 includes the objective of the investigation and the independence of investigations, the responsibility of the State of Occurrence for the protection of evidence, the safe custody and removal of the aircraft and its contents. It also defines how the State of Occurrence must handle requests for participation in the investigation from other States.

All States that may be involved in an investigation must be promptly notified of the occurrence. Chapter 4 contains procedures regarding notification. It also outlines the responsibilities for conducting an investigation depending on the location of the occurrence, for example, in the territory of an ICAO Contracting State, in the territory of a non-Contracting State or outside the territory of any State. Chapter 5 addresses the responsibility for instituting and conducting the investigation, the investigation process, *inter alia*, the provisions regarding the investigator-in-charge, flight recorders, autopsy examinations, coordination with judicial authorities, informing aviation security authorities, disclosure of records and reopening of an investigation.

States of Registry, the Operator, Design and Manufacture who participate in an investigation are entitled to appoint an accredited representative to take part in the investigation. Advisers may also be appointed to assist these representatives. The State conducting the investigation may call on the best technical expertise and equipment available from any source to assist with the investigation.

Chapter 6 contains SARPs dealing with the development and publication of the Final Report of an investigation. The recommended format of the Final Report is contained in the Annex Appendix. States shall not circulate, publish, or give access to a draft report or any part thereof, or any documents obtained during an investigation of an accident or incident, without the express consent of the State which conducted the investigation, unless such reports or documents have already been published or released by that latter State. Computerized databases greatly facilitate the storing and analyzing of information on aircraft accidents and incidents. The sharing of as complete safety information as possible is regarded as vital to accident prevention.

Recipient States are mentioned in Article 6.4:

> The Final Report of the investigation of an accident shall be sent with a minimum of delay by the State conducting the investigation to:
> 1. the State that instituted the investigation;
> 2. the State of Registry;
> 3. the State of the Operator;
> 4. the State of Design;
> 5. the State of Manufacture;
> 6. any State that participated in the investigation;
> 7. any State having suffered fatalities or serious injuries to its citizens; and
> 8. any State that provided relevant information, significant facilities or experts.

Chapter 7 addresses the reporting requirements of the Accident/Incident Data Reporting-system which is by means of Preliminary Reports and Accident/Incident Data Reports. Depending on the maximum mass of the aircraft involved in an accident, or when airworthiness or other matters are considered to be of interest to other States, the State conducting the investigation shall send the Preliminary Report to the State of Registry or the State of Occurrence, as appropriate, the State of Design, the State of Manufacture and any State that provided relevant information, significant facilities or experts, as well as to ICAO, only when the maximum mass of the aircraft is over 2250 kg.

When the aircraft involved in an accident has a maximum mass over 2250 kg, the State conducting the investigation shall send the Accident Data Report after the investigation as soon as practicable to ICAO. In case of an incident with an aircraft with a maximum mass over 5700 kg, the same procedure applies.

Chapter 8 deals with accident prevention measures such as incident reporting systems, both mandatory and voluntary, and the necessity for a non-punitive environment (just culture) for the voluntary reporting of safety hazards. Free exchange of information on actual or potential safety deficiencies is of paramount importance. In this context, Safety Management Systems (SMS) in all Contracting States are aimed to reduce the number of accidents and serious incidents worldwide.

Annex 14 Aerodromes

First of all, the definition of an aerodrome is a defined area on land or water (including any buildings, installations and equipment) intended to be used either wholly or in part for the arrival, departure and surface movement of aircraft. Airports, aerodromes certificated for commercial flight operations, are high-risk environments. Due to air traffic density, a significant number of all fatal air accidents and incidents, such as runway incursions and excursions, occur at or around airports. This complex issue involves a variety of aspects: airport design and infrastructure, lighting, markings, wildlife control, obstacle clearance and infringements, among other things, must be carefully considered in order to make the airport area as safe as possible.

Annex 14 forms the basis for the standardization of the use and design of aerodromes. From 27 November 2003, States must certify their aerodromes, which are used for international air transport operations, according to the criteria of Annex 14 and other relevant ICAO documents (e.g., Manual on Certification of Aerodromes). Certification of aerodromes contributes to enhancing aviation safety, since the owner of the aerodrome is obliged in this way to adhere to the relevant ICAO SARPs, which were first adopted by the Council on 29 May 1951.

Annex 14 is one of the most rapidly changing documents. The impact of the broad range of numerous subjects on the Annex is compounded by the rapidly changing industry which airports must support. New aircraft models, increased aircraft operations, operations in very low visibility and technological advances in airport equipment and design together, make Annex 14 one of the most rapidly changing Annexes. Its coverage is rather extensive. It extends from the planning of airports and heliports to such crucial details as switch-over times for secondary power supply, from civil engineering to illumination engineering, from provision of sophisticated rescue and fire-fighting equipment to simple but essential requirements for keeping airports clear of birds. From 9 March 1990, Annex 14 includes Volumes I and II.

Volume I deals with aerodrome design and operations. It is applicable to all airports open to public in accordance with the requirements of Article 15 of the Chicago Convention.

Article 15:

> Airport and similar charges.
> Every airport in a Contracting State which is open to public use by its national aircraft shall likewise, subject to the provisions of Article 68, be open under uniform conditions to the aircraft of all the other Contracting States. The like uniform conditions shall apply to the use, by aircraft of every Contracting State, of all air navigation facilities, including radio and meteorological services, which may be provided for public use for the safety and expedition of air navigation. Any charges that may be imposed or permitted to be imposed by a Contracting State for the use of such airports and air navigation facilities by the aircraft of any other Contracting State shall not be higher,
> – As to aircraft not engaged in scheduled international air services, than those that would be paid by its national aircraft of the same class engaged in similar operations, and
> – As to aircraft engaged in scheduled international air services, than those that would be paid by its national aircraft engaged in similar international air services.
>
> All such charges shall be published and communicated to the International Civil Aviation Organization, provided that, upon representation by an interested Contracting State the charges imposed for the use of airports and other facilities shall be subject to review by the Council, which shall report and make recommendations thereon for the consideration of the State or States concerned. No fees, dues or other charges shall be imposed by any Contracting State in respect solely of the right of transit over or entry into or exit from its territory of any aircraft of a Contracting State or persons or property thereon.

Article 68:

> Designation of routes and airports.
> Each Contracting State may, subject to the provisions of this Convention, designate the route to be followed within its territory by any international air service and the airports which any such service may use.

The contents of Annex 14 reflect, to a varying extent, the planning and design, as well as operation and maintenance of aerodromes, commonly called airports. Along with defining the ground environment of an airport such as runways, taxiways and aprons, specifications are also required to define its airspace requirements. Airports must have airspace free from obstacles in order for aircraft to approach and depart safely from that airport. It is also important that the volume of this space is defined so that it may be protected to ensure the continued growth and existence of the airport, or to prevent the airport from becoming unusable by the growth of obstacles. Obstacle limitation surfaces define the limits to which objects at and around airports may project into the airspace.

Aerodrome lighting is another striking feature at aerodromes, primarily used to guide and control aircraft movements in a safe and orderly manner. Other specifications are meant to improve the safety of equipment installed at airports. The objective of most specifications is to improve the safety of aviation, especially the rescue and fire-fighting services which are of critical importance to the operation of any airport.

To manoeuvre safely at and around an airport, aircraft require accurate information on the condition of facilities at airports. Adequate information is provided by NOTAMs and AIPs, set out in Annex 15 – Aeronautical Information Services. Volume I does not include specifications relating to the overall planning of aerodromes, such as separation between adjacent aerodromes or capacity of individual aerodromes, impact on the environment, or to economic and other non-technical factors that need to be considered in the development of an aerodrome. These subjects are described in the Airport Planning Manual (ICAO Doc 9184) Part I, and guidance material on the environmental aspects of the development and operation of an aerodrome is included in Part II.

Volume II includes provisions for heliports. The specifications complement those in Volume I, which, in some cases, are also applicable for heliports. The provisions address the physical characteristics and obstacle limitation surfaces required for helicopter operations from surface level and elevated on-shore heliports and helidecks, under both visual and instrument meteorological conditions.

ICAO issued many publications related to the specifications of Annex 14, such as: Airport Planning Manual (ICAO Doc 9184), Aerodrome Design Manual (ICAO Doc 9157), Airport Services Manual (ICAO Doc 9137), STOL (Short Take-off and Landing) port Manual (ICAO Doc 9150), Heliport Manual (ICAO Doc 9261), Manual of the ICAO Bird Strike Information System (IBIS) (ICAO Doc 9332), Manual of Surface Movement Guidance and Control Systems (SMGCS) (ICAO Doc 9476), Manual on Certification of Aerodromes (ICAO Doc 9774), Safety Management Manual (SMM) (ICAO Doc 9859) and PANS-Aerodromes (ICAO Doc 9981).

Annex 15 Aeronautical Information Services

The objective of the Aeronautical Information Services (AIS) is to ensure uniformity and consistency in the flow of aeronautical information/data to satisfy the needs of safety, regularity and efficiency for the operational use of international air navigation. Annex 15 defines how an aeronautical information service shall receive and/or originate, collate or assemble, edit, format, publish/store and distribute specified aeronautical information/data.

In 1953, the ICAO Council first adopted the SARPs of Annex 15, which has its origins in Article 37 of the Convention. A vast number of amendments updated Annex 15 over the years to meet the rapid changes brought about by air travel and associated information technology. The amendments reflected the increased need for the timely provision of quality aeronautical information/data and terrain data as they have become critical components of data-dependent on-board navigation systems.

The Annex now contains many provisions aimed at preventing corrupt or erroneous aeronautical information/data which can potentially affect the safety of air navigation just because of the direct dependence upon it by both airborne and ground-based systems. It is therefore imperative that each State will ensure that users (aviation industry, air traffic services, etc.) receive timely and qualitative aeronautical information/data for the period of intended use.

To demonstrate to those users the required information/data quality, Annex 15 provides that States must establish a quality system and put in place quality management procedures at all stages of the aeronautical information/data process.

Any aircraft operator, flying a private aircraft or a fleet of air transport aircraft, must have available a multitude of information concerning the air navigation facilities and services expected to be used in the planning and operating phase. Availability ranges from regulations related to entry and transit procedures in the airspace-structure of each State flying to or from its aerodromes, navigation aids, meteorological services, communication services and air traffic services and their associated regulations and procedures in relation to specific regions where the operations are carried out. This information, added with airspace restrictions, hazards which might affect the operation of flights and serviceability of facilities to be used, must be available during flight planning, and in case of *ad hoc* situations, during flight.

The philosophy of Annex 15, which stems from Article 28 of the Convention, is that each State is responsible for making available to civil aviation interests any and all information which is pertinent to and required for the operation of aircraft engaged in international civil aviation within its territory, as well as in areas outside its territory in which the State has air traffic control duties or other responsibilities.

Annex 15 Article 2.1.1 states that each Contracting State shall:
1. provide an Aeronautical Information Service; or

2. agree with one or more Contracting State(s) for the provision of a joint service; or

3. delegate the authority for the provision of the service to a non-governmental agency, provided that the SARPs of this Annex are adequately met.

The SARPs are to be used in conjunction with the Procedures for Air Navigation Services-ICAO Abbreviations and Codes (ICAO Doc 8400). An aeronautical information service shall obtain information to enable it to provide pre-flight information service and to meet the need for in-flight information from the aeronautical information services of other States and from other sources that may be available.

In today's digital era, AIS is transforming to an information management service, changing duties, responsibilities and scope to satisfy the new requirements as the computer-based navigation systems, Area Navigation (RNAV), Required Navigation Performance (RNP) and Air Traffic Management (ATM), and to cope with and to manage the provision of information. The definition of a future high-level view as to the shape, nature and content of a strategy for the evolution from traditional product-centric AIS to the enlarged scope of data-centric Aeronautical Information Management (AIM) started, and ICAO took the lead at the global level with regard to the transition from AIS to AIM.

The AIS will have to transform into a broader concept of AIM, with a different method of information provision and management given its data-centric nature as opposed to the product-centric character of AIS, however, with the aim to establish only few changes in terms of the scope of information to be provided. The major change will be the increased emphasis on data distribution, which should place the AIM in a position to better serve airspace users and air traffic management in terms of their information management requirements.

The need, role and importance of aeronautical information/data have changed significantly with the evolution of the Communications, Navigation and Surveillance/Air Traffic Management (CNS/ATM) systems. The implementation of RNAV, RNP and airborne-computer-based navigation systems has brought about exacting requirements for the quality, which includes accuracy, resolution and integrity of aeronautical information/data and terrain data. A special study group, the ICAO Secretary Study Group on Legal Aspects of CNS/ATM systems, reviewed the 2004 current legal framework applicable to the CNS/ATM systems to finalize a concept of a contractual framework, and a roadmap to its implementation.[46]

---

46 CNS/ATM is a comprehensive system in which enhanced capabilities of satellite-based navigation and digital data link communication systems will permit the next generation of ATM systems to combine the features of Automatic Dependent Surveillance (ADS) and Controller-to-Pilot Data Link Capability (CPDLC) with the conventional ATC functions. The combination of these enabling CNS technologies and their application to ATM has become known as CNS/ATM (Source Skybrary: www.skybrary.aero/index.php/Communication_Navigation_Surveillance/Air_Traffic_Management_(CNS/ATM). *See also* Brisibe, T., *Aeronautical Public Correspondence by Satellite*, Essential Air and Space Law, Volume 3, Series Editor Benkö, M.E., Utrecht: Eleven International Publishing, 2006, pp. 208-210.

The information handled by an AIS may vary widely in terms of the duration of its applicability. The validity of information related to airports and its facilities might significantly differ from changes in the availability of those facilities. Information may be valid for a long period of time or for as short a time as days or hours.

The urgency attached to information may vary as well as the extent of its applicability in terms of the number of operators or types of operation affected. Information could be lengthy or concise or include graphics. Therefore, aeronautical information is handled differently depending on its urgency, operational significance, scope, volume and the length of time it will remain valid and relevant to users.

Amendment 40 to Annex 15 was adopted by the Council on 9 March 2018, representing a major restructuring to ensure that high-level requirements are embodied in the Annex, that technical specifications and operating procedures are incorporated into the new PANS-AIM and that guidance material is developed to support implementation.

Annex 15 consists of 6 Chapters:

Chapter 1 – General; Chapter 2 – Responsibilities and Functions; Chapter 3 – Aeronautical Information Management; Chapter 4 – Scope of Aeronautical Data and Aeronautical Information; Chapter 5 – Aeronautical Information Products and Services and Chapter 6 – Aeronautical Information Updates.[47]

Annex 15 specifies that aeronautical information should be published as an (electronic) Integrated Aeronautical Information Package (IAIP), composed of the following elements:

- The Aeronautical Information Publications (AIP) including amendment services
- AIP supplements
- Aeronautical Information Circulars (AIC)
- NOTAM (Notice to Airmen), that alerts aircraft pilots of any hazards en route or at a specific location (additional types of notices are: SNOWTAM to notify hazardous conditions due to snow, ice, slush and standing water associated with snow on the airport movement area, and ASHTAM to notify volcanic activity, volcanic eruption or volcanic ash cloud that is of significant importance to aircraft operations)
- Checklists and lists of valid NOTAM
- Pre-flight Information Bulletins (PIB)

A NOTAM is defined as a notice distributed by means of telecommunication containing information concerning the establishment, condition or change in any aeronautical facility, service, procedure or hazard, the timely knowledge of which is essential to personnel concerned with flight operations.

---

47 Introduction to Annex 15 (16th Edition 2018), AIM SG/5 Cairo, Egypt, 22-24 January 2019, by Abbas Niknejad, ICAO Regional Officer.

Each element is used to distribute specific types of aeronautical information.

Each Contracting State shall ensure that the provision of aeronautical information/data covers its own territory and those areas over the high seas for which it is responsible for regulating the provision of air traffic services, and that the aeronautical information/data provided is complete, timely and of required quality, and that arrangements are established between originators of aeronautical information/data and the aeronautical information service in relation to the timely and complete provision of aeronautical information/data.

The quality system must be documented and demonstrable for each function stage, ensuring that the organizational structure, procedures, processes and resources are in place in order to detect and remedy any information/data anomalies during the phases of production, maintenance and operational use. Explicit in such a quality management regime is the ability to trace all information/data from any point, back through the proceeding processes, to its origin.

The information management resources and processes established by an aeronautical information service shall be adequate to ensure the timely collection, processing, storing, integration, exchange and delivery of quality-assured aeronautical information/data within the ATM system.

Detailed specifications for the collection of aeronautical information/data are contained in the PANS – Aeronautical Information Management Document (PANS-AIM, Doc 10066, First edition, 2018). The scope of the aeronautical information/data provides for the minimum requirement to support digital data exchange and data services. Contracting States should take care to identify all originators of aeronautical information/data particularly under those circumstances where more than one organization or authority is responsible for its provision.

As the aviation industry has been changing significantly and air traffic volume is expected to increase in an unprecedented manner in the next 15 years, air traffic control uses strictly organized procedures to ensure safe course of operations. In complex environments to be expected, any deviation from basic procedures in order to expedite air traffic should be carefully considered against the extent of coordination required and the associated risk.

With crowded skies, new tools in the domain of air traffic services must be introduced to keep air transport safe. Trajectory prediction, medium-term conflict detection, European Air Traffic Control Harmonization and Integration Programme (EATCHIP), ATM Surveillance Tracker and Server system (ARTAS), management of departure and arrival traffic flows, minimum safe altitude warning and area proximity warning are some of the tools to raise safety levels while still being cost-competitive in the field of aeronautical information/data services.

Annex 16 Environmental Protection

The Chicago Convention was drafted at a time when the international community was not even aware that greenhouse gas emissions would one day be deemed to be a threat to sustainable development. It is obvious that there was not any guidance in the Convention for problems that did not exist at the time of its adoption. However, over the years a great deal has changed in the field of aviation.

Air transport has become an integral part of global society in the late twentieth century and especially in the years thereafter, enabling both passengers and cargo to travel over long distances at subsonic speeds to virtually any location on Earth, encouraging global integration and enhancing international economy. On a 24-hour basis, thousands of commercial aircraft are cruising at high altitudes to many congested airports, located in metropolitan areas, through a relatively narrow layer within the Earth's atmosphere. In the long run, if the current trends in air traffic growth continue, civil aviation with its ever expanding fleet, will become a major contributor to air pollution and noise.[48]

It is estimated that aviation contributes more than 2% of the global CO_2 emissions. Aircraft contrails and associated cirrus cloud formations at high altitudes possibly create an additional impact on global warming. Perceived damaging effects from aviation will only increase in the future unless drastic measures are taken.[49]

Emissions from international air transport that contribute to environmental issues, such as climate change and global warming, remain to a great extent unregulated. A multilateral solution to address the impact on the environment is not easy to accomplish. On the other hand, there are natural additions to the atmosphere like the emission of gases and ash from volcanoes, smoke from forest fires, pollen and volatile organic compounds emitted by plant growth and even ozone and nitrogen oxides from thunderstorm activities. Although quite harmful, these substances form a natural part of the environment. Rather unnatural is the increasing air pollution by human activities as a result of a significant growth of the world population, industrialization, modern agriculture techniques and global transport, including international civil aviation.

Environmental protection has become one of the biggest challenges to civil aviation in the twenty-first century. Since its adoption, Annex 16 has further been developed to meet new environmental concerns and to accommodate new relevant technology. ICAO will continue to keep Annex 16 under review consistent with its intention of achieving max-

---

48 Ahmad, T. Md, *Climate Change Governance in International Aviation: Towards Regulating Emissions Relevant to Climate Change and Global Warming*, Essential Air and Space Law Volume 17, Series Editor, Benkö, M.E., The Hague: Eleven International Publishing, 2016, The Contribution of Aviation to Climate Change and Global Warming, pp. 16-23.

49 *See also* Kaar, van 't, D., Schnitker, R.M., Contrails: Silver Lines or Black Clouds? The Climatic and Chemical Impacts of Aviation Emissions, *ZLW* 61. Jg. 3/2012, pp. 365-383.

imum compatibility between the safe and orderly development of civil aviation and the quality of the environment.

Improving the environmental performance of aviation is a challenge ICAO takes very seriously. In fulfilling these responsibilities, ICAO developed a range of SARPs, policies and guidance material for the application of integrated measures to address aircraft noise as well as aircraft engine emissions. Annex 16 deals with the protection of the environment from the effect of aircraft noise and aircraft engine emissions, two topics which were virtually unknown or untreated matters when the Chicago Convention was signed in 1944.

Aircraft noise, a real concern during the years following the creation of ICAO, but limited to the noise caused by propeller tips rotating at speeds approaching that of sound, increased dramatically with the introduction of the first-generation jet aeroplanes, equipped with turbojet and turbofan engines in the early 1960s. Since then the seriousness of aircraft noise, especially in the vicinity of airports, severely accelerated with the growth in the number of jet aircraft in international operations.

Aircraft noise is a function, among other things, of the power of the jet engines, in particular, that propel aircraft through the atmosphere. Reduce the power, and you reduce the noise, but at the same time you may affect the safety characteristics of the jet aircraft. As aircraft engine noise production is found to be dominant, airframe noise is considered to have a significant contribution to the aircraft noise levels, especially during the approach and landing phase.

Aircraft noise is a source of disturbance to the public, especially in the vicinity of airports (Assembly Resolution A16-3). Apart from being annoying, noise pollution can also lead to health problems, which makes it one of the main issues the aerospace industry is facing today and will face in the future. Today, noise levels are typically around 20 dB lower than they were about 45 years ago (Stage 1 compliant aircraft), representing a significant reduction in the perceived noise level. Nevertheless, due to the continuous growth of air traffic in the past, the overall impact has not decreased. Technical and operational advancements are deemed necessary to compensate for this adverse environmental impact.

Annex 16 (Volumes I and II, First Edition) deals with various aspects of aircraft noise problems and was adopted in 1971 on the basis of recommendations of the 1969 Meeting on Aircraft Noise in the Vicinity of Aerodromes. These aspects included: procedures for describing and measuring aircraft noise, human tolerance to aircraft noise, aircraft noise certification, criteria for the establishment of aircraft noise abatement procedures, appropriate airport planning and land use control and ground run-up noise abatement procedures.

Volume I basically contains provisions related to aircraft noise, while Volume II contains provisions related to aircraft engine emissions.

Shortly after the 1969 Meeting, the Committee on Aircraft Noise (CAN) was established to assist ICAO in the development of noise certification requirements for different aircraft classifications. In Volume I different aircraft classifications form the basis of noise certification. For each classification of aircraft type, a noise evaluation measure has been standardized. Except for propeller-driven aircraft not exceeding 5700 kg maximum certificated take-off mass, the noise evaluation measure is the effective perceived noise level, expressed in decibels (EPNdB), being a single number indicator of the subjective effects of aircraft noise on people, taking into account the instantaneous perceived noise level and duration.

During subsequent meetings the CAN developed noise certification standards for future subsonic jet aircraft and propeller-driven aircraft, and for future production of existing supersonic transport aircraft types and helicopters. It also developed guidelines for noise certification of future supersonic and propeller-driven STOL (Short Take-off and Landing) aircraft as well as installed APUs (Auxiliary Power Units) and associated aircraft systems when operating on the ground.

A resolution adopted by the ICAO Assembly in 1971 led to specific action on the issue of engine emissions and detailed proposals for ICAO Standards for the control of engine emissions from certain types of aircraft engines. The Committee on Aircraft Engine Emissions (CAEE) was subsequently established with a view to develop specific ICAO Standards for aircraft engine emissions, finally adopted in 1981. These Standards set limits for the emission of smoke and certain gaseous pollutants for large turbojets and turbofan engines to be produced in the future and they prohibit the intentional venting of raw fuels to the atmosphere from the fuel nozzle manifolds of all turbine engine-powered aircraft manufactured after 18 February 1982, as stated in Volume II. In 1983, the CAN and CAEE Committees were amalgamated to form the new Committee on Aviation Environment Protection (CAEP) as a Technical Committee of the ICAO Council.

Since its establishment, CAEP has further developed the Annex 16 Standards for both aircraft noise and aircraft engine emissions. CAEP assists the Council in formulating new policies and adopting new SARPs related to aircraft noise and engine emissions, and more in general to aviation environmental impact. In the 1990s, more stringent ICAO Standards were adopted by the Council concerning the reduction of aircraft noise and new emission limits in view of global atmospheric problems, as recommended by CAEP.

The ICAO noise Standards are published in the SARPs in Volume I, Part II, with each new Standard published as a new chapter. Concerning aircraft noise, on the basis of recommendations by CAEP, the ICAO Council adopted in 2001 a new Chapter 4 noise Standard (Stage 4 compliant aircraft), more stringent than that contained in Chapter 3. Stage 4 noise Standard required a cumulative reduction of 10 EPNdB from the Chapter 3 limit. Commenced on 1 January 2006, the Chapter 4 noise Standard will apply to newly certificated aircraft and to Chapter 3 aircraft for which re-certification to Chapter 4 is requested. The Chapter 4 noise Standard was adopted at about the same time as the

Assembly endorsed the concept of a balanced approach to noise management developed by CAEP that is comprised of four elements, namely reduction of noise at source, land-use planning, operational measures and operation restrictions.

The latest noise Standard (Stage 5 compliant aircraft) is contained in Chapter 14, which entered into force on 14 July 2014. It is intended for newly designed aircraft. Stage 5 noise Standard requires a cumulative reduction of 7 EPNdB from Stage 4 Standard. Chapter 5 follows the three other noise Standards: Chapters 2, 3 and 4. However the sequence is disturbed since Chapter 5 is already used for a different Standard. The next available was 14 after Chapter 13 – Tilt-rotor aircraft.

Concerning aircraft engine emissions, there has been a change in the focus of the work of ICAO. While it was initially based on concerns regarding air quality in the vicinity of airports, in the 1990s it was expanded to include global atmospheric problems, such as climate change, to which aircraft engine emissions contribute. As a result, consideration is being given to further development of the ICAO emissions Standards to take account of emissions not only in the landing and take-off (LTO) cycle, but also during the cruise phase of operations.

Regarding CO_2 emissions from international aviation, ICAO Contracting States agreed in a plan to reduce the emission of pollutants. Paragraph 5 of Assembly Resolution A39-3 (39th Session of the ICAO Assembly, held from 27 September to 7 October 2016) decided to implement a global Market-Based-Measure (global-MBM) scheme in the form of a Carbon Offsetting and Reduction Scheme for International Aviation (CORSIA), considered to be binding under the Chicago Convention, to address any annual increase in total CO_2 emissions from international civil aviation above the 2020 levels, which form the basis for carbon neutral growth from 2020, taking into account special circumstances and respective capabilities.

On 6 March 2017, the ICAO Council has adopted a new aircraft CO_2 emissions standard which will reduce the impact of aviation greenhouse gas emissions on the global climate. This CO_2 standard for aircraft confirms the air transport community's leadership and concrete actions towards ensuring a sustainable and environmentally responsible future for global civil aviation.

Contained in a new Volume III to Annex 16 – Aeroplane CO_2 Emissions (First Edition March 2017, CO_2 Certification Requirement), the aircraft CO_2 emissions measure represents the world's first global design certification standard governing CO_2 emissions for any industry sector. The ICAO Standard shall apply to new aircraft type designs from 2020 and to existing aircraft type designs already in production as of 2023. However, if the latter aircraft do not meet the standard by 2028, production will be seized unless their designs are sufficiently modified.

CORSIA, the world's first global market-based climate measure for a sector, implemented in a new Volume IV to Annex 16, is designed to complement the basket of mitigation measures the air transport community is already pursuing to reduce CO_2

emissions from international aviation.[50] These include technical and operational improvements and advances in the production and use of sustainable alternative fuels for aviation. With the technical contribution of CAEP, SARPs and related material are developed for the implementation of the CORSIA Monitoring and Reporting and Verification (MRV) system by all ICAO Member States in domestic regulation or legislation on a national level, in order to be able to make the necessary arrangement from 1 January 2019, in accordance with the SARPs.

MRV consists of three components: first, the purpose of monitoring fuel use is to collect accurate information on the fuel burn of each flight. CO_2 emissions are being calculated from the fuel burn by multiplying by 3.16, which is a constant factor, representing the number of tonnes of CO_2 produced by burning a tonne of aviation fuel. After monitoring aircraft operators' total fuel burn and calculating CO_2 emissions, necessary information will be reported through the State Authority to ICAO, which consolidates the CO_2 emissions data, calculates the annual sectoral growth factor and communicates the outcome to the States/aircraft operators.[51]

Participation in both of the early stages, the pilot phase from 2021 through 2023 and the first stage from 2024 through 2026, will be voluntary and the next stage from 2027 to 2035 will have more of a compelling character, except for Least Developed Countries (LDCs), Small Island Developing States (SIDS), Landlocked Developing Countries (LLDCs) and States with very low levels of international aviation activities. The success of CORSIA depends on its implementation and enforcement through ICAO. It is only one component of the action needed to make international aviation compliant with the objectives of the Paris Agreement adopted in 2015 by nearly 200 States Parties to the United Nations Framework Convention on Climate Change (UNFCCC). CORSIA has the full support of IATA.[52]

Annex 17 Security – Safeguarding International Civil Aviation against Acts of Unlawful Interference

Aviation security refers to measures taken to keep aircraft and their passengers and crew members safe. Various events throughout most of aviation history after World War II have led to heightened security for those travelling on board aircraft. The drafters of the 1944 Chicago Convention did not foresee security threats such as acts of sabotage, unlawful seizure of aircraft and the use of civil aircraft in terrorist attacks. Aviation security did not become a serious issue until the late 1960s.

---

50 Volume IV to Annex 16 – Carbon Offsetting and Reduction Scheme for International Aviation (CORSIA) was adopted by the ICAO Council on 27 June 2018, effective on 22 October 2018.
51 *See also* www.icao.int/environmental-protection/Pages/A39_CORSIA_FAQ4.aspx.
52 Mestral, A.L.C. de, Fitzgerald, P.P., Ahmad, T.Md (Eds.), *Sustainable Development, International Aviation, and Treaty Implementation*, Cambridge: Cambridge University Press, 2018, p. 153.

The dramatic increase in crimes of violence which adversely affected the safety of civil aviation since that time, resulted in an Extraordinary Session of the ICAO Assembly in June 1970. There was a need to adopt an international framework for addressing acts of unlawful interference.

One of the resolutions of that Assembly called for specifications in existing or new Annexes to the Chicago Convention to specifically deal with the problem of unlawful interference, in particular with unlawful seizure of aircraft. It became clear that ICAO assumed a leadership role in developing aviation security policies and measures at the international level.

Following the work of the Air Navigation Commission, the Air Transport Committee, and the Committee on Unlawful Interference, and as a result of the comments received from Contracting States and interested international organizations, to whom draft material had been circulated, SARPs on aviation security were adopted by the Council on 22 March 1974, pursuant to the provisions of Article 37 of the Chicago Convention, and designated as Annex 17.[53]

The material included in this Annex was developed by the Council pursuant to the following two resolutions of the Assembly: Resolution A17-10 Implementation by States of Security Specifications and Practices, adopted by this Assembly and further work by ICAO related to such specifications and practices, and Resolution A18-10 Additional Technical Measures for the Protection of the Security of International Civil Air Transport.

This Annex is intended to set out the basis for the ICAO civil aviation security programme and seeks to safeguard commercial aviation and its facilities against acts of unlawful interference. Of critical importance to the future of civil aviation and the international community at large are the measures taken by ICAO to prevent and suppress all acts of unlawful interference against civil aviation throughout the world.

Annex 17 is primarily concerned with administrative and coordination aspects and with technical measures for the protection of the security of international air transport, requiring each Contracting State to establish its own civil aviation security programme with such additional security measures as may be proposed by other appropriate bodies. It is recognized that airline operators themselves have a primary responsibility for protecting their passengers, assets and revenues, and therefore States must ensure that the carriers develop and implement effective complementary security programmes compatible with those of the airports out of which they operate.

Annex 17 also established guidance on key security issues like for instance: training programmes, isolation of security processed passengers, inspection of aircraft for concealed weapons and other dangerous devices, cargo and mail screening, incorporation of security considerations into airport design, background checks for aviation employees,

---

53 *See* Foreword of Annex 17, Tenth Edition, April 2017.

passenger and baggage reconciliation, new standards for passenger carry-on and checked baggage screening and security measures for catering supplies and operators.[54]

Following the tragedy of 9/11, a number of changes were recommended to Annex 17 applicable to international and domestic flights to withstand the changing nature of terrorist threats. Special security features have been included in aircraft design to improve the protection of the aircraft, passengers, crew and cargo such as protection of the flight deck as well as cabin in-flight security personnel.

The strategic objective to enhance global aviation security and facilitation reflects the need for ICAO's leadership in aviation security, facilitation and related border security issues. To address future threats, ICAO and its Council continue to treat the subject of aviation security as a matter of the highest priority. Still, acts of unlawful interference continue to pose a serious threat to the safety and regularity of civil aviation operations, whether it is an aircraft, an airport or another object related to aviation.

An important initiative in the strategy of ICAO is the Universal Security Audit Programme for strengthening aviation security worldwide. This programme was based on the central element of the ICAO strategy, namely the ICAO Aviation Security Plan of Action which included mandatory, regular, systematic and harmonized audits to enable the evaluation of civil aviation security in all Contracting States. Project 3 of the Plan of Action, adopted by the Council in June 2002, provides for the promotion of global aviation security through auditing of Contracting States. Audits are divided into documentation-based audits, oversight-focused audits and compliance-focused audits. Implementation of USAP commenced with the first aviation security audit in November 2002.

Annex 17 encourages States to have a security clause in their air transport agreements. To help States in improving their aviation security systems by identifying deficiencies and providing suitable recommendations, the USAP audits are expected to provide useful feedback concerning the provisions of Annex 17. ICAO has developed and continues to update legal and technical regulations and procedures to prevent and suppress acts of unlawful interference, which however continue to pose a serious threat to the safety and regularity of civil aviation.

Annex 17 has been amended and updated several times to reflect the practical experience and the changing nature of the threats to civil aviation. By means of a Task Force on Improvised Explosive Devices (IED), the threat posed by IEDs concealed in personal belongings, including portable electronic devices, must be addressed. One of the topics in modern times is cyber threats to critical aviation information and communication technology systems. Cybersecurity is a growing concern for civil aviation.[55] Today, organizations and airline operators increasingly rely on electronic systems for critical parts of their operations and infrastructure, including safety-critical functions. Malicious

---

54 Price, J.C., Forrest, J.S., *Practical Aviation Security: Predicting and Preventing Future Threats*, Burlington, MA: Butterworth-Heinemann, 2009, p. 86.
55 *See* ICAO Assembly Resolution A29-19 – Addressing Cybersecurity in Civil Aviation.

electronic attacks (unlawful interference) could possibly disrupt advanced aviation systems, such as air traffic control computers, aircraft electronic instruments and other most essential equipment.

Annex 17, the principal document concerning security measures, contains detailed provisions regarding the establishment of security measures. Its uniform and consistent application is paramount to making the aviation security system successful. Today, the further enhancement of global aviation security is a key objective of ICAO.

Annex 18 The Safe Transport of Dangerous Goods by Air

More than half of the cargo carried by all modes of transport in the world is dangerous cargo such as explosive, corrosive, flammable, toxic and even radioactive material. Dangerous goods are defined as those things which may cause danger to aircraft and/or its occupants if they are carried, and must therefore either be prohibited altogether or carried only when subject to specific restrictions on their packaging, quantity carried, stowage location, proximity to other items or category of flight.

The dangerous goods are essential for a wide variety of global industrial, commercial, medical and research requirements and processes. A great deal of dangerous goods are carried by aircraft, due to the advantages of the rather fast air transport system.

ICAO recognizes the importance of this type of cargo and has taken steps to ensure that such cargo can be carried in a safe way. This has been done by adopting Annex 18, together with the associated document: Technical Instructions for the Safe Transport of Dangerous Goods by Air (ICAO Doc 9284). Annex 18 specifies the broad SARPs which determine whether items are acceptable for airlifting, while the Technical Instructions will amplify the basic provisions of Annex 18 and contain all the detailed and numerous instructions necessary for the safe international transport of dangerous goods by air.

The Technical Instructions are intended to facilitate transport while giving a level of safety such that dangerous goods can be carried without placing an aircraft or its occupants at risk, provided all the requirements are fulfilled. These instructions require frequent updating as developments occur in the medical, manufacturing and packaging industries, and a special procedure has been established by the Council to allow these instructions to be revised and reissued regularly to keep up with new products and advances in technology.

The Technical Instructions contain a comprehensive set of requirements which is based upon a classification of dangerous goods and includes a list of all those defined. The list identifies those goods which are:
– forbidden under any circumstances;
– forbidden on both passenger and cargo flights in normal circumstances subject to exemption by the States concerned;

– forbidden on passenger aircraft but permitted on cargo aircraft in normal circumstances; and
– permitted on both passenger and cargo aircraft in normal circumstances.

The Technical Instructions require that all dangerous goods be packaged appropriately, and usually restrict the quantity per package according to the degree of hazard and the type of aircraft on which the items are being loaded. The Instructions also specify the packing methods to be used and the packaging permitted, together with the specifications for that packaging including the stringent testing regime before loading. Moreover, there are precise requirements for the marking and labelling of dangerous goods packages and in respect of the documentation which must be prepared whenever such packages are consigned by air. The Technical Instructions are designed to ensure, should an incident occur, that the arisen situation cannot lead to an aggravating case like a serious accident.[56]

The ICAO requirements for dangerous goods have been largely developed by a panel of experts, the Dangerous Goods Panel (DGP), preceded by the Study Group, which was established in 1976. This panel continues to meet and recommends the necessary revisions to the Technical Instructions. As far as possible, these Technical Instructions are kept aligned with the recommendations of the United Nations Committee of Experts on the Transport of Dangerous Goods and with the Regulations for the Safe Transport of Radioactive Materials of the International Atomic Energy Agency (IAEA). The use of these common bases by all forms of transport allows cargo to be transferred safely and smoothly between air, sea, rail and road modes.

The ICAO requirements for the safe handling of dangerous goods firstly identify a limited list of those substances which are unsafe to carry in any circumstances and then show how other potentially dangerous articles or substances can be transported safely.

The United Nations Committee of Experts determined the nine hazard classes which are used for all modes of transport.

The nine hazard classes are as follows:
– Class 1 includes explosives of all kinds such as sporting ammunition, fireworks and signal flares;
– Class 2 comprises compressed or liquefied gases which also may be toxic or flammable. Examples are cylinders of oxygen and refrigerated liquid nitrogen;
– Class 3 substances are flammable liquids constituting a wide range including gasoline, lacquers, paint thinners, etc.;
– Class 4 covers flammable solids, spontaneously combustible materials and materials which, when in contact with water, exit flammable gases. Examples are some powdered metals, cellulose type film and charcoal;

---

56 *See also* Skybrary Dangerous Goods www.skybrary.aero/index.php/Dangerous_Goods.

- Class 5 covers oxidizing materials including organic peroxides which are both oxygen carriers and very combustible, oxidizing materials including bromates, chlorates or nitrates. This class also covers organic peroxides which are both oxygen carriers and very combustible;
- Class 6 includes poisonous or toxic substances, pesticides, mercury compounds and infectious substances which must sometimes be shipped for diagnostic or preventative purposes;
- Class 7 covers radioactive materials, mainly radioactive isotopes needed for medical or research purposes but are sometimes contained in manufactured articles such as heart pacemakers and smoke detectors;
- Class 8 covers corrosive substances which may be dangerous to human tissue or which pose a hazard to the structure of an aircraft. These substances are, for example, caustic soda, battery fluid and paint remover;
- Class 9 is a miscellaneous category for other materials which are potentially hazardous in air transport, such as magnetized materials which could affect the aircraft's navigation systems.[57]

Annex 18 and the Technical Instructions were adopted by the Council on 26 June 1981, setting 1 January 1983 as its effective date and 1 January 1984 as its applicable date when all of the Contracting States were expected to conform to the ICAO requirements and to give them legislative recognition.

The dangerous goods documents contain detailed instructions and specifications on the labelling, packaging, handling, carrying and processing of dangerous materials. Both documents have enhanced the ability of air carriers to transport dangerous goods safely with the minimum amount of disruption.

The successful application of regulations concerning dangerous goods in air transport greatly depends on the appreciation by all individuals concerned of the risks involved and on a highly detailed understanding of the relevant regulations which are extremely important with respect to possible infringement of safety. While all Annexes to the Chicago Convention are normally directed to Contracting States, Chapters 7, 8 and 9 of Annex 18 include obligations for the shipper and the operator with references to the Technical Instructions.

Annex 19 Safety Management (Since 14 November 2013)

Civil air transport is globally recognized as one of the most convenient, fastest and safest modes of travel. In fact, of all transport modalities, civil aviation is statistically the safest way to travel. This magnificent mode of transportation has evolved from executive to

---

57 *See also* The IATA Dangerous Goods Regulations.

mass transport and makes it possible for mankind to regard the world in a new way, namely in terms of time rather than distance. Each year millions of flights, carrying a multitude of passengers all over the world, are successfully completed. In order to accomplish such an outstanding achievement, a high general level of safety should be maintained. The aviation industry has made extraordinary progress regarding technology and research, operational procedures, training and expertise, all significant for aviation safety.

In May 2005, during a meeting between the ANC and the aviation industry, it was identified that there was a need for a broad plan that would provide a common frame of reference regarding aviation safety for all stakeholders. Such a plan would allow a more proactive approach to aviation safety and help to coordinate and guide safety policies and initiatives worldwide to reduce the accident risk for civil aviation.

It was then decided that a group of aviation industry representatives (Industry Safety Strategy Group (ISSG)) of various companies and organizations like Boeing, Airbus, Airports Council International (ACI), the international Civil Air Navigation Services Organization (CANSO), IATA, International Federation of Air Line Pilot's Associations (IFALPA) and the Flight Safety Foundation (FSF), would work together with ICAO to develop a common approach for aviation safety. The Global Aviation Safety Roadmap that was developed by the ISSG provided the foundation upon which the expansion of the 1997 Global Aviation Safety Plan was based. GASP is a broad-based approach to improve aviation safety and was very well received and widely supported by a convincing majority of ICAO Contracting States. Through the Safety Roadmap, ICAO began a major revision of GASP, whose objectives are to reduce the number of accidents and fatalities worldwide irrespective of the volumes of air traffic and achieve a significant reduction of accident rates especially in regions where these remain high.

The ICAO High-Level Safety Conference (HLSC), held in Montreal from 29 March to 1 April 2010, provided the impetus for the development of a new Annex dedicated to the subject of aviation safety management. The Conference, attended by around 600 participants from 150 Contracting States, and observers representing 32 international organizations, recommended that the new Annex should contain safety responsibilities framed under the ICAO State Safety Programme (SSP), the framework of which also included the implementation of a Safety Management System (SMS) for a number of aviation service providers. A typical Safety Management System is structured upon four components of safety management: policy, safety risk management, safety assurance and safety promotion.[58]

The Conference concluded that a single, new Annex should focus States' attention on the importance of integrating their safety management activities, and contain safety management processes under the direct responsibility of States that are critical to civil aviation safety, and should:

---

58   Postal History of ICAO, Annex 19. www.icao.int/secretariat/PostalHistory/annex_19_safety_management. htm.

– include the State Safety Programme framework and the eight critical elements of a State Safety Oversight (SSO) system;
– cover general and business aviation activities; and
– retain the Safety Management System requirements specific to one area of activities in individual Annexes.

The benefits of a new Annex included:
– address safety risks proactively, given the increasing complexity of the global air transport system and its inter-regulated aviation activities required to assure the safe operation of aircraft;
– manage and support regulatory and infrastructure developments;
– reinforce the role played by the State in managing safety at the State level, in accordance with service providers; and
– stress the concept of overall safety performance in all domains.

On 25 February 2013, at the fourth meeting of its 198th Session, the ICAO Council adopted Annex 19 dedicated to safety management.

With air traffic projected to increase tremendously in the next 15 years, safety risks must be addressed proactively to ensure that the significant capacity expansion is carefully managed and supported through strategic regulatory and infrastructure development.

The ANC recommended in this context that the new Annex be divided in two phases:

Phase I: This involved the consolidation of existing safety management provisions currently contained in as many as six different Annexes into a single, new Annex.

Phase II: The development of enhanced requirements will be the focus of this Annex, once it becomes applicable.

The ICAO Council approved this two-phase approach.

The basis of the new Annex is the transfer of overarching safety management provisions from the following Annexes:
– Annex 1 – Personnel Licensing;
– Annex 6 – Operation of Aircraft, Part I International Commercial Air Transport, Part II International General Aviation – Aeroplanes and Part III International Operations – Helicopters;
– Annex 8 – Airworthiness of Aircraft;
– Annex 11 – Air Traffic Services;
– Annex 13 – Aircraft Accident and Incident Investigation; and
– Annex 14 – Aerodromes – Volume I Aerodrome Design and Operations.[59]

---

59 Stolzer, A.J., Goglia, J.J., *Safety Management Systems in Aviation*, Second Edition, Milton Park, Abingdon, Oxon: Routledge, 2016, Regulatory Oversight ICAO, pp. 227-228.

Annex 19 overview (First Edition):
– Chapter 1 – Definitions
– Chapter 2 – Applicability
– Chapter 3 – State Safety Management responsibilities
– Chapter 4 – Safety Management Systems
– Chapter 5 – Safety data collection, analysis and exchange
– Appendix 1 – State Safety Oversight system
– Appendix 2 – SMS framework
– Attachment A – SSP framework
– Attachment B – Legal guidance for the protection of information of safety data collection and processing systems

Chapter 1 includes 12 existing definitions and six new definitions specific to the management of safety.

Chapter 2 includes SARPs which are applicable to safety management related to, or in direct support of, the safe operation of aircraft.

Chapter 3 outlines safety management responsibilities directly applicable to the State, including that the SMS requirements be implemented by the following service providers:
– Approved Training Organizations (ATO), in accordance with Annex 1 that are exposed to safety risks related to aircraft operators during the provisions of their services;
– Operators of aeroplanes or helicopters authorized to conduct international commercial air transport, in accordance with Annex 6, Part I and Part II, Section II, respectively;
– Approved Maintenance Organizations (AMO) providing services to operators of aeroplanes or helicopters engaged in international commercial air transport, in accordance with Annex 6, Part I or Part III, Section II, respectively;
– Organizations responsible for the type design or manufacture of aircraft, in accordance with Annex 8;
– Air Traffic Services providers, in accordance with Annex 11; and
– Operators of certified aerodromes in accordance with Annex 14.

Chapter 3 also addresses the components of the State Safety Programme, namely: State safety and policy objectives, State safety risk management, State safety assurance and State safety promotion. The State Safety Programme framework is described in Attachment A and the State Safety Oversight system in Appendix 1.

Chapter 4 (SMS) outlines the safety management responsibilities of service providers described in Appendix 2 (SMS framework) and includes the safety management responsibilities of international general aviation operators, conducting operations of large or turbojet aeroplanes in accordance with Annex 6, Part II, Section 3.

Chapter 5 outlines specifications of which the objective is to support safety management activities by collection and analysis of safety data and by exchange of safety information, as part of the SSP. Legal guidance for the protection of information from safety
data collection and processing systems is described in the complementary Attachment B.

The main benefits of Annex 19 are that it:

– highlights the importance of safety management at the State level;
– enhances safety by consolidating safety management provisions applicable to multiple
  aviation domains;
– facilitates the evolution of safety management provisions;
– provides an opportunity to further promote the implementation of SMS and SSP
  provisions; and
– establishes a process to analyse feedback received regarding Annex 19 and safety
  management implementation.

The implementation of safety management provisions are additionally highlighted in
ICAO's newly amended GASP. The GASP prioritizes the implementation of a SSO system, including proper governance arrangements, as a prerequisite to the establishment of
a SSP.

During the second ICAO High-Level Safety Conference, held in Montreal from 2 to
5 February 2015, attended by representatives of 155 Contracting States as well as representatives of the aviation industry and international aviation organizations, there was
strong and united support for the ICAO's short- and long-term strategic planning and
priorities for global aviation safety. Next to forging global consensus on two particularly
challenging emerging safety issues, namely flight tracking and conflict zone risk mitigation, the event also delivered clear affirmations for the objectives now being pursued in
every world region under the ICAO GASP.

2.3   FREEDOMS OF THE AIR

World air transport is operating in a quite complex and thoroughly regulated regime of
law and policy. This regime consists of a few multinational treaties, a rather large number
of bilateral air transport agreements and informal arrangements as well as a mass of
national laws, regulations and policies, all mainly based on customary law which includes
the principle of national sovereignty in airspace.

When the 1919 Paris Convention accepted that States have sovereign rights in the
airspace above their respective territories, direct government intervention in cross-border
air transport became inevitable. In other words, whilst sovereignty over the airspace
above their territories was asserted as a right of all States under customary law, freedom

of passage for foreign aircraft was merely explained as a contractual right under the 1919 Paris Convention.[60]

The 1944 Chicago Conference attempted to reach an agreement on the mutual granting of traffic rights for scheduled international air services between States on a multilateral basis. However, general consensus among the delegates of the States could not be reached. Especially, the United States and the United Kingdom were unable to reach an agreement on the subject of the fifth freedom. Although their views on the subject were both aimed at restricting this freedom of the air, finding of an adequate method to actually restrict it failed due to divergent approaches. The elementary principal restriction of Article 1 of the Chicago Convention, however, was tempered by a solution-oriented blueprint for supplementary agreements concerning the free transit of scheduled international air services, as subsequently proposed by the United States.[61]

In this respect, the need to establish freedoms of the air unfortunately illustrates the rather restrictive and protectionist character of international civil aviation. Thus, while general consensus on the granting of traffic rights could not be accomplished, as far as scheduled international air services are concerned, the U.S. government made a proposal that the freedoms of the air should be incorporated in two supplementary agreements. These significant documents, accepted at the Chicago Conference, were referred to as respectively the two freedoms agreement, formally the International Air Services Transit Agreement (IASTA) and the five freedoms agreement, consisting of the two freedoms and three additional freedoms, associated with commercial transport set forth in the International Air Transport Agreement (IATA).

In fact, the five freedoms of the air were relegated to the separate IATA, which was accepted by relatively few States. In 1944, at the decisive turning point of the war, the United States was in favour of such an agreement, despite its protectionist air policy in the years preceding World War II. The consideration was that it would facilitate the United States to play a dominant role in post-war international air transport. Remarkably, it denounced the IATA (not to be confused with the International Air Transport Association) in 1946 for reasons of strong opposition by the U.S. Senate, originating from discussions concerning the 1944 Chicago Convention. Agreeing to the IATA could jeopardize the ratification of the Chicago Convention, since it would involve a serious threat to the predominance of the United States in civil aviation by providing other States too many air traffic rights.[62]

However, the two Agreements can be seen as the starting point and framework for today's bilateral and multilateral system of the exchange of air traffic rights, although

---

60 Johnson, D.H.N., *Rights in Air Space*, Manchester: Manchester University Press, 1965, p. 33. *See also* Convention Relating to the Regulation of Aerial Navigation, 1 *J. Air L. & Com.* 94 (1930).

61 Honig, J.P., *The Legal Status of Aircraft*, Proefschrift ter verkrijging van de graad van Doctor in de Rechtsgeleerdheid aan de Rijksuniversiteit te Leiden (Dissertation to obtain the degree of Doctor at the Leiden University), The Hague: Martinus Nijhoff, 1956, pp. 20-29.

62 Honig, J.P., *The Legal Status of Aircraft*, The Hague: Martinus Nijhoff, 1956, pp. 30-32.

both IASTA and IATA did not receive the widespread support that was anticipated. Due to the lack of a decisive number of ratifications, international air transport could not benefit from these Agreements. In practice, international air transport is still highly regulated from a national perspective.[63]

Article 5 of the Chicago Convention:

Right of non-scheduled flight.
Each Contracting State agrees that all aircraft of the other Contracting States, being aircraft not engaged in scheduled international air services shall have the right, subject to the observance of the terms of this Convention, to make flights into or in transit non-stop across its territory and to make stops for non-traffic purposes without the necessity of obtaining prior permission, and subject to the right of the State flown over to require landing. Each Contracting State nevertheless reserves the right, for reasons of safety of flight, to require aircraft desiring to proceed over regions which are inaccessible or without adequate air navigation facilities to follow prescribed routes, or to obtain special permission for such flights.
Such aircraft, if engaged in the carriage of passengers, cargo, or mail for remuneration or hire on other than scheduled international air services, shall also, subject to the provisions of Article 7 (Cabotage), have the privilege of taking on or discharging passengers, cargo, or mail, subject to the right of any State where such embarkation or discharge takes place to impose such regulations, conditions or limitations as it may consider desirable.

Freedoms are practically referred to as privileges to emphasize their extraordinary nature. A privilege is a right or freedom to fly through airspace, however, subject to set conditions. After all, there is no general freedom of the air. The intention of Article 5 of the Chicago Convention to clear the way for free international non-scheduled air traffic hardly received any consent from the Contracting States. The conception of a multilateral agreement for the granting of traffic rights failed at Chicago, leaving negotiations to establish agreements on this matter to the States concerned.[64]

---

63 *See* Milde, M., *International Air Law and ICAO*, Essential Air and Space Law Volume 4, Series Editor Benkö, M.E.,Utrecht: Eleven International Publishing, 2008, Chapter VI Legal Regime of International Air Transport.

64 Mankiewicz, R.H. (Ed.), *Yearbook of Air and Space Law 1967 Annuaire de Droit Aérien et Spatial*, Institute of Air and Space Law, McGill University, Montreal: McGill-Queen's University Press, ICAO after Twenty Years, p. 9.

In practice, most of the States violate the scope of Article 5. Among the Contracting States, three distinct groups with different views regarding the aim of Article 5 can be identified.

In the first place, there are States which admit non-scheduled commercial and non-commercial air traffic without prior permission. Second are States which insist on prior permission even though they recognize the fact that Article 5 is not intended to create the possibility of requiring prior permission for non-scheduled air traffic, and in the third place, there are States which act on the assumption that Article 5 entitles them to require prior permission for non-scheduled air traffic. In principle, and certainly nowadays because of far-reaching security measures, all international commercial air transport services are forbidden except to the extent that they are permitted. Similarly, the first two freedoms do not involve rights to take on or to put down passengers, cargo or mail, and therefore, were not traffic rights in the strict sense.

The ICAO Council adopted in 1952 the following definition of scheduled international air service:

> A scheduled international air service is a series of flights that possesses all of the following characteristics:
> – it passes through the airspace over the territory of more than one State;
> – it is performed by aircraft for the transport of passengers, mail or cargo for remuneration, in such a manner that each flight is open to be used by members of the public;
> – it is operated so as to serve traffic between the same two or more points, either
>   1. according to a published timetable, or
>   2. with flights so regular or frequent that they constitute a recognizable systematic series.

This definition is merely an interpretation of the terms used in Article 6 of the Convention as formulated by the ICAO Council. However, in the present liberalized and Open Skies air transport regime, the difference or dissimilarity between scheduled and non-scheduled international air services, ranging from short-haul to even long-haul operations, has become a very thin line.

Article 6 of the Chicago Convention:

> Scheduled air services.
> No scheduled international air service may be operated over or into the territory of a Contracting State, except with the special permission or other author-

ization of that State, and in accordance with the terms of such permission or authorization.

The freedoms of the air are as follows:

First freedom of the air: the right or privilege, with respect to scheduled international air services, granted by one State to another State or States to fly across its territory without landing (also known as the first freedom right).

Second freedom of the air: the right or privilege, with respect to scheduled international air services, granted by one State to another State or States to land in its territory for non-traffic purposes (also known as the second freedom right).

Third freedom of the air: the right or privilege, with respect to scheduled international air services, granted by one State to another State to put down, in the territory of the first State, traffic coming from the home State of the carrier (also known as the third freedom right).

Fourth freedom of the air: the right or privilege, with respect to scheduled international air services, granted by one State to another State to take on, in the territory of the first State, traffic destined for the home State of the carrier (also known as the fourth freedom right).

Fifth freedom of the air: the right or privilege, with respect to scheduled international air services, granted by one State to another State, traffic coming from or destined to a third State (also known as the fifth freedom right).

ICAO characterizes all freedoms of the air beyond the fifth freedom as so-called freedom rights because only the first five freedoms have been officially recognized as such by international treaty. The so-called or additional freedoms are not included in the multilateral Chicago Convention, but are occasionally agreed to on a State-by-State basis through bilateral agreements.

The so-called sixth freedom of the air: the right or privilege, in respect of scheduled international air services, of transporting via the home State of the carrier, traffic moving between two other States (also known as the sixth freedom right). The so-called sixth freedom of the air, unlike the first five freedoms, is not incorporated as such into any widely recognized air services agreements such as the Five Freedoms Agreement.

The so-called seventh freedom of the air: the right or privilege, in respect of scheduled international air services, granted by one State to another State, of transporting traffic between the territory of the granting State and any third State without requirement to include on such operation any point in the territory of the recipient State, i.e., the service need not connect to or be an extension of any service to/from the home State of the carrier (also known as the seventh freedom right).

The so-called eighth freedom of the air: the right or privilege, in respect of scheduled international air services, of transporting cabotage traffic between two points in the territory of the granting State on a service which originates or terminates in the home State of the foreign carrier (in connection with the so-called seventh freedom of the air) outside the territory of the granting State (also known as the eighth freedom right or consecutive cabotage).

The so-called ninth freedom of the air: the right or privilege of transporting cabotage traffic of the granting State on a service performed entirely in the territory of the granting State (also known as the ninth freedom right or stand-alone cabotage).[65]

2.4 INTERNATIONAL AIR SERVICES TRANSIT AGREEMENT (IASTA) 1944

The International Air Services Transit Agreement, referred to as the Two Freedoms Agreement, was signed at Chicago on 7 December 1944. It entered into force on 30 January 1945 (for the United States on 8 February 1945, as is the date of deposit of second instrument of acceptance). Depository is the government of the United States.

The Agreement provides for the multilateral exchange of the first two freedoms of the air with regard to scheduled international air services. It also deals with designation of routes and airports, charges, revocation of permits and settlement of disputes.

Article 1.

Section 1.

Each Contracting State grants to the other Contracting States the following freedoms of the air in respect of scheduled international air services:
1. The privilege to fly across its territory without landing.
2. The privilege to land for non-traffic purposes.

The privileges of this section shall not be applicable with respect to airports utilized for military purposes to the exclusion of any scheduled international air services. In areas of active hostilities or of military occupation, and in time of war along the supply routes leading to such areas, the exercise of such privileges shall be subject to the approval of the competent military authorities.

Section 2.

The exercise of the foregoing privileges shall be in accordance with the provisions of the Interim Agreement on International Civil Aviation and, when it comes into force, with the provisions of the Convention on International Civil Aviation, both drawn up at Chicago on 7 December, 1944.

---

65   Source: ICAO Manual on the Regulation of International Air Transport, Part 4.1 (Doc 9626).

Section 3.

A Contracting State granting to the airlines of another Contracting State the privilege to stop for non-traffic purposes may require such airlines to offer reasonable commercial service at the points at which such stops are made. Such requirement shall not involve any discrimination between airlines operating on the same route, shall take into account the capacity of the aircraft, and shall be exercised in such a manner as not to prejudice the normal operations of the international air services concerned or the rights and obligations of a Contracting State.

Section 4.

Each Contracting State may subject to the provisions of this Agreement,

1. Designate the route to be followed within its territory by any international air service and the airports which any such service may use;
2. Impose or permit to be imposed on any such service just and reasonable charges for the use of such airports and other facilities; these charges shall not be higher than would be paid for the use of such airports and facilities by its national aircraft engaged in similar international services; provided that, upon representation by an interested Contracting State, the charges imposed for the use of airports and other facilities shall be subject to review by the Council of the International Civil Aviation Organization established under the above-mentioned Convention, which shall report and make recommendations thereon for the consideration of the State or States concerned.

Section 5.

Each Contracting State reserves the right to withhold or revoke a certificate or permit to an air transport enterprise of another State in any case where it is not satisfied that substantial ownership and effective control are vested in nationals of a Contracting State, or in case of failure of such air transport enterprise to comply with the laws of the State over which it operates, or to perform its obligations under this Agreement.

The first two freedoms concern the passage of civil aircraft engaged in international scheduled air services through foreign airspace and airports. They represent the basic and elementary terms for the privileged right to fly internationally in respect of scheduled air services. States, that are not Parties to the IASTA, have to seek permission for overflight of foreign territory in international scheduled air service by a series of bilateral agreements with other States.

2.5 International Air Transport Agreement (IATA) 1944

The International Air Transport Agreement, referred to as the Five Freedoms Agreement, was signed at Chicago on 7 December 1944. It entered into force on 8 February 1945. Depository is the government of the United States.

Article 1.

Section 1.

Each Contracting State grants to the other Contracting States the following freedoms of the air in respect of scheduled international air services:
1. The privilege to fly across its territory without landing (basic privilege of IASTA).
2. The privilege to land for non-traffic purposes (basic privilege of IASTA).
3. The privilege to put down passengers, mail and cargo taken on in the territory of the State whose nationality the aircraft possesses.
4. The privilege to take on passengers, mail and cargo destined for the territory of the State whose nationality the aircraft possesses.
5. The privilege to take on passengers, mail and cargo destined for the territory of any other Contracting State and the privilege to put down passengers, mail and cargo coming from any such territory.

With respect to the privileges specified under paragraphs 3, 4 and 5 of this Section, the undertaking of each Contracting State relates only to through services on a route constituting a reasonably direct line out from and back to the homeland of the State whose nationality the aircraft possesses.

The privileges of this Section shall not be applicable with respect to airports utilized for military purposes to the exclusion of any scheduled international air services. In areas of active hostilities or of military occupation, and in time of war along the supply routes leading to such areas, the exercise of such privileges shall be subject to the approval of the competent military authorities.

Section 2.

The exercise of the foregoing privileges shall be in accordance with the provisions of the Interim Agreement on International Civil Aviation and, when it comes into force, with the provisions of the Convention on International Civil Aviation, both drawn up at Chicago on 7 December 1944.

The fifth freedom, from a historical point of view, is considered the most important freedom because it is not geographically limited to one pair of States but enables taking on and discharging passengers, mail and cargo in any other State. The condition, however, is that all States concerned must be bound by an agreement permitting such flights.

In this context it must be noted that practice indicates that despite the traditional five freedoms of the air having their origins in the multilateral Chicago Conference's international legal instruments (IASTA and IATA), their most essential application is done by the method of bilateral air services agreements between States. The IATA is deemed to be of little significance because it attracted ratification by only 11 States.

With respect to the additional freedoms of the air, freedoms 6 and 7 are special applications of the fifth freedom and freedom 8 is cabotage in the sense of Article 7 of the Chicago Convention. The ninth freedom was invented to distinguish what is known as stand-alone cabotage. The foreign aircraft is presumably stationed or contracted to provide point-to-point service within another State, using the aircraft's foreign crew and governed in the first place by its own national rules.

Article 7 of the Chicago Convention:

> Cabotage.
> Each Contracting State shall have the right to refuse permission to the aircraft of other Contracting States to take on in its territory passengers, mail and cargo carried for remuneration or hire and destined for another point within its territory. Each Contracting State undertakes not to enter into any arrangements which specifically grant any such privilege on an exclusive basis to any other State or an airline of any other State, and not to obtain any such exclusive privilege from any other State.

Cabotage is the transport of goods or passengers between two places in the same State by a transport operator from another State. It applies originally to shipping along coastal routes, but also to aviation and other modes of transport. Cabotage is the right to operate within the domestic border of another State, and there are strict sanctions against it, for reasons of economical protectionism, national security, national prestige or public safety.[66] In the European Union all Member States grant cabotage rights to each other.[67]

The Chicago Convention prohibits Contracting States from granting cabotage on an exclusive basis, which has limited the availability of cabotage as a bargaining chip in bilateral air transport negotiations. Cabotage is not granted under most Open Skies agreements or treaties.

---

66 Mendes de Leon, P.M.J., *Cabotage in Air Transport Regulation*, Dordrecht: Martinus Nijhoff Publishers, 1992, pp. 17-19.
67 Havel, B.F., *Beyond Open Skies: A New Regime for International Aviation*, Alphen aan den Rijn: Kluwer Law International, 2009, pp. 122-124.

2.6   BILATERAL AGREEMENTS

Ever since the Chicago Convention of 1944 declared that "No scheduled international air service may be operated over or into the territory of a Contracting State, except with the permission or other authorization of that State, and in accordance with the terms of such permission or authorization" (Art. 6), scheduled civil air transportation, and in the course of the years non-scheduled air transportation likewise, in an ever-increasing number, both have been governed by so-called air services agreements (ASAs) between sovereign States on a strictly bilateral basis.

This was largely due to the inability of the Chicago Conference to reach a multilateral agreement on the economic regulation of air transport. Bilateral air services agreements between a State and a union of States, like the European Union as a supranational entity, acting as a single entity under authority granted to it by its Member States, are certainly possible.

When Brexit becomes formally a reality, EU Member States will not be allowed to negotiate or to enter in bilateral air services agreements with the United Kingdom. In this most complicated case, the European Commission, representing the remaining 27 Member States, shall negotiate with the United Kingdom. To be prepared for a worst-case scenario, a hard 'no deal' Brexit, where there will be no time to negotiate a comprehensive air services agreement between the United Kingdom and the European Union, the European Commission proposed earlier a so-called Basic Connectivity Air Traffic Plan containing two legislative short-term measures to cover basic needs as to limit disruption to air traffic and to extend membership of the European Aviation Safety Agency (EASA) in order to continue the validity of certain aviation-related licenses, certificates, approvals, and regarding airspace, the Single European Sky project.

The United Kingdom has the largest aviation industry in Europe and its geographical position in the air transport network is crucial, with approximately 90% of air traffic passing through Europe's North Atlantic gateway. If the UK-Ireland Functional Airspace Block (FAB), controlled airspace and part of the Single European Sky, will cease, it could have potentially considerable implications which means, from an economical (capacity/delays/cost inefficiency) and environmental (off-optimum routing) point of view, a huge setback.

By withdrawing all existing air transport services, the UK air carriers will lose their current rights to operate freely within the European Union. Their rights will be restricted to the third and fourth freedoms only. Renegotiations on issues such as traffic rights, routes, capacity, frequencies of flights, leasing of aircraft, ownership and control, border management and change of gauge, on the basis of reciprocity, may need to be conducted, preferably during a short transitional period which has been recognized by the aviation industry for a long time.[68]

On the other hand, a concluded Withdrawal Agreement, allowing for a transitional implementation period in which to complete extensive negotiations on future relationships regarding aviation, *in casu* a collective EU-UK air services agreement including the full range of key issues, could give more clarity. Either by failure to agree to a collective deal, or by choice to return to Chicago Convention traditions, the United Kingdom or the European Union might prefer negotiating individual agreements with each EU Member State, probably including restrictions for flights of UK-owned airlines within the European Union up to fifth freedom rights. However, this will involve considerable diplomatic activity within Europe. A long-term option for the United Kingdom would be to continue as an affiliate member of the European Union and/or a third country member of EASA as well as to remain Party to the European Common Aviation Area (ECAA) Agreement, a single market in aviation services, in order to retain certain aviation rights similar to Norway as a non-EU Member State.

The European Union has either exclusive competency to conclude international agreements on behalf of EU Member States, or that competency is shared with its Member States. In that case it will be mixed agreements like the EU/U.S. Open Skies agreement. Upon the United Kingdom ceasing to be a member of the EU, it will cease to conditionally benefit from the EU/U.S. Open Skies agreement.

Air services agreements rely almost completely on the trade policy principle of reciprocity and personify an exchange of mutual traffic rights and obligations between two parties bound to the agreement. A majority of the traditional types of bilateral air services agreements reflect protectionist attitudes. The discriminatory side to this form of agreement is that these exchanges not only do not include rights for third parties, but the actual rationale is to exclude them.

The goal of bilateral regulation in the international air transport area, the legal structure composed of several thousand bilateral agreements and understandings, and thus a part of public international law, is typically the conclusion, implementation or continuance of some kind of intergovernmental agreement or understanding concerning air services between the territories of the two parties. Although all these bilateral air transport and air services agreements generally tend to have the characteristics of a particular type of agreement, each one is unique. Nevertheless, these agreements typically have in common numerous types of essential provisions, most of which, while not identical, have a similar scope.[69]

---

68 Abeyratne, R.I.R., *Megatrends and Air Transport: Legal, Ethical and Economic Issues*, Cham: Springer International Publishing, 2017, pp. 103-107.

69 *See also* ICAO Doc 9626 Manual on the Regulation of Air Transport, Third Edition 2016, Chapter 2.2. Structure of Bilateral Regulation, Basic Document Types and Typical Provisions of Bilateral Air Transport (Services) Agreements.

The 1944 Chicago Conference concluded with the signature of the final act containing the following primary legal instruments: the Interim Agreement on International Aviation, the Convention on International Civil Aviation, being the organic constitution of ICAO for the orderly and safe development of international air transport, together with the draft of 12 Technical Annexes, the International Air Services Transport Agreement, the International Air Transport Agreement and a standard form of a Bilateral Agreement.

During the Conference, the State delegates were not able to reach agreement on any but the most fundamental two freedoms of the air. The failure to agree on more freedoms of the air was largely due to the considerable disagreement between the United States and the United Kingdom, as mentioned before, being at the time the two largest carriers of civilian air traffic internationally.

A further attempt towards a multilateral agreement on traffic rights, pricing and capacity was made at the 1947 Geneva Conference, but this failed as well. Governments and air carriers eventually found a way to circumvent the discomfitures of Chicago and Geneva. Exchange of traffic rights became the subject of bilateral air services agreements between States.

Highly competent negotiators of States and air carriers usually came up with attractive *quid pro quo*, innovative and smart approaches to achieve market access, but also used intimidation and, above all, perseverance. Major airlines, but also new generation Low Cost Carriers (LCCs) in recent years, put pressure on their respective national aviation authorities to apply protectionist policies. The control of capacities and frequencies became in most cases a matter of inter-airline negotiations and subsequent agreements. The International Air Transport Association (IATA) became the regulating body for tariffs.[70]

At Bermuda, a remote island location situated between the United States and the United Kingdom, the proposed meeting between the two wartime allies had the intention to facilitate the development of post-war air traffic across the Atlantic Ocean and the Pacific.

Representatives of both States negotiated during that meeting in 1946 a bilateral understanding that is well known as the Bermuda I Agreement, a rather significant agreement because it represented a compromise between widely divergent positions taken at the 1944 Chicago Conference. Bermuda I, the new intergovernmental air services agreement, would become the framework for the world's bilateral air transport agreement, and was considered a benchmark for a period of some 30 years until Bermuda II replaced it in 1977.

The desire of American carriers to increase the frequency to London was the cause for Bermuda I. The Bermuda I Agreement, signed and becoming effective on 11 February 1946, was based on the standard Chicago Agreement non-binding model for bilateral air transport agreements drafted by the Chicago Conference. Two historical events, the 1944

---

70 Doganis, R., *Flying Off Course: The Economics of International Airlines*, Third Edition, London: Routledge, 2002, pp. 30-31.

Chicago Conference and the founding of IATA in 1945, were the underlying causes behind making Bermuda I a sustainable and decisive agreement.

The United States favoured a relatively liberal approach to the issue of the way in which international air transportation should be developed in the aftermath of World War II. The U.S. conditions were no arbitrary restrictions or predetermined formulas on capacity, frequency, carriage of so-called fifth-freedom traffic and fixed rates. Bermuda I became the model for a large number of bilaterals; however, eventually, imbalance of capacity-sharing between States, like the United States and the United Kingdom, turned out to be the reason to abandon this particular model. In 1976, the United Kingdom announced its denunciation of Bermuda I.

In 1977, negotiations between the United States and the United Kingdom started in order to redress the balance of air service advantage, which at that time lay within the United States, by limiting the number of air carriers that could be designated to operate on certain routes and the excess provision of capacity by some U.S. carriers.[71]

During the negotiations to get to Bermuda II, the United States tried to put pressure on the United Kingdom to maintain a competitive system, but at the same time they were reluctant to allow these negotiations to turn into a major British-U.S. political crisis. The British negotiating team, having a fundamentally different policy, defended its interests in a professional way and was not prepared to go that far.

The intended liberal, but at first sight rather restrictive, Bermuda II Agreement established a framework within which British and relatively dominant U.S. air carriers could compete on broadly equal terms, like the so-called Bermuda II 50/50 capacity rule. Under the original version of Bermuda II, British Airways, Pan American World Airways and Trans World Airlines were the only carriers allowed to operate flights between London Heathrow Airport and the United States. However, the capacity rules increased the number of U.S. gateways for air services to the United Kingdom, but restricted entry at those U.S. gateways for air services from London and placed additional restrictions on air services to London Heathrow, the gateway to Europe for most air passengers from the United States. Only New York and Los Angeles were to be allowed air services by two air carriers of both States.

A more stringent capacity control clause was also incorporated in Bermuda II and additionally fifth freedom rights were substantially reduced. Flight frequency, code-sharing and tariffs were also restricted, subject to government approval.[72]

Bermuda II would become the new ultimate model for bilateral air transport agreements. However, the U.S. government changed to a more competitive air services policy. Through deregulation it introduced a more liberal playing field in its domestic air trans-

---

71 Cheng, C-J. (Ed.), *The Use of Airspace and Outer Space for All Mankind in the 21st Century*, The Hague: Kluwer Law International, 1995, pp. 24-25.

72 Kaufman, W., Slettedahl Macpherson, H. (Eds.), *Britain and the Americas: Culture, Politics, and History: A Multidisciplinary Encyclopedia*, Volume I, Santa Barbara, CA: ABC-CLIO, 2005, pp. 71-73 Air Transport.

port system, soon after to be extended to the international air transport sector. By early 1978, the United States had concluded a much more liberal bilateral air services agreement with the Netherlands, followed by Belgium and Germany in late 1978, including flexibility for multiple designation of U.S. air carriers, and country of origin rules as well as the elimination of restrictions on capacity, frequency and sixth freedom rights.[73]

Bilateral air services agreements became the principal vehicles with which to authorize international scheduled air services. The bilateral air services agreement is typically concluded between two States, but there are exceptions.[74] The main objective of a bilateral agreement is to regulate and stimulate the direct flow of traffic between the two Contracting States, and to exchange reciprocal air transport privileges. It just turned out to be only feasible to exchange fifth freedom rights on a strictly equitable basis or *quid pro quo* regime, because of severe competition between the major international legacy airlines, often flag carriers, but also with LCCs. In essence, bilateral air services agreements are discriminatory. They discriminate against and exclude third parties. Even the United States, with its liberalized bilateral Open Skies agreements with a number of States and the European Union, which involve eliminating most of the restrictions on capacity and routes, are still banning foreign air carriers from transporting domestic passengers within the United States.[75]

In the 1990s, partly as a reaction to the signs of an increasingly inadequate, rather restrictive bilateral system, two important developments became ground-breaking, namely the third package of the European Community, as a result of which every EU air carrier was free to operate between any two points in the European Union, without any restriction as to frequency, capacity, routing and pricing or code-sharing, and on the other hand the Open Skies policy of the U.S. government which, as mentioned earlier, introduced deregulation in its domestic aviation market already in the mid-1970s.

Bilateral agreements between EU Member States regarding air transport have disappeared by 1997. With respect to air transport with States outside the European Union, the EU Council did not make any decisions in that direction yet, thus each individual EU Member State retained its exclusive competence to conclude classic bilateral air services agreements pursuant to the Chicago Convention.

Open Skies and thus open access into the U.S. market was obtained by a number of EU Member States by means of individual bilateral agreements. In addition, it created the possibility of entering into air carrier alliances of their respective national carriers with their U.S. partners. However, it took the European Union together with its Member States

---

73 Doganis, R., *The Airline Business*, Second Edition, Milton Park, Abingdon, Oxon: Routledge, 2006, pp. 32-33.

74 The United States negotiated with the EU Commission on behalf of the Member States of the European Union on Atlantic air transport. Sweden, Denmark and Norway represent the interests of Scandinavian Airlines (SAS) in the field of bilateral air services agreements with other States.

75 Ito, T., Krueger, A.O. (Eds.), *Trade in Services in the Asia-Pacific Region*, Chicago: University of Chicago Press, 2003, pp. 80-82.

years of successive negotiation attempts to reverse this situation in a single combined bilateral agreement with the United States.[76]

In 2007, the EU-U.S. Air Transport Agreement was signed, and provisionally applied from 30 March 2008 between, on the one hand, the European Union and all of its Member States, and on the other hand, the United States. This factual bilateral agreement (the First Stage Agreement) represents important steps towards the normalization of the international aviation industry. The ultimate EU objective has been to create a transatlantic Open Aviation Area, in other words, a single air transport market between the European Union and the United States with free flows of investment and no restrictions whatsoever on air services, which means access to the domestic markets of both parties. Through this ambitious Open Skies agreement, European air carriers (Community airlines concept) could fly from any point in the European Union to any point in the United States, and *vice versa* for U.S. air carriers. It means international routes between the European Union and the United States on third and fourth freedom rights, and routes beyond the European Union and the United States on fifth freedom rights without restriction of flights and type of aircraft, as well as unlimited operation of seventh freedom cargo services.

This First Stage Agreement caused a dramatic increase in air services as well as much closer alliance agreements between hub carriers, particularly in those parts of the transatlantic market that were previously subject to significant restrictions on operations arising from the pre-existing bilateral agreements.

Since its implementation, the First Stage Agreement established closer regulatory cooperation between the European Union and the United States to achieve a strong and effective combined response to varying challenges like the threat to aviation security, the environmental impact and the application of environmental measures, mitigation of inconvenient delays, facilitating airport and airline operations and a roadmap to continue negotiations on a Second Stage Agreement.[77]

This Second Stage Agreement, the Protocol to amend the valid EU-U.S. Air Transport Agreement, signed and provisionally applied as from 24 June 2010, builds on the meaningful benefits of the ground-breaking First Stage Agreement by providing for considerable further advances including additional investment and market access opportunities. It

---

76 The so-called 'Open Skies' judgments of 5 November 2002 of the Court of Justice of the European Union marked the start of the EU external aviation policy (Cases: C-466/98, C-467/98, C-468/98, C-469/98, C-471/98, C-472/98, C-475/98 and C-476/98). Whereas, traditionally, international air services have always been governed by bilateral agreements between States, the 2002 judgments paved the way for the EU, a new important player with certain exclusive competences in external relations in the field of civil aviation.
77 Air Transport Agreement, *OJ EU* L134/4, 25.5.2007.

also strengthens the framework of cooperation in regulatory areas as security, safety and the impact on the environment.[78]

Noteworthy is Article 18(5) in which the Air Transport Agreement will be extended to include third parties (Iceland and Norway, as though they were members of the European Union, accession to the Air Transport Agreement as amended by the Protocol is provisionally applied as from 21 June 2011) in order to maximise the benefits for consumers, airlines, labour and communities on both sides of the Atlantic.

2.7   OPEN SKIES

The term 'open skies' is an international policy concept that calls for the liberalization, to a greater or lesser extent, of the rules and regulations of the international aviation industry, in order to create a free-market environment for the commercial airline sector. In other words, the concept refers to a bilateral or multilateral air services agreement that liberalizes the rules for international aviation markets and minimizes government intervention.

Open Skies agreements are in principle bilateral agreements that have vastly expanded international passengers and cargo flights between States and regions around the world.

Open Skies agreements promote increased travel and trade, enhance productivity and globalization, and provide for maximum operational flexibility for air carrier alliances throughout the world by allowing air carriers from a single State or a group of States, such as the European Union being a supranational entity, unlimited market access to partner markets and the right to fly to intermediate and beyond points. Furthermore, Open Skies agreements will develop cooperative marketing opportunities between air carriers, liberalize charter regulations, commit governments on both sides to high standards of safety and security and facilitate numerous new cultural links worldwide.

The potentials of the fifth freedom and the third State code-sharing of Open Skies agreements can best be achieved where, in this particular case, transatlantic regions (North America-European Union) or alliances of neighbouring States (EU) are all in harmony with the policy of the Open Skies system for Full-Service Carriers (FSCs). These carriers are still maintaining a dominant role, although low cost carriers of those participating States are increasingly trying to successfully compete using the system within their own regions.

---

78 International Agreements. 2010/465/EU: Decision of the Council and the Representatives of the Governments of the Member States of the European Union, meeting within the Council of 24 June 2010, on the signing and provisional application of the Protocol to Amend the Air Transport Agreement between the United States of America, of the one part, and the European Community and its Member States, of the other part. Protocol to amend the Air Transport Agreement between the United States of America and the European Community and its Member States, signed on 25 and 30 April 2007. *OJ EU* L 223/3, 25.8.2010.

LCCs are even operating regular intercontinental flights (North Atlantic routes, and routes between all continents starting from 2018 and expanding in the foreseeable future), not without being vulnerable, however, to fierce competition and significant cost overruns. To generate ancillary revenue as part of their business models, LCCs use *à la carte* pricing such as charging separate fees for checked baggage, meals, etc. However, a growing number of FSCs started to unbundle their services, as well as to set up subsidiary LCCs, often operating on short-, medium-, even long-haul, indirectly subsidized, thin air routes as well as profitable trunk routes in order to gain additional market share and revenue.[79]

In Europe and the United States, a huge step was taken when the Netherlands, as a Member State of the European Union, signed the first Open Skies agreement in 1992 with the United States, in spite of objections posited by EU authorities. The agreement gave both States unrestricted landing rights in each other's territory. Normally landing rights are granted for a fixed number of flights a week to a designated destination.

Each adjustment in the regular (Bermuda) bilateral agreement will take a lot of negotiation, often between diplomatic representatives of the governments rather than the air carriers involved. The United States Department of Transportation (DOT) subsequently granted antitrust immunity to the alliance of Northwest Airlines and KLM Royal Dutch Airlines, which started in 1989. In April 1995, DOT issued the U.S. International Aviation Policy Statement in which the agency advocated a global open aviation system. This position committed the United States to an Open Skies approach and endorsed the growing trend towards alliances between the United States and foreign air carriers. The U.S. Open Skies policy consisted of a liberalized bilateral and multilateral structure that would enable the negotiation of civil air services agreements with foreign aviation partners and alliances such as the alliance between United and Lufthansa in 1996.[80]

This liberalized structure has been designed to accomplish this progressiveness by eliminating government interference in the decision making and commerce of air carriers concerning routes, capacity and pricing in international markets and to allow air carriers to provide more affordable, convenient and efficient air service for consumers. The objective was to promote increased travel and trade, enhancing productivity, efficiency and encouraging employment in specialized fields, and not least economic growth.

The Open Skies agreement between the European Union and the United States is a monumental new type of agreement; there are numerous truly innovative elements and since it came into effect, it has led to a considerably more logical and liberal structure of air services between the two continents. There are three remarkable key elements that

---

79 Forsyth, P., *et al.* (Eds.), *Liberalization in Aviation: Competition, Co-operation and Public Policy*, Milton Park, Abingdon, Oxon: Routledge, 2016, Chapter 10.

80 *See* International Aviation: Competition Issues in the U.S.-U.K. Market, Statement of John H. Anderson, Jr., Director, Transportation Issues, Resources, Community, and Economic Development Division. Testimony before the Subcommittee of Aviation, Committee on Commerce, Science and Transportation, U.S. Senate, June 4, 1997, p. 3.

certainly will contribute to the future of global air transport:

1. Recognition of all European airlines as Community air carriers. All European airlines are classified identically without any discrimination based on their EU State of origin.
2. Community air carriers are allowed to fly from any point in the European Union to any point in the United States, and *vice versa* for U.S. air carriers.
3. Flights are now possible beyond the United States towards third States. Community air carriers are allowed to go beyond the United States and provide destinations using the United States as a stopover.

These rules apply to cargo flights between the U.S. and third States as well.[81]

While the United States liberalized its national market already in 1978 and introduced its Open Skies policy in 1992, the European Union started the process of an internal common aviation market in the 1990s.[82] However, regarding air transport with States outside the European Union, the EU Council of Ministers did not make any decisions on the basis of Article 70 (2) EC yet in this respect. Hence, each individual EU Member State retained its exclusive competence to conclude bilateral air services agreements pursuant to the Chicago Convention.[83]

Up till 1992, the EU aviation market was fragmented among the national markets of its Member States, each State remaining faithful to a rather restrictive bilateral agreement with each of the other Member States. From 1992, all national markets of the EU Member States were merged into a single EU aviation market and all national air carriers are considered as EU carriers based on the so-called third package of measures, one of three successive stages of measures on liberalizing the European air transport sector. The third package was adopted in July 1992.

This process of liberalization was effected in 1993 by the common implementation of Council Regulation (EEC) No. 2408/92 of 23 July 1992, later repealed by Regulation (EC) No. 1008/2008 of the European Parliament and of the Council of 24 September 2008. On 1 April 1997, the final result was a true intra-European Common Aviation Area, established on the basis of a regulated internal Open Skies aviation market in which European Community air carriers will operate intra-Community air services. Consequently, all bi-

---

81 Cento, A., *The Airline Industry: Challenges in the 21st Century*, Heidelberg: Physica-Verlag, 2009, pp. 8, 16-17.
82 U.S. DOT issued Final Order 92-8-13, Docket 48130, on 5 August 1992, establishing a definition of Open Skies and outlining the basic elements that should be encompassed in an Open Skies regime.
83 Art. 70 (2) EC Treaty/TFEU (Art. 90 TEU): The Council may, acting by a qualified majority, decide whether, to what extent and by what procedure appropriate provisions may be laid down for sea and air transport.

lateral air service agreements between the EU Member States have expired and cannot be reverted, at least, according to the European Commission.[84]

Many European States entered into independent liberal Open Skies agreements with the United States. When in a given geographical region, like Europe, EU Member States, as a combined entity, agree to an Open Skies agreement with a State outside the European Union, the resulting commercial chances seem to be more comprehensive than the total sum of all those independent bilateral Open Skies agreements involved. This opinion was one of the factors why an integral Open Skies agreement, the Air Transport Agreement, being one of the most ambitious air service agreements ever negotiated, was concluded on 30 April 2007 between the 27 EU Member States and the United States, effective from 30 March 2008.[85]

Norway and Iceland, as Member States of the European Economic Area (EEA), became both Party to the Air Transport Agreement.[86] Created in 1994, the EEA combines, as a free trade zone, the EU Member States and Member States of the European Free Trade Association (EFTA) to facilitate participation in the European market trade and movement without having to apply to become one of the EU Member States. Trade agreement details stipulated by the EEA include liberties on products, persons, services and money movement between States.

The EEA consists of all EU Member States and three of the four Member States of the EFTA, namely Norway, Iceland and Liechtenstein, a small neighbouring State of Switzerland (Swiss Confederation), albeit without an international air transport industry. The U.S. government concluded on 21 June 2010 an Open Skies air traffic agreement with Switzerland, an EFTA Member State. However, Switzerland is neither a Member State of the EU nor of the EEA.

With respect to the Air Transport Agreement, it was an arduous trajectory to finally achieve an extremely liberalized agreement on the world's most important international market, the North Atlantic.

Under the Lisbon Treaty, the latest primary treaty at EU-level, signed on 13 December 2007 and entered into force on 1 December 2009, the European Union has been given a single legal personality. Previously, the European Community (EC) and the European Union had different statutes and did not operate the same decision-making rules. The

---

84 *See* Council Regulation (EEC) No. 2408/92 of 23 July 1992 on access of Community air carriers to intra-Community air routes, *OJ EC* L240/8, 24.8.92. Regulation (EC) No. 1008/2008 of the European Parliament and of the Council of 24 September 2008 on common rules for the operation of air services in the Community, *OJ EU* L 293/3, 31.10.2008.

85 Westra, C., The April 2007 U.S.-EU 'Open Skies' Agreement: A Dream of Liberalization Deferred, *32 B.C. Int'l & Comp. L. Rev.* 161 (2009). *See also*: (2007/339/EC) Decision of the Council and the representatives of the governments of the Member States of the European Union, meeting within the Council of 25 April 2007 on the signature and provisional application of the Air Transport Agreement between the European Community and its Member States, on the one hand, and the United States of America, on the other hand (*OJ EU* L 134/1).

86 *OJ EU* L 283/16, 29 October 2011, Ancillary Agreement, 2011/708/EU.

European Union is quite unique. It is not a federal State because its Member States remain independent sovereign nations; however, the Member States have the opportunity to pool some of their sovereignty by taking joint decisions, and thus gain greater collective strengths and influence.

As a powerful entity, the European Union is a rather strong negotiator, for example in the field of international aviation. But in order to have the right to negotiate Community-level agreements with third countries, the European Commission needs a mandate of the EU Member States.

Before that time, in 1999, 10 EU Member States were successful in obtaining open access into the vast U.S. air transport market. Nine of these bilateral agreements incorporated the antitrust immunity provision which gave rise to alliances of national carriers of the EU Member States concerned with their U.S. partner air carriers. Alliances could provide an economic boost in the sense of direct participation through code-share programmes in their partners' networks and joint ventures.

Attempts by the European Commission to obtain a meaningful mandate from the Member States to negotiate an Open Skies agreement between the European Union as a whole and the United States, however failed.

Eventually, the disputes between eight Member States and the Commission were submitted to the European Court of Justice (ECJ) that has ruled in its so-called Open Skies decisions in November 2002. While the Court actually did not reject the rights of Member States to conclude bilateral air services agreements, the Court's decision made the broad finding that such existing arrangements were to be an infringement of Community law causing an imminent unworkable situation legally. Therefore, such agreements, containing a provision that limited formal access in international markets to carriers owned and controlled by the designated Member States and/or its nationals, should be amended to be in conformity with Community law.[87]

Following the decision of the Court, the European Council approved three legislative texts aimed at establishing a new framework for relations in the aviation sector with the United States and other third countries. This framework was based on principles of Community law as laid down in the judgements of the Court, offering, especially in this case, a pragmatic solution to this difficult legal question raised by the judgement.

The most important elements of the so-called Open Skies decisions were: on the one hand, regarding traffic rights, the Member States are competent to negotiate with third countries, the Community has none, and on the other hand, the nationality clause in all eight agreements precludes EU air carriers from taking advantage of the opportunities of

---

87 Communication from the Commission on relations between the Community and third countries in the field of air transport (COM/2003/0094 final, Introduction 1.2). Cases C-466/98, C-467/98, C-468/98, C-469/98, C-471/98, C-472, C-475, C-476 Commission v. United Kingdom, Sweden, Finland, Belgium, Luxembourg, Austria and Germany (the so-called Open Skies cases).
See also C-523/04 Commission v. Kingdom of the Netherlands (the first European State that had signed an Open Skies Agreement with the United States of America).

other air services agreements than those entered into by their home-State. Therefore, it is in violation with one of the basic principles of the EC Treaty: the freedom of establishment.[88]

To resolve the impending unworkable situation, the European Commission received two mandates on 5 June 2003. First of all, a horizontal mandate to be able to negotiate the replacement of the classic nationality clause by the EU clause in the bilateral air services agreements that contravene Community law, and secondly, the vertical mandate to negotiate with the United States the establishment of a comprehensive Open Skies agreement.

The result of the horizontal mandate could be described as less impressive, mainly because of a lack of sufficient meaningful *quid-pro-quos* and limited negotiation flexibility, while the vertical mandate resulted in the concept of the Open Aviation Area. Hereafter, more in detail, the negotiations for a more open civil aviation market, the tipping point towards liberalization, and further developments in this respect.[89]

Part of the drive of the Community to reform international civil aviation towards more flexibility and liberalization was the establishment of a European external aviation policy. This policy should have its legal bases within the EC Treaty. The Open Skies judgements of the ECJ expressly confirmed the external competence of the executive bodies of the Community on the grounds of the exercise of their internal powers. This exclusive competence in the field of aviation mainly extended to automated booking systems, tariffs on intra-Community routes and slot allocations.[90]

The European external aviation policy took the final shape during a session of the Council on 5 and 6 June 2003 following the establishment of the framework for such a policy in May 2003. Eventually, a package of measures was adopted involving mandating.

After the Commission had previously presented a number of proposals for mandates, the Council ultimately granted the Commission mandates to deal with non-Member States to revise all bilateral agreements to be in compliance with the Open Skies judgements by inserting clauses in conformity to Community law, and to negotiate with the United States a substantial Open Skies agreement, as well as the regulation on the negotiation and implementation of bilateral air services agreements between Member States and third countries.

The Commission negotiated at Community-level a progressive agreement with the United States, aimed at creating an open aviation market to replace the so-called individual Open Skies agreements, as well as other more restrictive agreements, bilaterally

---

88 Freedom of establishment, Art. 43 of the EC Treaty.
89 van het Kaar, D., The Sky has a Limit, Het communautaire externe luchtvaartbeleid en de Open-Skies verdragen (European Community External Aviation Policy and the Open Skies Agreements), Heerlen: *Open University of the Netherlands*, Thesis 2007.
90 Council Regulation (EEC) No. 95/93 of 18 January 1993 on common rules for the allocation of slots at Community airports (*OJ EC* L 14, 22.01.93), amended by Regulation (EC) No. 793/2004, *OJ EU* L 138/50, 30.04.2004.

agreed by the Member States. Moreover, the Council adopted a decision authorizing the Commission to negotiate Community-level agreements with third countries to replace certain specific provisions, agreed bilaterally by the Member States, and reached a general approach, pending the European Parliament's opinion in first reading, on a draft Regulation with respect to the negotiation and implementation of air services agreements between Member States and third countries.[91]

First of all, the Community-level agreement with the United States. The Council's mandate envisaged a comprehensive liberal agreement allowing air carriers from both the European Union and the United States to provide air services on a fair and equal basis. Secondly, Community agreements with third countries to replace bilateral provisions. The Community-level agreements envisaged by the Council's mandate would seek to bring existing bilateral agreements between Member States and third countries into conformity with Community law.

The Council's mandate established that new agreements would supersede conflicting texts under bilateral agreements between the Member States and third countries. During the negotiations, the Commission should use standard clauses developed jointly with the Member States, and it should establish, in a binding way, a list of third countries to be approached, indicating an order of priority.

The draft Regulation should create a framework within which the Member States may continue to negotiate with third countries with a view, *inter alia*, to reducing the vulnerability to legal challenge of their existing bilateral agreements.

Such negotiations would be permitted, subject to certain conditions as complying with (post-2002) EU law, and by following certain guidelines and using standard clauses, even where the Commission has received a mandate to negotiate a Community-level agreement. Member States should ensure a distribution of traffic rights among eligible Community carriers on the basis of a non-discriminatory and transparent procedure. Regulation (EC) No. 847/2004 reflects division of responsibilities of competence between the Community and EU Member States.

A mandate, agreed at the EU Transport Council of 5 June 2003 granted the Commission the authority to negotiate with the United States to reach an agreement. (Council Decision on authorizing the Commission to open negotiations with the United States in the field of air transport, 9 July 2003).

A number of negotiation rounds followed since July 2003. On 18 November 2005 the Commission and the U.S. delegation signed a draft text of an Air Transport Agreement.

In December 2005, the EU Transport Council expressed its unanimous satisfaction that the draft text represented significant improvements regarding its own considered proposals, in particular on issues regarding enhancement of regulatory cooperation, ad-

---

91 Regulation (EC) No. 847/2004 of the European Parliament and of the Council of 29 April 2004 on the negotiation and implementation of air service agreements between Member States and third countries, *OJ EU* L 157/7, 30.4.2004.

vanced market access and essential elements for a Stage One deal to be concluded such as ownership and control of air carriers. However, the U.S. Administration had to withdraw its important proposal to relax the rules governing control of U.S. air carriers by foreign nationals due to strong opposition in the United States.

Notwithstanding this critical situation, the EU Transport Council reaffirmed its strong wish to achieve a comprehensive first stage air transport agreement, and requested the Commission to urgently consult the United States to seek elements that could be used to restore a proper balance of interests. These negotiations settled some important elements and strengthened the commitment by both parties to a second stage agreement, on which negotiations had to begin within a defined timescale on delicate matters.

The negotiating mandate, which showed a purely innovative idea to deliver full market access, set the ultimate objective of the European Union to create a Transatlantic Common Aviation Area (TCAA), later called Open Aviation Area (OAA) regarding the EU-U.S. aviation market.[92]

This would:

1. Remedy the elements of the existing bilaterals that were found to be illegal by bringing all aspects of relations under the legal umbrella of a Community-level agreement and by ensuring that there is no discrimination between Community air carriers on the basis of nationality;

2. Create a single market for air transport between the United States and the European Union in which investment can flow freely and in which European and U.S. air carriers can provide air services without any restriction, including in the domestic markets of both parties.

On 2 March 2007, the Commission well accepted the text of a comprehensive first stage air transport agreement with the United States. This agreement would replace the existing bilateral agreements, being not anymore in conformity with Community law, which were previously concluded by the Member States.

The elaborated OAA concept extends full freedoms of the air to both parties by removing the constraints imposed by the outdated system of historic bilateral air services agreements. However, the unequal treatment of cabotage regarding EU air carriers remained an important issue. The concept further removes restrictions on investment by foreign entities and permits wet leasing of aircraft under non-discriminatory, transparent conditions. Furthermore, the concept embodies a general commitment to regulatory convergence, which would be a challenge to regulatory oversight. However, given the high

---

92 *See also* Proposal for a Decision of the Council and the representatives of the governments of the Member States of the European Union, meeting within the Council on the conclusion of the Air Transport Agreement between the European Community and its Member States, on the one hand, and the United States of America, on the other hand. COM(2006) 169 final – 2006/0058 (CNS), Brussels, 21 April 2006.

level of regulatory oversight in the United States and within the European Union, it would not harm aviation safety.

The OAA will establish the harmonization of high common level air transport standards regarding safety, security, competition, quality control and environmental issues. The intention of an OAA is to provide an all-encompassing framework that goes beyond the basic form of an Open Skies model.[93]

The main elements of the rather asymmetrical EU-U.S. Air Transport Agreement are:

– The Agreement allows any air carrier of the European Union to fly without restrictions between any point in the European Union and any point in the United States, mostly making use of tailored code-sharing.

– Removal of all restrictions on international routes between the European Union and the United States (third/fourth freedom rights), and routes beyond the European Union and the United States (fifth freedom rights).

– Removal of all restrictions on pricing on all routes between the European Union and the United States, except for U.S. air carriers which cannot price-lead on intra-Community routes.

– Removal of all restrictions on seventh freedom flights for all-cargo services operated by EU air carriers, but no additional seventh freedom for all-cargo flights for U.S. air carriers.

– Seventh freedom rights for passenger services for EU air carriers only, between the United States and any point in the European Common Aviation Area.

– Rights to enter into franchising and branding arrangements with other air carriers or companies.

– Commitment of the U.S. authorities to provide fair and expeditious consideration of antitrust immunity application and assurance that Community air carriers qualify for ATI under the Agreement.

– Unlimited code-sharing between EU, U.S. and third country air carriers.

– Creation of new opportunities for EU air carriers to wet-lease aircraft to U.S. air carriers for use on international routes between the United States and any third country, which was previously prohibited by the Federal Aviation Administration (FAA).

– Binding provisions, contained in a new Annex on ownership, investment and control, to the benefit of U.S. investments in the European Union and EU investors in the United States, subject to the two limitations defined by U.S. Statute (*1. Ownership by all foreign nationals of more than 25% of a corporation's voting equity is prohibited by U.S. law. 2. Actual control of foreign nationals is also limited by U.S. law*), on ownership, investment and control:

---

93   The Economic Impacts of an Open Aviation Area between the EU and the U.S., Final Report January 2007, prepared for: Directorate General Energy and Transport European Commission, by Booz/Allen/Hamilton (London) in association with Campbell Hill Aviation Group (Alexandria, VA) and Mr Erwin von der Stein, Dr Ingomar Joerss and Dr Pablo Mendes de Leon, pp. 14-16.

1. As much as 25% of the voting equity by EU investors and/or 49.9% of total equity of a U.S. air carrier shall not be deemed to constitute control of that air carrier.
2. Ownership of 50% or more of the total equity by EU nationals shall not be presumed to constitute control of that air carrier, subject to a case-by-case analysis.
3. Guarantee of fair and expeditious consideration of any transaction involving investment by EU nationals in U.S. air carriers.

– The Annex contains one-sided U.S. binding commitments with regard to EU investment and control of third countries' air carriers established in a number of States: the United States shall not exercise their rights to object to the operations to the United States of third countries' air carriers, being on a continuous updated list, which are owned and controlled by EU investors.

– The Annex provides for rights in the area of inwards foreign investment in Community air carriers by ECAA investors, whereby the Community air carriers, owned and controlled by ECAA citizens, will be treated by the United States as EU nationals.

– A role for the Joint Committee in matters concerning ownership and control regarding common understanding of the criteria used by the European Union and the United States in air carrier control decision making.

– Under the chapter 'Regulatory Cooperation', the following issues:
1. With respect to security, the United States agreed on compatible practices and standards and to minimise regulatory divergence in the security field.
2. Regarding safety, procedures for consultation in the event of safety concerns on both sides, and to recognize the development of safety responsibilities at EU level.
3. Regulation and arrangements for cooperation regarding air carrier alliances, and reducing the potential for conflicts in the application of competition laws of both sides, and thereby recognizing that government subsidies and support could distort competition, in which cases solution-oriented procedures have to be established by both sides.
4. Furthermore, the recognition of environmental issues like taxation of aviation fuel on certain routes and conditions flown by U.S. air carriers, and the fact that nothing in the Agreement will affect in any way the respective legal and policy positions on various aviation related environmental issues, thus keeping open the EU's options in respect of future environmental measures.
5. Mutual commitment to enhance climate change research and related technical development in order to enhance safety, fuel efficiency and the reduction of emissions (European Union and ICAO Emissions Trading Systems, ETS). In Novem-

ber 2008, the European Parliament and the Council adopted Directive 2008/101/ EC by virtue of which international aviation was included into the EU ETS. Airlines participating in ETS could trade the so-called European Union Aviation Allowances (EUAA), which were especially established by the European Commission, among themselves but could not sell these allowances to other sectors.[94]

6. The establishment of a Joint Committee, responsible for resolving issues relating to interpretation and application, review of implementation and of the Agreement, and facilitating greater cooperation, with dispute resolution as a last resort through formal arbitration procedures, as determined by the Agreement.

– Other issues are:

1. international cooperation with international organizations and third countries;
2. ground-handling services – Traditional provisions guaranteeing access to these services;
3. intermodal provisions, facilitating combinations of passenger and cargo air services with surface transportation providers;
4. the right to establish offices, to maintain staff, and to engage sales agents in the territory of the other party;
5. Computer Reservation Systems (CRS) – The United States accepted provisions to guarantee EU CRS providers the right to operate in the United States, depending on certain conditions.

Contrary to the right of U.S. air carriers to operate intra-Community flights, EU air carriers are however not permitted to operate intra-U.S. flights, nor are they allowed to purchase a controlling stake in a U.S. air carrier (asymmetrical elements). This form of liberalization between Europe and the rest of the world, is a key objective of the EU's external aviation policy. This EU policy, expressed as Open Skies agreements with third States will open up civil aviation markets, will lift restrictions to be able to grow faster and promote fair competition.

Another ambitious Open Skies air transport agreement between the European Union and a major partner in the world is the EU-Canada Air Transport Agreement, signed in December 2009. This Agreement was negotiated by the European Commission under a mandate received from the Council in October 2007, and has replaced bilateral air services agreements concluded between EU Member States and Canada.[95]

---

94 Directive 2008/101/EC of the European Parliament and of the Council of 19 November 2008 amending Directive 2003/87/EC so as to include aviation activities in the scheme for greenhouse gas emission allowance trading within the Community, *OJ EU* L 8/3, 13.1.2009. *See also* Valdés, A.P., *Greenhouse Gas Emissions from International Aviation: Legal and Policy Challenges*, Essential Air and Space Law Volume 14, Series Editor Benkö, M.E., The Hague: Eleven International Publishing, 2015, p. 124.

95 *See also*: COM (2006) 871 of 9 January 2007, Communication from the Commission developing a Community civil aviation policy towards Canada.

The European Union was of the opinion that Canada, with its market-oriented economic and transport policy and high regulatory standards, and being already a leading aviation partner of the European Union, should be a strong candidate for a new-generation liberalized air transport agreement with the European Union.

As a truly comprehensive ATA, it is ground-breaking in the air transport industry, providing for unprecedented levels of liberalization in terms of traffic rights as well as of foreign investment in air carriers. The EU-Canada ATA eventually will establish a fully OAA between the European Union and Canada. Citizens of EU Member States will be allowed to establish operations in Canada and freely invest in Canadian air carriers and vice versa.

More and more Open Skies agreements, with increasing liberalizing effect, have been concluded or are in the process of negotiations (e.g., EU-Morocco Aviation Agreement, as early as 2006, EU-Turkey Initial 'Horizontal' Aviation Agreement in 2010, the EU-Mediterranean Aviation Agreement with Israel in 2013, and a large number of African Union States (AU) concluded in January 2018 the Single African Air Transport Market (SAATM)).

The SAATM is an important project of the African Union, ensuring that aviation will play a major role in connecting Africa in order to achieve social, economic and political integration and to boost intra-African trade. Noteworthy in this respect is the Yamoussoukro Decision (YD), adopted on 14 November 1999 to counter the protectionist nature of bilateral air services agreements, and hence liberalize African air transport. The 1999 YD, evolving from the Yamoussoukro Declaration of 1988, commits its 44 signatory States to deregulate air services, and to promote regional air markets open to transnational competition in the form of a multilateral treaty.

The YD entered into force in 2000 and became fully binding in 2002, and remains the single most important air transport reform initiative by African governments. It calls for full liberalization of intra-African air transport services in terms of access, capacity, frequency, tariffs, and free exercise of first to fifth freedom rights for passengers and freight air services by eligible airlines, as well as liberalized tariffs and fair competition, all in compliance with ICAO safety SARPs.[96]

The YD defines an eligible airline as any African air transport company fulfilling the requirements set forth in Article 6, subparagraph 6.9, eligibility criteria. To be eligible an airline should:

1. be legally established in accordance with the regulations applicable in a State Party to this Decision;
2. have its headquarters, central administration and principal place of business physically located in the State concerned;
3. be duly licensed by a State Party as defined in Annex 6 of the Chicago Convention;

---

96   Open Skies for Africa-Implementing the Yamoussoukro Decision (YD). 2010 Study of the World Bank.

4. fully own or have a long-term lease exceeding six month on an aircraft and have its technical supervision;
5. be adequately insured with regard to passengers, cargo, mail, baggage and third parties in an amount at least equal to the provisions of the International Conventions in force;
6. be capable of demonstrating its ability to maintain standards at least equal to those set by ICAO and to respond to any query from any State to which it provides air services;
7. be effectively controlled by a State Party.

The objective of the YD is to strengthen aviation safety and security oversight in Africa, and to promote an atmosphere of cooperation among African air carriers through partnerships, mergers and consortiums.[97] Unfortunately, implementation, guaranteeing the creation of a larger aviation market and improved access to capital, has fallen short so far, so that the full potential has not been realized yet. Nevertheless, the YD makes African air transport leaders recognize that reliable, safe, and competitively priced air services are essential to better integrating Africa with the global economy, according to the 2010 World Bank Study, underlining the need for action on those commitments.

Today, 28 African States have signed up to SAATM, and 16 of them have signed a Memorandum of Implementation (MoI) that formally opens their air transport markets and commits these States to unconditional and immediate implementation of all the provisions of the YD. Nigeria and Burkina Faso have become the latest African States so far to sign the MoI for SAATM, removing all bilateral restrictions on intra-African flights.[98]

While the African Civil Aviation Commission (AFCAC) is the body responsible for implementing and operationalizing intra-African Open Skies, the MoI must pull the project out of a deadlock by simplifying intra-African air transport liberalization.[99] Most of the legal framework for SAATM has been finalized, including rules for consumer protection and a level playing field. Dispute settlement rules will follow. AFCAC strategy will include synchronization of its elaborated plan with other stakeholders, such as IATA.[100]

Throughout the world, more Open Skies negotiations and agreements have been concluded, such as the Multilateral Agreement on the Liberalization of International Air

---

97 www.iata.org/policy/promoting-aviation/Documents/single-african-air-transport-market.pdf. Benefits of Yamoussoukro Decision. Yamoussoukro is since 1983 the official capital of Ivory Coast (Côte d'Ivore). *See also* United Nations Economic and Social Council, Economic Commission for Africa, ECA/RCID/CM.-CIVAV/99/RPT, Annex 1, Decision Relating to the Implementation.
98 *Air Transport World*, 9 May 2019.
99 Dakar-based AFCAC is a specialized agency of the African Union on all matters in civil aviation and comprises 54 African States.
100 *Air Transport World*, 22 March 2019, Moores, A., New AFCAC chief looks to make African liberalization easier.

Transportation (MALIAT) between the United States and various States in the Pacific Rim.[101]

Key features of this multilateral agreement are:
- an open route schedule;
- open traffic rights, including seventh freedom cargo services;
- open capacity and frequency;
- operational flexibility, including change of gauge, aircraft type, co-terminalization and intermodal rights;
- unlimited airline designation;
- unlimited code-sharing, including third country code-sharing;
- open pricing and a minimal tariff filing regime.[102]

This multilateral agreement has some ground-breaking elements such as provisions that eliminate the traditional ownership provisions that require an air carrier to be substantially owned by either home country nationals or the homestead government, for conditional access to outside investments and eliminating the difference between charter and scheduled air services, and expanding the bilateral model to a multilateral template to effectively deal with accession, amendments, dispute resolution and the relationship with other agreements. Furthermore, the agreement standardizes and streamlines safety, security, CRS and facilitation clauses. A Protocol to the MALIAT allows parties to exchange seventh freedom passenger and cabotage rights under special conditions.[103]

The MALIAT represents the first successful multilateral effort based on the Open Skies template to remove barriers to improved air services. While the MALIAT is not an APEC agreement, the original signatory States are all APEC economies. Other APEC States are permitted to join, but membership is not restricted to APEC members.[104]

In Southeast Asia, ASEAN Member States have intensively participated in intra-ASEAN economic arrangements.[105] In the air transportation sector, the need emerged to develop a competitive air services policy with the possibility of leading towards an

---

101 The United States, Brunei Darussalam, New Zealand, Chile and Singapore met at Kona, Hawaii from 31 October to 2 November 2000 to negotiate and agree on a preliminary text of the MALIAT or Kona Agreement, which was agreed in principle and announced at Brunei on 15 November 2000 at the Leaders Meeting, and formally signed, together with the Protocol, at Washington DC on 1 May 2001 by five APEC States. MALIAT entered into force on 21 December 2001. New Zealand is designated as the Depositary State of the MALIAT. Mongolia, Samoa, the Cook Islands and Tonga joint later.

102 Change of gauge is a change of aircraft, at an en-route point on an international flight outside the home territory of the carrier, to (on an outbound trip) or from (on an inbound trip) another aircraft having a smaller capacity. Source: ICAO Doc 9626 Manual on the Regulation of International Air Transport, Chapter 4.1 Basic Market Access.

103 The MALIAT or Kona Agreement. See www.icao.int/Meetings/ATConf5/Documents/Kiser.pdf.

104 Asia-Pacific Economic Cooperation (APEC), an intergovernmental forum for 21 Pacific Rim Member economies that promotes free trade throughout the Asia-Pacific region, is established in 1989 at Canberra, Australia and is headquartered in Singapore.

105 Framework Agreement on Enhancing ASEAN Economic Cooperation, 28 January 1992, Singapore.

open sky policy. To date, the frameworks to achieve operation of ASEAN Open Skies have been completed, which include the ASEAN Multilateral Agreement on Air Services (MAAS), actually a precursor to the ASEAN Single Aviation Market (ASAM) also known as the ASEAN Open Skies policy, the ASEAN Multilateral Agreement for the Full Liberalization of Passenger Air Services (MAFLPAS), both agreements designed to allow unlimited air passenger services between ASEAN capital cities, secondary cities and sub-regions without limitations on capacity and frequency, and the ASEAN Multilateral Agreement on the Full Liberalization of Air Freight Services, part of the broader ASEAN Air Transport Integration and Liberalization Plan in Southeast Asia.[106]

These Multilateral Agreements and their associated Protocols create intra-ASEAN Open Skies for each of the ASEAN Member States to strengthen the economy of the ASEAN Community.[107]

Achieving Open Skies in the region is an important part of the bigger plan to implement a single aviation market. The ASAM Implementation Framework was a major step in liberalizing the air transport sector. The roadmap included economic elements such as market access, charters, airline ownership and control, tariffs, competition law and policy, consumer protection, airport user charges, dispute solution and technical elements including aviation safety, security and ATM.

The ASAM is intended to increase regional and domestic connectivity, encouraging higher traffic growth and air services quality while lowering airfares, gradually lifting certain key aviation barriers like restrictions on capacity and competition, integrating production networks and enhancing regional trade. Third-, fourth- and fifth-freedom restrictions are addressed in these Multilateral Agreements. However, due to persistent protective opposition from some Member States, for the time being there would not be a full implementation of fifth freedom rights.

The progress of liberalization in the 10 Member States, together forming ASEAN, has led to changes in regulations to achieve a regulatory situation similar to that of Europe, and the development of new regional and international routes to create a strong single aviation market in Southeast Asia. In this respect, agreements have been established with other strategic partners. Based on an approved aviation cooperation framework with China, the ASEAN-China Air Transport Agreement (AC-ATA) was established in 2010, providing unlimited passenger and cargo services between China and ASEAN Member States.[108]

Two years after announcing plans to establish a Comprehensive Air Transport Agreement (CATA), delegations representing the Member States of the European Union and

---

106 Association of Southeast Asian Nations (ASEAN), headquartered in Jakarta, Indonesia.
107 Review of Developments in Transport in Asia and the Pacific 2007, *Data and Trends*, New York: United Nations Economic and Social Commission for Asia and the Pacific.
108 *See also* Duval, D.T. (Ed.), *Air Transport in the Asia Pacific*, Milton Park, Abingdon, Oxon: Routledge, 2016, Chapter 7.

ASEAN will have a round of negotiations, starting late 2018, to resume dialogues regarding an Open Skies deal between the two economic regions. If finalized, the ASEAN-EU CATA will significantly ease connectivity and boost air traffic.[109]

Air transport liberalization also has its downside, which emerged after the United Kingdom made its decision to exit the European Union by early 2019, which, however, has been postponed. This means that there are concerns about the post-Brexit situation with respect to civil air transport rights. The almost inevitable Brexit will render it impossible for British air carriers to make use of the liberalized air services agreement within the European Union and between the remaining 27 EU Member States and the U.S. and Canada. Conversely, air carriers from outside the United Kingdom will experience the same problems with their liberalized air services to and from the United Kingdom.

A Brexit will definitely mean that the United Kingdom has to negotiate not only with the European Union but for its incredibly important North Atlantic route network with the United States and Canada for alternative Open Skies agreements.

2.8 PARIS AGREEMENT 1956 COMMERCIAL RIGHTS OF NON-SCHEDULED AIR SERVICES IN EUROPE

Multilateral Agreement on Commercial Rights of Non-Scheduled Air Services in Europe

The Paris Agreement (ICAO Doc 7695) between European Civil Aviation Conference (ECAC) States was reached within the framework of ECAC and was intended for the European region. It was signed at Paris on 30 April 1956. A similar agreement was concluded in Southeast Asia, namely the Multilateral Agreement on Commercial Rights of Non-Scheduled Air Services among the Association of Southeast Asian Nations, signed at Manila on 13 March 1971. The geographical scope of this Agreement is limited to Southeast Asia.[110]

These Agreements generally provided for a more liberalized regime with respect to the authorization of non-scheduled air services between the States Parties, such as charter flights flying routes not being directly served by scheduled air services.[111]

The absence of a clear definition of a non-scheduled air service raised some problems in regulating non-scheduled flights.

---

109 Meszaros, J., EU and ASEAN Head for New Round of Open Skies Talks, November 2018, and ASEAN-EU Air Transport Deal Near Completion, 6 December 2018, *AINonline Air Transport*.

110 The original signatory States were Indonesia, Malaysia, Philippines, Singapore and Thailand being Member States of ASEAN and ICAO in 1971, later followed by Brunei Darussalam, Cambodia, Lao PRD, Myanmar and Viet Nam (ASEAN and ICAO Member States).

111 Abeyratne, R.I.R., *Convention on International Civil Aviation: A Commentary*, Cham: Springer International Publishing, 2014, Art. 5 Right of Non-scheduled Flight, 1. Commercial Aspects.

The only starting point to come to the understanding of a non-scheduled air service is to observe and omit specific points in the definition of a scheduled air service, as adopted by the ICAO Council in 1952 (Council Definition, 1952). The definition adopted by the Council is previously mentioned in Chapter 2.3, Freedoms of the Air.

As a reminder, ICAO Doc 9587, Policy and Guidance Material on the Economic Regulation of International Air Transport, Fourth Edition 2017, Part I, Page 1-12, gives the same definition: An international scheduled air service is a series of flights that possesses all the following characteristics:

1. it passes through the airspace over the territory of more than one State;
2. it is performed by aircraft for the transport of passengers, mail or cargo for remuneration, in such a manner that each flight is open to use by members of the public;
3. it is operated, so as to serve traffic between the same two or more points, either
   a. according to a published timetable; or
   b. with flights so regular or frequent that they constitute a recognizable systematic series.

Characteristics of non-scheduled air services.

Non-scheduled air services may be performed by all types of air carriers and may be distinguished from scheduled services by the following characteristics. They are usually operated:

– pursuant to a charter contract on a point-to-point and often plane-load basis (but several charters may share the capacity of an aircraft);
– either an *ad hoc* basis or on a regular but seasonal basis;
– not subject to the public service obligations that may be imposed upon scheduled air carriers such as the requirement to operate flights according to a published timetable regardless of load factor;
– with more operational flexibility with respect to choices of airports, hours of operation and other operational and service requirements than scheduled services;
– with the financial risk for underutilized payload being assumed by the charterer rather than the aircraft operator;
– generally without the air carrier maintaining direct control over retail prices (the aircraft capacity is usually sold wholesale by the carrier to tour operators, freight forwarders or other entities); and
– subject to seeking permission, or giving prior notification, for each flight or series of flights, to/from the country of origin or destination or both.[112]

As for charter operations, the following practices could be noticed:

---

112 *See also* ICAO Doc 9626 Manual on the Regulation of Air Transport, Chapter 5.3 Air Services, for the definition of an international scheduled air service, and Chapter 4.6 Non-Scheduled Air Services, for the characteristics of non-scheduled air services.

- the tendency to apply national rules to incoming and outgoing charters unless there is a special agreement abrogating them;
- the tendency of charter companies to join forces, which has already resulted in the creation of a number of organizations;
- bilateral charter agreements (charter bilaterals) along the lines of those concluded for scheduled air transport;
- scheduled airline companies establishing subsidiary companies solely in order to capture their share of the non-scheduled charter traffic business;
- increased cooperation between scheduled airline companies and charter companies, especially on the issue of minimum fares and rates.

According to ICAO, a charter flight is a non-scheduled operation using a chartered aircraft. Though the terms non-scheduled and charter (i.e., a contractual arrangement between an air carrier and an entity hiring or leasing its aircraft) have come to be used interchangeably, it should be noted that not all commercial non-scheduled operations are charter flights. IATA extended, on 20 September 1974, its membership clause to include charter companies, thereby providing a forum for closer cooperation between the two sectors of air transport.

The conclusion of the Paris Agreement document by ECAC-States was based on their consideration that the policy of each of the States Parties is that aircraft engaged in non-scheduled commercial flights within Europe, which do not harm their scheduled services, may freely be admitted to their territories for the purpose of taking on or discharging traffic. Furthermore, that the treatment provided by the provisions of the first paragraph of Article 5 of the 1944 Chicago Convention, which applies to the international movements of private and commercial aircraft engaged in non-scheduled operations on flights into or in transit non-stop across the territories of the States Parties to the Convention and to stops therein for non-traffic purposes, is satisfactory, and furthermore based on their desire to arrive at further agreement as to the right of their respective commercial aircraft to take on and discharge passengers, cargo or mail, on international flights for remuneration or hire on other than international scheduled services, as provided in the second paragraph of Article 5 of the Convention.

Article 5 of the Chicago Convention:

> Right of non-scheduled flight.
> [...] Such aircraft, if engaged in the carriage of passengers, cargo, or mail for remuneration or hire on other than scheduled international air services, shall also, subject to the provisions of Article 7 (Cabotage), have the privilege of taking on or discharging passengers, cargo, or mail, subject to the right of any

State where such embarkation or discharge takes place to impose such regulations, conditions or limitations as it may consider desirable.

Pursuant to the Chicago Convention, facilities were granted for such services on the following conditions:

Article 1, 1956 Paris Agreement:

This Agreement applies to any civil aircraft:
1. registered in a State Member of the European Civil Aviation Conference, and
2. operated by a national of one of the Contracting States duly authorized by the competent national authority of that State, when engaged in international flights for remuneration or hire, on other than scheduled international air services, in the territories covered by this Agreement as provided in Article 11.

Article 11, 1956 Paris Agreement:

This Agreement shall apply to all the metropolitan territories of the Contracting States, with the exception of outlying islands in the Atlantic Ocean and islands with semi-independent status in respect of which any Contracting State, at the time of the deposit of its instrument of ratification or adherence, may declare that its acceptance of this Agreement does not apply.

Article 2, 1956 Paris Agreement:

1. The Contracting States agree to admit the aircraft referred to in Article 1 of this Agreement freely to their respective territories for the purpose of taking on or discharging traffic without the imposition of the 'regulations, conditions or limitations' provided for in the second paragraph of Article 5 of the Chicago Convention where such aircraft are engaged in:
   a. flights for the purpose of meeting humanitarian or emergency needs;
   b. taxi-class passenger flights of occasional character on request, provided that the aircraft does not have a seating capacity of more than six passengers and provided that the destination is chosen by the hirer or hirers and no part of the capacity of the aircraft is resold to the public;

c. flights on which the entire space is hired by a single person (individual, firm, corporation or institution) for the carriage of his or its staff or merchandise, provided that no part of such space is resold;

d. single flights, no operator or group of operators being entitled under this sub-paragraph to more than one flight per month between the same two traffic centres for all aircraft available to him.

2. The same treatment shall be accorded to aircraft engaged in either of the following activities:

a. the transport of freight exclusively;

b. the transport of passengers between region which have no reasonably direct connection by scheduled air services;

provided that any Contracting State may require the abandonment of the activities specified in this paragraph if it deems that these are harmful to the interests of its scheduled air services operating in the territories to which this Agreement applies; any Contracting State may require full information as to the nature and extent of any such activities that have been or are being conducted; and further provided that, in respect of the activities referred to in sub-paragraph (b) of this paragraph, any Contracting State may determine freely the extent of the regions (including the airport or airports comprised), may modify such determination at any time, and may determine whether such regions have reasonably direct connections by scheduled air services.

Nowadays, non-scheduled, charter companies or low cost subsidiaries of scheduled air carriers tend to increasingly switch to regular air transport operations, in a system of year-round quasi-scheduled international point to point flights between major and regional airports or even the same routes operated by scheduled carriers, but often in a role as a traffic feeder for the economic benefit of a legacy or national (flag) carrier to fill up its (inter)continental hub and spoke system. In other words, the slowly diminishing distinction between scheduled and non-scheduled air carriers is largely fading away due to the global progress in liberalization regarding international air transportation and the emergence of large (inter)continental low cost carriers.[113]

2.9 PARIS AGREEMENT 1960 CERTIFICATES OF AIRWORTHINESS FOR IMPORTED AIRCRAFT

Multilateral Agreement Relating to Certificates of Airworthiness for Imported Aircraft

---

113 Budd, L., Ison, S. (Eds.), *Low Cost Carriers, Emergence, Expansion and Evolution*, Milton Park, Abingdon, Oxon: Routledge, 2016, pp. 113-118.

The Chicago Convention does contain certain provisions concerning Certificates of Airworthiness. However, before 1960 there was no multilateral agreement for the issuing and validation of those certificates for aircraft imported from one State to another. Article 33 of the Chicago Convention has been amended by the 1960 Paris Agreement with regard to Certificates of Airworthiness for imported aircraft.

Article 33 does not cover the issuing and recognition of Certificates of Airworthiness of imported aircraft, but only provides for the mutual recognition of these documents.

Article 33:

> Recognition of certificates and licenses.
> Certificates of airworthiness and certificates of competency and licenses issued or rendered valid by the Contracting State in which the aircraft is registered, shall be recognized as valid by the other Contracting States, provided that the requirements under which such certificates or licenses were issued or rendered valid are equal to or above the minimum standards which may be established from time to time pursuant to this Convention.

To operate an aircraft, it must be in a state of airworthiness. All requirements such as weight and balance, type of fuel and other liquids, aircraft maintenance logs, proper functioning of all parts and instruments and approved spare parts (no inferior, bogus or counterfeit parts) must be satisfactorily fulfilled.[114]

The 1960 Paris Agreement (ICAO Doc 8056) was concluded at an international level between European States, in particular open for signature to Member States of ECAC. It was signed at Paris on 22 April 1960. Over time, the 1960 Paris Agreement opened for accession to signing by non-signatory ECAC Member States. Eventually nearly all ECAC Member States ratified the Agreement.

The Agreement shall apply to all the metropolitan territories of the Contracting States, and it refers to the issue and validation of Certificates of Airworthiness of aircraft imported from one State to another and the exchange of information on the requirements and regulations referred thereto.[115]

An important requirement for importing aircraft, determined by the Chicago Convention, is a Certificate of Registration related to the ownership and the responsibility assumed by the State for its activity, as well as for being the instrument that proves which is the State in charge of issuing the Certificate of Airworthiness.

---

114 Cheng, C.J., Kim, D.H. (Eds.), *The Utilization of the World's Air Space and Free Outer Space in the 21st Century*, Proceedings of the International Conference on Air and Space Policy, Law and Industry for the 21st Century held in Seoul from 23 to 25 June 1997, The Hague: Kluwer Law International, 2000, p. 201.
115 Kean, A. (Ed.), *Essays in Air Law*, The Hague: Martinus Nijhoff Publishers, 1982, p. 48.

Each Contracting State shall, to the greatest extent practicable, keep other Contracting States fully and currently informed of its laws, regulations and requirements relating to airworthiness, including any complementary operating regulations and any changes therein effected occasionally. Moreover, upon request by a Contracting State, which proposes to apply the provisions of Article 2 of this Agreement, another Contracting State shall supply, as far as practically possible, details of laws, regulations and requirements relating to airworthiness under which it was issued or validated a Certificate of Airworthiness (Art. 7, 1960 Paris Agreement).

A Contracting State in whose territory an aircraft is constructed and from which it is exported to another Contracting State that subsequently provides that aircraft with a valid Certificate of Airworthiness pursuant to Article 2 of the 1960 Paris Agreement, shall communicate to all other Contracting States (in practice between the competent authorities of those States), particulars of mandatory modifications to, and mandatory inspections of, that type of aircraft which may at any time be prescribed by it, and on request provide, as far as practicable, to any Contracting State information and advice on: the conditions on which the Certificate of Airworthiness was originally issued to that aircraft, as well as major repairs which cannot be dealt with by the relevant repair schemes, included in the maintenance manuals relating to that particular type of aircraft or by the fitment of spare parts and their history (serial numbers, etc.), highly important as to eliminate counterfeit aircraft parts (Art. 8, 1960 Paris Agreement).

ICAO Annex 8 – Airworthiness of Aircraft – indicates that in the interest of aviation safety, an aircraft must be designed, constructed and operated in compliance with the appropriate airworthiness requirements of the State of Registry of that particular aircraft. Consequently, the aircraft will be issued with a Certificate of Airworthiness declaring that the aircraft is suitable to fly. The Certificate of Airworthiness as mentioned in the SARPs of Annex 8 is the Certificate of Airworthiness referred to in Articles 29, 31 and 33 of the Chicago Convention.

Article 33 has been amended by the 1960 Paris Agreement relating to airworthiness for imported aircraft, as Article 33 only provides for the mutual recognition of the Certificates of Airworthiness, since it does not include imported aircraft, as mentioned earlier.

The 1960 Paris Agreement applies only to civil aircraft constructed in the territory of a Contracting State and imported from one Contracting State to another. Article 1 of the 1960 Paris Agreement imposes a number of conditions on such aircraft.

Imported aircraft must have been constructed in accordance with the applicable laws, regulations and requirements relating to airworthiness of the State of Construction (Manufacturer), and must comply with the applicable minimum standards relating to airworthiness established pursuant to the Chicago Convention. Furthermore, there is a rule that imported aircraft can comply with the requirements of the operating regulations of the State of Import, and comply with any other special conditions notified in accordance with Article 4 of this Agreement.

Article 2, 1960 Paris Agreement:

1. If a Contracting State receives an application for a Certificate of Airworthiness in respect of an aircraft imported or being imported into its territory and subsequently to be entered on its Register, it shall, subject to the other provisions of this Agreement, either:
   a. render valid the existing Certificate of Airworthiness of such aircraft, or
   b. issue a new certificate.
2. However, if that State elects to issue a new certificate, it may, pending the issue thereof, render valid the existing one for a period not exceeding 6 months or for the unexpired period of the existing certificate, whichever is lesser.

Article 4, 1960 Paris Agreement:

A Contracting State to which an application has been made pursuant to Article 2 of this Agreement shall have the right to make the validation of the certificate dependent on the fulfilment of any special conditions which are for the time being applicable to the issue of its own Certificates of Airworthiness and which have been notified to all Contracting States. The exercise of such right shall be subject to prior consultation:
1. with the State that provided the aircraft concerned with its current Certificate of Airworthiness; and
2. if requested by that State, also with the State in whose territory the aircraft was constructed.

Product liability is another important aspect of imported aircraft, directly related to aviation safety. Manufacturing of aircraft is a process of international cooperation, ranging from the supply of numerous hardware and software aircraft components to complete aircraft engines from various specialized companies all over the world. The aircraft manufacturer has to demonstrate that a newly designed aircraft fulfils specified minimum airworthiness standards to apply for a Certificate of Airworthiness. That means that all components, including engines, and eventually the aircraft as a whole, are extensively tested and shall function under all possible conditions in simulation and flight tests. One of the most important aspects regarding manufacture, submanufacture, import and operation of aircraft is product liability, determined by contract.[116]

---

116 See also 85/374/EEC. Council Directive of 25 July 1985 on the approximation of the laws, regulations and administrative provisions of the Member States concerning liability for defective products, OJ EC L 210/29 7.8.85.

Each application for the issue or validation of a Certificate of Airworthiness shall be accompanied by the documents listed in the Schedule to this Agreement (Art. 3, 1960 Paris Agreement). Required are: the Certificate of Airworthiness, the flight manual and maintenance manual pertaining to the particular aircraft, the weight schedule showing the ascertained empty weight and the corresponding centre of gravity and certain inspection and maintenance records.

2.10 TOKYO CONVENTION REGIME

Legal Instruments Related to Aviation Security

In the early days of civil aviation, no major incidents occurred as a result of criminal acts committed on board aircraft by individual or conspiracy terrorists. The first reported aircraft hijacking took place in May 1930, when Peruvian revolutionaries seized a Pan American World Airways mail plane. However, the vulnerability of civil aviation in this respect became especially evident from 1948 onwards when aircraft hijacking increased significantly. At the time of the Cold War, starting in the late 1950s, hijacking of aircraft was practically commonplace. In the 1960s and 1970s, the number of aircraft hijackings, sabotage and armed attacks rose to very serious proportions. The endless hijacking events culminated in the largest single attack involving the air transport industry on 11 September 2001. On that day, almost 3000 people were killed by terrorist attacks with commercial aircraft impacting the twin towers of the WTC in New York City, the Pentagon in Arlington, VA and another terrible intentional crash near Shanksville, PA.

The rise of extremely violent terrorism and the unlawful seizure of civil aircraft caused an irrevocable and abrupt end to the fundamental openness of the air transport industry, previously experienced by politicians, operators, air travellers and crew members. To restrain this altered reality, legal instruments were deemed to be urgently needed.[117]

The ICAO Legal Committee had officially established a subcommittee on the Legal Status of Aircraft in 1953 to study the problems associated with crimes on board aircraft in flight. A first ICAO draft Convention on the Legal Status of Aircraft was developed in 1958, expanding the scope of the issue to become, in 1959, a draft Convention on Offences and other Acts Occurring on Board Aircraft, followed by a final draft for consideration, finalizing and eventually adoption by the Diplomatic Conference on Air Law

---

117 Thomas, A.R. (Ed.), *Aviation Security Management: The Context of Aviation Security Management*, Volume 1, 2 and , Westport, CT: Greenwood Publishing Group, Preager Security International, 2008, Volume I, Chapter 10, A Chronology of Attacks against Civil Aviation by Mary F. Schiavo. *See also* Haberfeld, M.R., Von Hassell, A. (Eds.), *A New Understanding of Terrorism: Case Studies, Trajectories and Lessons Learned*, New York: Springer, 2009 (Ebook), Chapter 7, September 11 Terrorist Attacks Against the United States and the Law Enforcement Response.

convened at Tokyo by the ICAO Council from 20 August to 14 September 1963. The Tokyo Convention, formally called the Convention on Offences and Certain other Acts Committed on Board Aircraft, entered into force on 4 December 1969.

In the light of increased security, the Tokyo Convention, established by the successful work of the ICAO Council, was a first step in what would become a tremendous international effort to curb international aviation terrorism as far as possible. The Convention had its early origins in discussions and studies on the legal status of aircraft and of the aircraft commander rather than concerns regarding unlawful interference.

Whereas the Tokyo Convention mainly dealt with offences and certain other acts committed on board, the increase of unlawful seizure of aircraft, sabotage and armed attacks on civil aviation in the 1970s called for a wide range of security measures to safeguard passengers, crew members, ground personnel as well as the general public in each Contracting State. Amending and supplementing instruments were adopted and ratified to urgently undertake further efforts with a view to ensuring the security of air travel and preventing the acts of unlawful seizure, attacks and sabotage of civil aircraft.

On 25 November 1970, the United Nations General Assembly adopted Resolution 2645 which condemned, without exception whatsoever, all aerial hijackings or other interferences through threat or use of force on civil air traffic.[118]

To drastically address these horrific abuses, two new conventions were prepared. From 1 to 16 December 1970, 77 States and 12 international organizations met in The Hague for a Diplomatic Conference ending with the signing of The Hague Convention for the Suppression of Unlawful Seizure of Aircraft (the Anti-Hijacking Convention) which came into force on 14 October 1971. The Hague Convention, widely ratified, attempted to rectify shortcomings in the Tokyo Convention, and designated hijacking as a distinct criminal act.

The other convention, the Montreal Convention for the Suppression of Unlawful Acts against the Safety of Civil Aviation, was opened for signature at the 1971 Montreal Conference on Air Law.[119] The 1971 Montreal Convention was a multilateral treaty by which States agreed to prohibit and punish behaviour which may threaten the safety of civil aviation. It especially dealt with a different, emerging terrorist threat which was aircraft sabotage.

In the years to follow, the UN General Assembly and Security Council adopted a number of resolutions calling for international cooperation dealing with acts of international terrorism.[120]

---

118 United Nations General Assembly Resolution 2645 (XXV) Aerial Hijacking or Interference with Civil Air Traffic, 1914th Plenary Meeting on 25 November 1970.

119 The Postal History of ICAO, Legal Instruments related to Aviation Security, www.icao.int/secretariat/PostalHistory/legal_instruments_related_to_aviation_security.htm.

120 For instance: UN Security Council Resolution 286 (1970) of 9 September 1970, adopted at the 1552nd Meeting. The Security Council, gravely concerned at the threat to innocent civilian lives from the hijacking of aircraft and any other interference in international travel, 1. Appeals to all parties concerned for the immediate release of all passengers and crews without exception, held as a result of hijackings and other interference in international travel. 2. Calls on States to take all possible legal steps to prevent further hijackings or any other interference with international civil air travel.

To extend the provisions of the 1971 Montreal Convention to include attacks on airports, the Montreal Protocol was adopted in 1988. In 2010, the Beijing Convention and the Beijing Protocol, partly prompted by the terrorist attacks on 11 September 2001 on targets in the United States, were adopted, complementing the shortcomings in the existing international legal instruments. These instruments were followed by the 2014 Montreal Protocol to amend the outdated 1963 Tokyo Convention.

2.10.1 TOKYO CONVENTION 1963

Convention on Offences and Certain Other Acts Committed on Board Aircraft

International civil aviation safety and security have always been the goals of ICAO. However, protection from criminal acts in the early days of civil aviation was considered low priority. Due to a lack of adequate security measures, it was apparently easy in the 1960s to hijack an aircraft. With the advent of the Cold War, the Cuban Revolution (refugee-hijacking) and the Palestinian mass aircraft hijacking, relentlessly ending on a remote desert airstrip by name Dawson's Field in Jordan, the vulnerability of civil aviation became ruthlessly apparent. Due to the vast increase in the number of aircraft hijackings in the 1960s, aerial hijacking, based on different political ideologies, turned from a regional to a global problem, affecting a number of States in much the same way.

In particular, the Palestinian Liberation Organization (PLO) wanted to call worldwide attention to the deplorable situation of the Palestinians by means of aircraft hijacking. These hijackings were used as blackmail to achieve self-determination for the Palestinian people. Aircraft hijacking, also known as air piracy, especially within the special aircraft jurisdiction of the United States, is the unlawful seizure of an aircraft by an individual or a group.

In most cases, the aircraft commander is forced to fly according to the orders given by the hijackers. Occasionally, however, the hijackers have flown the aircraft themselves, which was the case with the devastating September 11 attacks in 2001 on iconic landmarks in Washington D.C. and Manhattan.

Especially after these most frightening hijackings in the United States, security measures in aviation were drastically scaled up worldwide, but in particular with regard to commercial flights to the United States. These extremely stringent security measures were not only intended to prevent potential hijackings in particular, but also, in general, offences against penal law and acts which, whether or not they are offences, may or do jeopardize the safety of the aircraft or of persons or property therein or which jeopardize good order and discipline on board.

At the 1944 Chicago Conference, the delegates could hardly have foreseen that one day sometime in the future, hijackers and terrorists could turn the operational vulnerability and the fundamental openness and easy access, so obvious in civil aviation history, to their advantage.

With the rise of extremely violent terrorism and the unlawful seizure of civil aircraft, aviation security became a key element of ICAO's role in the world. Together with a number of organization such as IATA, several regional and national bodies, other organizations like IFALPA, ACI, FAA and ECAC, ICAO made important progress in combatting unlawful interference in civil aviation.

The objectives of the 1963 Tokyo Convention, signed at Tokyo on 14 September 1963, cover a variety of subjects with the intention of providing safety in aircraft, protection of life and property on board, and generally protecting the security of civil aviation. In other words, it provides unification of rules on jurisdiction, maintaining law and order on board aircraft engaged in international air navigation, protection of persons acting in accordance with the Tokyo Convention, protection of the interests of disembarked persons and the quest of hijacking. The Tokyo Convention entered into force on 4 December 1969, bringing closure to ICAO's efforts on the subject since the 1950s.

In the years since 1968, the number of aircraft hijackings increased significantly. The total was further enlarged by politically motivated acts of sabotage against aircraft and passengers both in the air and on the ground. Deep concern prevailed in the world over these acts of unlawful interference with international civil aviation. This was the reason to convene an extraordinary ICAO Assembly (17th), which was held in Montreal from 16 to 30 June 1970, specifically on the subject of aviation security. It produced a series of resolutions dealing with a wide range of security measures, eventually leading to the adoption of a completely new Annex 17 – Security. On 22 March 1974, the ICAO Council adopted the First Edition of Annex 17.

Annex 17 lays down the objective that each Contracting State shall have as its primary objective the safety of passengers, ground personnel, crew and the general public in all matters related to safeguarding against acts of unlawful interference with civil aviation, that each Contracting State shall establish, in view of the foregoing, an organization and develop and implement regulations, practices and procedures taking into account the safety, regularity and efficiency of flights and that each Contracting State shall ensure that such an organization and such regulations, practices and procedures protect according to the primary objective, as well as be capable of responding rapidly to meet any increased security threat.[121]

The Tokyo Convention (ICAO Doc 8364) is applicable to offences against penal law and to acts which, whether or not they are offences, may or do jeopardize the safety of the aircraft or of persons or property therein or which jeopardize good order and discipline

---

121 ICAO Annex 17, Tenth Edition 2017, Chapter 2. General Principles, 2.1 Objectives.

on board civilian aircraft while in flight and engaged in international air navigation. Coverage includes, except as provided in Chapter III, offences committed or acts done by a person on board any aircraft registered in a Contracting State, while that aircraft is in flight or on the surface of the high seas or of any other area outside the territory of any State.[122]

Application of the Tokyo Convention is geographically not limited. However, the Convention does not create or define particular offences. They are left to be determined by national law.[123]

The Tokyo Convention has four principal purposes:

First, the Convention makes it clear that the State of Registry of an aircraft has the authority to apply its laws to events occurring on board its aircraft while in flight, no matter where it may be.

Secondly, the Convention provides the aircraft commander with the necessary authority to deal with persons who have committed, or are about to commit, a crime or an act jeopardizing safety on board his aircraft through use of reasonable force when required and without fear of subsequent retaliation through civil suit or otherwise.

Thirdly, the Convention delineates the duties and responsibilities of the Contracting State in which an aircraft lands after the commission of a crime on board, including its authority over, and responsibility to, any offenders that may be either disembarked within the territory of that State or delivered to its authorities.

Fourthly, the Convention is dealing with an emerging issue which is the crime of hijacking, however, not being prioritized.

Concerning the question of which penal law actually will be applicable, five theories can be distinguished:

(1) The territorial theory.

This follows the territorial basis in international law, on which each State is assumed to be sovereign in its overflying airspace.

The law of the State in whose airspace the offence has taken place will be applied by its national courts. In fact, the offence is subject to the concurrent jurisdiction between the State of Registry (Flag State) and the subjacent State. In principle, the State of Registry has the competence to exercise jurisdiction (Art. 3 paras. 2 and 3). The enforcement power of the subjacent State is restricted by Article 4, except in the case of defined conditions.

---

122 Chapter III, Art. 5.1 states: The provisions of this Chapter shall not apply to offences and acts committed or about to be committed by a person on board an aircraft in flight in the airspace of the State of Registration or over the high seas or any other area outside the territory of any State unless the last point of take-off or the next point of intended landing is situated in the State other than that of Registration, or the aircraft subsequently flies in the airspace of a State other than that of Registration with such person still on board.

123 Haanappel, P.P.C., *The Law and Policy of Air Space and Outer Space: A Comparative Approach*, The Hague: Kluwer Law International, 2003, pp. 50-51.

Article 4, 1963 Tokyo Convention:

A Contracting State which is not the State of registration (State of Registry) may not interfere with an aircraft in flight in order to exercise its criminal jurisdiction over an offence committed on board except in the following cases:

(a) The offence has effect on the territory of such State;

(b) The offence has been committed by or against a national or permanent resident of such State;

(c) The offence is against the security of such State;

(d) The offence consists of a breach of any rules or regulations relating to the flight or manoeuvre of aircraft in force in such State;

(e) The exercise of jurisdiction is necessary to ensure the observance of any obligation of such State under a multilateral international agreement.

However, the determination of the exact geographical position of the aircraft at the point of time the offence was actually committed is not always clear, a weakness due to the high speeds and altitudes of modern aircraft. For that reason, it is impracticable for a State to base its jurisdiction solely on this particular principle.

(2) The national theory.

The law of the State where the aircraft is registered is to be applied under all circumstances, according to this theory. The nationality rule is of special importance when over the high seas.

(3) The mixed basis theory.

The law of the nationality of the aircraft in flight, and or the law of the State over which the aircraft is flying, next to each other, are enforceable whenever the security or public order of such State is jeopardized by offences committed on board. This theory has already been described in a proposal concerning the resolution of conflicts of competence and jurisdiction contained in excerpts from the Draft Convention on Jurisdiction with Respect to Crime of the Harvard Research in International Law.[124]

---

124 Boyle, R.P., et al., 'The Tokyo Convention on Offences and Certain Other Acts Committed on Board Aircraft', 30 J. Air L. & Com. 305 (1964), pp. 313-314, Concurrent Jurisdiction. The 1935 Harvard Draft Convention on Criminal Jurisdiction would vest jurisdiction in States over crimes committed within their airspace and on aircraft which have their national character. The drafters specifically rejected any provision assigning priority to either State: Art. 3. A State has jurisdiction with respect to any crime committed in whole or in part within its territory. Art. 4. A State has jurisdiction with respect to any crime committed in whole or in part upon a public or private ship or aircraft which has its national character.

Thus with respect to all crimes on aircraft regardless where they might be, there would be two competent jurisdictions.

(4) The departure theory.

This is the theory of the law of the State of departure.

(5) The arrival or landing theory.

This is the theory of the law of the State of landing.

The last two theories confer jurisdiction on the State that the aircraft has departed from, or has landed in, respectively. The departure theory does not leave the aircraft commander any choice of jurisdiction, while the landing theory gives the aircraft commander the power to inform the appropriate authorities by any means of communication, and alert the airport for assistance and to scale up security measures (Art. 9).

In all cases, the aircraft commander will retain full authority in selecting which airport in what State is adequately equipped, and thus whose law will eventually be applied to the committed offence (Art. 8).[125]

Criminal jurisdiction may be exercised by Contracting States other than the State of Registry under limited conditions, *viz.* when the exercise of jurisdiction is required under multilateral international obligations, in the interest of national security and so forth.

The Convention recognizes, in the first time in the history of international aviation law, certain powers and immunities of the aircraft commander who, on international flights, may restrain any person(s) he has reasonable cause to believe is committing or is about to commit an offence liable to interfere with the safety of persons or property on board or who is jeopardizing good order and discipline.

Article 1, Paragraph 3 states that an aircraft is considered to be in flight from the moment when power is applied for the purpose of take-off until the moment when the landing run ends. And Article 1, Paragraph 4 states that this Convention shall not apply to aircraft used in military, customs or police services. Furthermore, Article 5, Paragraph 2 states that notwithstanding the provisions of Article 1, Paragraph 3, an aircraft shall for the purposes of Chapter III – Powers to the Aircraft Commander – be considered to be in flight at any time from the moment when all its external doors are closed following embarkation until the moment when any such door is opened for disembarkation. In other words, the powers of the pilot-in-command are equally applicable while on the ground.

In the case of a forced landing, the provisions of this Chapter shall continue to apply with respect to offences and acts committed on board until competent authorities of a State shall take over the responsibility for the aircraft and for the persons and property on board.

Both Article 11 and certain supplementary provisions are the only ones that are re-lated specifically to hijacking, but they do not oblige parties to prohibit or punish hijack-

---

125 Diederiks-Verschoor, I.H.Ph., Butler, M.A. (Legal adviser), *An Introduction to Air Law*, Eighth Revised Edition, Alphen aan den Rijn: Kluwer Law International, 2006, pp. 290-291.

ing. They merely require them to take all appropriate measures to restore control of the aircraft to its lawful commander or to preserve his or her control of the aircraft to permit its passengers and crew to continue their journey as soon as practicable, and to return the aircraft and its cargo.

These provisions were not nearly enough to combat hijacking of aircraft; in fact they contain weaknesses. Therefore, ICAO convened a conference at The Hague on the subject.

Article 11, Paragraph 1, Tokyo Convention:

> When a person on board has unlawfully committed by force or threat thereof an act of interference, seizure, or other wrongful exercise of control of an aircraft in flight or when such an act is about to be committed, Contracting States shall take all appropriate measures to restore control of the aircraft to its lawful commander or to preserve his control of the aircraft.

Article 11, Paragraph 2, Tokyo Convention:

> In the cases contemplated in the preceding paragraph, the Contracting State in which the aircraft lands shall permit its passengers and crew to continue their journey as soon as practicable, and shall return the aircraft and its cargo to the persons lawfully entitled to possession.

Article 10 of the Tokyo Convention deals with indemnity of liability:

> For actions taken in accordance with this Convention, neither the aircraft commander, any other member of the crew, any passenger, the owner or operator of the aircraft, nor the person on whose behalf the flight was performed shall be held responsible on account of the treatment undergone by the person against whom the actions were taken.

The Tokyo Convention actually deals with three major issues: penal jurisdiction, the powers and immunities of the aircraft commander and unlawful seizure of aircraft. In fact, it is the first global treaty on civil aviation security, or to be more precise, it is regarded as the first worldwide civil aviation treaty on counter-terrorism (Art. 3, para. 2).

The important contribution of the Convention regarding international law is not just the recognition of the competency of a State to exercise jurisdiction over offences and acts committed on board aircraft bearing its registration, but the commitment of the States Parties under Article 3, Paragraph 2 to establish such jurisdiction. Exactly who has legal authority to exercise control in any given situation is, however, often disputed. Basically, the State of Registry is the determining State in terms of penal law. The decision to deliver a person to a State of landing or disembarkation is based on the opinion of the aircraft commander that such person has committed a serious offence according to the penal law of the State of Registry of the aircraft.

The Tokyo Convention has set out detailed jurisdiction rules to ensure that offences and acts which jeopardize the safety of civil aircraft, persons or property, or good order and discipline on board civil aircraft should not go unpunished because of a lack of jurisdiction over those responsible. It has set the stage for many subsequent aviation security policies. The Convention addressed unlawful acts committed on board an aircraft that affect the safety of flight and, most importantly, allowed the aircraft commander to take reasonable measures to protect those on board, including the ability to have a passenger restrained or removed from the flight (Arts. 6 and 7). It also addressed in what way States should handle a hijacked aircraft.

The Convention does not create or define particular offences. They are left to be determined by national law. No provision of this Convention shall be interpreted as authorizing or requiring any action in respect of offences against penal law of a political nature or those based on racial or religious discrimination, without prejudice to the provisions of Article 4 and except when the safety of the aircraft or of persons or property on board so requires (Art. 2).

The Tokyo Convention did no more than to reformulate customary international law obligations already existing for quite some time. In fact, the anti-hijacking provisions, in particular Article 11, were considered to be too weak to provide effective sanctions for their enforcement. The Tokyo Convention only focused incidentally on the hijacking problem, making it not a pronounced anti-hijacking treaty. With the adoption of two major international conventions addressing terrorism against international civil aviation, the modern era of international counter-terrorism agreements, providing for assistance in law enforcement issues, began in 1970 and 1971.

The weaknesses of the provisions of the Tokyo Convention had left major questions unanswered regarding extradition enforcement, custody and prosecution of hijackers. It applied only to aircraft in flight without considering possible attacks or acts of sabotage on facilities and parked aircraft at airports. Moreover, the Tokyo Convention, and subsequent treaties on the subject, would only apply to those States that ratified it, which made it rather limited in its application.[126]

The Tokyo Convention was actually used as a starting point from which rules of international law, only occasionally referring to aircraft hijacking, could effectively be

---

126 Mackenzie, D., *ICAO: A History of the International Civil Aviation Organization*, Toronto: University of Toronto Press, 2010, pp. 253-255.

implemented. Basically, the Tokyo Convention obligated the Contracting States to establish jurisdiction over serious offences and crimes only committed on board aircraft of its own nationality. Its imperfections were translated into the strength of two subsequent international legal instruments dealing with counter-terrorism (1970 The Hague Convention, also known as the Anti-Hijacking Convention, fully focusing on the problems associated with aerial hijacking, and the 1971 Montreal Convention, also known as the Sabotage Convention).[127]

The Hague Conference resulted in a more stringent draft treaty which was concluded as The Hague Convention which, unlike the Tokyo Convention, makes aircraft hijacking a distinct offence and calls for severe punishment of any person found within the territory of a Contracting State who actually hijacked an aircraft. The Montreal Convention is in every aspect identical to The Hague Convention, as it contains similar provisions for punishment and extradition, but additionally, the Montreal Convention deals with terrorist acts of violence other than aircraft hijacking, such as sabotage attacks.

2.10.2 The Hague Convention 1970

Convention for the Suppression of Unlawful Seizure of Aircraft

In December 1969, the United Nations General Assembly adopted Resolution 2551 in which it emphasized its deep concern over acts of unlawful interference with international civil aviation.[128] On 9 September 1970, the United Nations Security Council adopted Resolution 286, calling upon States to take all possible legal steps to prevent further hijacking or any other interference with international air navigation. On 25 November 1970, the United Nations General Assembly condemned without exception whatsoever, by Resolution 2645, all aerial hijacking or other interference caused through criminal threat, usually accompanied by aggressive behaviour, use of force and or intimidation.[129]

The international community in this way condemned terrorism against air transport by giving official recognition to such condemnation and called upon all States to contribute to the eradication of the offence by taking decisive, effective, preventive and deterrent

---

127 Sweet, K.M., *Aviation and Airport Security: Terrorism and Safety Concerns*, Second Edition, Boca Raton, FL: CRC Press, Taylor & Francis Group, 2008, pp. 38-41. *See also* McWhinney, E., *Aerial Piracy and International Terrorism:The Illegal Diversion of Aircraft and International Law*, Second Revised Edition, Dordrecht: Martinus Nijhoff Publishers, 1987, pp. 36-40.

128 United Nations General Assembly Resolution 2551 (XXIV) Forcible Diversion of Civil Aircraft in Flight, 1831st Plenary Meeting on 12 December 1969. The Resolution was adopted by a vote of 77 in favour, 2 against and 17 abstentions

129 United Nations General Assembly Resolution 2645 (XXV) Aerial Hijacking or Interference with Civil Air Travel, 1914th Plenary Meeting on 25 November 1970. The Resolution was adopted by a vote of 105 in favour, none against and 8 abstentions.

measures. For this urgent reason, in the atmosphere of crisis, two new Conventions were prepared, namely The Hague Convention and the Montreal Convention.[130]

The Hague Convention for the Suppression of Unlawful Seizure of Aircraft was signed at The Hague on 16 December 1970, and entered into force on 14 October 1971. The Hague Convention (ICAO Doc 8920) is a multilateral treaty by which States agree to prohibit and punish aircraft hijacking. The Convention opens with a definition of the offence of unlawful seizure of aircraft:

Article 1, 1970 The Hague Convention:

> Any person who on board an aircraft in flight:
> (a) unlawfully, by force or threat thereof, or by any other form of intimidation, seizes, or exercises control of, that aircraft, or attempts to perform any such act, or
> (b) is an accomplice of a person who performs or attempts to perform any such act commits an offence (hereinafter referred to as 'the offence').

The definition of an offence as included in The Hague Convention is very similar to the notion of wrongful interference with aircraft in Article 11 of the Tokyo Convention, although that Convention created no offence. A further important difference between the two Conventions is that The Hague Convention makes provisions for the liability of accomplices. Subsequently, it imposes an obligation on the Contracting States to make the offence punishable by severe penalties.

Article 2, 1970 The Hague Convention:

> Each Contracting State undertakes to make the offence punishable by severe penalties.

There must be a seizure of, or the exercise of control over, an aircraft or an attempt to do so. These expressions taken together, clearly cover, *inter alia*, cases where a pilot (the commander) is replaced by a hijacker, and where a pilot is ordered to follow the hijacker's instructions or commands, either through the threat or use of force against the pilot or other members of the crew, passengers or, indeed, the aircraft itself. The threat or use of force must come from within the aircraft, thus only be committed by a person or persons on board the aircraft. Consequently, the offence does not extend to a case where an aircraft is forced to change course by the threat or application of force from another aircraft.

---

130 Hodgkinson, D.I., Johnston, R., *International Air Carrier Liability: Safety and Security*, Milton Park, Abingdon, Oxon: Routledge, 2017, pp. 209-210.

The States Parties to The Hague Convention considered in the preamble:

> The States Parties to this Convention, considering that unlawful acts of seizure or exercise of control of aircraft in flight jeopardize the safety of persons and property, seriously affect the operation of air services, and undermine the confidence of the peoples of the world in the safety of civil aviation; considering that the occurrence of such acts is a matter of grave concern; considering that, for the purpose of deterring such acts, there is an urgent need to provide appropriate measures for punishment of offenders; have agreed as follows: [...]

The Hague Convention made aerial hijacking a distinct offence, calling for severe punishment. The jurisdictional rules contained in the Convention provide a rationally comprehensive regime but, as usual, the actual exercise of the jurisdiction simply depends as much on the will of States as on the assignment of rights under international law.

The Convention does not apply to customs, law enforcement or military aircraft, and thus it applies exclusively to civil aircraft. The Convention only addresses situations in which an aircraft takes off or lands in a place different from its State of Registry. The Convention sets out the principle that a Contracting State must prosecute an aircraft hijacker if no other State requests his or her extradition for prosecution of the same crime.

Jurisdiction belongs first to the Contracting State in which the aircraft is registered. If that State refuses or is unable to respond, jurisdiction passes to the Contracting State where the aircraft first lands. Issues related to prosecution are in practice however more difficult to address, because many Contracting States refuse to extradite offenders to States that have the death penalty. The Hague Convention did not list the penalties that should be imposed for hijacking or specify policies against extradition or a refusal to prosecute hijacking which eventually made some Contracting States safe havens for hijackers.[131]

Especially when hijacking can be considered a political crime, the hijackers are, in the opinion of some States, actually not offenders.

The Hague Convention has been established because of the deepening of the aerial hijacking problem, especially after 1960, but also due to inadequate provisions contained in the 1963 Tokyo Convention which made The Hague Convention an unspoken anti-hijacking treaty.

One of the weaknesses of The Hague Convention is the absence of rules dealing with sabotage committed on the ground or unlawful interference with air navigation facilities, airports, air traffic control units or applicable radio communication.[132] Another weak-

---

131 Elias, B., *Airport and Aviation Security: U.S. Policy and Strategy in the Age of Global Terrorism*. Boca Raton, FL: CRC Press, Taylor & Francis Group, 2009, p. 6.
132 Mankiewich, R.H., The 1970 Hague Convention, 37 *J. Air L. & Com.* 195 (1971), p. 200.

ness lies in the fact that it does not impose a positive obligation to extradite an offender, although the offence is considered to be an extraditable offence within existing treaties. Furthermore, The Hague Convention obliges States to create the offence of hijacking in their national law, and it only addresses situations in which an aircraft takes off or lands in a place different from its State of Registry.[133]

The Convention sets out the principle of *aut dedere aut judiciare* (*Grotius: aut dedere, aut punire*) which essentially means either extradite or prosecute. In other words, a Contracting State to the Convention must prosecute an aircraft hijacker if no other State requests his or her extradition for prosecution of the same crime. The principle that combines the options of extradition and prosecution is contained in many other legal instruments adopted subsequently.[134]

Extradition would however not be necessary if all States exercised their universal jurisdiction. The Convention goes a long way in establishing hijacking as an offence of universal jurisdiction, at least for Contracting States, with any obligation to prosecute (Art. 7).

In conclusion, The Hague Convention provided for effective legal measures being taken to deter acts of unlawful seizure of aircraft through the cooperation of States throughout the world. The action taken by ICAO and the Contracting States resulted in a considerable reduction of hijackings during 1971.

2.10.3 MONTREAL CONVENTION 1971

Convention for the Suppression of Unlawful Acts against the Safety of Civil Aviation

From 8 to 23 September 1971, a full Diplomatic Conference under the auspices of ICAO was held at Montreal. It was attended by delegates from 60 Member States and the United Nations, as well as by observers from one State and six international organizations. The Convention was signed at Montreal on 23 September 1971, and entered into force on 26 January 1973.

The States Parties to the Montreal Convention (ICAO Doc 8966) consider that unlawful acts against the safety of civil aviation jeopardize the safety of persons and property, seriously affect the operation of air services and shall undermine the confidence of the peoples of the world in the safety of civil aviation, especially in the early 1970s when an exponential increase of hijackings and sabotage acts were dominating the news. The occurrence of such cruel acts is a matter of great concern and social instability. That is the

---

133 Harrison, J., *International Aviation and Terrorism: Evolving Threats, Evolving Security*, Milton Park, Abingdon, Oxon: Routledge, 2009, pp. 31-32.

134 Price, J.C., Forrest, J.S. *Practical Aviation Security: Predicting and Preventing Future Threats.* Third Edition, Cambridge, MA: Butterworth-Heinemann, 2016, pp. 104-106. *See also* Kittichaisaree, K., *The Obligation to Extradite or Prosecute*, Oxford: Oxford University Press, 2018, pp. 71-73, 173.

reason why, for the purpose of deterring such acts, there is an urgent need to provide appropriate measures for punishment of offenders.

The Montreal Convention is directed towards the prevention and discouragement of sabotage and acts of violence against civil aviation in general, including airports and air navigation facilities used in international air navigation. It expanded the criminalization of any attack on an aircraft, regardless of whether it occurred in flight or at an airport. The Tokyo Convention and, in particular The Hague Convention, were focused on hijacking and acts of unlawful seizure directed against aircraft. The Montreal Convention was intended as a supplement to the more specific prohibitions and protective controls contained in The Hague Convention, which in turn dealt with the complex issue of extradition and prosecution of offenders neglected by the Tokyo Convention.

Criminal elements changed their tactics due to stringent security measures worldwide, especially increased detection and prevention of aerial hijacking. The method of aerial hijacking to enforce demands turned to inconspicuous but extremely violent and devastating acts like sabotage attacks to achieve political objectives. Acts of sabotage, threatening offences to the law of nations, were, as opposed to aerial hijacking, harder to apprehend or to combat beforehand on the part of law-enforcement authorities.

This kind of terrorism caused significant changes to security strategies and practices around the world. Eventually, overall attacks on aviation decreased considerably. However, a possible false sense of trust in the aviation security system, induced by weakening terrorist activity and the cramped anticipation to collect and combine fragmented information by scattered intelligence bureaucracies within the United States, unfortunately led up to the horrific 9/11 attacks.[135]

The Montreal Convention essentially extends the legal regime of The Hague Convention to aircraft sabotage and other acts of violence against the civil aviation industry. However, the application of both Conventions will often overlap. The nature of hijacking and unlawful interference with civil aviation makes it essential that universal jurisdiction should be established (*aut dedere aut judicare*).

Since both the 1963 Tokyo Convention and the 1970 The Hague Convention dealt only with unlawful seizure committed on board aircraft, neither covered sabotage committed on the ground nor unlawful interference with air navigation facilities and services. The Montreal Convention was partly drafted to fill these gaps.[136]

The objectives of the Montreal Convention are best described as:

The primary aim of the Montreal Convention was to arrive at a generally acceptable method of dealing with alleged perpetrators of acts of unlawful inter-

---

135 Notten, van, Ph., *Writing on the Wall: Scenario Development in Times of Discontinuity*, Boca Raton, FL: Dissertation.com, 2005, p. 58.

136 McWhinney, E., *Aerial Piracy and International Terrorism: The Illegal Diversion of Aircraft and International Law*, 2nd Revised Edition, Dordrecht: Matinus Nijhoff Publishers, 1987, pp. 45-47.

ference with aircraft. In general, the States represented at the Montreal Conference agreed that acts of sabotage, or violence and related offences interfering with the safety and development of international civil aviation constituted a global problem which had to be combated collectively by concerned States of the international community.

A multilateral international convention had to be adopted which extended both the scope and efficacy of national legislation and provided the legal framework for international cooperation in the apprehension, prosecution and punishment of alleged offenders.[137]

The 1971 Montreal Convention defines (Art. 1, para. 1) the following as offences:

> Any person commits an offence if he unlawfully and intentionally:
> (a) performs an act of violence against a person on board a civilian aircraft in flight if it is likely to endanger its safety in flight; placing or causing to be placed devices or substances likely to destroy the aircraft; or
> (b) destroys an aircraft in service or causes damage to such an aircraft which renders it incapable of flight, or which is likely to endanger its safety in flight; or
> (c) places or causes to be placed on an aircraft in service, by any means whatsoever, a device or substance which is likely to destroy that aircraft, or to cause damage to it which is likely to endanger its safety in flight; or
> (d) destroys or damages air navigation facilities (only if these facilities are used in international air navigation) or interferes, if any such act is likely to endanger the safety of aircraft in flight; or
> (e) communicates information which he knows to be false, thereby endangering the safety of an aircraft in flight.

In addition, any person is also committing an offence (Art. 1, para. 2) if he:
(a) attempts to commit any of the offences mentioned in Paragraph 1 of Article 1; or
(b) is an accomplice of a person who commits or attempts to commit any such offence.

A new term, aircraft in service, is introduced by the Montreal Convention, while the definition of an aircraft in flight, as defined in Article 3.1 of The Hague Convention, applies to the Montreal Convention as well. The term aircraft in service is defined in Article 2 (b).

---

137 Abeyratne, R.I.R., *Aviation Security Law*, Berlin, Heidelberg: Springer-Science & Business Media, 2010, p. 237.

Article 2, 1971 Montreal Convention:

> For the purpose of this Convention:
>
> (a) An aircraft is considered to be in flight at any time from the moment when all its external doors are closed following embarkation until the moment when any such door is opened for disembarkation; in the case of a forced landing, the flight shall be deemed to continue until the competent authorities take over the responsibility for the aircraft and for persons and property on board (authentic text).
>
> (b) An aircraft is considered to be in service from the beginning of the preflight preparation of the aircraft by ground personnel or by the crew for a specific flight until twenty-four hours after any landing; the period of service shall, in any event, extend for the entire period during which the aircraft is in flight as defined in Paragraph (a) of this article.[138]

The Convention applies, whether the aircraft is engaged in an international or domestic flight, only if the point of take-off or landing, actual or intended, is outside the territory of the State where the aircraft is registered; or if the offence is committed outside of the State of Registry. States Parties may establish jurisdiction in cases when the offence takes place in the territory of that State; the State is the State of Registry of the aircraft; the aircraft lands in the State's territory with the alleged offender still on board or when the offence is committed against or on board an aircraft leased without crew to a lessee whose primary place of business or permanent residence is in that State. Criminal jurisdiction exercised in accordance with the national law is not excluded by this Convention.

In the context of international terrorism, especially aircraft hijacking, a Joint Statement was produced during the Bonn Economic Summit Conference on 17 July 1978. The States attending the Conference, indicating their concern about terrorism and the taking of hostages, declared that their governments would intensify their joint efforts to combat international terrorism.

To this end, in cases where a country refuses extradition or prosecution of those who have hijacked an aircraft and/or do not return such aircraft, the heads of State and government are jointly resolved that their governments should take immediate action to cease all flights to that country.

At the same time, their governments will initiate action to halt all incoming flights from that country or from any country by the airlines of the country concerned. The

---

138 United Nations Treaties No. 14118, Multilateral Convention for the Suppression of Unlawful Acts against the Safety of Civil Aviation (with Final Act of the International Conference on Air Law held under auspices of the International Civil Aviation Organization at Montreal in September 1971, concluded at Montreal on 23 September 1971. Vol. 974, 1-14118.

heads of State and government urge other governments to join them in this commitment.[139]

2.10.4 MONTREAL PROTOCOL 1988

Protocol for the Suppression of Unlawful Acts of Violence at Airports Serving International Civil Aviation, Supplementary to the Convention for the Suppression of Unlawful Acts against the Safety of Civil Aviation

The 1971 Montreal Convention is supplemented by the Protocol for the Suppression of Unlawful Acts of Violence at Airports Serving International Civil Aviation (so-called Airport Protocol), done at Montreal on 24 February 1988 (ICAO Doc 9518). The Airport Protocol extends the provisions of the Montreal Convention to encompass terrorist attacks, qualified as unlawful and intentional acts of violence against persons at an airport serving international civil aviation which cause or are likely to cause serious injury or death, and such acts intended to destroy or seriously damage facilities on international airport premises including air navigation installations, or aircraft not in service located thereon or disrupt the services of the airport.

The Montreal Protocol was done at Montreal as a result of the International Conference on Air Law held between 9 and 24 February 1988. The main reason for this amendment to the 1971 Montreal Convention was the tragedy caused by two major terrorist attacks against the Rome and Vienna international airports, simultaneously carried out on 27 December 1985.[140]

The Protocol came into force on 6 August 1989 (Art. VI). As between Parties to the Protocol, the Convention and the Protocol are to be read and interpreted as one single instrument (Art. I). A State that is not a Party to the Convention may ratify or accede to the Protocol only if at the same time it ratifies or accedes to the Convention (Arts. V (2) and VII (2)).

Between those Parties to the Convention which are not Parties to the Protocol, the Convention will continue to apply in its original, unmodified form. The Protocol makes use of the scheme and methods of the Convention. In particular, Article II extends the scope of the offences as mentioned in Article 1 of the Convention by adding some new offences, and Article III provides for the establishment of jurisdiction over the Protocol offences.

---

139 The 1978 Bonn Declaration. A Joint Statement of the heads of State and government of Canada, the Federal Republic of Germany, France, Italy, Japan, the United Kingdom and the United States, together with the President of the EU Commission at the 4th G7 Summit.
140 Twin Attacks at the Airports of Vienna and Rome (27 December 1985). Israeli Security Agency.

For the Protocol offences, the situation is more straightforward: the majority of the provisions of the Convention apply to the Protocol offences. The explanation of Article I makes this clear. Accordingly, references in the Convention to the concepts of offence and alleged offender must, as between Parties to the Protocol, be read as referring, in addition, to the Protocol offences and those alleged to have committed them. Article II of the Protocol states:

1. In Article 1 of the Convention, the following shall be added as new Paragraph 1 *bis*:
   1 *bis* (a): A person commits an offence if he, unlawfully and intentionally, using any device, substance or weapon:
   – performs an act of violence against a person at an airport serving international civil aviation which causes, or is likely to cause, serious injury or death; or
   – destroys or seriously damages the facilities of an airport serving international civil aviation or aircraft not in service located thereon or disrupts the services of the airport, if such an act endangers or is likely to endanger safety at the airport.
2. In Paragraph 2 (a) of Article 1 of the Convention, the following words shall be inserted after the words 'Paragraph 1': 'or Paragraph 1 *bis*.'

The offence must involve a device, substance or weapon, unlawfully and intentionally used to perform an act of violence against a person at an international airport and must cause, or is likely to cause, serious injury or death to a person (or persons), or on the other hand to destroy or inflict serious damage to the airport facilities, or aircraft not being in service, or to disrupt the services of the airport.

The requirement that the act should be both intentional and unlawful might give rise to the question of which law governs the legality of the conduct. It is a fact that difficulties may arise in determining the unlawful character of activities within Article 1 of the Convention because of the possibility that such activities may occur in circumstances where different Parties have competing claims to regulate conduct.

However, no such difficulty is likely to arise in the case of Protocol offences since the acts will take place at an airport, and the legality of such conduct will fall to be determined by the law of the Party in whose territory the international airport, including airport buildings, aprons, taxiways, runways and air navigation facilities used in international air navigation, is located. Therefore, such an act is first of all a domestic judicial case, but the universal jurisdiction of the Montreal Convention as amended by the Protocol will apply. That means, if the alleged offenders are able to flee the territory of the State in which the crime was committed, foreign authorities will exercise jurisdiction and will take them into custody to either prosecute or extradite.[141]

---

141 Guimulla, E.M., Weber, L. (Eds.), *International and EU aviation law: Selected Issues*, Alphen aan den Rijn: Kluwer Law International, 2011, p. 292.

Article III of the Protocol requires each Party to take such measures as may be necessary to establish its jurisdiction over Protocol offences where the alleged offender is present in its territory and it does not extradite him pursuant to Article 8 of the Convention. Whereas the obligation under Article 5.2 of the Convention does apply only when there has been no extradition to one of the Parties mentioned in Article 5.1 of the Convention, the obligation under Article 5.2 *bis* (Protocol supplement) applies only when there has been no extradition to the Party mentioned in Article 5.1 (a) of the Convention. This conforms to the analysis of the applicability of Article 5.1 of the Convention, as suggested above.

Article 5, 1971 Montreal Convention:

1. Each Contracting State shall take such measures as may be necessary to establish its jurisdiction over the offences in the following cases:
   (a) when the offence is committed in the territory of that State;
   (b) when the offence is committed against or on board an aircraft registered in that State;
   (c) when the aircraft on board which the offence is committed lands in its territory with the alleged offender still on board;
   (d) when the offence is committed against or on board an aircraft leased without crew to a lessee who has his principal place of business or, if the lessee has not such place of business, his permanent residence, in that State.
2. Each Contracting State shall likewise take such measures as may be necessary to establish its jurisdiction over the offences mentioned in Article 1, Paragraph 1(a), (b) and (c), and in Article 1, Paragraph 2, in so far as that paragraph relates to those offences, in the case where the alleged offender is present in its territory and it does not extradite him pursuant to Article 8 to any of the States mentioned in Paragraph 1 of this article.
3. This Convention does not exclude any criminal jurisdiction exercised in accordance with national law.

Article III of the Protocol:

In Article 5 of the Convention, the following shall be added as Paragraph 2 bis:
2 bis. Each Contracting State shall likewise take such measures as may be necessary to establish its jurisdiction over the offences mentioned in Article 1, paragraph 1 bis, and in Article 1, paragraph 2, in so far as that paragraph relates to those offences, in the case where the alleged offender is present in its terri-

tory and it does not extradite him pursuant to Article 8 to the State mentioned in paragraph 1 (a) of this Article.

The offences created by the Montreal Convention (Art. 1) relate to aircraft in flight and to aircraft in service, while the corresponding Protocol offence applies to activities in relation to aircraft not in service when located at an airport serving international civil aviation, which remedies the deficiency in the text of the Convention.

A person also commits an offence if he attempts to commit one of the Protocol offences, or if he is the accomplice of a person who commits or attempts to commit one of the Protocol offences.

The Protocol has the significant effect of imposing an international treaty obligation to either extradite or to assume domestic jurisdiction and to extend international cooperation. The Protocol inserts into the Montreal Convention, at least for States Parties to both agreements, additional offences relating to acts of violence against the facilities of, or persons or aircraft not in service at the premises of an airport serving international civil aviation. In these cases, it is necessary that such acts endanger or are likely to endanger the safety at that airport.

It is therefore apparent that a Party to the Protocol is required to establish its jurisdiction over the Protocol offences when committed in the territory of that Party and, probably, also when Protocol offences are committed on board or against aircraft in the circumstances described in Article 5 of the Convention.

Until September 2001, the international community had not sought to amend or update The Hague Convention, which addresses hijackings of civil aircraft in international aviation. By contrast, the Montreal Convention, dealing with the sabotage of aircraft in flight, was amended by the Protocol in 1988 to enhance the international legal framework on terrorist acts affecting international civil aviation. It became obvious that terrorist groups altered their tactics from seizing or destroying aircraft in flight to inflicting serious injury, death and devastating damage in airport terminals to achieve maximum chaos, intimidation and fear.

The Protocol, negotiated in the aftermath of terrorist attacks to deliberately kill innocent people in international airport terminals at the airports of Rome and Vienna in December 1985, carried out by the Abu Nidal Organization (ANO), a Palestinian nationalist militant group, expanded the reach of the Montreal Convention to extend beyond aircraft in flight and include airports serving international civil air transport where aircraft passengers are assembled before and after their itinerary. It is clear that passengers on the ground were easy targets of terrorist machine-gun fire, suicide bombings with explosive belts and other devices, which gave rise to great concern and the demand for the increased need for adequate ground security.[142]

After the terrorist attacks on 11 September 2001, the international community started to consider whether any aspects of the legal framework for international cooperation in combating terrorist acts should be updated to address issues raised by the attacks. Because the terrorist attacks were committed by persons piloting aircraft, the ICAO Assembly took a leading role and directed a study of existing international instruments. The review of appropriate existing law and other international dialogue sparked a negotiating process spanning almost nine years and leading to a successful Diplomatic Conference in Beijing in September 2010.

During this Conference, two international air law instruments were adopted: the Convention on the Suppression of Unlawful Acts Relating to International Civil Aviation (2010 Beijing Convention), prevailing over the 1971 Montreal Convention and the 1988 Montreal Protocol, and at the same time the 2010 Beijing Protocol, supplementary to the 2010 Beijing Convention, amending The Hague Convention.

The weaknesses of the Tokyo Convention were translated into the strength of the other hijacking Conventions. The provisions of the Tokyo Convention had left major questions unanswered regarding custody and prosecution of hijackers. It was mainly used as a viewpoint from which an international law of hijacking could effectively be implemented.

Nevertheless, the Montreal Convention and its Protocol of 1988 maintained the template of the Tokyo Convention and The Hague Convention regarding ultimate State discretion with respect to prosecution and extradition. The Montreal Convention, in a much broader perspective if it comes to serious aviation crimes, criminalizes any act or attempted act of violence against a person on board an aircraft in flight, if that act is likely to endanger the safety of that aircraft as well as any attempted act that destroys or damages an aircraft while it is in service, including placing an explosive device on the aircraft and jeopardizing the safety of an aircraft through sabotage of ground-based air navigation facilities, or providing false information that comprises flight safety.[143]

These principles were extended to apply to unlawful and intended acts of violence at international airports. The legal instruments on aviation security, complemented by

---

142 Sweet, K.M., *Aviation and Airport Security: Terrorism and Safety Concerns*, Second Edition, Boca Raton, FL: CRC Press Taylor & Francis Group, 2008, p. 80. Nasr, K.B., *Arab and Israeli Terrorism: The Causes and Effects of Political Violence, 1936-1993*, Jefferson, NC: McFarland & Company Publishers, 1997, pp. 157-158. Dempsey, P.S., Jakhu, R.S. (Eds.), *Routledge Handbook of Public Aviation Law*, Milton Park, Abingdon, Oxon: Routledge, 2017, pp. 147-148. *See also* Rubin, B.M., Rubin, J.C., *Chronologies of Modern Terrorism*, New York: M.E. Sharpe, 2008, p. 200.

143 Montreal Convention 1971, Arts. 1, 7 and 8. *See also*: Havel, B.F., Sanchez, G.S., *The Principles and Practice of International Aviation Law*, New York: Cambridge University Press, 2014, pp. 205-206.

ICAO SARPs on the subject (Annex 17-Security, Safeguarding International Civil Aviation against Acts of Unlawful Interference), and the implementation of decisions by ICAO Member States and other international organizations, have proved to be an effective safeguard of aviation security. The terrorist attacks on 11 September 2001, causing an alarming wake-up call, gave rise to a reconsideration on aviation security and the urgent question of how to modernize the relevant legal framework in order to cope with changing conditions.

2.10.5 BEIJING CONVENTION 2010

Convention on the Suppression of Unlawful Acts Relating to International Civil Aviation

The Convention on the Suppression of Unlawful Acts Relating to International Civil Aviation was adopted on 10 September 2010 during a Diplomatic Conference on Aviation Security, held from 30 August to 10 September 2010 at Beijing. The Convention entered into force on 1 July 2018.

At the same Conference, the Protocol Supplementary to the Convention for the Suppression of Unlawful Seizure of Aircraft was adopted.

Immediately prompted by the terrorist attacks in 2001, the international community started to consider reviewing and updating the legal framework for international cooperation on terrorist acts and counter-terrorism.

The Convention is the result of collective efforts of the international community to modernize the legal framework for civil aviation security. These efforts started in 2001 pursuant to the adoption of ICAO Assembly Resolution A33-1 which directed the Council and the Secretary General to act urgently to address the new and emerging threats to international civil aviation, in particular to review the adequacy of the existing aviation security conventions (the Tokyo regime).[144]

These new and emerging threats are:
1. misuse of civil aircraft as a weapon;

---

144 ICAO Assembly Resolution A33-1 Declaration on misuse of civil aircraft as weapons of destruction and other terrorist acts involving civil aviation. *The Assembly*: 1. *Strongly condemns* these terrorist acts as contrary to elementary considerations of humanity, norms of conduct of society and as violations of international law; 2. *Solemnly declares* that such acts of using civil aircraft as weapons of destruction are contrary to the letter and spirit of the *Convention on International Civil Aviation*, in particular its preamble and Arts. 4 and 44, and that such acts and other terrorist acts involving civil aviation or civil aviation facilities constitute grave offences in violation of international law; 3. *Urges* all Contracting States to ensure, in accordance with Art. 4 of the Convention, that civil aviation is not used for any purpose inconsistent with the aims of the *Convention on International Civil Aviation*, and to hold accountable and punish severely those who misuse civil aircraft as weapons of destruction, including those responsible for planning and organizing such acts or for aiding, supporting or harbouring the perpetrators; [...].

2. use of civil aircraft to unlawfully spread biological, chemical and nuclear (NBC) substances;
3. attacks against civil aviation using such substances;
4. electronic attacks using radio transmitters or other devices that may jam or alter signals used for air navigation;
5. computer-based attacks to destroy data essential for operation of the aircraft;
6. the unlawful and intentional delivery, placing or discharging of a lethal device at an airport or on board aircraft; and
7. the threatening of the use of a lethal device.[145]

States Parties that ratify the Beijing Convention (ICAO Doc 9960) agree to criminalize a number of acts, including preparatory acts of offences, constituting those new and emerging threats against international civil aviation. Both instruments will strengthen the capacity of States to prevent the commission of the newly inserted and already existing offences and to prosecute and punish those who commit such offences.

The Beijing Convention (and the Beijing Protocol), adopted to complement the shortcomings in the existing international instruments pertaining to the subject, addresses these threats which could disrupt society by means of new ruthless methods like terrorists able to not only hijack aircraft, but to pilot those aircraft as well to fulfil their abhorrent missions. The Beijing Convention helps to modernize and reinforce the legal framework for aviation security, including through the criminalization of a variety of terrorist acts additional to the 1971 Montreal Convention.

These additional acts range from using an aircraft, including Unmanned Aerial Systems or Remotely Piloted Aerial Systems (RPAS) in service as a lethal weapon for the purpose of causing death, serious injury or serious damage to property or the environment or to obstruct or destabilize aviation through jamming or cyber hacking, especially on air navigation facilities.[146]

A complete spectrum of criminalized acts is given in Article 1 of the Convention:

1. Any person commits an offence if that person unlawfully and intentionally:
   a. performs an act of violence against a person on board an aircraft in flight if that act is likely to endanger the safety of that aircraft; or
   b. destroys an aircraft in service or causes damage to such an aircraft which renders it incapable of flight or which is likely to endanger its safety in flight; or

---

145 Piera, A., Gill, M., Will the New ICAO-Beijing Instruments Build a Chinese Wall for International Aviation Security?, *Vanderbilt Journal of Transnational Law*, January 2014, Vol. 74:145, p. 154.
146 Završnik, A. (Ed.), *Drones and Unmanned Aerial Systems, Legal and Social Implications for Security and Surveillance*, Cham: Springer International Publishing, 2016, pp. 205-207.

c. places or causes to be placed on an aircraft in service, by any means whatsoever, a device or substance which is likely to destroy that aircraft, or to cause damage to it which renders it incapable of flight, or to cause damage to it which is likely to endanger its safety in flight; or

d. destroys or damages air navigation facilities or interferes with their operation, if any such act is likely to endanger the safety of aircraft in flight; or

e. communicates information which that person knows to be false, thereby endangering the safety of an aircraft in flight; or

f. uses an aircraft in service for the purpose of causing death, serious bodily injury or serious damage to property or the environment; or

g. releases or discharges from an aircraft in service any BCN (biological-chemical-nuclear) weapon or explosive, radioactive or similar substances in a manner that causes or is likely to cause death, serious bodily injury or serious damage to property or the environment; or

h. uses against or on board an aircraft in service any BCN weapon or explosive, radioactive or similar substances in a manner that causes or is likely to cause death, serious bodily injury or serious damage to property or the environment; or

i. transports, causes to be transported or facilitates the transport of, on board an aircraft:
    –   any explosive or radioactive material, knowing that it is intended to be used to cause, or in a threat to cause, with or without a condition, as is provided for under national law, death or serious injury or damage for the purpose of intimidating a population, or compelling a government or an international organization to do or to abstain from doing any act; or
    –   any BCN weapon, knowing it to be a BCN weapon as defined in Article 2; or
    –   any source material, special fissionable material or equipment or material especially designed or prepared for the processing, use or production of special fissionable material, knowing it is intended to be used in a nuclear explosive activity or in any other nuclear activity not under safeguards pursuant to a safeguards agreement with the International Atomic Energy Agency (IAEA); or
    –   any equipment, materials or software or related technology that significantly contributes to the design, manufacture or delivery of a BCN weapon without lawful authorization and with the intention that it will be used for such purpose [...].

2. Any person commits an offence if that person unlawfully and intentionally, using any device, substance or weapon:
   a. performs an act of violence against a person at an airport serving international civil aviation which causes or is likely to cause serious injury or death; or
   b. destroys or seriously damages the facilities of an airport serving international civil aviation or aircraft not in service located thereon or disrupts the services of that airport, if such an act endangers or is likely to endanger safety at that airport.

Furthermore, a person that makes a threat to commit or attempts to commit any of the aforementioned offences is punishable, just as organizing or directing others, individuals or a group, to commit these offences, or participating as an accomplice, or unlawfully and intentionally assisting another person that, to the knowledge of the person, committed an act constituting a specific offence set forth in this article or is wanted for criminal prosecution or has been sentenced for such an offence, to evade investigation, prosecution or punishment.

To protect the public and international civil aviation, non-standard provisions found in modern counter-terrorism conventions are incorporated.[147]

The Beijing Convention shall prevail over the following instruments: the 1971 Montreal Convention and the 1988 Montreal Protocol (Beijing Convention, Art. 24).

2.10.6 BEIJING PROTOCOL 2010

Protocol Supplementary to the Convention for the Suppression of Unlawful Seizure of Aircraft

The Beijing Protocol, done at Beijing on 10 September 2010 (ICAO Doc 9959), supplements the Convention for the Suppression of Unlawful Seizure of Aircraft, done at The Hague on 16 December 1970 (The Hague Convention). The Protocol expands the scope of The Hague Convention to cover different forms of aircraft hijacking and certain preparatory acts for the offence, including through modern technological means.[148] The Protocol will also contribute to the implementation of the United Nations Global Coun-

---

147 *See* International Convention for the Suppression of Terrorist Bombings, done at New York on 15 December 1997, entered into force on 23 May 2001. http://treaties.un.org/doc/db/Terrorism/english-18-9.pdf. *See also* International Convention for the Suppression of the Financing of Terrorism, done at New York on 9 December 1999, entered into force on 10 April 2002. https://www.un.org/law/cod/finterr.htm.

148 Guimulla, E.M., Weber, L. (Eds.), *International and EU Aviation Law*, Selected Issues, Alphen aan den Rijn: Kluwer Law International, 2011, pp. 293-294.

ter-Terrorism Strategy, adopted on 8 September 2006 by enhancing the global treaty regime on counter-terrorism.[149]

The Protocol entered into force on 1 January 2018. It expands the grounds of jurisdiction by requiring each State Party to establish jurisdiction when the offence is committed by its national, and by enabling each State Party to establish jurisdiction when the victim of the offence is its national.

It also affirms the principles of fair treatment and non-discrimination. Moreover, the Protocol contains a clause that a State cannot refuse to extradite an offender on the sole ground that the offence would be political in nature.

In addition, it specifically provides for the criminal liability of directors and organizers of an offence, as well as the liability of those who knowingly assist an offender to evade investigation, prosecution or punishment. Any person making a threat to commit an offence may be criminally accountable when the circumstances indicate that the threat is credible.

Under certain conditions, agreement to contribute or the contribution to an offence, whether such an offence is actually committed or not, may well be punishable. A legal entity (organization) may also be criminally liable if the applicable national law so provides.

The Hague Convention focuses on a fairly specific offence, namely, the unlawful seizure of an aircraft engaged in international civil air transport. It achieved its original aim and quickly became one of the most subscribed international instruments addressing international aerial terrorism.

The Beijing Protocol to The Hague Convention elaborates on the hijacking offence and strengthens its provisions in several specific but useful ways. Some highlights of the new instrument include:

1. The Beijing Protocol significantly expands the scope of the hijacking offence to include hijackings that occur pre- or post-flight, hijackings through modern technological means, as well as a wide variety of ancillary offences, such as attempt to commit the offence, accomplice liability, conspiracy and assistance after the criminal fact. Whereas The Hague Convention limited the offence to individuals on board the flight, the Beijing Protocol eliminates such a requirement, recognizing that not all persons involved in aircraft hijackings will physically board the aircraft.

2. The Beijing Protocol includes more detailed extradition and legal assistance provisions than the underlying The Hague Convention. Particularly, it provides that a request for extradition or legal assistance may not be denied on the sole ground that it is a political offence or an offence inspired by political motives. The Protocol also includes an exclusion clause which permits denial of assistance if the requested State

---

149 A/RES/60/288, Sixtieth Session: The United Nations General Assembly adopted the Global Counter-Terrorism Strategy on 8 September 2006. The strategy is a unique global instrument to enhance national, regional and international efforts to counter terrorism. Reviewed every two years.

has substantial grounds to belief that the request was made to prosecute a person on account of that person's race, religion, nationality, ethnic origin, political opinion or gender.

There are some minor adjustments such as Article 3, or complete replacements or substantial additions such as Articles 2, 4 and 8.[150]

Article IV of the Protocol states:

The following shall be added as Article 2 *bis* of the Convention (The Hague Convention):

1. Each State Party, in accordance with its national legal principles, may take the necessary measures to enable a legal entity located in its territory or organized under its laws to be held liable when a person responsible for management or control of that legal entity has, in that capacity, committed an offence set forth in Article 1. Such liability may be criminal, civil or administrative.

2. Such liability is incurred without prejudice to the criminal liability of individuals having committed the offences.

3. If a State Party takes the necessary measures to make a legal entity liable in accordance with Paragraph 1 of this article, it shall endeavour to ensure that applicable criminal, civil or administrative sanctions are effective, proportionate and dissuasive. Such sanctions may include monetary sanctions.

The main reason for ratification with respect to the Protocol is the result of collective efforts by the international community to modernize the legal framework for aviation security. Both the Convention and the Protocol retain the principle of prosecute or extradite. The two legal instruments address, after years of negotiations by States at a global level, the immense threat and public vulnerability following the 9/11 terrorist attacks when global civil aviation safety was seriously at stake.

The direct response was the incorporation of modern counter-terrorism provisions criminalizing terrorist acts causing death, serious injury or substantial damage to property or the environment.

Next to these provisions, a variety of strict security measures were introduced like reinforced and locked cockpit doors and intensified use of armed covert law enforcement or counter-terrorist agents on board commercial aircraft (sky marshals, also known as air marshals or in-flight security officers (IFSO), serving since the 1960s) as well as Advance Passenger (Pre)Screening Systems (APPS), hold baggage scanning, Explosives Detection

---

150 Shaw, M.N., *International Law*, Eighth Edition, Cambridge: Cambridge University Press, 2017, pp. 507-509.

Systems (EDS) such as high altitude simulation test chambers for high-risk cargo and mail to minimize the dangers of barometric-pressure detonating bombs.[151]

2.10.7 MONTREAL PROTOCOL 2014

Protocol to Amend the Convention on Offences and Certain Other Acts Committed on Board Aircraft

ICAO has identified unruly passengers as a major issue for civil aviation since they endanger the safety of both passengers and crew members, requiring a stronger international legal framework to deal with unruly passengers.

The Tokyo Convention was considered ineffective, no longer up-to-date and too easily avoided to empower air carriers to take remedial actions against unruly passengers. It failed to provide a suitable deterrent to unruly passengers as under its terms the State of Registry of the aircraft concerned was the State of Jurisdiction to try the unruly passenger. This rule had become obsolete by the complex leasing agreements which modern aircraft are subject to. The 2014 Montreal Protocol (ICAO Doc 10034) or the Unruly Passenger Protocol, an amendment to the Tokyo Convention, was adopted by ICAO on 4 April 2014.

As the trade organization for the world's airlines, IATA propagated its position regarding the issue of unruly passengers on board aircraft in an IATA Position Paper of November 2013 called *Reform of the Tokyo Convention 1963*. IATA was of the opinion that the Tokyo regime should be amended to better deal with the growing trend of unruly passenger behaviour.

Although ICAO has developed guidance material in the form of Circular 288 (Guidance Material on the Legal Aspects of Unruly/Disruptive Passengers), that document has

---

151 *See also* Regulation (EC) No. 300/2008 of the European Parliament and of the Council of 11 March 2008 on common rules in the field of civil aviation security and repealing Regulation (EC) No. 2320/2002, *OJ EU* L 97/72, 9.4.2008, and Commission Regulation (EC) No. 272/2009 of 2 April 2009 supplementing the common basic standards on civil aviation security laid down in the Annex to Regulation (EC) No. 300/2008 of the European Parliament and of the Council, *OJ EU* L 91/7, 3.4.2009, and amended by a number of Commission Regulations concerning alternative security measures.
See Guidance material on security measures can be found in the ICAO Aviation Security Manual (ICAO Doc 8973-Restricted).
High-risk cargo and mail are defined in ICAO Annex 17:
Cargo or mail presented by an unknown entity or showing signs of tampering shall be considered high risk if, in addition, it meets one of the following criteria:
1. specific intelligence indicates that the cargo or mail poses a threat to civil aviation; or
2. the cargo or mail shows anomalies that give rise to suspicion; or
3. the nature of the cargo or mail is such that the baseline security measures alone are unlikely to detect prohibited items that could endanger the aircraft.
Regardless of whether cargo or mail comes from a known or unknown entity, a State's specific intelligence about a consignment may render it as high risk.

hardly been implemented and imposed, with no obligation upon States so far to take remedial action. Thus, amendments to the Tokyo regime are highly required, especially on jurisdiction, immunity standard, offences, scope and right of recourse for air carriers, according to IATA.

The objectives of the Montreal Protocol are to redefine elements of the Tokyo Convention in order to be able to strengthen the position of the aviation industry by effectively empowering air carriers to better deal with unruly passengers, but not in the last place to improve civil aviation security and, potentially, aviation safety.

Unruly passenger incidents on board aircraft which threaten safety and security have been more or less the order of the day in recent years, but nowadays, the frequency is increasing dramatically and worse, there is an escalation of violence. According to a survey conducted by ICAO among a number of Contracting States, incidents concerning unruly passengers involved various types of offences and reprehensible acts, including, assault, intimidation or threat, whether physical or verbal, against crew members and passengers, fights among intoxicated passengers, child molestation, sexual harassment and assault, illegal consumption of drugs on board, refusal to stop smoking, likely to endanger the safety of the aircraft, or excessively consuming alcoholic beverages, refusal to comply with safety instructions or other lawful instructions, tampering with safety-related devices on board or operating a portable electronic device when such an act is prohibited, ransacking and sometimes vandalizing of aircraft seats and cabin interiors.[152]

These particular behaviours often cause disruption, diversions, delays and significant costs for air carriers. Taken together with the operational measures already being implemented by air carriers to prevent and manage unruly incidents, the Protocol will provide a more effective deterrent by making the consequences of unruly behaviour clear and enforceable.

Whereas the Tokyo Convention only grants jurisdiction over offences and other acts committed on board aircraft to the State of Registry of the aircraft concerned, the Montreal Protocol gives mandatory jurisdiction to the intended State of landing, however, with two included safeguards to reflect the concerns of some States concerning legal certainty and proportionality. First of all, the character of the offence must be sufficiently serious, in the sense that the safety of the aircraft or of persons or property therein, or good order and discipline on board are expressly jeopardized. Secondly, the State of landing must consider if the offence is an offence in the State of the Operator.

The Montreal Protocol states that if the aircraft concerned diverts, should the need arise from the unruly behaviour, to a third State, other than the scheduled destination or

---

152 ICAO Circular 288-LE/1, Guidance Material on the Legal Aspects of Unruly/Disruptive Passengers, June 2002, Chapter 1 Introduction 1.1 and Chapter 2, Para. 2 The Content of the List, 2.1.1. A uniform list of offences is considered desirable for two reasons: firstly, in order to provide a common dominator for offences as a basis for national prosecution; and, secondly, in order to offer uniform criteria for States to extend their respective jurisdiction.

the State of Registry, that State is given the competence to exercise jurisdiction at its discretion. Since in many cases, the State of Registry is necessarily not the State of the Operator, due to increasing numbers of long-term lease aircraft, mandatory jurisdiction for the State of the Operator is established by the Protocol.

The Protocol clearly identifies certain behaviours which should at least be considered as an offence which in turn gives rise to taking appropriate criminal or other legal proceedings by States. These include physical assault or a threat to commit such assault against a crew member, and refusal to obey a lawful instruction given by or on behalf of the aircraft commander in view of aviation safety.

This definition and simplification make the powers of the aircraft commander (pilot-in-command) much clearer and certainly will increase the likelihood that the commander shall feel properly empowered to take the appropriate and legitimate action against the unruly passenger(s).

In order to assist aircraft commanders in exercising their powers under Article 9 of the Tokyo Convention, it may be desirable to arrive at a common understanding as to what constitutes a serious offence. The Secretariat Study Group was of the view that due to the need to offer enhanced legal protection for the crew and the type of the risks involved as well as their potential consequences covered by Section 1 of the model legislation, namely, assault and other acts of interference against a crew member on board a civil aircraft, should be considered as serious offences within the meaning of Article 9 of the 1963 Tokyo Convention (ICAO Circular 288-LE/1, 4.4.2.).

The high burden on the commander who was required to have reasonable grounds to believe that unruly behaviour constituted a serious offence under the penal law of the State of Registry, was thus taken away by the Protocol.

The Protocol recognizes that air carriers may have a right, the right of recourse, to seek compensation for substantial costs incurred as a result of unruly passenger behaviour, because in all cases the air carriers have to bear the costs involved in diversions in order to disembark that unruly passenger. The presence of such a clause should have strong deterrent value.

The Protocol represents a clear opportunity for governments to put in place an international legal instrument which gives them the means to deal with disruptive or unruly passengers more effectively, and to deter future incidents.

Summarizing, the Tokyo regime, comprising all relevant legal instruments, was purely necessary to prevent the commission of various criminal offences related to safety and security in civil aviation, whether it is on board or against an aircraft or at an airport or relevant facilities. Criminal offences committed on board international flights are governed by the Tokyo Convention itself. It provides the guidelines for what principles States should follow, and also gives the aircraft commander the power to take all reasonable steps against unruly passengers to protect the safety of those on board.

Especially in the 1960s, the number of aircraft hijackings increased dramatically. Admittedly, the Tokyo Convention contained an anti-hijacking provision in Article 11, but it proved to be inadequate to combat this aggressive form of criminal act. The lack of sophisticated detection units at airports to identify the presence of weapons carried by persons embarking an aircraft, as well as other undersized security measures posed to be an enormous problem. Once the armed hijackers were on board they could seize or exercise control over the aircraft when all external aircraft doors had closed, a situation not quite covered by the Tokyo Convention.[153] Anti-hijacking became the focal point of The Hague Convention.

The Hague Convention exclusively deals with acts of international hijacking committed by persons on board an aircraft in flight which means, unlike the provision of the Tokyo Convention, at any time from the moment when all its external doors are closed following embarkation until the moment when any such door is opened for disembarkation.[154]

The 1971 Montreal Convention deals with acts other than those covered by the Tokyo and The Hague Conventions. The Convention contains detailed provisions on jurisdiction, custody, prosecution and extradition of the alleged offender on matters of sabotage and other acts of violence against civil aviation, not only on board or against an aircraft in service, but also against air navigation facilities used in international aviation. The Convention attempts to establish a form of universal jurisdiction over the offender.

The 1988 Montreal Protocol (Airport Protocol) adds to the definition of offence given in the 1971 Montreal Convention, unlawful and intentional acts of violence against persons at an airport serving international civil aviation which cause or are likely to cause serious injury or death and such acts which destroy or seriously damage the facilities of such an airport or aircraft not in service located thereon or disrupt the services of the airport. The Protocol enhances aviation security by including airports serving international civil aviation.

The 2010 Beijing Convention and Protocol, adopted in Beijing, further criminalize the act of using civil aircraft as a weapon, and of using or threatening to use dangerous materials to attack aircraft or other targets on the ground. The unlawful transport of biological, chemical and nuclear (BCN) weapons and their related materials has been declared punishable under the two treaties. The criminal liability of directors and organizers of an offence under the treaties is specifically stated. The treaties also update provisions to promote cooperation between States in combating the unlawful acts directed

---

153 Tokyo Convention, Chapter IV Unlawful Seizure of Aircraft, Art. 11. Art. 1.3 For the purpose of this Convention, an aircraft is considered to be in flight from the moment when power is applied for the purpose of take-off until the moment when the landing run ends.

154 Bantekas, I, Nash, S., *International Criminal Law*, Third Edition, London: Routledge-Cavendish, 2007, Taylor & Francis e-Library, 2009, pp. 199-200.

against civil aviation, while emphasizing the human rights and fair treatment of the suspects.

The 2014 Montreal Protocol, however still ineffective, is an amendment to the Tokyo Convention which failed to provide a suitable deterrent to unruly passengers, as under its conditions, the State of Registry of the aircraft was the State with jurisdiction to judge the unruly passenger. The Protocol extends jurisdiction to the States in which the operator is located and the State of destination of the flight. It clarifies what constitutes unruly behaviour, which makes the powers of the aircraft commander much clearer. Moreover, it strengthens the position of the aviation industry by providing purposeful deterrents to be able to prevent unruly behaviour, which has risen sharply in recent years, or if this behaviour does occur to recover costs incurred by unruly passengers.

On 5 June 2019, Uruguay deposited the instrument of ratification, which means that the Protocol is only two ratifications short of official entry into force. New guidance material, released by IATA and ICAO, is intended to assist national governments in legislating for more appropriate and harmonized legal measures to prevent and deter unruly and disruptive behaviour on flights.

2.11 Paris Tariffs and Capacity Agreements

2.11.1 Paris Multilateral Agreement 1967

Tariffs for Scheduled Air Services
International Agreement on the Procedure for the Establishment of Tariffs for Scheduled Air Services

The International Agreement on the Procedure for the Establishment of Tariffs for Scheduled Air Services (1967 Paris Multilateral Agreement), signed at Paris on 10 July 1967, entered into force on 30 May 1968. The provisions of this Paris Multilateral Agreement (ICAO Doc 8681) are preceded by the following:

> The Governments signatory hereto,
> Considering that the establishment of tariffs of scheduled international air services is governed in different ways by numerous bilateral air transport agreements, or is not provided for at all between States,
> Desiring that the principles and procedures for establishing such tariffs should be uniform and that wherever possible use should be made of the procedures of the International Air Transport Association,
> Have agreed as follows [...].

This Paris Multilateral Agreement, the only agreement in force in the international rate-making field, establishes tariff provisions between any two States which have no bilateral agreement, or where an agreement exists, contains no tariff clause. It also replaces the tariff clause in any bilateral agreement already concluded between two States, for as long this agreement remains in force between the two States.

The term tariff means the prices to be paid for the carriage of passengers, baggage and freight and the conditions under which those prices apply, including prices and conditions for agency and other auxiliary services, but excluding remuneration or conditions for the carriage of mail (Art. 2.1).

The tariff clause is essentially similar to the Bermuda I-type of bilateral agreements on air transport, with the following significant differences:

1. Tariffs are defined as including the conditions under which prices apply and the charges and conditions of agency services.
2. Tariffs shall, if possible, be agreed by the air carriers concerned of both Parties, after consultation with the other air carriers operating over the whole or part of the route, and such agreement shall, wherever possible, be reached, by the use of the procedures of the IATA for the working out of tariffs (Art. 2.3).
3. Tariffs must be submitted to the aeronautical authorities of both Parties for at least 90 days before their proposed introduction; in special cases this period may be reduced subject to the agreement of the said authorities (Art. 2.4); this approval may be given expressly. If neither of the aeronautical authorities has expressed disapproval within 30 days of the submission, in accordance with Article 2.4, these tariffs shall be considered as approved. In the event of the period for submission being reduced, as provided for in Article 2.4, the aeronautical authorities may agree that the period within which any disapproval must be notified shall be less than 30 days (Art. 2.5).
4. A tariff established in accordance with the provisions of Article 2 shall remain in force until a new tariff has been established. Nevertheless, a tariff shall not be prolonged by virtue of this paragraph for more than 12 months after the date on which it otherwise would have expired (Art. 2.8).

Whereas the importance of the Paris Multilateral Agreement does not lie in an innovation of a new ratemaking mechanism for scheduled international air transport, and in fact is based on an existing system, its provisions lead to harmonization and unification of tariff clauses in existing bilateral agreements. The 1967 Paris Multilateral Agreement was one of the first achievements of ECAC.[155]

---

155 Havel, B.F., *Beyond Open Skies: A New Regime for International Aviation*, Alphen aan den Rijn: Kluwer Law International, 2009, p. 231.

2.11.2 PARIS TARIFFS AGREEMENT 1987

Replacing the Paris Agreement of 1967
International Agreement on the Procedure for the Establishment of Tariffs for Intra-European Scheduled Air Services

In 1987, the International Agreement on the Procedure for the Establishment of Tariffs for Intra-European Scheduled Air Services (1987 Paris Tariff Agreement), was concluded and signed at Paris on 16 June 1987, entered into force on 5 June 1988, 30 days after five signatory States had deposited their instruments of ratification or notifications of approval or acceptance with ICAO, in accordance with Article 11(1). When this Agreement enters into force, the 1967 Paris Multilateral Agreement shall become inoperative between the Parties to this Agreement in respect of the procedures for the establishment of tariffs for intra-European scheduled air services (Art. 11(3)).

The 1987 Paris Tariff Agreement superseded the 1967 Paris Multilateral Agreement, and created two different dispute settlement mechanisms within each bilateral agreement effected. The Paris Tariff Agreement and the Paris Capacity Agreement were both concluded at the Paris ECAC-Sixteenth Intermediate Session from 16 to 18 June 1987. The Paris Tariff Agreement was registered by ICAO on 13 June 1988.

The objective of ECAC, based on its intra-European air transport policy work, was to achieve liberalization for both sharing of capacity and tariffs within Europe. With the development of the two international agreements in 1987, which permitted partial capacity and tariff liberalization, ECAC, with its outstanding civil aviation expertise, took the first steps in Europe towards liberalizing the air transport market, despite the fact that initially there has been some criticism from IATA. On the other hand, a number of pro-liberal Member States preferred ECAC to fulfil its unmodified liberalization policy in Europe.

Still, the power in air transport matters shifted from ECAC to the European Union. It was within the European Union, as a supranational entity with stronger binding force than ECAC as an autonomous intergovernmental institution, that the real progress towards full liberalization was made, supported by the institutional framework and its general urge towards economic integration, by the creation of a real single civil aviation market providing air carriers greater scope to develop markets and better meet passengers and shippers needs.[156] Eventually, the ECAC Tariffs Agreements were overtaken by the European Union.

Following growing litigation between Member States and air carriers, resulting in rulings to comply with the principles of the single European market, air transport liberal-

---

156 *See* Council Directive 87/601/EEC of 14 December 1987 on fares for scheduled air services between Member States, *OJ EC* L 374/12, 31.12.87.

ization was enhanced by three successive aviation liberalization packages, the first one adopted in December 1987, the second one in July 1990, while the third package was agreed in 1992 by the European Council of Ministers. The third package was the culmination of a gradual process of liberalization of the Community air transport market to which EU Member States committed themselves in 1986.

The provisions of the Paris Tariffs Agreement are preceded by the following:

The governments signatory hereto,
Considering that the principles and procedures for the establishment of tariffs for intra-European scheduled air services should be uniform; and
Considering that for such services it is desirable to replace the International Agreement on the Procedure for the Establishment of Tariffs for Scheduled Air Services, signed at Paris on 10 July 1967 (hereinafter referred to as the 1967 Agreement) by a new Agreement,
Have agreed as follows [...].

1987 Paris Tariffs Agreement, Article 2 states:

In this Agreement:

Article 2 (a):

The term 'intra-European' applies exclusively to the territories within Europe of Member States of the European Civil Aviation Conference.

Article 2 (b):

The term 'tariff' means the prices to be charged for the carriage of passengers, baggage or cargo (excluding mail), including any significant additional benefits to be furnished or made available in conjunction with such carriage; and the commission to be paid on the sales of tickets for the carriage of persons, or on corresponding transactions for the carriage of cargo. It includes also the conditions that govern the applicability of the price for carriage or the payment of commission.

Article 2 (c):

The term 'zone of flexibility' means a range in terms of price levels and conditions as defined in the Annex to this Agreement, within which passenger tariffs qualify for automatic approval.

There are two flexibility zones, one for discount fares and one for deep discount fares, plus conditional additional flexibility.

Council Directive 87/601/EEC of 14 December 1987 (no longer in force, date of end of validity: 01/11/1990) gives the following descriptions in Article 2:

> For the purposes of this Directive:
> (a) scheduled air fares means the prices to be paid in the applicable national currency for the carriage of passengers and baggage on scheduled air services and the conditions under which those prices apply, including remuneration and conditions offered to agency and other auxiliary services.
> (b) zone of flexibility means a pricing zone as referred to in Article 5, within which air fares meeting the conditions in Annex II quality for automatic approval by the aeronautical authorities of the Member States. The limits of a zone are expressed as percentages of the reference fare.
> (c) reference fare means the normal economy air fare charged by a third- or fourth-freedom air carrier on the routes in question; if more than one such fare exists, the average level shall be taken unless otherwise bilaterally agreed; where there is no normal economy fare, the lowest flexible fare shall be taken. [...].

2.11.3 PARIS CAPACITY AGREEMENT 1987

Sharing of Capacity on Intra-European Scheduled Air Services
International Agreement on the Sharing of Capacity on Intra-European Scheduled Air Services

The Chicago Convention states clearly that international civil aviation should be developed in an orderly manner, that international air transport services should be operated soundly and economically, that the rights of Contracting States should be fully respected, and that every Contracting State should have a fair opportunity to operate international air carriers. That means a more balanced coexistence with other air carriers of any Contracting State engaged in bilateral air services agreements, with progressive results of switching from a restrictive capacity determination method to a more liberal one.

The Paris Capacity Agreement was concluded at the same Conference in 1987 as was the Paris Tariffs Agreement. While the impact of the Paris Capacity Agreement on existing bilateral air services agreements is quite considerable, the Paris Tariffs Agreement has more influence on these bilateral agreements.[157]

The Paris Capacity Agreement allows any designated air carrier of two States concerned to submit to the competent authorities of both States their capacity proposals for the air services operated by all designated air carriers on all routes between two States for any given traffic season within a certain bandwidth on the total capacity proposed by all designated air carriers.

The Paris Capacity Agreement is the first multilateral agreement regarding sharing of capacity to introduce flexibility in the provision of capacity.[158]

In the European Union, Council Decision 87/602/EEC of 14 December 1987 was the first step forward in the direction of strengthening its economic and social cohesion and further liberalization in respect of capacity sharing and market access, including new fifth-freedom traffic rights between Community airports.[159] This Council Decision was succeeded by Council Regulation (EEC) No. 2343/90 of 24 July 1990 on access for air carriers to scheduled intra-Community air service routes and on the sharing of passenger capacity between air carriers on scheduled air services between Member States.[160]

The 1987 Paris Agreements covered intra-European scheduled air services. However, liberalization of air transport tariffs extended to other continents. Whereas regulatory liberalization was initially exclusively linked to the United States, on the other side of the Atlantic Ocean, ECAC recommended various liberalized proposals to its Member States resulting in the two instruments regarding tariffs and sharing of passenger capacity.

On 1 April 1987, a new Memorandum of Understanding) between ECAC and the United States came into operation representing the continuation of a constructive dialogue on North Atlantic fares matters, instituted with the signing of the first MoU in 1982. In addition a dialogue was initiated with the U.S. authorities on CRS (Computer Reservation Systems) issues.

---

157 Stadlmeier, S., *International Commercial Aviation: From Foreign Policy to Trade in Services*, Forum for Air and Space Law, Volume 5, edited by Marietta Benkö in cooperation with Willem de Graaff, Paris: Editions Frontières, 1998, pp. 419-420.

158 www.ecac-ceac.org/ecac-documents.

159 Council Decision 87/602/EEC of 14 December 1987 on the sharing of passenger capacity between air carriers on scheduled air services between Member States and on access for air carriers to scheduled air service routes between Member States, *OJ EC* L374/19, 31.12.87.

160 Council Regulation (EEC) No. 2343/90, *OJ EC* L 217/8, 11.8.90.

2.12   INTERNATIONAL COSPAS-SARSAT PROGRAMME AGREEMENT 1988

COSPAS is the acronym for the Russian words: Cosmicheskaya Sistema Poiska Avariy-nyh Sudov, which means "Space System for the Search of Vessels in Distress." SARSAT is the abbreviation of Search and Rescue Satellite-Aided Tracking.

On 6 May 1977, the former Union of Soviet Socialist Republics (USSR) and the United States initiated and signed a Cospas-Sarsat Agreement covering deployment of an international system of emergency beacon receivers on board aircraft. In 1979, four countries, the USSR, the United States, Canada and France came together to jointly develop a worldwide system of satellite based search and rescue.

The successful implementation of the Cospas-Sarsat Search and Rescue Satellite System was established under a Memorandum of Agreement (MoA) on 23 November 1979 among the Ministry of Merchant Marine of the USSR, the Department of National Defence of Canada, the National Oceanic and Atmospheric Administration of the United States and the *Centre National d'Études Spatiales* of France, which was signed on 5 October 1984 and came into effect on 8 July 1985. By 1985, the global system known as Cospas-Sarsat was fully operational.

Three years of tough negotiations, mainly because of divergent space policies and incompatible constraints among the four founding States, were necessary to achieve a consensus on the appropriate institutional arrangements required to satisfy the international community. The International Cospas-Sarsat Programme, formally constituted as a treaty-based, non-profit, humanitarian cooperative intergovernmental organization, was established under the International Cospas-Sarsat Programme Agreement (ICSPA) at Paris on 1 July 1988.

This Agreement secured the future Cospas-Sarsat System and cleared the path for its adoption by the International Maritime Organization as part of the Global Maritime Distress and Safety System (GMDSS). The founding States, Canada, France, the former USSR and the United States, all provide the satellites which form the heart of the system. In January 1992, the Russian Federation replaced the USSR as Party to the Agreement.[161]

Including the four Parties to the Agreement, 40 States and two organizations are now currently formally associated with the Programme and actively participate in the management and the operation of the Cospas-Sarsat System.[162] However, the associated participants are not considered legally equal to the four founding States. One representative from each of the four Parties form the Council, next to the Secretariat, headquartered in Montreal. The international Cospas-Sarsat Programme provides accurate, timely and

---

161 www.cospas-sarsat.int.
162 www.cospas-sarsat.int.

reliable distress alert and location data to help search and rescue authorities who assist persons in distress.[163]

Prior to the introduction of Cospas-Sarsat, civil aircraft were already using the 121.5 MHz frequency for distress calls, while military aircraft utilized the 234.0 MHz frequency as the primary emergency frequency together with the 121.5 MHz frequency as a back-up.

Already in the 1960s, small aircraft and some marine vessels started carrying small battery-powered radio transmitters, operating at the international distress frequency of 121.5 MHz, that could be activated in an emergency situation. These transmitters, Emergency Locator Transmitters (ELTs) on board aircraft, emitted a low-power signal that could be picked up by a receiver in a nearby air traffic control facility or by an aircraft in the vicinity, providing only line-of-sight coverage if it would be actively searching in that particular area.[164]

The four founding States led the development of the 406 MHz marine Emergency Position-Indication Radio Beacon (EPIRB), a key advancement in search and rescue technology, for detection by the system. Years later, due to technological progress, the system is now used worldwide, using state-of-the-art technical tools as the incorporated Global Positioning System (GPS).

As a number of States and organizations started to participate in the Cospas-Sarsat System, as being a space/ground segment provider, a Party-space segment provider or as user States, the geographical SAR-distribution took shape, which would provide and operate satellites and the ground segment equipment, to especially enable space-based relay, which in turn improved the detection and location of distress alerts significantly, compared to the 121.5 MHz ELTs, lacking a global monitoring system.[165]

However, in the early days of cooperative space projects, the international SAR community was concerned by the lack of a firm institutional basis to guarantee an open access to the satellite system and its continuity in the long term. Although the unique cooperative framework of the Cospas-Sarsat System allowed other countries' participation and

---

163 Dunk, von der, F.G., Tronchetti, F. (Eds.), *Handbook of Space Law*, Cheltenham: Edward Elgar Publishing, 2015, pp. 116-117.

164 ELT: a generic term describing equipment that broadcasts distinctive signals on designated frequencies and, depending on application, may be automatically activated by impact or be manually activated (ICAO Annex 6 & 10). Distress tracking: ELT for ICAO specified in-flight distress tracking (Cospas-Sarsat Glossary C/S G. 004-Issue 2).

165 In the 1980s, 150,000 ELT's operating at 121.5 MHz were already deployed in the United States and Canada. Unfortunately, the 121.5 MHz analogue technology frequency of those ELTs imposed severe limitations on the expected performance of the satellite system in terms of coverage, capacity and location accuracy. By the year 2000, the number of 121.5 MHz beacons had grown to over 600,000 and continued to grow until 1 February 2009 following a decision from Cospas-Sarsat to terminate the satellite processing of the frequency (Phase-out plan to prepare for transition to the new 406 MHz). Source: Levesque, D. (Ed.), *The History and Experience of the International Cospas-Sarsat Programme for Search and Rescue*, Paris: International Astronautical Federation (IAF), 30 July 2016.

contribution to the system, it was considered inadequate for the management of an inter-national operational system.

The mission of the Programme is to provide accurate, timely and reliable distress alert and location data to help SAR authorities assist persons in distress. The objective of the Cospas-Sarsat System is to reduce, as far as possible, delays in the provision of distress alerts to SAR services, and the time required to locate a person in distress at sea or on land and provide assistance to that person, all of which have a direct impact on the probability of survival. The distress alert and location data is provided by Cospas-Sarsat Participants to the responsible SAR services.[166]

Cospas-Sarsat cooperates with United Nations-affiliated agencies such as ICAO for worldwide civil aviation related distress alert, the International Telecommunication Un-ion for radio frequency allocations and IMO for worldwide shipping related distress alert, and will become a component of ICAO's Global Aeronautical Distress and Safety System (GADSS) of which the network and service will be indispensable and essential for the safety of air operations over vast water areas.[167]

ICAO will be a key client of Cospas-Sarsat. The Cospas-Sarsat System, designed to detect and locate activated distress beacons transmitting in the frequency band of 406.0-406.1 MHz and to distribute these alerts to Rescue Coordination Centers, will, as a GADSS component, especially focus on autonomous distress tracking.

The GADSS concept was developed because recent distress events with commercial aircraft showed deficiencies in the current air navigation tracking system (1 June 2009, Air France flight AF 447; 8 March 2014, Malaysian Airlines flight MH 370). Timely identification and localization of aircraft in distress is of paramount importance. When an accident occurs, rescuing of possible survivors has the highest priority, followed by the recovery of casualties, the wreckage or parts of it, together with the Digital Flight Data Recorder (DFDR) and the Cockpit Voice Recorder (CVR), in that order. Each recorder is equipped with an Underwater Locator Beacon (ULB).[168]

Both data carriers are playing a key role in the aircraft accident investigation process. Analyzing of indispensable data such as cockpit voice, cockpit sound and communication recordings as well as technical flight data, in conjunction with other investigation meth-ods, may significantly contribute to determining the probable cause of the accident and to enhancing aviation safety.

ICAO has identified that the current effectiveness of search and rescue services could be enhanced by developing and implementing the GADSS concept, which shall be able to

---

166 www.cospas-sarsat.int.

167 Olla, Ph. (Ed.), *Commerce in Space: Infrastructures, Technologies, and Applications*, Hershey, PA: Informa-tion Science Reference, 2008, pp. 73-74.

168 The Underwater Locator Beacon (ULB) assists in locating the aircraft wreckage in the event of an overwater accident. The ULB or 'pinger' is activated when the recorder is immersed in water. It transmits an acoustical signal on 37.5 KHz that can be detected with a special receiver. The beacon can transmit from depths down to 14,000 feet (Source: National Transportation Safety Board-NTSB).

address all flight phases under all circumstances, including the distress phase. This system, through its main functions, aircraft tracking, autonomous distress tracking and post flight localization and recovery, will maintain an up-to-date record of the aircraft progress.

Aircraft flight tracking means a process, established by the operator, that maintains and updates, at standardized intervals, a ground-based record of the four-dimensional (4D) position of individual aircraft in flight in all airspaces. In case of a crash, forced landing or ditching in oceanic areas, the location of survivors, the aircraft and recoverable flight data will be identified and coordinated (dissemination of information). An improved and effective method of alerting search and rescue services is essential.[169]

The consequent objectives of the GADSS are to:
- initiate SAR actions in a timely manner;
- ensure tracking of aircraft in distress and timely and accurate location of end of flight;
- accurately direct SAR actions;
- enable efficient and effective SAR operations;
- ensure timely retrieval of flight recorder data.[170]

The Cospas-Sarsat System is a worldwide international satellite-based search and rescue system and service, which is able to detect and locate transmissions from ELTs carried by ships, aircraft or people. The system operates 24/7, year-round which is important for the efficient operation of search and rescue services. Use of the system is free to beacon operators. Once the distress signals are detected and the location is verified by the system, search and rescue can be initiated. The system utilizes a network of satellites that provide coverage anywhere on Earth.

This space segment includes Low-altitude Earth Orbit satellites for Search and Rescue (LEOSAR), Geostationary Earth Orbit satellites for Search and Rescue, often referred to as Geosynchronous Equatorial Orbit satellites (GEOSAR) at 36,000 km above the Earth covering large fixed areas, and the relatively new, improved Medium-altitude Earth Orbit satellites for Search and Rescue (MEOSAR). MEO satellites have similar size footprints as GEO satellites, but provide continuous global coverage (including the Poles) by moving slowly. The MEOSAR system is based on the use of SAR transponders on new global positioning systems, Global Navigation Satellite Systems (GLONASS) as well as GALILEO satellites and updated ground segment equipment. MEO satellites calculated the location of EgyptAir flight MS 804 in the Mediterranean Sea.[171]

---

169 www.icao.int/safety/globaltracking. Concept of Operations, Global Aeronautical Distress and Safety System, Version 6, 2017.

170 GADSS Concept of Operations, Version 6.0. ICAO GADSS Advisory Group.

171 EgyptAir flight MS 804 was a regular scheduled passenger flight from Paris Charles de Gaulle Airport to Cairo International Airport. On 19 May 2016 at 02.33 Egypt Standard Time (UTC+2) the Airbus A-320 crashed in the Mediterranean Sea between Crete and Alexandria, killing 56 passengers, three security officers and seven crew members. No mayday call was received.

The system detects, locates and forwards information to almost all States and territories at no cost whatsoever to the 406 MHz beacon owners or the receiving government agencies. For satellite reception of alerts by Cospas-Sarsat, the beacon must be a (next generation) model that transmits at 406 MHz.

ICAO's main requirements are as follows (Annex 6):

- Allow the location of an aircraft site within 6 NM (Cospas-Sarsat provides redundant, encoded Global Navigation Satellite System (GNSS) and independently calculated positions).
- Allow the position of an aircraft in distress to be determined at least once every minute (Cospas-Sarsat will exceed this reporting-frequency requirement).
- Able to operate in the event of aircraft power loss (All ELTs have built-in battery power supply).
- Commence no more than 5 seconds after detection of abnormal flight conditions (Cospas-Sarsat will meet or exceed that specification).

The State and Agencies Parties recognize that it is desirable to operate the Cospas-Sarsat System in accordance with international law, so as to endeavour to provide long-term alert and location services in support of search and rescue and access to the system to all States on a non-discriminatory basis, and free of charge for the end-user in distress.

2.13 MONTREAL CONVENTION 1991

International Convention on the Markings of Plastic Explosives for the Purpose of Detection

On 21 December 1988, a bomb exploded in the cargo hold of Pan Am flight 103, a Boeing 747 on the way from Frankfurt to New York with an intermediate stop in London. The aircraft was climbing out of London Heathrow to its scheduled cruising level, readying for its North Atlantic crossing.

After levelling off at FL 310, just before 19.03 hours, the last secondary radar return was received by the Scottish ground radar station. The primary returns at the radar screens then showed the immediate breakup of the aircraft causing a trail of debris.

Major portions of the wreckage fell on the town of Lockerbie and the countryside. 259 passengers and crew were killed as well as 11 residents of the Scottish town of Lockerbie, the place of impact of the wreckage. Shortly after the so-called Lockerbie bombing, several groups claimed responsibility. Following a three-year investigation, arrest warrants were issued for two Libyan nationals. In April 1999, Libya handed over the Libyan nationals, an intelligence officer and a station manager, accused of the bombing, for a long-lasting trial in the Netherlands before a panel of Scottish judges at a former U.S. military base known as Camp Zeist.[172]

The Lockerbie disaster drew urgent attention to the dangerously growing trend of acts of unlawful interference, in particular through the use of plastic explosives, aimed at the total destruction of civil aircraft in commercial service while in flight and consequently the death of all occupants on board. The destruction of Pan Am flight 103 is the latest in a series of such acts of sabotage which resulted in great loss of life.

Sabotage is clearly now as great a threat to international aviation as hijacking and demands a similar international response. Against this background, the United Kingdom and the United States, in the belief that aviation security must be treated as the highest priority issue for ICAO, urged for a strong Resolution and associated Plan of Action to be founded by the ICAO Council on this issue, as soon as possible in 1989.

On 30 January 1989, the ICAO Council established an *ad hoc* group of experts on the detection of explosives to address this horrifying problem. One important finding of this group concerned the feasibility of placing an identifying additive in certain explosives to ensure easier detection.

On 14 June 1989, the United Nations Security Council stated that a new threat to civil aviation was an issue, caused by plastic explosives that escape detection in security devices normally used at airports throughout the world at that time.[173]

The United Nations Security Council unanimously adopted Resolution 635 after taking note of the applicable ICAO Resolution on 16 February 1989. The Council expressed deep concern regarding incidents of terrorism and condemned all acts of unlawful interference against the security of civil aviation, calling on all its Member States to cooperate in devising and implementing universal measures to combat terrorism.

The unprecedented potential threat of the use of devastating plastic explosives targeting the aviation industry must by all means be halted. The Council urged organizations like ICAO and Member States as well as the producers of plastic explosives to intensify research into making such explosives easier to detect and in the prevention of international terrorism in general.

At the 27th Session of the ICAO Assembly held in September-October 1989, a proposal was made on the initiative of the governments of the United Kingdom and of Czechoslovakia to draft an international instrument on the marking of plastic explosives, which was fully endorsed by the United Nations Security Council in Resolution 635. A special subcommittee of the Legal Committee prepared a preliminary draft in 1990 and an ICAO Conference was held at Montreal from 12 February to 1 March 1991 to adopt

---

172 Marquise, R.A., *Scotbomb: Evidence and the Lockerbie Investigation*, New York: Algora Publishing, 2006, Prologue of the Verdict. *See also* Wallis, R., *Lockerbie: The Story and the Lessons*, Westport, CT: Praeger Publishers, 2001, pp. 27-28

173 United Nations Security Council Resolution 635 (1989) on Markings of Plastic or Sheet Explosives for the Purpose of Detection.

the International Convention on the Markings of Plastic Explosives for the Purpose of Detection (ICAO Doc 9571), also known as the MEX Convention 1991.

The 1991 Montreal Convention is a multilateral anti-terrorism agreement that aims to prohibit and prevent the manufacture or storage of unmarked plastic explosives. The Convention was concluded at the ICAO International Conference on Air Law at Montreal on 1 March 1991, and it entered into force on 21 June 1998.

The provisions of this agreement for the most intrusive surveillance and detection relate, among other things, to possible terrorist acts of sabotage on the air transportation system. The States Parties to this Convention express deep concern regarding terrorist acts aimed at destruction of aircraft, other means of transportation and other potential targets by means of plastic explosives.

The States Parties furthermore consider that the marking of such explosives for the purpose of detection would contribute significantly to the prevention of such unlawful acts, and recognize that for the purpose of deterring such acts there is an urgent need for an international instrument obliging States to adopt appropriate measures to ensure that plastic explosives are duly marked.[174]

A State that ratifies the Convention agrees to prohibit the manufacture, storage, transport or entry of unmarked plastic explosives in its territory (Arts. 2 and 3), and to exercise strict and effective control over the possession and transfer of possession of any existing stocks of unmarked plastic explosives or unmarked explosives which have been manufactured in or brought into its territory prior to the entry into force of this Convention in respect of that State, so as to prevent their diversion or use inconsistent with the objectives of the Convention (Art. 4).

In general, plastic explosives are not prohibited by this Convention, but it requires States Parties to prohibit and prevent the manufacture in their territories of unmarked explosives, as well as the movement of such material into or out of their territories. In other words, the Convention mandates that when they are produced, they are marked with any one of the four designated detection agents (taggants) agreed upon by the Conference, and specified in the Technical Annex to the Convention, which in turn can facilitate future identification purposes.[175]

These detection agents are intended to be used to enhance the detectability of explosives by vapour detection means. In each case, the introduction of a detection agent into an explosive shall be done in such a manner as to achieve homogeneous distribution in the finished product.

---

174 *Technology Against Terrorism: The Federal Effort*, Congress of the United States Office of Technology Assessment, Washington DC: Government Printing Office, July 1991, pp. 7-10. *See also* Hodgkinson, D.I., Johnston, R., *International Air Carrier Liability: Safety and Security*, Milton Park, Abingdon, Oxon: Routledge, 2017, pp. 210-211.

175 Cheng, C-J. (Ed.), *The Use of Airspace and Outer Space for All Mankind in the 21st Century*, The Hague: Kluwer Law International, 1995, pp. 151-153.

The minimum concentration of a detection agent in the finished product at the time of manufacture shall be as shown in the Technical Annex (Table). The chemical detection agents shown in this Table are: Ethylene glycol dinitrate (EGDN) $C_2H_4(NO_3)_2$, 2,3-dimethyl-2,3 dinitrobutane (DMNB) $C_6H_{12}(NO_2)_2$ (the most popular marking agent), para-mononitrotoluene (p-MNT) $C_7H_7NO_2$ and ortho-mononitrotoluene (o-MNT) $C_7H_7NO_2$.[176]

Stocks of plastic explosives not held by authorities performing military and police functions are to be destroyed or consumed for purposes not inconsistent with the objectives of the Convention, marked or rendered permanently ineffective, with a period of three years from the entry into force of the Convention in respect of the State concerned.

The Convention also established an International Explosives Technical Commission (IETC), consisting of experts in the field of manufacture or detection of, or research in, explosives. This Commission evaluates technical developments relating to the manufacture, marking and detection of explosives, reports its findings, through the ICAO Council, to all States Parties and international organizations concerned and proposes amendments to the Technical Annex to the Convention as required (Arts. 5 and 6).

The Convention assigns specific functions to the Council with respect to, *inter alia*, the appointment of members to the IETC, the procedure regarding amendments to the Technical Annex and measures to facilitate the implementation of the Convention.

---

176 *See also*: Technical Annex to the Montreal Convention 1991, Part 2: Detection Agents, Table, Molecular Name of detection.

CHAPTER III: ESSENTIAL PRIVATE INTERNATIONAL AIR LAW

3.1 WARSAW SYSTEM

Air Carrier Liability under the Warsaw Regime

As the first airlines capable of carrying passengers, mail and cargo were established early in the civil air transport era starting shortly after World War I, unification of private air law with respect to international carriage by air became a priority topic. The Warsaw Convention on air carrier liability, dating from 1929, and subsequent amending legal instruments together form the Warsaw System, or the Warsaw Regime.

The 1929 Warsaw Convention was the first comprehensive legal framework governing international aviation and has been playing an essential role in regulating liability in the event of accidents. For the purpose of international carriage by air, it established a set of principles, most of which are still effective and constitute the basis of modern aviation law. The definition of air carrier has been somewhat unclear over the years.

A carrier means he who, either as proprietor, charterer or conductor of the aircraft, uses it individually or jointly, for the carriage by air of persons, luggage or goods, within the meaning of the Warsaw Convention, and in conformity with the national regulations. During the Warsaw Conference, the Brazilian delegates argued that according to the Brazilian Air Code carrier means the natural or judicial person who performs carriage by air for reward. However, this description was rejected by the conference for reasons that it would be premature to lock the notion of an air carrier into a formula.[1]

The Warsaw Convention was amended by The Hague Protocol on 28 September 1955. This Protocol raised the limit of liability regarding persons, and included some minor adjustments and clarifications and contributed to some simplifications of the documents of carriage. Further amendments were done by the Guadalajara Convention

---

[1] Goedhuis, D., *National Airlegislations and the Warsaw Convention*, Dordrecht: Springer Science and Business Media, Originally published by Martinus Nijhoff, The Hague,1937, pp. 132-133. The Warsaw Conference, from 4 to 12 October 1929, was the Second International Private Air Law Conference (*II Conférence International de Droit Privé Aérien*) after the 1926 Paris Conference.

in 1961. This instrument was necessitated by the modern modalities of air transport such as the development of charter flights and code-sharing operations, when a person was not a party to the agreement for carriage, in other words, the distinction between contracting carrier and actual carrier.[2]

As the United States announced in 1965 that it denied the ratifying of The Hague Protocol, mainly because of the liability limits set in this Protocol being unacceptably low, it considered a withdrawal from the Warsaw Convention, which meant a serious crisis regarding the unification of private air law. After establishing a temporary solution in the form of the 1966 Montreal Inter-carrier Agreement, work had to be done quickly for a permanent alternative.[3]

Eventually, this was done by the adoption of the Guatemala City Protocol in 1971, a controversial legal instrument that contained a considerable increase in the liability limit for persons, but a removal of the *force majeure* defence regarding passenger claims.

In 1975, the four Montreal Protocols were adopted, amending the Warsaw Convention and The Hague and Guatemala Protocols by, among other things, introducing the Special Drawing Right (SDR).

In 1999, an innovative new Montreal Convention, formally entitled "Convention for the Unification of Certain Rules for International Carriage by Air," not being part of the Warsaw system, was signed and intended to replace the Warsaw system.

3.1.1 WARSAW CONVENTION 1929

Convention for the Unification of Certain Rules Relating to International Carriage by Air

Early in aviation history, unification of private air law became a priority as the first airlines, capable of carrying passengers, mail and cargo, were established and operating internationally very shortly after World War I (the Great War). At the initiative of the French government, the *Comité International Technique d' Experts Juridiques Aériens* (CITEJA), an organization of legal experts, was created during the First International Conference on Air Law, held at Paris from 27 October to 6 November 1925.

CITEJA, in charge of the continuation of the work of the Conference, subsequently held several sessions to draft a Convention for consideration at the Second International

---

2   Guadalajara Convention, Art. 1.b: "Contracting carrier means a person who as a principal makes an agreement for carriage governed by the Warsaw Convention with a passenger or consignor or with a person acting on behalf of the passenger or consignor." Art. 1.c: "Actual carrier means a person, other than the contracting carrier, who, by virtue of authority from the contracting carrier, performs the whole or part of the carriage contemplated in paragraph b, but who is not with respect to such part a successive carrier within the meaning of the Warsaw Convention. Such authority is presumed in the absence of proof to the contrary."

3   The first Inter-carrier Agreement, relating to the Warsaw System.

Conference on Private Air Law, held at Warsaw from 4 to 12 October 1929. The Warsaw Convention, the end result of this Conference, has evolved into one of the most important instruments of private international law. After coming into force on 13 February 1933, it resolved some conflicts of law and jurisdiction.

As a consequence of the continuously changing worldwide aviation industry, globalization and the increasing, complex mobility of air travellers, the Warsaw Convention was succeeded by several amending, supplementing and superseding legal instruments. The Warsaw System consists of the original Warsaw Convention and the following instruments:

1. 1955 The Hague Protocol, Protocol to Amend the Convention for the Unification of Certain Rules Relating to International Carriage by Air, signed at Warsaw on 12 October 1929 (Warsaw Convention), done at The Hague on 28 September 1955 (ICAO Doc 7632).

2. 1961 Guadalajara Convention, Convention Supplementary to the Warsaw Convention, for the Unification of Certain Rules Relating to International Carriage by Air Performed by a Person Other than the Contracting Carrier, signed at Guadalajara on 18 September 1961 (ICAO Doc 8181).

3. 1971 Guatemala City Protocol, Protocol to Amend the Convention for the Unification of Certain Rules Relating to International Carriage by Air, signed at Warsaw on 12 October 1929, as Amended by the Protocol done at The Hague on 28 September 1955 (The Hague Protocol), signed at Guatemala City on 8 March 1971 (ICAO Doc 8932).

4. Montreal Protocol No. 1: Additional Protocol No. 1 to Amend the Convention for the Unification of Certain Rules Relating to International Carriage by Air, signed at Warsaw on 12 October 1929 (Warsaw Convention), signed at Montreal on 25 September 1975 (ICAO Doc 9145).

5. Montreal Protocol No. 2: Additional Protocol No. 2 to Amend the Convention for the Unification of Certain Rules Relating to International Carriage by Air, signed at Warsaw on 12 October 1929, as Amended by the Protocol done at The Hague on 28 September 1955 (The Hague Protocol), signed at Montreal on 25 September 1975 (ICAO Doc 9146).

6. Montreal Protocol No. 3: Additional Protocol No. 3 to Amend the Convention for the Unification of Certain Rules Relating to International Carriage by Air, signed at Warsaw on 12 October 1929, as Amended by the Protocol done at The Hague on 28 September 1955 and at Guatemala City on 8 March 1971 (Guatemala City Protocol), signed at Montreal on 25 September 1975 (ICAO Doc 9147).

7. Montreal Protocol No. 4: Additional Protocol to Amend the Convention for the Unification of Certain Rules Relating to International Carriage by Air, signed at Warsaw on 12 October 1929, as Amended by the Protocol done at The Hague on 28 Septem-

ber 1955 (The Hague Protocol), signed at Montreal on 25 September 1975 (ICAO Doc 9148).

8. Various Inter-carrier Agreements relating to the Warsaw Convention, supplementing liability rules (only applicable to Art. 17) such as the 1992 Japanese Initiative establishing a strict liability regime for the first 100,000 SDRs of provable damages for passengers travelling on Japanese air carriers, the IATA Inter-carrier Agreements on passenger liability of 1995 (IIA), the 1996 Agreement on Measures to Implement the IATA Inter-carrier Agreement (MIA), the ATA (Air Transport Association of America) Inter-carrier Agreements IPA, IPA-2 of 1996 and 2005, and the Montreal Inter-carrier Agreement of 1966 (MA66) which was in fact the first inter-carrier agreement relating to the Warsaw Convention. MA66 was the result of the U.S. denunciation of the Warsaw Convention on 16 November 1965, effective 15 May 1966. IATA adopted, in a last attempt to preserve the Warsaw Convention, on 13 May 1966, with the approval of the U.S. Civil Aeronautics Board (CAB), the MA66, the Montreal Agreement Relating to Liability Limitations of the Warsaw Convention and The Hague Protocol.[4]

The 1999 Montreal Convention, the Convention for the Unification of Certain Rules Relating to International Carriage by Air, signed at Montreal on 28 May 1999 (ICAO Doc 9740) actually is not a part of the so-called Warsaw System. However, the 1999 Montreal Convention, also known as the new Warsaw Convention, modernized and consolidated, certainly prevails over all Warsaw System instruments, as between two States both Parties to the Montreal Convention. As between two States, not both Parties to the Montreal Convention, the relevant Warsaw System instruments will remain in effect, if such States are both Parties thereto. The 1999 Montreal Convention enhances the rights of claimants in cases involving the death or injury of passengers in international air transport.

The Warsaw Convention is an international Convention which regulates liability for international carriage of persons, luggage or goods performed by aircraft for reward. It established the legal framework for conditional carriage by air and unified an important sector of private international air law. It covers conditions of carriage that define liability of the carrier in case of loss, damage, injury or death due to an accident on international flights, spells out procedures for claims and compensation and lays down the requirements for the format and content of air transport documents such as tickets, baggage labels, air consignment notes, air waybills, etc.

---

4   Goldhirsch, L.B. (Ed.), *The Warsaw Convention Annotated: A Legal Handbook*, The Hague: Kluwer Law International, 2000, pp. 6-9.

3.1.2   THE HAGUE PROTOCOL 1955

Protocol to Amend the Convention for the Unification of Certain Rules Relating to International Carriage by Air

Over the years, after the Warsaw Convention was signed on 12 October 1929, several amendments and supplementary instruments have been established. For example, The Hague Protocol of 1955 was the result of a Diplomatic Conference convened under the auspices of ICAO, held in The Hague, Netherlands. The Hague Protocol to the Warsaw Convention was signed on 28 March 1955, and entered into force on 1 August 1963.

It encompassed the first amendments to the Warsaw Convention. Various reasons underlie the establishment of this agreement. First of all, there was a tremendous gap between 1929 and the 1950s, when the technological progress and the advance of law required a modification of the original text of 1929. Secondly, difficulties in the interpretation of the dictum of wilful misconduct in the Warsaw Convention and the low limits of liability led to the drafting of The Hague Protocol, in which the common law definition of wilful misconduct as recognized by the Warsaw Convention was merely confirmed.[5]

The amendments outline changes in practically all articles and paragraphs to be deleted and replaced over time. The text of Article 1 was updated in such a way that a more contemporary (mid 1950s) definition of international carriage by air was introduced.

The Hague Protocol doubled the hitherto meagre and arbitrary limits of liability regarding passenger death or bodily injury to 250,000 gold francs, the unit of account for the Bank for International Settlements (Art. 22).

Furthermore, the liability of an air carrier would be limited, under certain circumstances, during a stopover by a passenger in an agreed or indicated stopping place.

Article 3, Paragraphs 1 and 2 of the Warsaw Convention shall be deleted and replaced by the following:

1. In respect of the carriage of passengers a ticket shall be delivered containing:
   (a) an indication of the places of departure and destination;
   (b) if the places of departure and destination are within the territory of a single High Contracting Party, one or more agreed stopping places

---

5   Tompkins Jr., G.N., *Liability Rules Applicable to International Air Transport as Developed by the Courts in the United States, From Warsaw 1929 to Montreal 1999*, Alphen aan den Rijn: Kluwer Law International, 2010, p. 112. Wilful misconduct is the intentional performance of an act with knowledge that the performance of that act will probably result in injury or damage, or it may be the intentional performance of an act in such a manner as to imply reckless disregard of the probable consequences, or, the intentional omission of some act, with knowledge that such omission will probably result in damage or injury, or the intentional omission of some act in a manner from which could be implied reckless disregard of the probable consequences of the omission.

being within the territory of another State, an indication of at least one such stopping place;

(c) a notice to the effect that, if the passenger's journey involves an ultimate destination or stop in a country other than the country of departure, the Warsaw Convention may be applicable and that the Convention governs and in most cases limits the liability of carriers for death or personal injury and in respect of loss of or damage to baggage.

2. The passenger ticket shall constitute *prima facie* evidence of the conclusion and conditions of the contract of carriage. The absence, irregularity or loss of the passenger ticket does not affect the existence or the validity of the contract of carriage which shall, none the less, be subject of the rules of this Convention. Nevertheless, if, with the consent of the carrier, the passenger embarks without a passenger ticket having been delivered, or if the ticket does not include the notice required by Paragraph 1 (c) of this article, the carrier shall not be entitled to avail himself of the provisions of Article 22.

The Hague Protocol rephrased the wilful misconduct exception to limited liability (Art. 25) and introduced an extension to the claim period regarding damage and delay to luggage and goods. The amended text of Article 26 of the Warsaw Convention:

In the case of damage, the person entitled to delivery must complain to the carrier forthwith after the discovery of the damage, and, at the latest within seven days from the date of receipt in the case of baggage, and fourteen days from the date of receipt in the case of cargo. In the case of delay the complaint must be made at the latest within twenty-one days from the date on which the baggage or cargo have been placed at his disposal.

The Hague Protocol altered the circumstances under which a carrier would lose the protection of liability limitations, and it simplified the provisions on documents of carriage, but retained the prior limits for baggage and cargo and for possessions carried by the passenger. However, the overall effect of The Hague Protocol was weakened, in particular due to the position of the United States by refraining from participation. A few years later, The Hague Protocol was succeeded by another amending instrument on the Warsaw/The Hague Articles, the 1961 Guadalajara Convention.

3.1.3 GUADALAJARA CONVENTION 1961

Convention Supplementary to the Warsaw Convention for the Unification of Certain Rules Relating to International Carriage by Air Performed by a Person other than the Contracting Carrier

A supplementary Convention to the 1929 Warsaw Convention was developed at the Diplomatic Conference, held from 29 August to 10 September 1961 at Guadalajara, Mexico. The Guadalajara Convention was signed on 18 September 1961, and entered into force on 1 May 1964. It was formally called the Convention Supplementary to the Warsaw Convention for the Unification of Certain Rules Relating to International Carriage by Air Performed by a Person other than the Contracting Carrier (ICAO Doc 8181).

This supplementary instrument was necessitated by the modern modalities of air transport when a person was not a party to the agreement for carriage. The multilateral Guadalajara Convention amended the Warsaw System, particularly to address indirect carriage of cargo, the agreement between the freight forwarder or contractual carrier and the actual carrier. In fact, the Guadalajara Convention extends the protection of the Warsaw Convention to actual carriers.[6]

The actual carrier, who performs the carriage, can never be held liable for an unlimited sum. His liability is restricted to the Warsaw Convention limits. The total sum of money recoverable from the contracting carrier and the actual carrier and from their servants and agents acting within the scope of their employment, shall not exceed the highest amount which could be awarded against either the contracting carrier or the actual carrier under this Convention. None of the persons mentioned shall be liable for a sum in excess of the limit applicable to him (Art. VI).[7]

In the early 1960s, the United States considered the liability limits for carriage of persons set by the Warsaw Convention and The Hague Protocol far too low compared to the economic and social standards prevailing at the time, which was the reason for its dissatisfaction and subsequent withdrawal from the Warsaw Convention. The United States, the most important nation in international civil aviation with the largest market for international carriers in the world, submitted in November 1965 a notice of denunciation of the Warsaw Convention, effective on 15 May 1966. This reaction resulted in a serious situation with respect to the unification of private international air law. The preservation of the Warsaw System was at stake.

---

6   Ndikum, P.F., Ndikum, S-D., *Liability Rules Developed by European Union, Australian, United Kingdom and United States of America Courts According to European Community Treaty-Warsaw 1929-Montreal 1999. Cases and Materials*, Encyclopedia of International Aviation Law, Volume 3, 2013 Edition, London: Ndikum Publications, pp. 792-793.

7   Diederiks-Verschoor, I.H.Ph., Butler, M.A. (Legal adviser), *An Introduction to Air Law*, Eighth Revised Edition, 2006, pp. 157-158.

However, before the notification actually came into effect, the United States withdrew this notification in consideration of a private voluntary agreement negotiated under the auspices of IATA. An interim agreement called the 1966 Montreal Inter-carrier Agreement, formally the Agreement Relating to Liability Limitations of the Warsaw Convention and The Hague Protocol, turned out to be the solution.[8]

It was not a convention or a protocol but just an agreement adopted by IATA on 13 May 1966, signed by all major foreign and U.S. air carriers serving the United States, with the approval of the American Civil Aeronautics Board (approving Agreement CAB 18900), to alter the terms of international air carrier liability. It established the strict liability of the carrier for bodily injury but without disturbing or amending the Warsaw Convention, in particular Article 25.[9]

The 1966 Montreal Inter-carrier Agreement, formulated pursuant to Article 22.1 of the Warsaw Convention, ensured that accident victims on flights with a point in the United States, either as a point of origin, a point of destination or an agreed stopping place, are compensated for up to US$ 75,000, inclusive of legal fees and costs, of proven damages, whether or not due to the negligence of the carrier of the accident, within the meaning of Article 17 of the Warsaw Convention.

IATA member air carriers operating these particular services accepted the terms of the Montreal Inter-carrier Agreement and adjusted their conditions of carriage and the liability limits. The Inter-carrier Agreement was to be considered an interim agreement which, according to the U.S. authorities, would shortly be replaced by a revised international convention that came closer to providing adequate compensation to victims of air carrier accidents.[10]

Article 17 Warsaw Convention:

> The carrier is liable for damage sustained in the event of the death or wounding of a passenger or any other bodily injury suffered by a passenger, if the accident which caused the damage so sustained took place on board the aircraft or in the course of any of the operations of embarking or disembarking.

---

8   Manno, C., Liability Limitations of Warsaw Convention Applicable to the Carrier's Employees (*Reed v. Wiser*), *St. John's Law Review*: Vol. 52: No. 2, Art. 4 (1978), p. 212.

9   Hodgkinson, D.I., Johnston, R., *International Air Carrier Liability: Safety and Security*, Milton Park, Abingdon, Oxon: Routledge, 2017, pp. 11-12. Giemulla, E.M., Weber, L. (Eds.), *International and EU Aviation Law: Selected Issues*, Alphen aan den Rijn: Kluwer Law International, 2011, p. 250.

10 Message from the President of the United States Transmitting Protocol to Amend the Convention for the Unification of Certain Rules Relating to International Carriage by Air Signed at Warsaw on October 12, 1929, Done at The Hague, 28 September 1955 (The Hague Protocol), 17th Congress, Second Session, Senate, Treaty Doc 107-14, Letter of Submittal, The Secretary of State, Washington D.C.: U.S. Government Printing Office, 31 July 2002, pp. V-VIII.

Article 20.1 Warsaw Convention:

> The carrier is not liable if he proves that he and his agents have taken all necessary measures to avoid the damage or that it was impossible for him or them to take such measures.

Article 22.1 Warsaw Convention:

> In the carriage of passengers the liability of the carrier for each passenger is limited to the sum of 125,000 francs. Where, in accordance with the law of the Court seized of the case, damages may be awarded in the form of periodical payments, the equivalent capital value of the said payments shall not exceed 125,000 francs. Nevertheless, by special contract, the carrier and the passenger may agree to a higher limit of liability.

Article 25 Warsaw Convention:

> 1. The carrier shall not be entitled to avail himself of the provisions of this Convention which exclude or limit his liability, if the damage is caused by his wilful misconduct or by such default on his part as, in accordance with the law of the Court seized of the case, is considered to be equivalent to wilful misconduct.
> 2. Similarly the carrier shall not be entitled to avail himself of the said provisions, if the damage is caused as aforesaid by any agent of the carrier acting within the scope of his employment.

3.1.4 GUATEMALA CITY PROTOCOL 1971

Protocol to Amend the Convention for the Unification of Certain Rules Relating to International Carriage by Air as Amended by the Protocol done at The Hague

In the early 1970s, a permanent solution and further modernization of the Warsaw Convention as amended by The Hague Protocol was reached in Guatemala City. The International Conference on Air Law, convened under the auspices of ICAO, met in Guatemala City from 9 February to 8 March 1971, and adopted a Protocol to Amend the Convention for the Unification of Certain Rules Relating to International Carriage by Air signed at Warsaw on 12 October 1929, as amended by the Protocol done at The Hague on 28 September 1955. The 1971 Guatemala City Protocol (ICAO Doc 8932) reflected further efforts to advance the issue of passenger rights by introducing major amendments to carrier liability and documentation by greatly revising the legal rules governing the international carriage by air of passengers and baggage. All in all, the Protocol is a thoroughly carrier-oriented instrument.[11]

This rather ill-conceived Protocol, especially with regard to passenger liability, held carriers strictly liable for up to 1,500,000 francs (100,000 US$) of proven damages in the event of passenger death or injury, but that amount constituted an unbreakable limit on liability per passenger, even if the carrier engaged in wilful misconduct. However, the Protocol expressly recognized the right of States to supplement passenger recoveries through State-legislated insurance plans. Soon after the Guatemala Conference, another opportunity arose to negotiate a more favourable and more comprehensive revision of the Warsaw Convention.

This opportunity was the Diplomatic Conference on International Air Law held in September 1975 at Montreal, under the auspices of the ICAO. Four Protocols (the Montreal Protocols), amending the Warsaw Convention and The Hague and Guatemala City Protocols, were adopted and opened for signature on 25 September 1975. The Montreal Protocols amended the increased liability limit found in the Guatemala City Protocol, altered the monetary measurement from the Gold Standard to the Special Drawing Right as defined by the International Monetary Fund (IMF), and eliminated obsolete documentary requirements regarding the transport of cargo by air.[12]

The provisions of the Guatemala City Protocol are incorporated in the No. 3 Montreal Protocol by reference without actually bringing the Guatemala City Protocol as such legally into force.

3.1.5 MONTREAL CONVENTION 1999

Air Carrier Liability under the Montreal Convention
Convention for the Unification of Certain Rules for International Carriage by Air

The Montreal Convention, signed on 28 May 1999 (ICAO Doc 9740), was intended to replace the antique Warsaw Convention and its various amending instruments (Warsaw System). The world of civil aviation had changed rapidly. Increased mobility of passengers and the tremendous progress in globalization of the air transport industry made the Warsaw Convention and its related amending instruments rather fragmented and incoherent. The Montreal Convention (MC99), the Convention for the Unification of Certain

---

11 Cheng, C.-J. (Ed.), *The Use of Airspace and Outer Space for all Mankind in the 21st Century*. Proceedings of the International Conference on Air Transport and Space Application in a New World held in Tokyo from 2 to 5 June 1993, The Hague: Kluwer Law International, 1995, pp. 113-115.

12 A Special Drawing Right is an international reserve asset, created by the International Monetary Fund (IMF) in 1969, the value of which is currently based on the market exchange rates of five major currencies: the US dollar, the Euro, the British pound sterling, the Chinese renminbi and the Japanese yen.

Rules for International Carriage by Air, is a multilateral treaty adopted at a Diplomatic Meeting of ICAO Member States in 1999, and came into force on 4 November 2003.

Preamble,

> *The States Parties to this Convention:*
> *Recognizing the significant contribution of the Convention for the Unification of Certain Rules Relating to International Carriage by Air signed in Warsaw on 12 October 1929, hereinafter referred to as the 'Warsaw Convention', and other related instruments to the harmonization of private international air law;*
> *Recognizing the need to modernize and consolidate the Warsaw Convention and related instruments;*
> *Recognizing the importance of ensuring protection of the interests of consumers in international carriage by air and the need for equitable compensation based on the principle of restitution;*
> *Reaffirming the desirability of an orderly development of international air transport operations and the smooth flow of passengers, baggage and cargo in accordance with the principles and objectives of the Convention on International Civil Aviation, done at Chicago on 7 December 1944;*
> *Convinced that collective State action for further harmonization and codification of certain rules governing international carriage by air through a new Convention is the most adequate means of achieving an equitable balance of interests;*
> *Have agreed as follows: [...].*

The Montreal Convention was adopted to eliminate in their entirety the passenger liability limits. It modernized important provisions of the Warsaw Convention and The Hague Protocol concerning compensation for the victims of air disasters. This Convention is designed to be a special universal treaty to govern air carrier liability around the world. The rules affecting air carrier liability provide for greater certainty among air carriers.

The States Parties to this Convention recognize the importance of ensuring the protection of the interests of consumers in international carriage by air and the need for equitable compensation based on the principle of restitution. Passengers will benefit from fairer compensation and greater protection. Shippers and those involved in the cargo supply chain will benefit from the ability to make claims without the need for expensive and time-consuming litigation.

The provisions of the Convention reaffirm the desirability of an orderly and safe development of international air transport in order to handle the flow of passengers, baggage and cargo uninterrupted in accordance with the principles and objectives of the 1944 Chicago Convention. The transition to electronic versions of tickets and airway bills and other documents will facilitate efficiency and faster air cargo shipments.

The general belief is that collective State action for further harmonization and codification of certain rules governing international carriage by air through a new treaty will be the most adequate means of achieving a fair balance of interests. The main objective of this Convention is to bring the liability limitations and documentation requirements into line with the rapid economic, legal and commercial changes, occurring throughout the commercial aviation nations worldwide. These are credible reasons why IATA is calling for universal ratification.

In essence, the obvious innovation is that this Convention has tried to successfully address the problems that accumulated in the Warsaw System by means of substantially raising liability limits of air carriers, updating the language and terminology used and presenting the liability framework in a single consistent legal instrument. All in all, it is a modern treaty instead of the fragmented collection of six different legal instruments, together forming the Warsaw System, which implied a corresponding loss of relevance for the travelling public and the aviation industry.

Contrary to the 1929 Warsaw Convention, the 1999 Montreal Convention is expressed in all ICAO official languages.[13]

The IATA Inter-carrier Agreement on Passenger Liability (IIA) and the Montreal Protocol No. 4, facilitating the application of electronic commerce to international air cargo, represented together a reasonable interim position, a short-term solution, to the issue of creating a modernized uniform liability regime for international air transport, which is the Montreal Convention, as a replacement for the Warsaw System.

In 1995, IATA initiated studies on the cost impact on air carriers of an enhanced liability package, and considered effective and appropriate means to secure complete compensation for passengers, when needed. Subsequently, IATA convened a worldwide Airline Liability Conference in Washington D.C., from 19 to 23 June 1995. The conference established two working groups to further study and prepare drafts for a proposed inter-carrier agreement on liability. The resulting IIA was unanimously endorsed on 31 October 1995.

Consequently, certain benefits for passengers provided by the Montreal Convention were already provided under the IATA IIA, however, not embodied in law. The international air carriers who signed this Inter-carrier Agreement would undertake to waive the liability limits and limit the *force majeure* defence in regard to passenger claims. In fact, international air carriers have acted together on a voluntary basis under the IIA to in-

---

13 Tompkins Jr., G.N., *Liability Rules Applicable to International Air Transportation as Developed by the Courts in the United States, from Warsaw 1929 to Montreal 1999*, Alphen aan den Rijn: Kluwer Law International, 2010, Chapter 2 The Evolution of the Montreal Convention 1999. *See also* Budd, L., Ison, S. (Eds.), *Air Transport Management: An International Perspective*, Milton Park, Abingdon, Oxon: Routledge, 2017, p.10.

crease the inadequate limits of liability of the Warsaw System, to the benefit of airline passengers. IATA made an intense effort to elaborate acceptable provisions to implement the IIA by means of the IATA Agreement on Measures to Implement the Inter-carrier Agreement (MIA), effective on 1 April 1997.

The substantive principles of the MIA are as follows.

> The MIA was drawn up in an effort to provide some uniformity in the manner in which signatory carriers would implement the substantive principles of the IIA. The MIA obligates signatory carriers to incorporate in their conditions of carriage and tariffs, where necessary, the following provisions:
> 1. [Carrier] shall not invoke the limitations of liability in Article 22(1) of the Convention (Warsaw Convention) as to any claim for recoverable compensatory damages arising under Article 17 of the Convention;
> 2. [Carrier] shall not avail itself of any defence under Article 20(1) of the Convention with respect to that portion of such claim which does not exceed 100,000 SDRs.[14]

Incidentally, in the same year, ICAO started the immense task of creating a modernized liability regime for international air transport, resulting in the Montreal Convention, completed at the May 1999 International Conference on Air Law in Montreal. However, to achieve international consensus on modernization was a hard nut to crack, not only because of differences in the objectives and legal systems of ICAO Member States, but also, especially, the vastly different liability regimes originated by treaties and voluntary agreements, respectively signed by States and air carriers.

Air carriers that signed those voluntary agreements do not accept strict liability up to 100,000 SDRs, and no provisions are incorporated to protect against inflation. Furthermore, those agreements do not contain the invaluable fifth jurisdiction, supplementing the four bases of jurisdiction provided for under the Warsaw Convention, as codified in Article 33.2 of the Montreal Convention and do not assure passengers and cargo consignors of recourse against both the contracting carrier and the actual carrier operating the flight in case of code-sharing operations. A key element of the Montreal Convention is the benefit of uniformity.

Montreal Convention, Chapter III Liability of the Carrier and Extent of Compensation for Damage, Article 33, Jurisdiction:

1. An action for damages must be brought, at the option of the plaintiff, in the territory of one of the States Parties, either before the court of the domicile of the carrier or of

---

14 Dagtoglou, P.D., Ehlers, P.N. (Eds.), *Airline Liability: A Seminar on Liability and Claims Handling in the Airline and Aerospace Industries*, European Air Law Association Conference Papers 11, Athens: Ant.N. Sakkoulas Publishers, 1997, p. 26.

its principal place of business, or where it has a place of business through which the contract has been made or before the court at the place of destination.

2. In respect of damage resulting from the death or injury of a passenger, an action may be brought before one of the courts mentioned in Paragraph 1 of this article, or in the territory of a State Party in which at the time of the accident the passenger has his or her principal and permanent residence and to or from which the carrier operates services for the carriage of passengers by air, either on its own aircraft or on another carrier's aircraft pursuant to a commercial agreement, and in which that carrier conducts its business of carriage of passengers by air from premises leased or owned by the carrier itself or by another carrier with which it has a commercial agreement.

3. For the purpose of Paragraph 2,
   a) 'commercial agreement' means an agreement, other than an agency agreement, made between carriers and relating to the provision of their joint services for carriage of passengers by air;
   b) 'principal and permanent residence' means the one fixed and permanent abode of the passenger at the time of the accident. The nationality of the passenger shall not be the determining factor in this regard.

4. Questions of procedure shall be governed by the law of the court seized of the case.

The Montreal Convention provides for:
- unlimited liability in the event of death or injury of passengers;
- advanced payments to meet immediate needs;
- the possibility of bringing a law suit before the court in the passenger's principal place of residence;
- increased liability limits in the event of delay;
- the modernization of transport documents (electronic airway bills and tickets);
- the clarification of the rules on the respective liability of the contractual carrier and the actual carrier;
- the obligation for air carriers to maintain adequate insurance; and
- preservation of all key benefits achieved for the air cargo industry by Montreal Protocol No. 4.

The 1999 Montreal Convention, in force and widely ratified, was a success with respect to all key U.S. policy objectives, albeit contrary to the U.S. position with regard to the Warsaw System, with the exception of the Montreal Protocol No. 4 of which the United States has been a Party.[15]

In Europe, both Council Regulation (EC) No. 2027/97 of 9 October 1997 on air carrier liability in the event of air accidents and Regulation (EC) No. 889/2002 of the European Parliament and of the Council of 13 May 2002 deal with liability, a proper level of compensation for passengers involved in air accidents and the reinforcement of the protection of passengers and their dependants.[16]

Regulation (EC) No. 889/2002 amends Council Regulation (EC) No. 2027/97 in order to align it with the provisions of the Montreal Convention, thereby creating a uniform system of liability regarding international air transport. The Regulations harmonized liability limits and legal defences in respect of EU carriers, irrespective of whether the accident should happen on an internal, intra-Community or international flight.[17]

The Montreal Convention has maintained the core provisions which have served the international air transport community from 1929. Under this Convention, air carriers are strictly liable for proven damage up to 100,000 SDRs; where damages of more than 113,000 SDRs (approximately €125,000) are sought, the carrier may avoid liability by proving that the accident which caused the injury or death was not due to their negligence or was attributable to the negligence of a third party.

If a passenger is killed or injured, the air carrier must make an advance payment to cover immediate economic needs within 15 days from the identification of the person entitled to compensation. In the event of death, the payment shall not be less than 16,000 SDRs (approximately €20,000).

The limits of liability prescribed in Articles 21 (compensation in case of death or injury of passengers), 22 (limits of liability in relation to delay, baggage and cargo) and 23 (conversion of monetary units) shall be reviewed by the depositary at five-year intervals. The first such review of limits shall take place at the end of the fifth year following the date of entry into force of the Convention, or if the Convention does not enter into force within five years of the date at which it was first open for signature, within the first

---

15 *See also* Message from the President of the United States Transmitting Protocol to Amend the Convention for the Unification of Certain Rules Relating to International Carriage by Air signed at Warsaw on 12 October 1929, Done at The Hague, 28 September 1955 (The Hague Protocol), 17th Congress, Second Session, Senate, Treaty Doc 107-14, Letter of Submittal, The Secretary of State, Washington D.C., U.S. Government Printing Office, 15 June 2002, pp. V-XIV.

16 Council Regulation (EC) No. 2027/97 of 9 October 1997 on air carrier liability in respect of the carriage of passengers and their baggage by air, *OJ EC* L 285/1, 17.10.1997. This Regulation aims to harmonize the rules on air carrier liability and improve the level of compensation and protection of passengers involved in air accidents. Regulation (EC) No. 889/2002 of the European Parliament and of the Council of 13 May 2002 amending Council Regulation (EC) No. 202797 on air carrier liability in the event of accidents, *OJ EC* L 140/2, 30.5.2002.

17 *See also* Regulation (EC) No. 785/2004 of the European Parliament and of the Council of 21 April 2004 on insurance requirements for air carriers and aircraft operators, *OJ EU* L 138/1, 30.4.2004, and Commission Regulation (EU) No. 285/2010 of 6 April 2010 amending Regulation (EC) No. 785/2004, *OJ EU* L 87/19, 7.4.2010.

year of its entry into force, by reference to an inflation factor which corresponds to the accumulated rate of inflation since the previous revision or in the first instance since the date of entry into force of the Convention. For the most recent review (2014), the inflation factor was determined to be below the threshold stipulated to trigger an adjustment. Accordingly, the limits of liability will remain at their present levels for the next five years.

Limits of liability in relation to delay, baggage and cargo are outlined as follows:

In case of passenger delay, the air carrier is liable for damage unless it took all reasonable measures to avoid the damage or it was impossible to take such measures. The liability for passenger delay is limited to 4,694 SDRs (approximately €5,100). The liability for baggage delay under the same conditions is limited to 1,131 SDRs (approximately €1,230).

The air carrier is liable for destruction, loss or damage to baggage up to 1,131 SDRs. In the case of checked baggage it is liable even if not at fault, unless the baggage was defective. In the case of unchecked baggage, the carrier is liable only if at fault.

If the air carrier actually performing the flight is not the same as the contracting air carrier, the passenger has the right to address a complaint or to make a claim for damages against either. If the baggage is damaged, delayed, lost or destroyed, the passenger must write and complain to the air carrier as soon as possible. In the case of damage to checked baggage, the passenger must write and complain within seven days, and in the case of delay within 21 days, in both cases from the date on which the baggage was placed at the passenger's disposal.

Montreal Convention, Chapter V, Carriage by Air Performed by a Person other than the Contracting Carrier,

Article 45, Addressee of claims:

> In relation to the carriage performed by the actual carrier, an action for damages may be brought, at the opinion of the plaintiff, against that carrier or the contracting carrier, or against both together or separately. If the action is brought against only one of those carriers, that carrier shall have the right to require the other carrier to be joined in the proceedings, the procedure and effects being governed by the law of the court seized of the case.

Article 46, Additional jurisdiction:

> Any action for damages contemplated in Article 45 must be brought, at the opinion of the plaintiff, in the territory of one of the States Parties, either before a court in which action may be brought against the contracting carrier, as provided in Article 33, or before the court having jurisdiction at the place where the actual carrier has its domicile or its principal place of business.

For passengers travelling to/from States which have not ratified the Montreal Convention, the Warsaw Convention and its subsequent amending legal instruments may govern air carriers' liability for accidents and other incidents in international carriage by air. The applicable treaty, however, is determined based on the most advanced regime that is in effect in both the origin and destination of each passenger and not that of the particular flight. If a specific passenger transits a State that has not ratified the Montreal Convention on a journey between two States that have ratified the treaty, the Montreal Convention will apply throughout that journey.

Summarizing, it can be said that the Montreal Convention modernizes and consolidates the international legal regime which has been established pursuant to the 1929 Warsaw Convention and its various amending instruments, the Warsaw System. The Montreal Convention facilitates the use of simplified and modernized documents of carriage, passenger tickets and air waybills, thus enabling the utilization of electronic or computerized data processing for the issuance of these documents.[18]

The Warsaw System, apart from the Montreal Convention, consists of a number of legal instruments which apply individually, partially or entirely, depending on whether or not signed by States, independent from applicable domestic law in certain cases. This patchwork of still existing liability regimes, causing unsatisfactory and economically dependent liability limits, insufficient ratifications of legal instruments, practically not yet in force, intended to amend the Warsaw Convention and The Hague Protocol, resulted in unfairness, confusion and complexity as well as unnecessarily complicated claim handling and litigation.

In 2016, the ICAO Assembly, recognizing the importance of achieving a universal regime to govern airline liability to passengers and shippers on international flights, and the desirability of an equitable, fair and convenient system for compensation for losses, urges all Contracting States, through a promotional statement, to support and encourage the universal adherence to the 1999 Montreal Convention, and urges all Contracting States that have not done so to become Parties to this Convention as soon as possible, and directs the Secretary General to provide assistance, as appropriate, with the ratification process if so requested by a Contracting State.[19]

3.2 GENEVA CONVENTION 1948

Convention on the International Recognition of Rights in Aircraft

---

18 Lawrence, R.Z., Drzeniek-Hanouz, M., Moavenzadeh, J. (Eds.), The Global Enabling Trade Report 2009, Smith, S., Moosberger, M., Chapter 1.4, *IATA e-Freight: Taking the Paper out of Air Cargo*.

19 ICAO Assembly Resolution A39-9 Promotion of the Montreal Convention of 1999 – 39th Session Montreal, 27 September-6 October 2016.

As early as 1931, CITEJA began to study the question of the development of a convention on aircraft mortgages. With the knowledge that financing aircraft would be crucial for the development and expansion of the post-war aviation industry, the manufacturers and air carriers agreed to work on this issue. While World War II was entering its final stages in 1944, the convened Chicago Conference recommended the early adoption of a special convention dealing with the transfer of title to aircraft. It was mainly the U.S. delegation that, convinced of the fact that extensive post-war aircraft sales would take their course, submitted Resolution V that the Conference adopted in its Final Act and Related Documents (ICAO Doc 2187).[20]

In the interest of the future increase in international civil air transport, it seems obvious that rights in aircraft should be recognized internationally. Shortly after the war, this important issue was studied by the Interim Assembly of PICAO in 1946. A year later, the CITEJA drafts were studied by the ICAO Legal Committee during its first full Session at Brussels from 10 to 25 September 1947.

The result was a document which was deliberated at Geneva during the Second Assembly Session from 1 to 21 June 1948. The final document, formally called the Convention on the International Recognition of Rights in Aircraft (Geneva Convention), was adopted by the Assembly on 19 June 1948. It came into force on 17 September 1953.[21]

The Preamble to the Geneva Convention refers explicitly to the recommendation done by the Chicago Conference. This particular Geneva Convention (ICAO Doc 7620) addresses legal questions arising in the ownership, financing and leasing of aircraft. It also sets forth principles for seizure of aircraft, lien priority and other creditors' rights, and judicial sales. In other words, it provides for the recognition by the Contracting States of the rights of property in aircraft, the rights to acquire aircraft by purchase coupled with possession and the rights to possession of aircraft under leases of six months or more.

Those rights must be continuously constituted in accordance with the law of the Contracting State in which the aircraft was registered as to nationality at the time of their constitution, and the rights are regularly recorded in a public record of the Contracting State in which the aircraft is registered as to nationality.

The overall objective of the Geneva Convention is to enhance the international financing and leasing of aircraft. Leasing of engines, considered as main components to be installed in aircraft, in view of the accession doctrine, is subject to risk, and not clearly covered by the Convention. The question concerning the legal status (lease contract) of an engine if installed in or on a specific aircraft or temporarily separated therefrom, shall

---

20 Milde, M., *International Air Law and ICAO*, Essential Air and Space Law Vol. 4, Series Editor Benkö, M.E., Utrecht: Eleven International Publishing, 2008, pp. 260-261.
21 www.icao.int/secretariat/postalhistory/other_international_legal_instruments.htm.

be dealt with in the more recent 2001 Cape Town Convention and additional Aircraft Protocol.[22]

The 1948 Geneva Convention was the first product of ICAO's work in air law.

Preamble,

Whereas the International Civil Aviation Conference, held at Chicago in November-December 1944, recommended the early adoption of a Convention dealing with the transfer of title to aircraft.

Whereas it is highly desirable in the interest of the future expansion of International Civil Aviation that rights in aircraft be recognized internationally.

The undersigned, duly authorized, have agreed, on behalf of their Governments, as follows: [...].

The purpose of this Convention is:

To facilitate the financing for the purchase of aircraft employed in international air services.

To protect secured creditors (banks) who lend money on the security of aircraft (through the standard form of a mortgage).

To protect third parties dealing in or with aircraft against hidden charges.

To define and protect privileged and priority claims against aircraft.

To facilitate the transfer of aircraft from one nationality to another.

Article XVI:

For the purpose of this Convention the term 'aircraft' shall include the airframe, engines, propellers, radio apparatus, and all other articles intended for the use in the aircraft whether installed therein or temporarily separated therefrom.

In general, this Geneva Convention deals with the international recognition of rights in aircraft and is designed to secure recognition on an international basis of property and other rights in aircraft so that when an aircraft crosses a frontier, the interests of holders of such rights will be still protected. It encourages investors to make financial assistance possible for the purchase of new aircraft to be employed in international civil aviation.[23]

---

22 Mendes de Leon, P.M.J. (Ed.), *From Lowlands to High Skies: A Multilevel Jurisdictional Approach towards Air Law*, Leiden: Koninklijke Brill, 2013, p. 220.
23 IATA Bulletin Volumes 24-25 (1956), p. 68.

Article I:

1. The Contracting States undertake to recognize:
   (a) Rights of property in aircraft.
   (b) Rights to acquire aircraft by purchase coupled with possession of the aircraft.
   (c) Rights to possession of aircraft under leases of six months or more.
   (d) Mortgages, hypothèques and similar rights in aircraft which are contractually created as security for payments of the indebtedness;
   provided that such rights:
   i.   have been constituted in accordance with the law of the Contracting State in which the aircraft was registered as to nationality at the time of their constitution, and
   ii. are regularly recorded in a public record of the Contracting State in which the aircraft is registered as to nationality.
   The regulation of successive recordings in different Contracting States shall be determined in accordance with the law of the State where the aircraft was registered as to nationality at the time of each recording.
2. Nothing in this Convention shall prevent the recognition of any right in aircraft under the law of any Contracting State; but Contracting States shall not admit or recognize any right as taking priority over the rights mentioned in Paragraph 1 of this article.

The Geneva Convention provides that the law of the State of Registry of the aircraft in question is the applicable law for rights and interests covered by it but gives no guidance as to whether such law is the domestic law only of that State or includes that State's private international law rules.

The Convention on International Interests in Mobile Equipment, signed at Cape Town on 16 November 2001 (Cape Town Convention), together with the Protocol on International Interests in Mobile Equipment on Matters Specific to Aircraft Equipment, signed at Cape Town on 16 November 2001 (Aircraft Protocol) provide that references therein to applicable law are to the domestic law of the State in question. However, relevant references therein to applicable law are few and international interests under the Cape Town Convention are *sui generis* interests not dependent on national law.

The Cape Town Convention shall, for a Contracting State that is a Party to the Geneva Convention, supersede that Convention as it relates to aircraft, as defined in the Aircraft Protocol, and to aircraft objects. However, with respect to rights or interests not covered or affected by the present Cape Town Convention, the Geneva Convention shall not be superseded.[24]

The Geneva Convention has been described as ill-suited to handle the demands of modern asset-based and lease-based financing. It must be considered as a stage or intermediate phase in the development of an effective system of international protection for securities on aircraft.

The relationship between the Geneva Convention and the Cape Town Convention, together, in the context of aircraft, with the Aircraft Protocol is not always fully understood.

3.3   ROME CONVENTION REGIME

Air Carrier Liability to Third Parties Regime

The first attempt to establish a worldwide uniform regime relating to liability for damage caused by foreign aircraft to third parties on the surface was the conclusion of the 1933 Rome Convention. The starting point of this liability regime, the burden of near absolute liability on the operator of the aircraft, was the protection of innocent humans and random property on the ground. The 1933 Rome Convention and the second attempt, the 1952 Rome Convention, were not widely accepted or ratified for various reasons, however, mainly due to the low interest of leading aviation States. The Rome Conventions were amended by the 1978 Montreal Protocol, which regulated some insurance aspects, for example raising the liability limits.

It was followed by the 2009 Convention on Compensation for Damage to Third Parties, Resulting from Acts of Unlawful Interference Involving Aircraft (Unlawful Interference Compensation Convention), as well as the 2009 Convention on Compensation for Damage Caused by Aircraft to Third Parties (General Risk Convention). The horrific terrorist attacks on targets in New York and Washington D.C. on 11 September 2001 were undoubtedly the impetus for the conclusion of these Conventions, although neither of these instruments received the required quorum with regard to ratification and entry into force. The opinion of some States is that the issue of ground damage is adequately covered by their existing national laws, which often creates unlimited strict liability.

---

24   Protocol to the Convention on International Interests in Mobile Equipment on Matters Specific to Aircraft Equipment, Art. XXIII – Relationship with the Convention on the International Recognition of Rights in Aircraft.

3.3.1 ROME CONVENTION 1933

Convention for the Unification of Certain Rules Relating to Damage Caused by Foreign Aircraft to Third Parties on the Surface
Convention for the Unification of Certain Rules Relating to the Precautionary Attachment of Aircraft

The advent of flying machines, but above all the unbridled development of commercial air transport after World War I gave rise to an oppressive awareness and concern regarding the possibility of human death or injury and damage to property on the ground caused by foreign aircraft. In other words, the operation of aircraft could cause damage on the surface to persons who are not in a contractual relation with the operator of the aircraft.

The 1933 Rome Convention was a consequence of the fact that in the late 1920s the League of Nations formally recognized the need for agreement on rules regarding liability for surface damage caused in international flight, which at that time was not covered by any international regulation to have formal assurance of any redress.[25]

The Rome Convention covers damage caused directly to persons and property on the ground in a Contracting State by aircraft registered in a foreign State that is also Party to the Convention. In the case of damage caused to persons and property in the territory of a Contracting State by an aircraft from a non-Party, or by an aircraft registered in that Contracting State, compensation would be governed by domestic law. In those particular cases, the compensation would not be limited by the Rome Convention, but it may be limited by applicable domestic legislation.

This deficiency, from a legal point of view, gave rise to the need to guarantee that sufficient funds would be available to compensate for the damage on the ground, caused by the operation of aircraft.

CITEJA already started to work on the issue as early as 1930. The Third International Diplomatic Conference on Private Air Law (the previous ones had been held in 1925 at Paris and in 1933 at Warsaw), held at the *Accademia dei Lincei, Palazzo Corsini*, Rome, adopted in 1933 two Conventions simultaneously on the subjects of liability in case of damage on the ground caused by foreign aircraft and of safeguarding aircraft from precautionary arrest:

---

25 Brown, E.G., The Rome Convention of 1933 and 1952: Do They Point a Moral, 28 *J. Air L. & Com.* 418 (1962), pp. 421-441.

1. The Convention for the Unification of Certain Rules Relating to Damage by Foreign Aircraft to Third Parties on the Surface; and
2. The Convention for the Unification of Certain Rules Relating to the Precautionary Attachment of Aircraft.[26]

Both Conventions were signed on 29 May 1933 by 20 States. The intention of the Rome Convention (Precautionary Attachment of Aircraft) was to immunize air transport, or at least to play a preventive role in safeguarding of aircraft from precautionary attachment by means of enumerating the categories of aircraft not liable to attachment (Art. 3), and indicating the manner in which such action may be prevented (Art. 4). Prevention was extremely important to ward off the air transport operation of an air carrier coming to a possible halt.

The purpose of the other Rome Convention (Damage to Third Parties) was to ensure adequate compensation for persons who suffer damage caused on the surface by foreign aircraft while limiting the liabilities of those responsible for such damage in a reasonable manner with a view not to hinder the highly probable development of international air transport. In short, it provided liability imposed on the responsible operator of the aircraft, while the liability limits depended on the weight of the aircraft and it required financial guarantees or insurance coverage from the operator.[27]

The 1933 Conventions did not achieve wide acceptance, as was the case with the international unification of private air law due to the outbreak of World War II. Just before the outbreak of this war, the Rome Convention (Damage to Third Parties) was amended by the Brussels Protocol, adopted by the Fourth International Conference on Private Air Law, signed on 29 September 1938 (Protocol Supplementing to the Convention for the Unification of Certain Rules Relating to Damage Caused by Foreign Aircraft to Third Parties on the Surface), though this did not achieve wide acceptance either.

This Protocol permitted insurers to use some basic defences and regulated certain insurance aspects of the Rome Convention (Damage to Third Parties). This Rome Convention and the Brussels Protocol were superseded by the new 1952 Rome Convention on the same subject as a result of several years of work by the ICAO Legal Committee. The 1952 Rome Convention embraced the principles laid down in the former Rome Convention and the Brussels Protocol.[28]

The Protocol to the Convention on International Interests in Mobile Equipment on Matters Specific to Aircraft Equipment (Aircraft Protocol) of 2001 states that the 2001

---

26 Art. 2(1): By precautionary attachment within the meaning of the present Convention shall be understood any act, whatever it may be called, whereby an aircraft is seized, in a private interest, through the medium of agents of justice or of the public administration, for the benefit either of a creditor, or of the owner, or of the holder of a lien on the aircraft, where the attaching claimant cannot invoke a judgement and execution, obtained beforehand in the ordinary course of procedure, or an equivalent right of execution.
27 www.icao.int/secretariat/PostalHistory/the_rome_convention_and_its_modernization.htm.
28 Kean, A. (Ed.), *Essays in Air Law*, The Hague: Martinus Nijhoff Publishers, 1982, pp. 181-183.

Cape Town Convention shall, for a contracting State that is Party to the Convention for the Unification of Certain Rules Relating to the Precautionary Attachment of Aircraft, supersede that Convention as it relates to aircraft, as defined in this Protocol. However, a Contracting State Party to the above Convention may declare, at the time of ratification, acceptance, approval of, or accession to this Protocol, that it will not apply this article.[29]

The 1938 Brussels Conference simultaneously adopted a Convention entitled: Convention for the Unification of Certain Rules Relating to the Assistance and Rescue of Aircraft or by Aircraft at Sea. However, this Convention never came into effect.

3.3.2 Rome Convention 1952

Convention on Damage Caused by Foreign Aircraft to Third Parties on the Surface

After the war, ICAO returned to the subject when it requested the Legal Committee to resume the studies of liabilities to third parties. In the fall of 1952, ICAO convened a Diplomatic Conference on International Air Law at Rome, attended by representatives and observers from 30 States and seven different international organizations, at the invitation of the Italian government.

The Rome Convention, formally called the Convention on Damage Caused by Foreign Aircraft to Third Parties on the Surface, was signed at Rome on 7 October 1952. It entered into force on 4 February 1958, and as of 2013 has been ratified by 49 States. However, Canada, Nigeria and Australia, as previous States Parties, have denounced the treaty, mainly because they deemed the limits of liability no longer appropriate. Another important argument was that the geographical size of a State is relevant in the context of ratifying the Rome Convention, since this Convention deals with damage done on the surface of the Earth by aircraft.

This is in contrast to the Warsaw System liability which deals not with the territory, but with liability towards passengers and shippers. The latter form of liability can be on a contractual or tortious basis in nature, while the Rome Convention liability is a form of third party liability which is considered always tortious (unlawful act) in nature.

Aircraft collisions are hardly covered at all by both Rome Conventions. Only Article 7 indicates that when two aircraft have collided or interfered with each other in flight and damage for which a right to compensation results, or when two or more aircraft have jointly caused such damage, the operator of each aircraft shall be liable to a third party.[30]

---

29 Chapter V, Relationship with other Conventions, Art. XXIV of the Cape Town Protocol 2001. Art. I (a): 'aircraft' means aircraft as defined for the purposes of the Chicago Convention which are either airframes with aircraft engines installed thereon or helicopters.

30 Hodgkinson, D.I., Johnson, R. (Eds.), *International Air Carrier Liability: Safety and Security*, Milton Park, Abingdon, Oxon: Routledge, 2017, p. 208.

The 1952 Rome Convention (ICAO Doc 7364) was an amended version of the original 1933 Rome Convention and was intended to unify, at an international level, the law relating to recovery by persons who suffer damage caused on the surface by foreign aircraft, while limiting the liabilities of those responsible for such damage. Furthermore, the latest Rome Convention deals with a large number of related matters like apportionment of claims, financial security requirements, jurisdiction and enforcement of judgements.

The 1952 Rome Convention actually addresses the rights of third parties which suffered damage from events involving aircraft. In other words, any person who suffers damage on the surface, shall, upon proof only that the damage was caused by an aircraft in flight or by any person or thing falling out or separated from it, be entitled to compensation. Liability for death or personal injury is rather limited, however, with the values expressed in 'gold francs' and varying by the weight of the aircraft involved.

The United States, The United Kingdom and France never became Parties to the Convention, for several compelling reasons. Especially the U.S. delegation opposed the content of the draft at an early stage by considering the low liability limits as being unrealistic.[31]

The first two articles of the original text of the 1952 Rome Convention:

Chapter I Principles of liability.

Article 1:

1. Any person who suffers damage on the surface shall, upon proof only that the damage was caused by an aircraft in flight or by any person or thing falling there from, be entitled to compensation as provided by this Convention. Nevertheless there shall be no right to compensation if the damage is not a direct consequence of the incident giving rise thereto, or if the damage results from the mere fact of passage of the aircraft through the airspace in conformity with existing air traffic regulations.
2. For the purpose of this Convention, an aircraft is considered to be in flight from the moment when power is applied for the purpose of actual take-off until the moment when the landing run ends. In the case of an aircraft lighter than air, the expression 'in flight' relates to the period from the moment when it becomes detached from the surface until it becomes again attached thereto.

---

31 Haanappel, P.P.C., *The Law and Policy of Air Space and Outer Space, A Comparative Approach*, The Hague: Kluwer Law International, 2003, pp. 85-88.

Article 2:

1. The liability for compensation contemplated by Article 1 of this Convention shall attach to the operator of the aircraft.
   (a) For the purposes of this Convention the term 'operator' shall mean the person who was making use of the aircraft at the time the damage was caused, provided that if control of the navigation of the aircraft was retained by the person from whom the right to make use of the aircraft was derived, whether directly or indirectly, that person shall be considered the operator.
   (b) A person shall be considered to be making use of an aircraft when he is using it personally or when his servants or agents are using the aircraft in the course of their employment, whether or not within the scope of their authority.
2. The registered owner of the aircraft shall be presumed to be the operator and shall be liable as such unless, in the proceedings for the determination of his liability, he proves that some other person was the operator and, in so far as legal procedures permit, takes appropriate measures to make that other person a party in the proceedings.

If the Rome Convention is not applicable, then the local law of a State, either general tort law, usually based upon fault or negligence, or law specifically developed for damage done by aircraft on the surface, usually based upon strict liability, will be applicable. However, in many States, not being Party to the Rome Convention, the national law is applicable to strict liability regarding damage caused by aircraft, whether it is national- or foreign-registered, on the surface of the Earth. In fact, national law will always apply in circumstances where damage is caused on the surface to persons or property by national aircraft.

In view of modernizing the 1952 Rome Convention, the ICAO Legal Committee created in the 1960s a subcommittee on this Convention to determine why States were not ratifying it, and to make proposals to overcome apparent obstacles.

ICAO continued studies related to this Convention. Many years later, an International Conference on Air Law was convened at Montreal from 6 to 23 September 1978. The Montreal Protocol, formally the Protocol to Amend the Convention on Damage Caused by Foreign Aircraft to Third Parties on the Surface was adopted and signed on 23 September 1978 (ICAO Doc 9257). It especially increased the limits of liability as determined by the 1952 Rome Convention, and expressed these limits in SDRs, a unit of account based on a basket of currencies. The 1978 Montreal Protocol entered into force on 25 July 2002.[32]

However, neither the 1952 Rome Convention nor the 1978 Montreal Protocol have received wide acceptance, mainly because of the fact that the limits of liability, the regime

---

32 www.icao.int/sevretariat/PostalHistory/the_rome_convention_and_its_modernization.htm.

of absolute liability, the jurisdictional clauses and provisions relating to financial security in both documents are perceived as inadequate and regarded as most unsatisfactory.

Another compelling reason, apart from the maximum liability amounts being considered as too low, was the controversial but also unsolved subject expressed by some States to define clear regulations in the Rome Convention to compensate for (environmental, structural) damage caused by (supersonic) aircraft noise and sonic boom, the sound associated with shock waves created when an aircraft travels at supersonic speeds.[33]

3.3.3 MONTREAL CONVENTION 2009

Convention on Compensation for Damage Caused by Aircraft to Third Parties
Convention on Compensation for Damage to Third Parties, Resulting from Acts of Unlawful Interference Involving Aircraft

The current effort to revise the 1952 Rome Convention began soon after the adoption of the 1999 Montreal Convention, a treaty as a replacement of the 1929 Warsaw Convention and its various amending instruments. The ICAO Legal Committee started the modernization cycle coincidentally in a turbulent and dramatic time period. The terrorist attacks on New York and Washington D.C. on 11 September 2001 demonstrated that the potential for death, injury and damage was euphemistically a bit bigger than previously thought. Civil aircraft were used as lethal weapons. This horrific scenario has sharpened the need for a modernized regime that accounts for both ordinary accidents as a result of safety-related matters and accidents as the results of unlawful interference.

The modernization was initiated by a Swedish proposal containing text to be included in the ICAO Legal Committee work programme on the subject: Consideration of the Modernization of the Convention on Damage Caused by Foreign Aircraft to Third Parties on the Surface, signed at Rome on 7 October 1952.

A study was carried out by a Special Group after an approval of the Council for priority, followed by a questionnaire of the ICAO Secretariat with a number of replies prompted by the developments in the wake of the attacks on 11 September 2001. The majority of the respondents argued that they would support a liability regime similar to the adopted 1999 Montreal Convention with a two-tier system with a strict liability regime up to a fixed limit, with unlimited liability on top based on presumed fault of the operator. The Special Group on the modernization of the 1952 Rome Convention developed two draft Conventions:

---

33 Giemulla, E.M., Weber, L., *International and EU Aviation Law: Selected Issues*, Alphen aan den Rijn: Kluwer Law International, 2011, pp. 274-275. *See also* Videla Escalada, F.N., *Aeronautical Law*, Alphen aan den Rijn: Sijthoff & Noordhoff International Publishers, 1979, pp. 602-608.

1. Convention on Compensation for Damage to Third Parties, Resulting from Acts of Unlawful Interference Involving Aircraft (Unlawful Interference Compensation Convention) (ICAO Doc 9920); and
2. Convention on Compensation for Damage Caused by Aircraft to Third Parties (General Risks Convention) (ICAO Doc 9919).

The two draft conventions (incorporated in the 2009 Montreal Convention) were considered and adopted at the International Conference on Air Law on Compensation for Damage Caused by Aircraft to Third Parties Arising from Acts of Unlawful Interference or from General Risks, held at Montreal from 20 April to 2 May 2009.[34]

The States Parties to this Convention recognized the need to ensure adequate compensation for third parties who suffer damage resulting from events involving an aircraft in flight, and to modernize the 1952 Rome Convention and the 1978 Montreal Protocol.[35] Furthermore, they recognized the importance of ensuring the protection of the interests of third-party victims and the need for equitable compensation as well as enabling the continued stability of the aviation industry.

The States Parties reaffirm the desirability of an orderly development of international air transport operations and the smooth flow of passengers, baggage and cargo in accordance with the principles and objectives of the Chicago Convention, and are convinced that collective State action for further harmonization and codification of certain rules governing the compensation of third parties who suffer damage resulting from events involving aircraft in flight through a new Convention is the most desirable and effective means of achieving an equitable balance of interests.

The first legal instrument adopted by the Conference is the Unlawful Interference Compensation Convention (ICAO Doc 9920), which encompasses acts of terrorism, and caps the operator's liability in return for strict liability. This Convention applies to damage to third parties which occurs in the territory of a State Party caused by an aircraft in flight as a result of an act of unlawful interference when the operator is based in another State whether or not a Party to the Convention. The Convention also applies, in certain circumstances, to damage to third parties in a non-State Party where the operator, causing the damage, was a State Party operator.

The air operator's liability is capped according to the weight of the aircraft. If an event involves two or more aircraft operated by the same operator, the limit of liability in respect of the aircraft with the highest maximum mass shall apply (Art. 4, Limit of the operator's liability). Further claims in excess of the fixed cap are to be paid from the International Civil Aviation Compensation Fund (the International Fund), a created

---

34 www.icao.int/secretariat/PostalHistory/rome_convention_and_its_modernization.htm.
35 Montreal Convention 2009, Art. 1- Definitions, For the purpose of this Convention: (c) an aircraft is considered to be 'in flight' at any time from the moment when all its external doors are closed following embarkation or loading until the moment when any such door is opened for disembarkation or unloading.

compensation fund reluctantly contributed to by the operators. Victims are provided compensation from this fund, in addition to that paid by the operator, up to an amount of three billion SDRs (approximately US$ 4.5 billion). In other words, where there is damage for which the operator is liable, the operator will pay up to the level of its cap, and the International Fund will pay additional compensation above and beyond the level of the cap. It is expected that operators will be able to obtain insurance up to the amount of the cap.[36]

The other legal instrument adopted by the Conference is the General Risks Convention (ICAO Doc 9919), which modernizes the current legal framework provided for under the 1952 Rome Convention and the related 1978 Montreal Protocol. It covers cases of damage caused by aircraft as a result of safety-related issues and thus not involving an act of unlawful interference, and provides for full compensation for victims.

The General Risks Convention applies to damage to third parties which occur in the territory of a State Party caused by an aircraft in flight on an international flight other than as a result of an act of unlawful interference. However, if a State Party so declares to the Depository, this Convention shall also apply where an aircraft in flight other than on an international flight causes damage in the territory of that State, other than as a result of an act of unlawful interference (Arts. 2.1 and 2.2, Scope).

This Convention indicates that the operator is subject to strict liability for damage up to a limit and thereafter the operator is only liable in so far as it is negligent.

Air carrier liability to third parties is thus subject to a variety of regimes, whether limited or unlimited and whether based on fault or strict liability.

The comprehensive draft working paper was essentially a consolidation of the 1952 Rome Convention and its 1978 Montreal Protocol, but incorporated a number of aspects from the structure of the 1999 Montreal Convention. However, liability remained the central problem. Although there never has been a functioning global system, and although liability may be strict or fault-based, limited or unlimited, depending on where the accident takes place, the liability regime in each State is relatively clear.

---

36 Mendes de Leon, P.M.J. (Ed.), *From Lowlands to High Skies: A Multilevel Jurisdictional Approach towards Air Law,* Essays in Honour of John Balfour, Leiden: Koninklijke Brill, 2013, p. 235. *See also* ICAO Working Paper A37-WP/31 LE/2, 2. Outcome of the Diplomatic Conference, 3.1 Resolutions 3.1.3. Resolution No. 2 relates to the Unlawful Interference Compensation Convention and the need to undertake preparatory work regarding the International Fund to ensure that it is operational by the time the Convention enters into force. In this regard, the Conference decided to set up, pending the entry into force of the Convention, a Preparatory Commission for the Establishment of the International Civil Aviation Compensation Fund (PCIF), composed of persons nominated by 16 States listed in the Resolution, and Appendix A.5. Pursuant to Art. 8, it is envisaged to create an organization called the International Civil Aviation Compensation Fund (the International Fund) with the principle purposes of paying compensation to persons suffering damage in the territory of a State Party, of providing financial support where an operator from a State Party causes damage in a State non-Party and of deciding whether to provide supplementary compensation to passengers on board an aircraft involved in an event.

The rules of this Convention shall prevail over any rules in the following instruments which would otherwise be applicable to damage covered by the Convention:

1. The Convention on Damage Caused by Foreign Aircraft to Third Parties on the Surface, signed at Rome, on 7 October 1952 (Rome Convention), or
2. The Protocol to Amend the Convention on Damage Caused by Foreign Aircraft to Third Parties on the Surface, signed at Rome, on 7 October 1952, signed at Montreal, on 23 September 1978 (Montreal Protocol).

The objective of this new two-tier Convention structure is to ensure equitable benefits for victims (damages arising from death and bodily injury and for property) while not unduly increasing the economic and regulatory burden on civil air carriers. Combating the effects of terrorism and improving the status of aircraft victims form the fundament of the two new legal air law instruments. The States Parties to the Montreal Convention are convinced that collective State action for further harmonization and codification of certain rules governing the compensation of third parties who suffer damage resulting from events involving aircraft in flight through a new agreement is the most desirable and effective means of achieving an equitable balance of interests.[37]

Overall, the 1952 Rome Convention has received minor interest by States because relevant domestic legislation is already well established with the operator's liability being limited to insurable levels. In addition, noise and sonic boom damage was not covered by the Rome Convention regime.

3.4. CAPE TOWN CONVENTION 2001 AND CAPE TOWN PROTOCOL ON AIRCRAFT EQUIPMENT 2001

Convention on International Interests in Mobile Equipment / Protocol to the Convention on International Interests in Mobile Equipment on Matters Specific to Aircraft Equipment

The Convention on International Interests in Mobile Equipment, and its Protocol on Matters Specific to Aircraft Equipment or the Cape Town Convention and the Aircraft Protocol are together, in general terms, known as the Cape Town Convention.

The Cape Town Convention (ICAO Doc 9793) is an international treaty intended to standardize transactions involving movable property and create international standards for registration of contracts of sale, security interests, leases and conditional sales contracts, and various legal remedies for default in financing agreements, including repossession and the effect of particular bankruptcy laws of States.

---

37 ICAO DCCD Doc No. 43, 1/5/09 (Unlawful Interference Convention). See also ICAO DCCD Doc 42, 1/5/09 (General Risks Convention). Both adopted at the International Diplomatic Conference on Air Law (Montreal, 20 April to 2 May 2009).

There are three specific protocols (aircraft equipment, railway equipment and space assets) to this comprehensive Cape Town Convention of which the Aircraft Protocol (ICAO Doc 9794) applies to movable aviation equipment.

Both the Cape Town Convention and Aircraft Protocol are considered private international air law agreements, but in certain respects they relate to responsibilities of States such as the required International Registration, and as such these legal instruments contain characteristics of public international air law.[38]

The Convention resulted from a Diplomatic Conference held in Cape Town, South Africa in 2001. The Convention was signed on 16 November 2001, and came into force on 1 April 2004. The Aircraft Protocol was signed immediately with the Convention, but took effect on 1 March 2006. As of April 2006, the Protocol has 65 Contracting Parties, which includes 64 States and the European Union.

The Protocol applies to aircraft (airframes) which are type certificated to transport at least eight people or 2750 kilograms of cargo, jet propulsion aircraft engines with thrust exceeding 1750 pounds-force or its equivalent (7800 N) and turbine-powered or piston-powered aircraft engines with at least 550 rated take-off shaft horsepower or its equivalent (410 kW), and helicopters that are type certificated to transport at least five or more persons including crew or goods in excess of 450 kilograms (990 pounds).[39]

In practice, this means that all but the very smallest commercial jet airframes will fall within the application of the Convention. It is important to remember that the engines must be considered separately from the airframe, so that it is possible for the Convention to apply to the engines even if it does not apply to the airframe itself, or the other way around. However, it is fairly unlikely that this will be the case, as an airframe capable of carrying eight persons will ordinarily have installed jet propulsion engines with over 1750 pounds of thrust or its equivalent (Art. I.2).

If the airframe falls outside the Convention but the engines fall within it, then it would be necessary to make a registration within the national register of the State (depending on whether such a register exists) in relation to the airframe and a registration in the International Registry in respect of each engine.

Aviareto Ltd, based in Dublin, Ireland, a joint venture between SITA SC (*Société Internationale de Télécommunications Aéronautiques*) and the Irish government, has a contract with ICAO to establish and operate the International Registry under the legal framework of the Cape Town Convention and the Aircraft Protocol. Aviareto draws on the strengths of SITA and the Irish aviation sector, and performs these functions on a not-for-profit, cost recovery basis, as required by the Cape Town Convention.[40]

---

38 Hanley, D.P., *Aircraft Operating Leasing: A Legal and Practical Analysis in the Context of Public and Private International Air Law*, Second Edition, Alphen aan den Rijn: Kluwer Law International, 2017, Chapter I, Paragraph 1.03 Aim and Methodology.
39 Protocol to the Convention on International Interests in Mobile Equipment on Matters Specific to Aircraft Equipment, Chapter I, Art. 1.
40 www.aviareto.aero/.

Registration takes place in the following way: either party to a particular transaction can register an interest with the consent of the other party. Strictly speaking, registration may only be affected on the International Registry's website by an approved user. However, the Convention provides that Contracting States may at any time designate an entity or entities in its territory as a designated entry point, through which the information for registration is submitted to the International Registry; for example, in the United States, the FAA is the exclusive designated entry point for authorizing the transmission of information to the International Registry.

The Cape Town Convention recognizes the International Registry as an additional place for the filing of interests, including prospective interests, in certain airframes, aircraft engines and helicopters (defined as aircraft objects). It establishes the right for owners of these aircraft to grant an Irrevocable De-Registration and Export Request Authorization (IDERA) to a secured party. IDERA is a remedy to procure the de-registration of the aircraft concerned, and to procure the export and physical transfer of an aircraft object from the territory in which it is situated.[41]

Furthermore it reduces from 750 to 550 rated take-off shaft horsepower the size threshold for aircraft engines eligible to be recorded as collateral in security instruments, and it establishes the Civil Aviation Registry as the Authorizing Entry Point.[42]

The objectives of the Cape Town Convention are:

1. to facilitate the acquisition and financing of international mobile assets by creating rights recognized in all Contracting States;
2. to give creditors resource to basic default and insolvency-related remedies designed to offer rapid relief;
3. to establish an electronic registry of international interests which serves to give notice to third parties and ensures priority;
4. to ensure that the specific needs of the aircraft industry are met; and
5. to give prospective creditors a greater degree of confidence when extending credit to borrowers.

To meet these objectives, the Convention creates the following:

1. an international interest which is recognized in all Contracting States,
2. an electronic international register of interests; and
3. standard rights for creditors on default.

---

41 Kozuka, S. (Ed.), *Implementing the Cape Town Convention and the Domestic Laws on Secured Transactions*, Cham: Springer International Publishing, 2017, 2.1.2.2. The Remedies Available Under the Cape Town Convention.

42 *See also*: The Cape Town Convention and its Protocol on Matters Specific to Aircraft Equipment, 16 November 2001, as adopted in the United States by the Cape Town Treaty Implementation Act of 2004- 9 August 2004.

The principle objective of international aviation finance and lease law is to facilitate the efficient purchase and use of aircraft objects. The special laws make the expensive aircraft, engines and helicopters more available and will reduce their cost. Moreover, the mortgagors and lessors obtain more legal security, which lowers the economic risk.

Chapter IV: International Aviation Institutions and Programmes

4.1   Introductory Note

In this chapter, a number of leading international institutions and programmes related to the regulation of air navigation and aviation safety are being treated. It remains arguable, however, whether or not acts of these institutions or organizations and programmes should be part of the topic international air law. In this regard, the question is if the institutions, organizations or commissions mentioned are vested with regulatory powers, and if aviation safety programmes impose legal obligations on participating States. Although acts of aviation organizations do not fall within the scope of Article 38.1 of the ICJ Statute, it still deserves consideration through a somewhat more extensive explanation. The Statute does not mention the concept of sources of international law, but rather spells out how the court is to decide disputes which may be submitted to it for settlement. The Statute provides for the application of the law.[1]

As far as ICAO is concerned, Assembly resolutions have a legal effect internally, although internal resolutions contain external elements which do have a considerable impact on the regulation of the safety and efficiency of international air navigation. Regulatory material such as resolutions or even guidelines and recommendations could not be attributed to one of the 'axiomatic' sources of international law listed in Article 38(1) of the ICJ Statute, but could fit in the category of quasi-legislation. Assuming that the ICAO regulations are considered quasi-law and therefore, in practice, determine the way in which entities should act, they cover rules which are not usually legally binding but may include some legal force.

First and foremost, the provisions of quasi-law should be prescriptive and not descriptive. Quasi-law provisions must contain specific and precise requirements to do or refrain from doing something. In ICAO, most quasi-law provisions are formulated to specify requirements in the daily operation of aviation activities or to supplement the existing law. [...] The requirement of specificity distinguishes quasi-law from the so-called soft law, which may include vague and imprecise provisions.[2]

---

1   Wallace, R.M.M., *International Law*, Third Edition, London: Sweet & Maxwell, 1997, pp. 7-8.
2   Huang, J., *Aviation Safety through the Rule of Law: ICAO's Mechanism and Practices*, Alphen aan den Rijn: Kluwer Law International, 2009, pp. 192-193.

Soft law exists in international law as well, but it would not necessarily be labelled as a new source of international law.[3] Soft law participates in international law-making and, according to some authors, it contains certain possible legal effects. It makes provisions not precise, but it may modify the meaning, interpretation or content of existing treaty law.

Nevertheless, the challenging question remains if acts of international organizations, unilateral acts of States and soft law are considered potential new sources of international law outside of Article 38 of the ICJ Statute. Malgosia Fitzmaurice (Professor of Public International Law, Department of Law, Queen Mary University of London) observes the following disquisitions concerning acts on the topic:

> Michel Virally (French Professor of International Law) analysed the powers of the United Nations and other international organizations such as ICAO. He examined in particular the internal and external powers of international organizations to adopt unilateral acts. He found that the powers of an international organization to adopt acts which are directed to States was the most complex legal issue.

Related to acts of international organizations are the decisions of the organs set up under Multilateral Environmental Agreements (MEAs), which do not enjoy separate international legal personality but are nonetheless the highest organs established by MEAs. Their decisions, which are directed to States Parties, make general obligations more precise, and even fill gaps in the agreements. This new phenomenon was called 'autonomous institutional arrangements'. The legal status of the decisions is unclear. From a strictly legal point of view, they are not binding. However, they are sometimes referred to as *de facto* law-making, and States endeavour to implement them. Therefore, such practice bypasses the classical consent of States, which, having decided to conclude MEAs, also agree to some future unspecified obligations which arise not from the treaty but from decisions of the treaty-based organs.

There are several possible classifications of unilateral acts of States, which is one of the most daunting tasks, given their various natures and purposes. For example, Virally has classified unilateral acts into acts which are part of the treaty-making process, acts which contribute to the formation of customs and acts which have independent significance in international law. The difficulties of identification and classification of unilateral acts were highlighted in the context of the ILC's 2006 Guiding Principles applicable to uni-

---

3   Soft law, in written form, embraces treaties containing general obligations and non-binding or voluntary resolutions, statements of intent and codes of conduct produced by international and regional organizations and statements by individuals, for example, groups of eminent international lawyers, purporting to articulate international practices (Wallace, R.M.M., *International Law*, Third Edition, London: Sweet & Maxwell, 1997, p. 30).

lateral declarations of States capable of creating legal obligations, the major weakness of which was arguably the absence of practical guidance concerning the juridical character of a unilateral act which leaves the legal framework pertaining to unilateral acts disappointingly opaque. Because of such a great number of unresolved legal issues, unilateral acts may constitute a new source of obligations in international law only in very rare circumstances.

Soft law is even more problematic as a new source of international law, and its character remains inconclusive. The quest for a clear classification has not changed much, as the evolving informality of international law and exponential growth of various soft law declarations blur the distinction between the legal and non-legal, which may be considered dangerous from the point of view of the rule of law.

Samantha Besson (Professor of Public International Law and European Law at the University of Fribourg):

> It is a kind of intermediate international legal outcome whose legality might be questioned and hence whose normativity qua law is almost inexistent.
> Certain provisions of soft law instruments are legally binding and have a normative content due to their evolution into norms of customary international law. Soft law is an important auxiliary mechanism for treaty interpretation, application and development.[4]

ICAO Standards are not fully binding as well, because there is an opt-out rule (Chicago Convention, Article 38, Departures from international standards and procedures), according to which a Contracting State immediately must notify ICAO of the differences between its own practice and that established by the international standard. On the other hand, ICAO possesses formal legislative authority for civil aviation over the high seas, thus in that particular area, no deviation is allowed by virtue of Article 12 of the Chicago Convention. In every respect, ICAO Standards, recognized as minimum international safety standards, are highly authoritative in practice.[5]

Article 12 Chicago Convention

Rules of the Air.

---

4   Besson, S., Aspremont, J. d'. (Eds.), Knuchel, S. (Assistant), *The Oxford Handbook of the Sources of International Law*, Oxford: Oxford University Press, 2017, Chapter 8, The History of Article 38 of the Statute of the International Court of Justice: The Journey from the past to the Present, Part IV, The Past without the Present, by Malgosia Fitzmaurice.

5   Huang, J., *Aviation Safety Through the Rule of Law: ICAO's Mechanism and Practice*, Alphen aan den Rijn: Kluwer Law International, 2009, pp. 192-193. *See also* Joyner, C.C. (Ed.), *The United Nations and International Law*, Cambridge: Cambridge University Press, 1997, pp. 171-177.

> [...] Over the high seas, the rules in force shall be those established under this Convention. Each Contracting State undertakes to insure the prosecution of all persons violating the regulations applicable.

As far as aviation safety is concerned, the ICAO Assembly urges Contracting States to agree to (mandatory) safety audits regulated by the Universal Safety Oversight Audit Programme, but always with the consent of the State to be audited. There is no distinct legal binding force, although Contracting States have a duty to cooperate with the ICAO initiatives, decided by the Assembly and brought into effect by the Council. Theoretically, a State could frustrate or refuse to adhere to audits, although this behaviour certainly will elicit a message of disapproval from the global aviation industry. After all, the ICAO Standards are mainly safety rules which must be as uniform as possible to protect and enhance safety of international civil air transport.

Implementation procedures of ICAO Standards vary from State to State. In addition, Contracting States are not legally bound to act in accordance with the ICAO Standards, which in some cases will lead to deviations from these international standards. Contracting States rather decide whether to transform the ICAO Standards into national laws or regulations, or in some cases deviate from these international standards or not implement them at all. ICAO has no real enforcement powers which implies that non-compliance by Contracting States and its aviation industry, especially air carriers and airports, could have serious consequences, such as being subjected to increased insurance costs.

Even worse, structural non-compliance or neglect of relevant international safety standards, which means ICAO Standards, will cause negative effects in the field of aviation safety that undeniably leads towards any form of blacklisting or possible exclusion from the international air transport system. Such a detrimental situation will immediately affect the operations of a State's air carriers, rather than the State itself.[6]

The European Aviation Safety Agency is a specialized agency of the European Union with regulatory responsibility for civil aviation safety and possesses actual decisional power in individual cases. One of its tasks is to draft implementing rules in all fields pertinent to ensure, among other things, the highest common level of safety protection especially for EU citizens, based on the provisions of the new Basic Regulation. This Regulation (EU) 2018/1139 of the European Parliament and of the Council of 4 July 2018 on common rules in the field of civil aviation and establishing a European Union Aviation Safety Agency, is the most recent revision and has superseded the original Basic Regulation (EC) No. 216/2008 on 11 September 2018.

A European Regulation is a legal act of the EU, having exclusive effect, that becomes immediately enforceable as law in all EU Member States simultaneously as enshrined in

---

6 *See* Mendes de Leon, P.M.J., The Legal Force of ICAO SARPs in a Multilevel Jurisdictional Context, *Journaal Luchtrecht*, No. 2-3, June 2013, Special Edition, Liber Amicorum in Honour of Roderick D. Van Dam, The Hague: Sdu Publishers, pp. 16-17.

Article 249 EEC Treaty, Article 288 TFEU (Treaty on the Functioning of the European Union). The same Treaty allows for a sort of enforcement action by the European Commission (Arts. 169/170 EEC Treaty, Arts. 185/186 TFEU).

While the technical expertise of EASA is reflected in the aviation rulemaking process, the European Commission still retains the overall formal regulatory powers. At the same time, the influence of EASA on EU Member States and beyond regarding implementation, monitoring and interpretation of regulations is to be considered significant. The mandate of EASA covers a variety of regulatory (hard law), certification specifications, acceptable means of compliance and guidance material (soft law) as well as monitoring, investigation and standardization tasks.

EASA's mandate was expanded, among other things, by the SAFA (Safety Assessment of Foreign Aircraft) programme, originally a voluntary programme set up by ECAC in 1996, focusing on air carrier operational performance and compliance.[7]

IATA resolutions could have an internal binding effect. If an IATA resolution is approved by National Aviation Authorities (NAAs), under conditions or restrictions, the other IATA members must decide within 30 days whether the resolution shall be void or whether it shall be binding upon all members with the restrictions or conditions incorporated. Disapproval by a government authority of a resolution or a portion thereof shall normally be considered disapproval of the entire resolution or conditionally only a particular portion.[8]

Both ECAC and EUROCONTROL do not have regulatory powers. Resolutions, recommendations and documents adopted, approved and produced by ECAC as well as guidance material are non-binding. On the other hand, ECAC established under its auspices two international agreements in 1987, dealing respectively with capacity sharing and tariffs, and one international agreement in 1956 on commercial rights of non-scheduled air services as well as another international agreement in 1960 relating to certificates of airworthiness for imported aircraft.[9]

If the qualification of these institutions and programmes, considered to be subsidiary sources of international law, has been designated as overvalued, then at least they are outstanding contributors to and prominent influencers of comprehensive legislative procedures to enhance international civil aviation safety.

---

7   Directive 2004/36/EC of the European Parliament and of the Council of 21 April 2004 on the safety of third-country aircraft using Community airports, *OJ EU* L 143/76 30.4.2004. *See also* Art. 11 Implementation. Member States shall bring into force the laws, regulations and administrative provisions necessary to comply with this Directive by 30 April 2006. They shall forthwith inform the European Commission thereof.

8   Rinck, G., The International Factors in German Air Transport, 33 *J. Air L. & Com.* 102 (1967), p. 107.

9   Multilateral Agreement on Commercial Rights of Non-Scheduled Air Services in Europe (Paris, 30 April 1956). Multilateral Agreement Relating to Certificates of Airworthiness for Imported Aircraft (Paris, 22 April 1960). International Agreement on the Procedure for the Establishment of Tariffs for Scheduled Air Services (Paris, 10 July 1967). International Agreement on the Procedure for the Establishment of Tariffs for Intra-European Scheduled Air Services (Paris, 16 June 1987).

4.2 ICAN/CINA

International Commission for Air Navigation/Commission Internationale de Navigation Aérienne

The first concrete step in effecting international regulation of air navigation was taken by the Aeronautical Commission of the Peace Conference in 1919 (the Aeronautical Commission had its origin in the Inter-Allied Aviation Committee, created in 1917), when it organized the International Air Navigation Conference of 13 October 1919 at Paris, to conclude the 1919 Paris Convention, formally called the Convention Relating to the Regulation of Aerial Navigation, and to begin the process of creating an International Commission for Air Navigation, an international governing body.

In the early years of international civil air transport, numerous conferences, congresses, commissions and committees appeared to deal with multiple issues relating to air navigation at an international level, either exclusively or secondarily. ICAN was one of them, albeit with a permanent status.

ICAN, the precursor of ICAO, under the coordinating direction of the League of Nations, although practically operating autonomously, was to develop international regulations in the field of air navigation in line with the technical progress and the extraordinary expansion of civil aviation. ICAN was particularly working in the field of public international air law. It consisted of representatives of the Contracting States and was provided with a permanent secretariat, located at Paris, from 11 July 1922, when it came into being, until 1946.

ICAN was organized in sub-commissions dealing with various civil aviation-related categories (operational, legal, wireless telegraphy, meteorology, medicine, cartography and equipment), and in Committees (standardization and customs). Article 34 of the Paris Convention outlined the duties of the Commission:

– To receive proposals from or to make proposals to any of the Contracting States for the modification or amendment of the provisions of the Paris Convention, and to notify changes adopted.
– To carry out duties imposed upon it by the Articles 9, 13, 14, 15, 17, 28, 34, 36 and 37 of the Paris Convention.
– To amend the provisions of the Annexes A-G to the Paris Convention.
– To collect and communicate to the Contracting States information of every kind concerning international air navigation.
– To collect and communicate to the Contracting States all information relating to wireless telegraphy, meteorology and medical science which may be of interest to air navigation.
– To ensure the publication of maps for air navigation in accordance with the provisions of Annex F.

–   To give its opinion on questions which the Contracting States may submit for examination, subject to weighted consent by the Contracting States (except modifications of Annex provisions).

As mentioned above, one of ICAN's tasks was to keep up-to-date the technical provisions of the Paris Convention. The Annexes to the Convention were declared to have the same effect as the Convention itself (Art. 39), contrary to the Annexes to the 1944 Chicago Convention. ICAN was given limited quasi-legislative powers through its voting system in amending the Annexes, which turned out to be a significant phase in the evolution of international institutions.

Several duties of the later formed ICAO Air Navigation Commission (Chicago Convention, Chapter X) correspond with the ICAN duties.

ICAN was by no means the first and only international organization designed to foster the growth of civil aviation. Some early existing organizations were already dealing exclusively with aviation, such as the International Aeronautical Federation/*Fédération Aéronautique Internationale* (FAI), created on 14 October 1905, an international organization in the field of non-commercial, private aviation. Furthermore, there were the Aircraft International Register (AIR), and the International Air Traffic Association, formed at The Hague in 1919 as the precursor of the International Air Transport Association founded on 19 April 1945 at Havana, as a non-governmental trade association of the world's airlines.[10]

ICAN possessed administrative, legislative, executive and judicial powers, and was an advisory body and a centre of documentation. Until World War II, it was a significant instrument for legislative and regulatory unification, since the Contracting States had to model their domestic legislation and regulations on the provisions of the Paris Convention and its Annexes. Unfortunately, ICAN could not achieve a worldwide scope, due to the fact that the United States, faced with increasingly isolationist policies, and other non-European States, ultimately did not participate in the League of Nations and its institutions.[11]

Under international agreement by Member States of the International Telecommunication Union and ICAN, the application of standardized uniform ground station location identifiers and radio navigation codes (Q-Codes) was established. The work of ICAN and its sub-commissions proved to be very useful and essential in the drafting of the technical Annexes to the 1944 Chicago Convention. From 1944, during the initial phase of ICAO (PICAO), former standards and procedures of ICAN and the ITU were consequently

---

10 FAI: www.fai.org/history. IATA: www.iata.org/history. At its founding, IATA had 57 members from 31 States, mostly in Europe and North America. Today, it has some 280 members from 120 States in every continent of the world.

11 Milde, M., *International Air Law and ICAO*. Essential Air and Space Law, Volume 4, Series Editor Benkö, M.E.,Utrecht: Eleven International Publishing, 2008, p. 12 and p. 120.

refined, extended and published in these Annexes. The Paris offices of the ICAN secretariat were taken over by ICAO on its foundation and remained there for its first 19 years in the capacity of the EUR Region Office of ICAO until August 1965. Previously, the focus of the European Office was expanded to include the North Atlantic (EUR/NAT office), and eventually changed location in Paris.[12]

4.3 CITEJA

Comité International Technique d'Experts Juridiques Aériens

With the rapid expansion of the network of international scheduled air services, and consequently the inevitable increase in aircraft accidents and serious incidents, disputes likewise increased with regard to associated damage and loss of life, claims by duped passengers and owners of lost or damaged cargo and aircraft. In the years following World War I, there was a lack of uniform regulations governing private air law. Without adequate international consultation, a patchwork of rules emerged in national aviation regulations.

From an international perspective, this rather chaotic situation needed the formulation of a uniform system of regulation regarding private air law, as had been done by a number of States in the field of public air law, resulting in the 1919 Paris Convention. The French government was the first to become interested in (international) private air law, or conflict of laws in aviation, especially concerning the liability of the carrier in civil air transport, although it was realized that this issue could only be solved by an international agreement.

A proposal to submit the issue of liability of the air carrier to the International Commission for Air Navigation, being considered as fully qualified to make preparatory work for a private air law conference scheduled to be held in Paris, was initially accepted. But at that time, ICAN represented only 17 States which did not match with the intention to call upon as many States as possible.

The French government convened the First International Conference on Private Air Law in 1925, after earlier suspensions, in order to address the problems associated with conflict of laws in aviation.[13]

Next to the principal subject of liability of the air carrier, some other legal subjects were added to the agenda and raised for study and discussion:
- Damage caused by aircraft to goods and persons on the ground

---

12 ICAO/European and North Atlantic (EUR/NAT) Office/History: The beginning. In July 2016, major contributions over the last 70 years to the safety, security and sustainable development of international civil aviation, on behalf of ICAO's European and North Atlantic (EUR/NAT) Office, were celebrated in Paris.
13 Giemulla, E.M., Weber, L. (Eds.), *International and EU Aviation Law*, Selected Issues, Alphen aan den Rijn: Kluwer Law International, 2011, p. 224.

- Compulsory insurance
- Establishment of aeronautical registers on ownership of aircraft, vested rights and mortgages
- Seizure of aircraft
- Renting (leasing) of aircraft
- Aerial collisions
- Legal status of the aircraft commander
- Air consignment note
- Uniform rules for the determination of the nationality of aircraft

The Conference then passed a resolution including the intention to accomplish a swift formation of a committee of legal experts, specialized in aviation, responsible for preparing the continuation of the work of the Conference. Various reasons formed the basis for the realization of such a legal expert team, like the complexity, significance, urgency and the legal technicalities of these particular issues.

Formally, this special committee of experts, The *Comité International Technique d'Experts Juridiques Aériens* (CITEJA), a body appointed by different governments, acting in their individual capacity, was created pursuant to a recommendation adopted on the basis of the resolution. Its general task was to develop a code of private air law.

Therefore, CITEJA was designated to examine the issues relating to the responsibility of international air carriers and to commence with the comprehensive task of codifying the rapidly expanding area of private air law, especially through the preparation of draft international conventions for final adoption at periodic international conferences on private air law. CITEJA went well beyond the initiative of the French government and dealt not only with the issue of liability in international carriage by air, but also established uniform rules regarding the documents of carriage and their connection with liability, rules of liability and limitation of liability as well as rules concerning the jurisdiction of courts.

This comprehensive and ground-breaking work formed the basis for the Convention for the Unification of Certain Rules Relating to International Carriage by Air, the 1929 Warsaw Convention, which was recognized many years later as a monumental piece of international law-making.[14]

A total number of four International Conferences on Private Air Law were held until World War II interrupted the work of CITEJA and further unification of private air law. CITEJA was active until May 1947.

The first session to be held since the outbreak of World War II, the 14th Plenary Session of CITEJA, was convened at Paris from 22 to 29 January 1946. It adopted several resolutions taking into consideration the creation of PICAO in 1946, and agreed in prin-

---

14 www.mcgill.ca/iasl/files/iasl/C08-Michael_Milde-Warsaw_System_and_Montreal_1999.pdf.

ciple to a liaison and cooperation with PICAO and to transmit to the Council of PICAO the drafts on international air law conventions. The First Interim Assembly of PICAO, held in Montreal from 21 May to 7 June 1946, adopted Resolution 31 foreseeing the establishment of a permanent committee on international air law (Legal Committee) following the creation of ICAO. CITEJA fully agreed with the view of PICAO and recommended in its last working meeting in 1947 that a committee on international air law was to be established within ICAO. During the First Session of the ICAO Assembly, held in Montreal from 6 to 27 May 1947, Resolution A1-46 was adopted creating the Legal Committee as a permanent body, replacing CITEJA.[15]

On 23 May 1947, the Legal Committee came into being as a committee of the ICAO Assembly but operated largely under the direction of the Council and its duties were to study any legal matters referred to it by the Council. It was comprised of legal experts appointed by the ICAO Member States.

Any draft convention which the Legal Committee considers as ready for presentation to States as a final draft is to be transmitted to the ICAO Council. Such draft conventions are considered with a view of approval by a diplomatic conference or international conference on air law, following consultation through circulation to Contracting States to give their comments for fine-tuning.

The resulting legal instrument is then open for signature at the conclusion of the conference. ICAO has been very productive in international law-making. Since 1947, the Legal Committee has prepared many drafts which led to the adoption of air law instruments.

Ever since 1947, the Legal Committee has, unlike the earlier CITEJA, considered questions of both private and public international air law. The Legal Committee, along with the Air Navigation Commission and the Air Transport Committee became the central permanent committees of ICAO.[16]

4.4 ICAO

International Civil Aviation Organization

In the period before World War II, in the *interbellum*, two international conventions regulated air navigation: the 1919 Paris Convention whose permanent body was the International Commission of Air Navigation, and the 1928 Havana Convention as a counterpart for air navigation in the Western Hemisphere, albeit without a permanent office.

---

15 Ide, J.J., The History and Accomplishments of the International Technical Committee of Aerial Legal Experts (CITEJA), 3 *J. Air L. & Com.* 27 (1932).

16 www.icao.int/secretariat/PostalHistory/the_first_years_of_the_legal_committee.htm (The Postal History of ICAO. The first years of the Legal Committee).

The unparalleled growth during the *interbellum* clearly demonstrated the possibilities of civil air transport. The advent of World War II, while interrupting civil air transport to a large extent, did not really stop the international aerospace industry. In those dreadful times aviation undeniably made use of significantly advanced technical and operational possibilities of air transport in a world that eventually would find peace again. Already during the course of this war, it was apparent that civil air transport would play a tremendous and important role in international relations in the coming years after 1945.

ICAO was created to promote the safe, efficient and orderly development of civil aviation, and in this capacity it was to become the world's rulemaking body for international civil aviation. However, first of all, PICAO carried out the basic purposes of the Chicago Convention until 4 April 1947 when ICAO came into operation once 26 States ratified the Chicago Convention.[17]

From its start, ICAO's vision has been for international civil aviation to promote friendship and understanding among the peoples of the world, as well as peace and prosperity based on a global air transport system that would be operated soundly and economically, with equality of opportunity for mankind, without discrimination between Contracting States, and to ensure the safe and orderly growth of international civil aviation throughout the world.

The Organization should furthermore encourage the arts of aircraft design and operation for peaceful purposes, the development of aviation infrastructure to meet the needs of the peoples of the world for safe, regular, efficient and economic air transport, and ensure that the rights of Contracting States are fully respected and that every Contracting State shall have a fair opportunity to operate international airlines.[18]

Economic cooperation between Contracting States is carried out under the regime of bilateral air services agreements, or under regional agreements. The European Union, as a supranational entity, is such a region.

The Standards and Recommended Practices in the Annexes to the Chicago Convention, alongside the tremendous technological progress achieved in the intervening years, have enabled the realization today of what must be recognized as one of mankind's great-

---

17   Folly, M.H., Palmer, N.A., The *A to Z of U.S. Diplomacy from World War I through World War II*, Lanham, MD: Scarecrow Press, Rowman & Littlefield, 2010, p. 54.
18   Chicago Convention, Art. 44 Objectives.

est cooperative achievements and a crucial operating system of the modern international air transport network which enhances global prosperity.

The consensus-building approach of ICAO plays a major role in addressing the greatest challenges faced by the development of global aviation in all capacities. The core mandate of ICAO, at the time and nowadays, was and is to assist States to achieve the highest possible degree of uniformity in civil aviation regulations, standards, procedures and organization.[19]

ICAO is a specialized agency of the United Nations. Its headquarters are located in the Quartier International at Montreal, Quebec, Canada.

ICAO codifies the principles and techniques of international air navigation and fosters the planning and development of international air transport to ensure safe and orderly growth. ICAO, as a largely advisory and consultative organization with moderate regulatory competencies, mainly based on voluntary cooperation by Member States, lacks a real enforcement mechanism to be able to issue mandatory rules to legally bind its Member States, thus without having the opt-out clause for non-compliance.[20]

However, when it comes to USOAP and USAP audits, namely specifically with regard to aviation safety, the assessment of the effective implementation of the eight critical elements of a safety oversight system and the current status of a State's implementation of all safety-relevant SARPs, associated procedures, guidance material and safety-related practices, and on the other hand with regard to aviation security, compliance of a Contracting State with Annex 17 and other aviation security-related provisions contained in other Annexes, the somewhat controversial mandatory requirement is contradictory to the principle of sovereignty, expressed in Article 1 of the Chicago Convention.

Sovereignty regarding safety and security audits is fully respected through a bilateral Memorandum of Understanding expressing the consent of the audited State. The question remains if ICAO legally may impose a mandatory audit upon Member States. The requirement of consent, being a formality, and the quasi-mandatory (persuasive) force of ICAO will commit States to accept audits in order to create an exemplary impression of themselves in the field of aviation safety and security. Regarding USAP audits, the principle of confidentiality is paramount. No State other than the audited State is provided

---

19 *See also* Rhoades, D.L., *Evolution of International Aviation: Phoenix Rising*, Third Edition, Milton Park, Abingdon, Oxon: Routledge, 2016. Chapter 12, The Slippery Legal Slope, pp. 145-146, The key to understanding ICAO is in realizing that like the UN in general it has no independent enforcement power; it cannot make its members implement any of its Standards. Its main bodies may act to support or condemn certain actions by members that relate to aviation, but this is an exercise in public relations and free expression. When or if a vote is taken on the issue of SARPS or PANS, it is the perfunctory end to months or years of consensus building at ICAO. If consensus is not initially achieved on certain issues, then all parties revise, rework or reframe the issue until consensus is obtained. It is a painstaking process, but it has and is producing some very positive results.

20 Antwerpen van, N., *Cross-Border Provisions of Air Navigation Services with Specific Reference to Europe, Safeguarding Transparent Lines of Responsibility and Liability*, Alphen aan den Rijn: Kluwer Law International, 2008, pp. 236-237.

with any information, practically always of a sensitive nature, contained in the classified USAP report, unless bilateral agreements have been made to deviate from this standing policy. States absolutely do not want information about their security measures and policy to be disclosed unauthorized as that would undermine public security. Safety issues, on the other hand, have to be shared internationally to enhance aviation safety.[21]

ICAO is comprised of an Assembly, a Council and such other bodies as may be necessary like a Secretariat. The Secretariat is headed by the Secretary General, elected by the Council. The Secretariat consists of five Bureaus corresponding to the committees and commissions of the Council: the Air Navigation Bureau, the Air Transport Bureau, the Technical Cooperation Bureau, the Legal Affairs & External Relations Bureau and the Bureau of Administration and Services.

The Council, being a permanent body of ICAO and accountable to the Assembly, is composed of 36 Member States elected by the Assembly for a three-year term. The Council convenes the Assembly.

The Council, which has numerous functions, appoints and defines the duties of the Air Transport Committee, as well as the Committee on Joint Support of Air Navigation Services, the Finance Committee, the Committee on Unlawful Interference, the Technical Cooperation Committee and the Human Resources Committee. It appoints the members of the Air Navigation Commission and it elects the members of the Edward Warner Award Committee.[22]

The ICAO Legal Committee which is composed of legal experts, being representatives of the Contracting States and designated by these States, is open to participation by all Contracting States and certain international or global organizations, invited by the Council. The Legal Committee along with the Air Navigation Commission and the Air Transport Committee became the central permanent committees of ICAO.

As one of the two governing bodies of ICAO, the Council gives continuing direction to the work of ICAO. In this regard, one of its major duties is to adopt international

---

21   Huang, J., *Aviation Safety and ICAO*. Dissertation to obtain the degree of Doctor at the Leiden University, 2009, pp. 73-77, Chapter 2.3 Auditing of State Compliance with Technical Regulations, Paragraph 2.3.3 Legal Issues Arising from ICAO Audits, and Paragraph 2.3.3.1 The Principle of Consent and the Mandatory Nature of Audits.

22   The Edward Warner Award, conferred by ICAO, is the highest honour in the world of civil aviation and recognizes individuals or organizations for their outstanding contribution to the development of international civil aviation. Dr. Edward Pierson Warner (1894-1958) was one of the leading figures in the post-war development of international civil aviation, realizing his dream of a structured and modern world air transport system based on international cooperation. His achievements are commemorated by the world's civil aviation community in this international award.

    Edward Warner was an American aviation pioneer, educator in aeronautical engineering, author, scientist and statesman. In 1944, he was Vice Chairman of the U.S. Aeronautical Board and was a member of the U.S. Delegation to the 1944 Chicago Conference and contributed to the realization of the Convention on International Civil Aviation. He became the first President of the Council of PICAO and ICAO from 1945 until 1957.

SARPs to be included as Annexes to the Chicago Convention. The Council may also amend existing Annexes as necessary.

On occasion, the Council may act as an arbiter between Contracting States on matters concerning aviation and the implementation of the provisions of the Chicago Convention. In general, the Council may take all necessary steps to maintain the safety and regularity of international civil air transport.

Challenges faced by the Council today include maintaining and improving aviation safety and air navigation efficiency, introducing advanced systems while integrating increased air traffic into the current aviation infrastructure and devising mitigation measures, in accordance with the Global Aviation Safety Plan and the Global Air Navigation Plan. Where previously aviation safety improved through trial and error and the resulting lessons, either directly or from accident investigation reports, today, the safety focus has undoubtedly shifted to a proactive approach to be able to identify and mitigate the risks in advance.

A more recently established ICAO section, although almost three decades ago (established in 1983), is the Committee on Aviation Environmental Protection, a merger of the Committee on Aircraft Noise and the Committee on Aircraft Engine Emissions.

CAEP, a body of interdisciplinary experts, is first and foremost a technical committee of the Council. CAEP will assist the Council in formulating new policies and adopting new SARPs related to international aviation environmental impact, which is an extremely serious, contemporary, but certainly also a future, issue of global interest. CAEP has been given an extensive mandate to expand its work plan to include climate change issues associated with aviation activities, and in that respect to have close coordination with other international environmental organizations like the United Nations Framework Convention on Climate Change and the Intergovernmental Panel on Climate Change (IPCC).

CAEP is composed of 25 members from all regions of the world and 17 observers (six States and 11 organizations). More than 600 internationally renowned experts are involved in CAEP activities and working groups. The Council reviews and adopts CAEP's recommendations on the reduction of aircraft noise and on engine emission limits in view of global atmospheric questions, including amendments to SARPs, and in turn reports to the ICAO Assembly where the main policies on environmental protection are ultimately defined.[23]

---

23 Mestral, A.L.C. de, Fitzgerald, P.P., Ahmad, T.Md (Eds.), *Sustainable Development, International Aviation, and Treaty Implementation*, Cambridge: Cambridge University Press, 2018, pp. 257-259. *See also* www.icao. int/environmental-protection/pages/caep.aspx.

4.5   IATA

International Air Transport Association

The International Air Transport Association, the worldwide non-governmental organization of scheduled airlines, a trade organization for the world's airlines, a forum for international pricing agreements and a substitute for a multilateral government agreement, was established at Havana on 19 April 1945.

In March 2019, the organization included some 290 member airlines from about 120 States in every part of the globe, representing approximately 83% of total air traffic and is headquartered in Montreal, Canada with executive offices in Geneva, Switzerland, and over 90 regional offices.[24]

IATA represents the member airlines in negotiating with ICAO, governments and airport authorities on various matters ranging from airport charges, airport slots (specific times allotted for an aircraft to land or take off), environment and infrastructure to taxation, consumer and passenger issues, tariff structure, aviation safety regulation, worldwide security measures and value and future of aviation. The group works both as a forum for inter-airline discussions on key aviation issues and as a pressure medium to represent the interests of substantially all of the international airlines.

It means to be the force for value creation and innovation driving a safe, secure and profitable air transport industry that sustainably connects and enriches our world. One of its main tasks is to coordinate, innovate and standardize a variety of aspects covering many areas of international air transport.

A downside to rapidly increasing air traffic is that the number of slot coordinated airports is expected to grow significantly versus limited capacity, due to lack of expansion in airport infrastructure, to cope with strongly increased demand, often causing long delays.

IATA is leading the way in ensuring a fair, neutral and transparent allocation of airport slots at the most congested airports in the world through the application of the Worldwide Slot Guidelines (WSG). These guidelines, remaining the best long-term solution to manage scarce capacity, allow airlines to plan their whole network and schedule, and provide choice, flexibility and connectivity to the passengers.[25]

IATA membership is open to any operating company which has been licensed to provide international air service. IATA active membership is open to airlines engaged directly in international operations, while IATA associate membership is open to domestic airlines. The IATA Annual General Meeting (AGM) is the sovereign body of the

---

24   www.iata.org/publications/Documents/iata-annual-review-2018.pdf.
25   Doganis, R., *Flying off Course: The economics of international airlines*, Third Edition, London: Routledge, 2002, pp. 39-43. *See also* Czerny, A.I., Forsyth, P., Gillen, D., Niemeier, H-M. (Eds.), *Airport Slots: International Experiences and Options to Reform*, Milton Park, Abingdon, Oxon: Routledge, 2016, pp. 9-11.

organization. All active members have an equal vote in its decisions. It is convened every year as the so-called World Air Transport Summit in recognition of its status as the premier, industry-wide platform for the debate of essential issues at the highest level. Year-round IATA policy direction is provided by the Board of Governors (BG), composed of Chief Executives of member airlines, that is advised by Special Committees, subcommittees and working groups, and IATA Standing Committees (four committees specialized in the fields of finance, industry affairs, operations and cargo), supported by the Secretariat, headed by the Director General and Chief Executive Officer.

Today's organization is the successor to the pre-war International Air Traffic Association which was founded in the Netherlands at The Hague in 1919, the year of the world's first international scheduled air services.[26]

As the 1919 International Air Traffic Association was able to start small and grow gradually, the post-war (which was World War II) IATA immediately had to handle worldwide responsibilities with a more systematic organization and a much larger infrastructure. In the early days, the old pre-war IATA was limited to the European continent until 1939 when the North American air carrier Pan American (World) Airways joined IATA.

The failure of States to ratify the International Air Transport Agreement, adopted by the Chicago Conference in 1944, left international civil aviation without a general set of rules governing airline operations. IATA soon filled the void. It became an overseas representative for a large number of world airlines and a partial substitute for government restrictions on international airline operations. IATA has established agreements on pricing, on inter-airline connections, on procedures for interline clearing of ticket revenue and on airports, maintenance, training and safety.[27]

The most important tasks of IATA during its earliest days were technical, because safety and reliability are fundamental to airline operations. These require the highest standards in air navigation, in airport infrastructure and flight operations. The IATA member airlines provided vital input to the work of ICAO, as that intergovernmental agency drafted its SARPs. By 1949, the drafting process was largely complete and reflected in the Annexes to the Chicago Convention.

---

26 The first national fixed-wing scheduled airline was started on 1 January 1914, from St. Petersburg, Florida to Tampa, Florida. In 1919, the first international scheduled air services were started between London and Paris, and from Amsterdam to London.

27 The Economic Effects of Significant U.S. Import Restraints, Phase III: Services. With a Computable General Equilibrium Analysis of Significant U.S. Import Restraints, Report to the Committee on Finance of the United States Senate on Investigation No. 332-262 Under Section 332 of the Tariff Act of 1930, USITC (United States International Trade Commission) Publication 2422 September 1991, p. 1-2-2 The International Air Transport Association.

The aims of IATA have always been, right from its establishment in 1945:

1. to promote safe, regular and economical air transport for the benefit of the peoples of the world, to foster air commerce and to study the problems connected therewith;
2. to provide means for collaboration among the air transport enterprises engaged directly or indirectly in international air transport service; and
3. to cooperate with ICAO, and other international organizations.

IATA's mission, today and in the future, is to represent, lead and serve the airline industry, especially by improving understanding of the air transport industry among decision-makers and increasing awareness of the benefits that aviation brings to national and global economies. Furthermore, it does this by challenging unreasonable rules and charges, holding regulators and governments to account and striving for sensible and acceptable regulations for the interests of airlines across the globe.

So far, IATA has been able to coordinate and standardize practically every aspect of international airline operation, due to the comprehensive work done by airline experts being part of specialized IATA committees and subcommittees. For over 70 years, it has developed global commercial standards upon which the air transport industry is built, while the coherent goal is to assist airlines by simplifying processes and increasing passenger convenience, and at the same time reduce costs and improve efficiency.

Moreover, IATA helps airlines to operate safely, securely, efficiently and economically under clearly defined rules. Professional support is provided to all aviation industry stakeholders with a wide range of products and expert services. IATA also represents airlines in negotiations with airport authorities, governments, State regulators and ICAO on a wide range of aviation issues. In this respect, its most important function, throughout the years, has been to set airline fares and cargo rates.

Another seemingly controversial aspect is the IATA multilateral interline system, introducing benefits for consumers with regard to connecting flights in order to save a significant amount of time and to be more flexible with travel plans. However, the relevance of this instrument is decreasing because of increasing code-share arrangements and the expansion of strategic airline alliances with their extensive networks around the world, offering a variety of connecting flights around the clock.[28]

The IATA-fixed tariff procedures in bilateral air services agreements lost their strength because of aviation deregulation that set in from 1978 onwards. Deregulation caused charter or non-scheduled air services to grow significantly in those years, offering much lower fares on routes within Western Europe and on the North Atlantic route system than the IATA scheduled tariffs.[29]

---

28 www.iata.org/about/pages/index.aspx. Programmes, Policy, Publications and Services.
29 Doganis, R., *The Airline Business*, Second Edition, Milton Park, Abingdon, Oxon: Routledge, 2006, pp. 30-33.

Noteworthy IATA services which are related to air transport regulation are:

- the IATA Schedules Conference, held twice yearly, where airlines coordinate their schedules and airport slots;
- the Billing and Settlement Plan (BSP), which provides for the computerized processing of accounts between airlines and their passenger agents;
- the Cargo Accounting Settlement System (CASS), which provides for the computerized processing of account between airlines and their cargo agents;
- the Clearing House, which includes proration services and enables airlines (and suppliers) to settle credits and debits between themselves at one location, thus minimizing the need to make actual transfers of money on a worldwide basis;
- the IATA/SITA baggage tracing (BAGTRAC) system,[30] to recover checked baggage that is lost or misdirected; and
- the Multilateral Interline Traffic Agreement (MITA), a legally binding agreement relating to the issuance of passenger tickets and cargo airway bills and the acceptance of each other's passengers, baggage and cargo.[31]

A safety audit programme within IATA is the IATA Operational Safety Audit (IOSA) programme, created in 2003, which is an internationally recognized and accepted evaluation system designed to assess the operational management and control systems of an airline. In the international airline industry, the most important certification mechanism is based on this programme, the standard for safety management. Another important auditing programme, modelled on the IOSA framework, is the IATA Safety Audit of Ground Operations (ISAGO).

The IOSA audit creates a standard that is comparable on a worldwide basis, enabling and maximizing the joint use of audit reports. This has saved the air transport industry over 6,400 redundant audits and continues to lead to extensive cost-savings for IOSA participating airlines.

IATA requires that its members pass an IOSA audit as a condition for IATA membership. All IATA members are IOSA-registered and must remain registered to maintain IATA membership. In 2018, the IOSA programme was 15 years operational, presently digitalized and has become a global standard.

The benefits for airlines and regulators are:

- quality audit programme under the stewardship of IATA;
- continuous updating of standards to reflect regulatory revisions and best practices;
- elimination of audit redundancy, reducing costs and audit resource requirements;
- accredited training organizations with auditor training courses; and

---

30 SITA, *Societé Internationale de Télécommunications Aéronautiques*, is a Swiss multinational information technology company, founded in 1949 by 11 airlines, providing IT and telecommunication services to the air transport industry.

31 ICAO Manual on the Regulation of International Air Transport (Doc 9626), Third Edition, 2016.

 − structured audit methodology and standardized checklists.

IOSA audits consist of questions that are Standards and Recommended Practices, referred to as ISARPs. These auditing standards have been developed in collaboration with a number of civil aviation regulatory authorities. IOSA is divided into eight main areas: Organization and Management (ORG), Flight Operations (FLT), Operational Control and Flight Dispatch Procedures (DSP), Engineering and Maintenance (MNT), Ground Handling Services (GRH), Passenger Cabin Operations (CAB), Cargo Operations (CGO) and Security (SEC).[32]

The three strategic pillars of IOSA are safety, efficiency and integrity. By establishing the IOSA programme, the whole audit environment has become more efficient. Its main purpose is to enable airline companies to share the results of their quality audits. A negative outcome will oblige the airline company concerned to present a recovery plan at short notice.

IATA uses a comprehensive safety strategy. The Six Point Safety Strategy is an elaborated approach to identify organizational, operational and emerging safety issues. It has been established in close cooperation with member airlines and strategic partners through the IATA Safety Group (SG) and the Operations Committee (OPC). The six key areas regarding actions to ensure safety are:

1. Reduce Operational Risk
2. Enhance Quality and Compliance
3. Advocate for Improved Aviation Infrastructure
4. Support Consistent Implementation of Safety Management Systems
5. Support Effective Recruitment and Training
6. Identify and Address Emerging Safety Issues

Environmentally, IATA is playing its part in furthering ICAO Carbon Offset Reduction Scheme for International Aviation phased implementation through workshops in various parts of the world to enable airlines to comply with CORSIA from 1 January 2019. From that date, all air carriers are required to monitor and report their CO_2 emissions on an annual basis. Offsetting is an action by a company or individual to compensate for their emissions by financing a reduction in emissions elsewhere. However, the aviation industry is committed to advances in technology, operational and infrastructure to reduce carbon emissions by the sector. Offsetting is not intended to replace these tremendous efforts.

Meanwhile, IATA is finalizing FRED+, a platform developed to support and facilitate CO_2 emissions reporting for aircraft operators and States. FRED+ is based on the IATA

---

32 Stolzer, A.J., Halford, C.D., Goglia, J.J. (Eds.), *Implementing Safety Management Systems in Aviation*, Farnham, Surrey: Ashgate Publishing, 2013, p. 301.

Fuel Reporting and Emissions Database (FRED), used to improve aviation fuel efficiency.[33]

Recently, IATA launched its Turbulence Aware data resource to assist airlines in better avoiding turbulence when planning routes during flights. To mitigate the impact of turbulence (possibly causing passenger inconvenience or even injuries and damage), Turbulence Aware improves on the industry's capability by collecting open source data from multiple contributing airlines, while at the same time applying rigorous quality control.

Turbulence Aware, already generating significant interest among airlines, will enhance, in the near future, the capability to forecast and avoid areas of turbulence by pooling and sharing real-time turbulence data generated by participating airlines. This IATA platform will provide a real improvement for passenger comfort. Additionally, with respect to the environment and to the cost aspect, it provides for fuel savings.[34]

4.6   ECAC/CEAC

European Civil Aviation Conference/Conférence Européenne de l'Aviation Civile

The European Civil Aviation Conference (*Conférence Européenne de l'Aviation Civile*) is Europe's largest, longstanding aviation organization and is part of the ICAO air transport global community. Founded in 1955 as an intergovernmental autonomous organization, ECAC seeks to harmonize civil aviation policies and practices amongst its Member States and, at the same time, promote understanding on policy matters between its Member States and other parts of the world.

ECAC's long-established expertise in aviation matters, its pan-European membership and close relationship with ICAO, which is expressed as being part of the ICAO air transport global community, enables it to serve as a unique European forum for discussion of every major civil aviation topic.

It works closely and cooperatively with the European Commission, EUROCONTROL, JAA TO (Joint Aviation Authorities Training Organization), other regional organizations and individual Contracting States of ICAO, including the United States, and has particularly effectual links with industry and organizations representing all parts of the air transport industry.[35]

---

33   *IATA – Airlines. Magazine.* Analysis/16 October 2018, Count Down to CORSIA.
34   IATA Press release no. 73/12 December 2018, IATA launches platform enabling airlines to share turbulence data.
35   www.ecac-ceac.org/about-ecac. *See also* ICAO Assembly Resolution A10-5 Relationship of ICAO with the European Civil Aviation Conference and ICAO Assembly Resolution A27-17 on the relationship between ICAO and regional civil aviation bodies (superseding Resolution A10-5).

ECAC held its Inaugural Session in Strasbourg from 29 November to 16 December 1955. Its objective is the promotion of the continued development of a safe, efficient and sustainable European air transport system. Presently, ECAC includes 44 Member States. The most important action of the Conference was the establishment of a standing Committee on Coordination and Liberalization (COCOLI), which was to hold short informal meetings about twice a year to consider what measures might be taken by governments to liberalize European air transport and encourage cooperation between European airlines. ECAC has been providing the major focus for intergovernmental cooperation in air transport matters in Europe.

ECAC addresses issues affecting the European civil aviation sector, in particular in relation to safety, security, environment, air navigation and economics. To fulfil this role, the Conference has working relationships with a number of key European organizations which have aviation sector interests and responsibilities such as the European Union, including EASA, EUROCONTROL, EASTI (European Aviation Security Training Institute), JAA TO and industry associations.

ECAC's priorities to fulfil its mission are threefold:

1. To act as a pan-European aviation think tank. ECAC provides an excellent opportunity for free and open discussions between its Member States on key strategic issues, without binding implications. ECAC represents a think tank for many new concepts and innovative matters, not only during DGCA (Directors General of Civil Aviation) meetings, but also through the organization of the ECAC/EU dialogue with the air transport industry and the annual ECAC forum.

2. To support its Member States in developing harmonized pan-European positions and solutions in all areas of aviation policy and practice for delivery at major ICAO meetings, such as the Assembly, High-Level Conferences and Committees and other important world aviation fora.

3. To serve as a centre of expertise for its Member States. ECAC's working groups elaborate standards and good practices, perform analyses and draft position papers and policies to support its Member States. ECAC's activities are considered added value to its Member States, while preventing possible overlaps or duplication with other European organizations regarding the support.

ECAC has developed active work programmes on a variety of civil aviation-related subjects such as training, economic and legal matters, safety, security, facilitation, environmental activities and capacity building.[36]

The strategic priorities of ECAC therefore lie in these areas:

---

36 ECAC's Strategy for the Future: A Policy Statement, Endorsed by ECAC Directors General of Civil Aviation at GGCA/145, December 2015.

1. *Safety and Air Navigation.* While EASA covers safety activities not only for the EU Member States but also for those other ECAC Member States covered by the EASA regulatory framework, ECAC will focus on safety activities only when it comes to added value and no unnecessary overlap with activities of EASA, and in particular on the sharing of experience and good practices within the Air Accident and Incident Investigation Group of Experts (ACC). The investigation of aviation accidents and incidents is today recognized as a fundamentally important element of improving safety, and those responsible for investigations have come to be considered by national and international safety authorities as key partners, both on the policy and technical levels.[37]

ECAC will continuously play a supporting role in the field of air navigation matters, acting in concert with the European Union, including EASA and EUROCONTROL, while consolidating a pan-European approach within ECAC Member States.

2. *Security.* ECAC, as the European centre of expertise on aviation security, will further develop and refine its Audit and Capacity Building programmes to reflect a more risk-based approach. By identifying the most critical areas, ECAC establishes the basis for the implementation of appropriate mitigation measures, focusing on the main risks. The sharing of information on risks between its Member States is critical to the implementation of such mitigation measures.

Through security audits and a wide range of capacity-building activities, ECAC will continue to support its Member States in their implementation of European security requirements. The promotion of the One Stop Security concept between EU and non-EU Member States will also be continued.

International cooperation with key partners, whether individual States or (sub)regional oriented organizations, will remain a priority with the objective of building partnerships and sharing experiences with other parts of the world. The performance of security projects by ECAC, such as the one funded by the European Union for the benefit of Africa, will contribute to strengthening international working relationships with other regions.

ECAC will continue as a centre of expertise for Europe on the development of technical specifications and common testing methodologies for security equipment. This expertise is also widely recognized by ECAC's international partners. Furthermore, by avoiding any duplication with the European Union, it will maintain its high profile in developing recommendations in areas of emerging interest (for example, cyber security, unpredictability, behaviour detection) and in elaborating guidance material.

---

37 www.ecac-ceac.org/ecac-documents. Air Accident and Incident Investigation Group of Experts, Terms of Reference and Rules of Procedure, adopted in June 2016. The Group of Experts has as its main objectives: a. To enhance the effectiveness of ECAC Member States' safety investigation capabilities through the sharing of knowledge and experience in the field of air accident investigation; and, b. To promote European experience and know-how in safety investigation within the wider international aviation community.

3. *Facilitation.* Facilitation, very often linked to civil aviation security, supports the efficient and sustainable development of air transport. Being the only European organization dealing with all aspects of facilitation such as there are, for example, immigration, health and customs, ECAC will continue to pursue the development of effective, efficient and uniform aviation facilitation measures, especially for persons with reduced mobility and persons with disabilities, on a pan-European basis, and will support ECAC Member States in their harmonized implementation of such measures.

4. *Environment.* The environmental impacts of the civil aviation sector are, and will continue to be, of primary importance for the international aviation community. In particular, on the issue of climate change and the implementation of Global Market-Based Measures, ECAC's activity on environmental issues will continue to be performed in close cooperation with the European Commission.

    ECAC will especially focus its activities when and where there is an added value for ECAC Member States, in particular from the pan-European perspective. An efficient collaboration amongst European aviation organizations is of utmost importance in order to prevent overlaps or duplications with their respective activities on environmental matters, and create synergies, complementarities and targeted measures.

5. *Aviation and Economics.* ECAC is a meaningful forum for pan-European consideration of the economic dimension of international air transport, including future trends and challenges like global competition. Periodic dialogues between ECAC/EU and the air transport industry and the annual ECAC forum are important vehicles for debating economic issues.

    Mutual understanding and cooperation on economic matters of interests to ECAC Member States, such as competitiveness, connectivity and other relevant emerging economic issues regarding European air transport, are supported by ECAC.

6. *Training.* Training in issues such as safety and security is important to create an aviation culture. ECAC will promote aviation training through the continuation of the management of the Network of Training Organizations with the objective of creating conditions to share best practices amongst several European aviation training organizations, and by offering encouragement to JAA TO and EASTI, which are two associated bodies of ECAC. Newly developed training courses shall meet the demands of ECAC Member States and the needs of the wider aviation community.

7. *External Relations.* Over the years, ECAC has established and maintained cooperative relationships with non-ECAC States and organizations. These relationships were initially restricted to other European States, which over time became members of ECAC themselves, and to international and European organizations. Relationships have been extended progressively to all regions of the world, thus reflecting the international dimension of the air transport sector.

To date, ECAC has signed a series of formal agreements with international and regional aviation organizations and with a number of individual States. Basically, these agreements focus on a comprehensive cooperation based on the exchange of information and mutual participation in meetings and events, while a few agreements have a more limited scope focusing on aviation security. ECAC has established and actively maintains a framework of relations and dialogue with external partners, including major emerging States. The external relations of ECAC serve the following objectives:

1. To promote pan-European positions and priorities at ICAO and at other major international events, ensuring that they are well represented there; and
2. To learn from the influence of selected major aviation States and regional organizations through the establishment of new cooperative relationships and the strengthening of those with existing partners, within and beyond Europe.

Significant agreements concluded under the auspices of ECAC are: the Multilateral Agreement on Commercial Rights of Non-Scheduled Air Services in Europe (Paris, 30 April 1956), the Multilateral Agreement Relating to Certificates of Airworthiness for Imported Aircraft (Paris, 22 April 1960), the International Agreement on the Procedure for the Establishment of Tariffs for Scheduled Air Services (Paris, 10 July 1967) and the International Agreement on the Procedure for the Establishment of Tariffs for intra-European Scheduled Air Services (Paris, 16 June 1987).

ECAC made some important recommendations and resolutions on:
– Airworthiness Certificates or permits to fly of certain historical aircraft;
– Methods of emission calculations, on passenger health issues and an operating ban in Europe;
– Minimum level of insurance cover for passenger and third-party liability;
– Safety of foreign aircraft;
– Airline's liability with respect to passengers, expert participation in aviation accident and incident investigations;
– Procedures for obtaining read-out of flight recorders when conducting aviation accident and incident investigations;
– Mutual acceptance by ECAC Member States of airworthiness;
– Inclusion of environmental aspects in air services agreements;
– Wide application of the Community list of airlines, subjected to an operating ban or blacklist.

ECAC works in close cooperation with (inter)governmental organizations such as the Organization for Economic Cooperation and Development (OECD), the International Transport Forum (ITF), the Universal Postal Union (UPU) and a large number of airlines, airports and training organizations, next to the aforementioned European Union (EU Council, Commission and Parliament), and EASA, EUROCONTROL and ICAO.

ECAC has always had a special working relationship with ICAO and represents the interests of its Member States at ICAO Assembly sessions and other special events.

ECAC engages in regular dialogue with JAA TO and the (ICAO regional) EASTI, that was inaugurated on 19 November 1997 and situated at Haren, close to Brussels International Airport, as well as the European Regions Airline Association (ERA), the International Aircraft Owners and Pilots Association (IAOPA), the Airports Council International (European region, ACI Europe), the European Cockpit Association (ECA), the International Federation of Air Line Pilots' Associations (IFALPA), the International Federation of Air Traffic Controllers' Associations (IFATCA), the Airlines International Representation in Europe (AIRE), the European Business Aviation Association (EBAA), the European Express Association (EEA), the International Air Transport Association (IATA), the Singapore Aviation Academy (SAA), established in 1959, Airports Council International, the Airport International Group (AIG) and the European Organization for Civil Aviation Equipment (EUROCAE).

Furthermore, ECAC works closely and cooperatively with other regional organizations in the field of civil aviation, such as the African Civil Aviation Commission, the Arab Civil Aviation Commission (ACAC) and the Latin American Civil Aviation Commission (LACAC) on a wide range of civil aviation issues of common interest, but particularly on security, safety and environmental training activities.

ECAC's close relationships with organizations and associations representing airlines and airports are very important to ECAC. Comprehensive cooperation is a key factor. At regular intervals, ECAC also conducts international symposia, workshops, seminars and training events.

In the late 1980s, serious air traffic congestion called for urgent remedial action, resulting in a number of meetings between ECAC and Ministers of Transport in Europe. Through these meetings, a political impetus was given to the establishment of a European Central Flow Management Unit (CFMU), the European Air Traffic Control Harmonization and Integration Programme, covering the en route phase of flights, and the Airport/Air Traffic Systems Interface (APATSI) strategy, dealing with the airport aspects of Air Traffic Control, were adopted, followed by the emerging ATM Strategy for 2000+, leading to the construction of the Single European Sky (SES) project. In particular, through this comprehensive cooperative work, the political position of ECAC has significantly strengthened.

In 1996, ECAC launched a voluntary safety assessment programme, called ECAC SAFA (Safety Assessment of Foreign Aircraft programme), which was complementary to but slightly different from the ICAO audits. SAFA is based on the understanding that maintaining confidence in the safety oversight provided by other States was a prerequisite for the continued development of a well-functioning and reliable global air transport system.

The SAFA programme is based on a bottom-up approach, basically taking as its starting point random ramp inspections of commercial aircraft landing at international airports located in ECAC States, in order to be able to oblige operators and appropriate civil aviation authorities to take corrective measures in specific safety cases showing significant deficiencies and irregularities. Following a decision of the Directors General of ECAC Member States, the ECAC SAFA programme was transferred under the competency of the European Commission, assisted by EASA, as of 1 January 2007.

4.7   JAA

Joint Aviation Authorities

In 1970, a number of EU Member States convened to make appointments which would facilitate the review on airworthiness of jointly manufactured aircraft, as well as the import and export of aircraft and parts within Europe. The JAA started as the Joint Airworthiness Authorities and was created in the same year by the respective aviation certification and regulatory agencies in Europe who agreed to cooperate in developing and implementing common safety regulatory standards and procedures, and who later entered to this effect into formal arrangements (Arrangements Concerning the Development and Acceptance of Joint Airworthiness Requirements, signed on 21 March 1979 by 13 European Civil Aviation Authorities).

The Joint Airworthiness Requirements (JAR) were formulated and adopted as guidelines. However, this JAR system had no formal status, which was perceived by ECAC as a shortcoming, though there was a need to develop common European requirements for aircraft operations next to requirements of airworthiness and aircraft maintenance. As a first step towards full integration with ECAC, the JAA became an associated body of ECAC, and would play a role as the European counterpart of the U.S. FAA. Its objectives were only to produce common certification codes for large aircraft and aircraft engines in order to meet the needs of the European aerospace industry, in particular for aeronautical products of international aircraft-manufacturing consortia such as Airbus Industries.

Since 1987, the work of the JAA was extended to aircraft operations, aircraft maintenance, personnel licensing and certification/design standards for all categories of aircraft. Against this background, it was decided to convert the legacy JAR system into a more comprehensive indication. On 19 June 1987, its title changed to the Joint Aviation Authorities (JAA), in which the Directors General of the cooperating States were represented, and JAR (Joint Aviation Requirements) by a Memorandum of Understanding on Future Airworthiness Procedures.[38]

The main objectives of the JAA were:

- to achieve the standardization of aviation regulation in the field of aviation safety among the JAA members;
- to internationally promote JAA standards in order to improve the safety of aviation worldwide;
- to ensure, through the application of unified standards, a fair and equal competition among the JAA members; and
- to achieve a cost-effective system in order to contribute to the efficiency of the aviation industry.

The technical requirements which were prepared by the JAA were only legally binding after being implemented in the national legislation of the Member States. Emphasis was also placed on the need for harmonization of JAA requirements with those of the United States. In implementing the so-called FUJA (Future of JAA) report, the JAA transitioned into a new phase as of 1 January 2007. The former JAA became the JAA T (Transition) which consisted of a liaison office, JAA LO, and a training office, JAA Training Office.

After the disbanding of the JAA T, the JAA TO (Training Organization) continues to provide training courses as an associated body of ECAC. It is a self-financing body, initiated by the ECAC Member States, and works independently from regulators. The Training Organization helps not only in Europe, but worldwide, to improve aviation safety by providing training courses and supporting activities in multiple fields of civil aviation safety, and assists in promoting understanding of existing and new European aviation-related regulations.[39]

The JAA TO will continuously serve as an educational platform for the international aviation community to learn and to follow the latest developments, and to exchange views on aviation progress. The main training centre and headquarters are located in Hoofddorp in the Netherlands, with regional training centres in Vienna in Austria (Austrian Airlines Training Center) at the Vienna International Airport, Abu Dhabi and Dubai in the United Arab Emirates (in partnership with the Gulf Center for Aviation Studies) located at the Abu Dhabi Al Bateen Executive Airport, Luxembourg in Luxembourg (in partnership with EUROCONTROL Institute of Air Navigation Services) and St. Julians at Malta (in partnership with AeroNautica Ltd.).

With the publication of the revised Regulation (EC) No. 1592/2002 on 19 March 2008, EASA took over practically all regulatory responsibilities, which were previously

---

38 Diederiks-Verschoor, I.H.Ph., Butler, M.A. (Legal adviser), *An Introduction to Air Law*, Eighth Revised Edition, Alphen aan den Rijn: Kluwer Law International, 2006, pp. 85-86. Memorandum of Understanding on Future Airworthiness Procedures, signed on 19 June 1987 by 12 European Civil Aviation Authorities.
39 Florio, F. de, *Airworthiness: An Introduction to Aircraft Certification and Operations*, Third Edition, Oxford: Butterworth-Heinemann, 2016, pp. 16-17.

in the hands of the JAA. Some of the functions which were transferred are safety and environmental type-certification of aircraft, engines and parts, and approval of organizations involved in the design, manufacture and maintenance of aeronautical products as well as aircraft operations and flight crew licensing.[40]

At the ECAC Directors General meeting of 19 March 2008, it was decided that the liaison JAA LO in Cologne would be disbanded by 30 June 2009. In the same year, the JAA TO continued its activities in the legal form of a Dutch Foundation. JAA TO is an ICAO Regional Center of Excellence (RTCE), and a leading member of the EASA Virtual Academy (EVA).

4.8   EUROCONTROL

The European Organization for the Safety of Air Navigation, EUROCONTROL, was set up by an international convention. The EUROCONTROL International Convention relating to Cooperation for the Safety of Air Navigation, usually called the EUROCONTROL Convention, was signed on 13 December 1960 (523 UNTS 117) at Brussels by the Contracting Parties: Belgium, France, the German Federal Republic, Luxembourg, the Netherlands and the United Kingdom, later joined by Ireland.[41]

The Convention went into force on 1 March 1963 for a period of 20 years with the possibility of renewal after the next 20 years. In 1993, the Contracting Parties to this Convention initiated a process of its revision which was finalized in 1997. The objective of such a revision was to extend the competence of EUROCONTROL, as an intergovernmental organization, to all aspects of air traffic management and provide the organization with more efficient decision-making mechanisms, thereby reinforcing the disciplines of its Member States.

The functions of EUROCONTROL continued to undergo changes. In December 1992, it was decided to investigate what further amendments to the EUROCONTROL Convention were required. A draft of a revised Convention was examined by the Permanent Commission, the highest governing body of EUROCONTROL, by the end of 1995.

In 1997, a Conference of the EUROCONTROL partners was held. However, the 27 Member States did not opt for a completely new Convention but instead signed, at Brussels on 27 June 1997, a Protocol consolidating the existing Convention.[42] This way the Conven-

---

40 Regulation (EC) No. 1592/2002 of the European Parliament and of the Council of 15 July 2002 on common rules in the field of civil aviation and establishing a European Aviation Safety Agency, *OJ EC* L 240/1 7.9.2002.

41 Cogen, M., *An Introduction to European Intergovernmental Organizations*, Milton Park, Abingdon, Oxon: Routledge, 2016, pp. 40-42.

42 Protocol consolidating the Eurocontrol International Convention relating to Cooperation for the Safety of Air Navigation of 13 December 1960 as variously amended, Brussels, 27 June 1997. The Protocol has not been ratified by the United Kingdom.

tion was eventually amended by a document called the Final Act of the Diplomatic Conference on the Protocol consolidating the EUROCONTROL International Convention relating to Cooperation for the Safety of Air Navigation of 13 December 1960, as variously amended and as consolidated by this Protocol (EUROCONTROL Revised Convention).[43]

Taking into account that some of the aspects such as decision-making and Member State disciplines are Community competences, it was necessary for the European Community to become members of EUROCONTROL. As accession implies acceptance by the Community of obligations resulting from EUROCONTROL instruments in areas in which the adoption of internal measures is subject to the co-decision procedure, the European Parliament must give its assistance to the Council Decision, in conformity with Article 300(3) of the EEC Treaty. Article 40 of the revised Convention made possible the accession of the European Community and provides that the terms and conditions of the accession shall be contained in an additional Protocol to the Convention.

Accession of the European Community to EUROCONTROL is justified by the fact that the revised Convention authorizes EUROCONTROL to adopt measures which are binding on the Member States. The Community must participate in this organization to enable such measures to be adopted in areas where the Community has competence. The Protocol (Accession Protocol) sets out the arrangements for applying the provisions of the revised Convention to the European Community and its Member States.[44]

These provisions concern European Community representation in the bodies of EUROCONTROL (Art. 5) and its voting rights (Art. 6). They enable the European Community to exercise, within EUROCONTROL, the competences conferred on it by its Member States in matters covered by the revised Convention. The Accession Protocol sets out the legal provisions enabling the European Community to obtain full membership of EUROCONTROL, and, in addition, provides for joint membership of the European Community and its Member States in EUROCONTROL, with voting rights shared.

The voting rights will be exercised by the European Community or by the Member States, depending on whether a particular decision concerns matters in which competence lies with the former or with the latter. The Member States will have to coordinate their position on matters in which the European Community exercises voting rights. In such matters, the European Community will exercise its voting rights by cumulating the votes of its Member States (Art. 6(1)). Article 40(6) authorizes the accession of regional economic integration organizations, such as the European Community.

43　Final act of the Diplomatic Conference on the Protocol consolidating the Eurocontrol International Convention relating to Cooperation for the Safety of Air Navigation of 13 December 1960, as variously amended and consolidated by the Protocol of 27 June 1997, Brussels 8 October 2002. ec.europa.eu/transport/files/modes/air/single_european_sky/doc/eurocontrol_2002_10_08_final_act_en.pdf.

44　Protocol on the accession of the European Community to the Eurocontrol International Convention relating to Cooperation for the Safety of Air Navigation of 13 December 1960, as variously amended and as consolidated by the Protocol of 27 June 1997, OJ EU L 304/210, 30.9.2004.

The overall objective of the Accession Protocol, which was signed on 8 October 2002 at Brussels, is to allow for the accession of the European Community to EUROCON-TROL, in order that the European Community assists this organization in achieving its objectives as set out in the Convention, notably that of being a single and efficient body for air traffic management policy-making in Europe.

As a full member of EUROCONTROL, the European Community, nowadays the European Union, in particular the European Commission, will make it possible to reflect the common objectives of the EU Member States within EUROCONTROL.[45] This form of co-operation provides a platform for the contribution by EUROCONTROL to the Single European Sky initiative.

Since 2004, the European Union has gained competences in air traffic management and the decision-making process has moved away from an intergovernmental practice to the EU framework. The main objective of the European Union is to reform ATM in Europe in order to cope with sustained air traffic growth and operations under the safest, most cost- and flight-efficient and environmentally friendly conditions.

Through this European Union policy on the Single European Sky, EUROCONTROL's air traffic organization is profoundly being influenced. EUROCONTROL helps the European Commission, due to delegation of parts of the SES regulations, in drafting the Single European Sky regulatory framework and provides support to rulemaking, standards and safety and environmental legislation.[46]

The Single European Sky initiative implies defragmenting the European airspace, reducing delays, enhancing safety standards and flight efficiency to mitigate the aviation environmental footprint and reducing costs related to services. Achievements have already been made at operational, technological and institutional levels; efforts are ongoing to maximize the benefits of activities initiated under the SES framework.[47]

For the European Union, the EUROCONTROL Convention shall apply to en route air navigation services and related approach and aerodrome services for air traffic in the FIRs of its Member States listed in Annex II to the Convention, which are within the limits of the territorial applicability of the Treaty establishing the European Community.[48]

EUROCONTROL is an intergovernmental organization with 41 Member States and two Comprehensive Agreement States. It is able to control air traffic within various air-

---

45   In 2009, the European Community's institutions were absorbed into the European Union's wider framework.

46   Regulation (EC) No. 549/2004 of the European Parliament and of the Council of 10 March 2004 laying down the framework for the creation of the single European sky (the framework Regulation) *OJ EU* L 96/1, 31.3.2004 and Regulation (EC) No. 551/2004 of the European Parliament and of the Council of 10 March 2004 on the organization and use of the airspace in the single European sky (the airspace Regulation) *OJ EU* L 96/20, 31.3.2004.

47   European Commission, Mobility and Transport, Air, Single European Sky (last update: 9 April 2019).

48   *See* Consolidated version of the Treaty establishing the European Community, *OJ EC* C 325/33, 24.12.2002.

spaces of its Member States, above 20,000 feet. Below this horizontal dividing line, Member States can confide air traffic control tasks to EUROCONTROL. However, these tasks are only partially transferred to EUROCONTROL presently. Practically, it controls all flights within the Brussels and Luxembourg FIRs, the Amsterdam FIR as well as the northern part of the German FIR only at high altitudes.

The underlying principle was that due to the speed of contemporary aircraft, air traffic control at high altitudes can no longer be envisaged within the restrictive framework of national borders in Europe. Based on this consideration, it was thought expedient to create an international control organization operating in the upper airspace and extending beyond the territorial limits of, rather small, individual States. For the lower airspace it was considered to be useful to entrust air traffic control over parts of the territory of a Member State either to the air traffic control unit of another Member State (cross-border control delegation), or to entrust the control to the EUROCONTROL organization.

EUROCONTROL assists Member States to effectuate safe, efficient and environmentally friendly air traffic operations throughout the European region. The organization works together with the European Commission, its Member States and the aviation industry to develop an improved route network over Europe's busy skies, so that flights can go to their destination more directly, saving time, fuel and money. It is committed to building, together with its partners, a Single European Sky that will deliver the air traffic management performance required for the twenty-first century and beyond.

This coordinated initiative will help overcome the safety, capacity and performance challenges facing European high-level civil and military aviation in the twenty-first century. EUROCONTROL, through its network manager functions, balances airspace capacity with demand, optimizing the efficiency and safety of air traffic for Europe's rather inefficient and complex continental airway structure.

The Network Manager, recognized by the European Commission in 2011, has extended the role of the former Central Flow Management Unit, and nowadays proactively manages the entire ATM network, based on the concept of Flexible Use of Airspace (FUA), with nearly 10 million flights every year, in close liaison with the Air Navigation Service Providers (ANSP), the military and civil airspace users and airports.[49]

The Maastricht Upper Area Control Centre (MUAC) provides an air traffic control service for the Netherlands, Belgium, Luxembourg and northern Germany. The Central Route Charges Office (CRCO) handles the billing, collection and redistribution of air navigation charges. Regarding non-collectible air navigation charges, the first option to enforce EUROCONTROL rights is to seize the aircraft concerned at the first port of call,

---

49 Cogen, M., *An Introduction to European Intergovernmental Organizations*, Milton Park, Abingdon, Oxon: Routledge, 2016, pp. 48-50.

or to arrest the kerosene by precautionary attachment as the aircraft cannot be operated without the kerosene, all subject to applicable international legislation (1933 Rome Convention – Precautionary Attachment of Aircraft) or domestic law.[50]

In the meantime, the organization is using its experience to develop the Centralized Services initiative, which will open up some services to market competition on a pan-European level, generating significant savings and making for greater operational efficiency.

EUROCONTROL supports the European Commission, EASA and National Supervisory Authorities (NSAs) in their regulatory activities. Furthermore, it is involved in research, development and validation and provides a substantial contribution to the Single European Sky ATM Joint Undertaking (SJU). Its aim is to deliver tangible results which will improve the ATM system's performance in the medium- and long-term; at the same time it has a unique platform for civil-military coordination within Europe.

It will facilitate civil-military coordination and cooperation in European air traffic management, and will help States and stakeholders in the implementation of the Single European Sky and the SESAR programme so as to share airspace in the most beneficial way. EUROCONTROL is also working on the air traffic management infrastructure of the future, to ensure a fluid exchange of information between airspace users and to provide a harmonized and integrated common framework for the European air navigation system.[51]

4.9   EASA

European Aviation Safety Agency

EASA is an agency of the European Union with regulatory and executive tasks in the field of civil aviation safety, created on 15 July 2003. It reached full functionality in 2008, taking over functions of the JAA. EASA's founding and functioning were established by Regulation (EC) No. 216/2008 (Basic Regulation).[52]

Establishment and functioning of the Agency are laid down in Chapter III, the European Aviation Safety Agency, Section 1, Article 17 of the Basic Regulation. Countries which are members of the European Free Trade Association have been granted participation in the Agency. So far, the total number of European Member States is 32 (28 EU

50 Honnebier, B.P., Collecting EUROCONTROL air navigation charges by precautionary arresting the aviation fuel of aircraft in the European Netherlands, *Journaal LuchtRecht*, June 2013, No. 2-3, Special Edition, Liber Amicorum in Honour of Roderick D. van Dam, The Hague: Sdu Publishers, pp. 33-56.

51 www.EUROCONTROL.int. SESAR, Single European Sky Air Traffic Management Research programme.

52 Regulation (EC) No. 216/2008 of the European Parliament and of the Council of 20 February 2008 on common rules in the field of civil aviation and establishing a European Aviation Safety Agency, and repealing Council Directive 91/670/EEC, Regulation (EC) No. 1592/2002 and Directive 2004/36/EC, *OJ EU* L 79/1, 19.3.2008.

Member States plus four EFTA Member States: Iceland, Liechtenstein, Norway and Switzerland). Its head office is located in Cologne, Germany.[53] Its tasks are:
- drafting implementing rules in all fields pertinent to the EASA mission;
- certifying & approving products and organizations in fields where EASA has exclusive competence (e.g., airworthiness);
- providing oversight and support to Member States in fields where EASA has shared competence (e.g., air operations, air traffic management);
- promoting the use of European and worldwide standards; and
- cooperating with international actors in order to achieve the highest safety level for EU citizens globally (e.g., EU safety list, Third Country Operators authorization).

Its mission is to:
- ensure the highest common level of safety protection for EU citizens;
- ensure the highest common level of environmental protection;
- single regulatory and certification process among Member States;
- facilitate the internal aviation single market and create a level playing field; and
- work with other international organizations and regulators.

The responsibilities of EASA include drawing up common standards to ensure the highest level of aviation safety, conducting data collection, analysis and research to improve aviation safety, providing advice for the drafting of EU legislation on aviation safety, implementing and monitoring safety legislation and rules (including inspections and audits, training and standardization of programmes in its Member States), issuing type-certification of aircraft and component parts as well as approving specialized organizations involved in the design, manufacture and maintenance of aeronautical products.

As part of the Single European Sky II, the Agency has been given additional tasks. The Agency will now be able to certify Functional Airspace Blocks if more than three parties are involved.

EASA has, other than the JAA, legal regulatory authority within the EU through the enactment of its regulations by the European Commission, Council and Parliament, while most of the JAA regulatory products were harmonized codes without direct force of law.

EASA has jurisdiction over new type-certificates and other design-related airworthiness approvals for aircraft, engines, propellers and parts. It is working with the National Aviation Authorities of the EU Member states, but has taken over many of their functions in the interest of aviation standardization across the European Union.

EASA is also responsible for assisting the European Commission in negotiating international harmonization agreements with the rest of the world on behalf of the EU Mem-

---

53 On 13 November 2018, the European Commission published a contingency action plan in the event of a Brexit no-deal scenario with the United Kingdom.

ber States and also concludes technical agreements at a working level directly with its counterparts around the world, such as the U.S. FAA.

EASA also sets policies for aeronautical repair stations (Part 145 organizations in Europe and the United States, also known as Part 571 organizations in Canada) and issues repair station certificates to repair stations located outside the EU.

Regulation (EU) 2018/1139 (new Basic Regulation), which has superseded Regulation (EC) No. 216/2008 on 11 September 2018, sets out common rules in the field of civil aviation.[54] The new Basic Regulation is a thorough update and expands EASA's mandate in several aviation areas such as contributing to a wider EU aviation policy, a coordinating role in aviation cybersecurity, greater scope in environmental protection, research and development and international cooperation.

With respect to civil aviation, a high uniform level of protection of the European citizen should at all times be ensured in this sector by the adoption of common safety rules and by measures ensuring that products, persons and organizations in the European Community comply with such rules and with those adopted to protect the environment. In addition, third-country aircraft operated into, within or out of the territory where the Treaty applies should be subject to appropriate oversight at the European Community level within the limits set by the Chicago Convention.[55]

The European Community should lay down, in line with the SARPs set by the Chicago Convention, essential requirements applicable to aeronautical products, parts and appliances to persons and organizations involved in the operation of aircraft, and to persons and products involved in the training and medical examination of pilots. The European Commission should be empowered to develop the necessary implementing rules.

With respect to operating bans regarding third-country air carriers, Regulation (EC) No. 2111/2005, as amended by Commission Regulation (EC) 474/2006 of 22 March 2006

---

54 Regulation (EU) 2018/1139 of the European Parliament and of the Council of 4 July 2018 on common rules in the field of civil aviation and establishing a European Union Aviation Safety Agency, and amending Regulations (EC) No. 2111/2005, (EC) No. 1008/2008, (EU) No. 996/2010, (EU) No. 376/2014 and Directives 2014/30/EU and 2014/53/EU of the European Parliament and of the Council, and repealing Regulations (EC) No. 552/2004 and (EC) No. 216/2008 of the European Parliament and of the Council and Council Regulation (EEC) No. 3922/91, *OJ EU* L 212/1, 22.8.2018.

55 The 2007 Lisbon Treaty modified the decision-making system. It clarified for the first time the powers of the EU. It distinguishes three competencies: exclusive competence, where the EU alone can legislate, and Member States only implement, shared competence and supporting competence. The Lisbon Treaty gives the EU full legal personality which means the EU obtained the ability to sign international treaties in the areas of its attributed powers or to join international organizations. The European Community was a community formed in 1967 that consisted of three organizations in the European Union, the European Economic Community, the European Coal and Steel Community and the European Atomic Energy Community. They dealt with policies and governing, in a communal fashion, across all Member States.

and Regulation (EU) No. 2018/1139 of 4 July 2018, entered into force in January 2006.[56] In March 2006, the European Commission published an initial list of air carriers considered to be unsafe and which are therefore not permitted to fly passengers or cargo in the European Union or operate within European airspace. The list will be updated at least every three months.

An operating ban is the consequence of non-compliance with international safety standards following one or more random SAFA ramp inspections, subsequent groundings and consequent failure of the air carrier operator to take satisfactory corrective actions.

Regulation (EC) No. 2111/2005 imposes a duty on EASA to communicate all information that may be relevant for the updating of the European Community list of air carriers, which, for obvious safety reasons, are subject to that operating ban.[57]

If EASA refuses to grant an authorization to an air carrier under the terms of this Regulation, it should pass on to the European Commission all relevant information on which this refusal was based, so that the name of the air carrier may be entered, if applicable, on that particular list.

EASA is responsible for coordinating SAFA ramp inspections. Commission Regulation (EU) No. 965/2012 of 5 October 2012 and its subsequent amendments also establish detailed rules for ramp inspections of aircraft of operators under the safety oversight of another State when landed at aerodromes located in the territory subject to the provisions of the EC Treaty.[58]

EASA maintains close working relations with ICAO on a wide range of activities, such as:
– Working with the European Commission and EASA Member States to coordinate common positions on matters addressed at global level.
– Supporting its Member States in implementing ICAO Standards, for example through the compliance checklists.
– Exchanging safety information with ICAO in order to reduce the burden on its Member States. Specifically, EASA and ICAO have signed a Working Arrangement through which they coordinate their auditing activities. This means that, when inspecting a Member State, EASA may collect evidence needed by ICAO to close their own findings or assess the level of compliance with ICAO Standards.

---

56 Regulation (EC) No. 2111/2005 of the European Parliament and of the Council of 14 December 2005 on the establishment of a Community list of air carriers subject to an operating ban within the European Community and on informing air transport passengers of the identity of the operating air carrier, and repealing Art. 9 of Directive 2004/36/EC, *OJ EU* L 344/15, 27.12.2005.

57 Aviation safety audit programmes are: EU Safety Assessment of Foreign Aircraft (SAFA), ICAO Universal Safety Oversight Audit Programme (USOAP), U.S. FAA International Aviation Safety Assessment (IASA) and especially for airlines IATA Operational Safety Audit (IOSA).

58 Commission Regulation (EU) No. 965/2012 of 5 October 2012 laying down technical requirements and administrative procedures relating to air operations pursuant to Regulation (EC) No. 216/2008 of the European Parliament and of the Council, *OJ EU* L296/1, 25.10.2012, amended by Commission Regulation (EU) No. 800/2013 of 14 August 2013, *OJ EU* L227/1, 24.8.2013 and Commission Regulation (EU) No. 71/2014 of 27 January 2014, *OJ EU* L23/27, 28.1.2014.

– Providing technical expertise to ICAO activities. EASA experts take part in the work of around 50 ICAO panels, committees, working groups, study groups and task forces. Additionally, under the Working Arrangement, EASA staff members are trained as ICAO auditors and take part in USOAP audits in EASA Member States and elsewhere.

– Having a permanent representation in Montreal, that serves as a liaison office towards ICAO, by participating in ICAO meetings, informing on EASA policies and regulatory developments and maintaining a working relationship on technical matters with the ICAO Secretariat.

– Contributing to the so-called No Country Left Behind (NCLB) initiative, by coordinating its technical assistance activities with ICAO and other donors at global and regional level. EASA also co-chairs ICAO's Aviation Safety Implementation Assistance Partnership (ASIAP).[59]

The ASIAP was established in February 2015. It serves as a framework for coordinated efforts that contribute to the provision of assistance to States. Its objectives are information sharing, prioritizing assistance needs, collaborating on assistance activities, supporting a resource mobilization strategy and agreeing on outcome indicators.[60]

EASA works with other international organizations such as IATA to address issues of common interest and coordinate actions. A particular area of cooperation is the exchange of safety information, based on a Memorandum of Understanding signed by EASA and IATA in 2012. EASA also provides support to IATA's safety audit programme IOSA by taking part in its oversight committee.

4.10   SAFA, IASA and USOAP

Aviation Safety Assessment Programmes

Aviation safety oversight is the process of ensuring that airmen, air carriers, aircraft, manufacturers, national aviation authorities and numerous other actors engaged in civil aviation, perform their functions in a safe and responsible manner. Safety oversight also ensures that the national aviation industry provides a safety level that is equal to or better than the requirements of the ICAO Standards and Recommended Practices. The primary objective is to create the safest possible civil aviation culture in order to acquire public trust and willingness to universally use the air transport system. However, to achieve an

---

59   ICAO launched the No Country Left Behind (NCLB) initiative to assist States with the effective, globally harmonized, implementation of SARPs and Air Navigation Plans (ANPs) and policies (ICAO/Annual Report 2015/NCLB initiative).

60   ICAO/Safety/ASIAP.

acceptable, or rather an idealistic high-quality-level of aviation safety throughout the world, a global regulatory regime for aviation activities is a prerequisite.

Distinct attention is paid to the EU SAFA programme (replaced in 2012 by the EU Ramp Inspection programme SAFA/SACA), the U.S. FAA International Aviation Safety Assessment program and the ICAO USOAP, all three comprehensive aviation safety assessment programmes, albeit with different approaches.

IATA's IOSA is described in Chapter IV, Part 4.5 of this book.

About 25 years after the adoption of the 1919 Paris Convention, in 1944, during World War II, the Chicago International Civil Aviation Conference created the Convention on International Civil Aviation, the organic constitution of ICAO, the permanent international aviation organization established by this Convention (till 1947 preceded by PICAO). ICAO, a specialized agency of the United Nations, came into force on 4 April 1947.

ICAO promotes, among other objectives, the safe and orderly development of international civil aviation throughout the world. It sets standards and regulations necessary for aviation safety, security, efficiency and regularity, as well as for aviation environmental protection. Annexes to the Chicago Convention, containing detailed safety-related standards, recommended practices and associated procedures, were developed, adopted, extended and continually amended through ICAO.

Implementation of these internationally agreed safety standards is obligatory, although the legal status under international and national law is not quite distinct. There are contrasting views regarding the legal obligation to implement or to comply with the provisions contained in the 19 Annexes, which form the basis for most of the world's national aviation regulations. Immediate notification to ICAO, under Article 38 of the Chicago Convention, by Contracting States unable to identify themselves with the multidisciplinary content of the requirements, is an opt-out or departure from those standards.

According to Annex 6, it is mandatory that Contracting States have a system in place to monitor all flight-operation activities of its air carriers engaged in international air transportation. In this respect, the State of the Operator does have major obligations to ensure air traffic safety in general, and more specifically, the safe transport of passengers and cargo operated by air carriers of that State.

The ICAO SARPs deal with practically all these activities. By implementing those regulations, the States concerned adhere to their obligations as Contracting States to the Chicago Convention, and thus will establish a State's safety oversight system, which shall be required to fulfil these obligations.

The safe and orderly development of international civil aviation requires that all civil aviation operations, both on the ground and in the air, shall be conducted under internationally accepted minimum operating standards, procedures and practices.

Implementation of SARPs by an ICAO Member State must normally be effected under the rule of law promulgated by that State, which in turn will require an enactment of a specific legislative framework to be able to discharge its obligations and responsibilities and to develop and promulgate civil aviation regulations consistent with the acceptance by that State of provisions set in the ICAO SARPs. This specific legislative framework also addresses the necessary powers to ensure compliance with these provisions.[61]

Two fundamental principles are crucial for aviation safety oversight. First of all, every State has complete and exclusive sovereignty over the airspace above its territory (Chicago Convention, Art. 1 Sovereignty and Art. 2 Territory) and secondly, a State's responsibility for safety oversight is one of the tenets of the Chicago Convention, and individual States should reaffirm their safety oversight responsibilities and obligations under ICAO Assembly Resolution A29-13. If these obligations are not fully respected by States, aviation safety deficiencies may arise.[62]

With respect to the European Union and its Member States, together forming a modern transnational, even supranational structure based on the understanding of mutual interdependence, the classical concept of indivisible sovereignty does not fit in the political and legal realities of the European Community order, however, not without inherent, deep-rooted resistance.

State sovereignty is a constituent and rather fundamental idea of the modern age, arguably the most fundamental. Yet, within the European Union, a transfer and delegation of powers and responsibilities will take place. The Member States determine which powers are transferred to the European Union, which undoubtedly will strengthen the functioning of the European Union, especially through the Treaty of Lisbon, signed on 13 December 2007.

This Treaty established, among other things, the concept of shared competence in the transport sector. Member States cannot exercise competence in areas where the European Union has done so. In this perspective, the European Union has developed an air transport policy from as early as 1977 until present. This is a remarkable and unparalleled process, because for the first time in the world of civil aviation experience, a group of States together has developed a comprehensive mandatory air transport policy including the adoption of rules and legislation, of which aviation safety is a vital element.

This European Union legislation, essentially consisting of EU Regulations and Directives as legal instruments, will be applied with the force of national law and European law as appropriate, creating a unified safe air transport market, based on uniform and harmonized rules.

Harmonization of these EU Regulations and Directives will ensure that common rules regarding licensing, airworthiness, operations of aircraft, accident and incident investiga-

---

61   ICAO Doc 9734 AN/959 Safety Oversight Manual, Part A, The Establishment and Management of a State's Safety Oversight System (Second Edition 2006).
62   ICAO Assembly Resolution A29-13, Improvement of Safety Oversight. Adopted in 1992 by the 29th Session of the ICAO Assembly. Resolution A29-13 formed the basis for USOAP. ICAO Assembly Resolution A36-4 (September 2007) established a new approach to be applied in the USOAP beyond 2010 which is based on the concept of Continuous Monitoring Approach (CMA).

tion, aeronautical products, parts and appliances, etc., are applicable throughout the European Union. Therefore, the objective of aviation-related Community legislation is primarily intended to enhance air transport safety in all aspects.

As early as 1955, since the establishment of ECAC, this European cooperative aviation organization has had the objective of implementing internationally agreed safety standards in a uniform manner within the European region. ECAC still plays an important role in developing and harmonizing civil aviation policy in Europe. ECAC collaborates closely with ICAO and the European Union, while contacts are maintained with regional civil aviation organizations and States outside Europe.

Parallel to the developments within ICAO regarding auditing safety oversight, ECAC examined the safety of foreign aircraft. ECAC introduced the voluntary SAFA programme to be able to build a European database of reports, incidents and findings, both technical and operational, of foreign aircraft using Community airports.

The European Commission and the Parliament came to the same conclusion after some tragic civil aircraft accidents involving European citizens and expressed the need to take a more active stance and to develop a strategy to improve the safety of its citizens travelling by air or living in the vicinity of airports.

In 1996, the European Commission issued a Communication to the European Parliament and the Council, SEC(96) 1083, which clearly states that safety may be effectively enhanced by ensuring that aircraft fully comply with the international safety standards laid down in the Annexes to the Chicago Convention, with the overall intention to be able to introduce a harmonized approach to the effective enforcement of these international safety standards within the Community with the aim to establish and maintain a high uniform level of civil aviation safety within the European Union. Appropriate legislation has materialized this intention.[63]

In 2001, the European Commission further outlined the strategy regarding the European Community contribution to world aviation safety improvement (COM (2001) 390 final).[64] This strategy was based on two main streams of actions. On the one hand, the first action plan recommended intensifying work to maintain and further improve the safety of operations in Europe, including the creation of EASA. On the other hand, the second action plan aimed to verify that third countries actually shall apply internationally agreed aviation safety standards, and if applicable, to assist them in complying.

The result was the adoption of the so-called SAFA Directive on the safety of foreign aircraft using Community airports so that appropriate information can be gathered and

---

63 Communication from the Commission to the Council and the European Parliament, report by the High Level Group established by the Council Decision of 11 March 1996, addressed to the European Parliament and to the Council, Defining a Community Aviation Safety Improvement Strategy SEC(96) 1083 final, 12.6.1996.

64 COM (2001) 390 final. Communication from the Commission, A European Community contributing to World Aviation Safety Improvement, Brussels,16.07.2001.

analyzed, and actions taken by the Community and its Member States to rectify danger-ous situations caused by possible aircraft deficiencies.

Following the adoption and coming into force of the SAFA Directive, the former ECAC SAFA programme was transferred to the competence of European Community institutions, *inter alia*, the European Commission and EASA as from 1 January 2007.[65]

The purpose of the SAFA Directive shall be to contribute to the improvement of air safety ensuring that:

- information is collected and disseminated so that sufficient evidence can be estab-lished to decide on measures required to ensure the safety of the travelling public as well as of people on the ground;
- third-country aircraft, their operation and crew are inspected whenever there is rea-sonable suspicion that international safety standards are not being met and such air-craft are grounded if this is necessary to ensure immediate safety;
- appropriate measures for rectification of identified shortcomings (defects) are decided and implemented.

The European Commission was not the only entity or organization in the world con-fronted with this unmistakable aviation safety issue. Apart from IATA with its IOSA programme, intended to audit airlines, there are two prominent aviation agencies in the world, the U.S. FAA that developed the IASA program, an integral part of the continuing effort by the FAA to provide the safest, most efficient air transport system in the world, and ICAO that established USOAP, a globally applied assessment programme, both of which are dealing with State oversight auditing.[66]

Under the IASA program, established in 1992, following a series of accidents and findings of shortcomings of foreign aircraft during ramp inspections at U.S. airports, similar to the situation in Europe, the FAA determines whether another State's oversight of its air carriers that operate, or seek to operate, into the United States, or code-share with a U.S. air carrier, complies with ICAO Standards. An assessment does not evaluate the safety compliance of any particular air carrier, nor does it address aviation security, airports or air traffic management. The IASA program focuses on a State's ability, not the ability of individual air carriers of that State, to adhere to ICAO Standards for personnel licensing, operation of aircraft and airworthiness of aircraft, contained respectively in Annexes 1, 6 and 8 to the Chicago Convention. The IASA program is conducted under the provisions of the Chicago Convention and applicable air transport agreements. Arti-cle 6, Scheduled Air Services, of the Chicago Convention states that:

---

65 Directive 2004/36/EC of the European Parliament and of the Council of 21 April 2004 on the safety of third-country aircraft using Community airports, *OJ EU* L 143/76, 30.4.2004 (SAFA Directive). This legal instrument has been superseded by Commission Regulation (EU) No. 965/2012 of 5 October 2012, which has been amended by Regulation (EU) 2018/1139 of 4 July 2018 (new Basic Regulation).
66 The FAA IASA program was formally established in the Federal Register, Vol. 57, No. 164, 24 August 1992.

No scheduled international air service may be operated over or into the territory of a Contracting State, except with the special permission or other authorization of that State, and in accordance with the terms of such permission or authorization.

IASA's authority is derived from federal regulatory provisions mandating that aircraft operations within the United States be in compliance with Annex 6, Operation of Aircraft. Through bilateral air services agreements, this assessment method is imposed on other Contracting States.[67]

The IASA program categorizes the safety oversight level of a foreign Civil Aviation Authority (CAA), which involves the following technical permissions regarding economic authority:

If the foreign CAA concerned meets the ICAO Standards, the FAA gives that CAA a Category 1 rating.

Category 1 means that the air carrier from the assessed State may initiate or continue service to the United States in a normal manner and take part in reciprocal code-share arrangements with U.S. air carriers, in accordance with the U.S. Department of Transportation authorizations.

If the CAA does not provide safety oversight of its air carrier operators in accordance with the minimum safety oversight standards established by ICAO, the FAA gives that CAA a Category 2 rating. Category 2 rating is applied if one or more of the following deficiencies are identified:

- the State lacks laws and regulations necessary to support the certification and oversight of air carriers in accordance with minimum international standards;
- the CAA lacks the technical expertise, resources and organization to license or oversee air carrier operations;
- the CAA does not have adequately trained and qualified personnel;
- the CAA does not provide adequate inspector guidance to ensure enforcement of, and compliance with, minimum international standards; and
- the CAA has insufficient documentation and records of certification and inadequate continuing oversight and surveillance of air carrier operations.[68]

---

67 Dempsey, P.S., Jakhu, R.S. (Eds.), *Routledge Handbook of Public Aviation Law*, Milton Park, Abingdon, Oxon: Routledge, 2017, pp. 80-81.

68 Milde, M., *International Air Law and ICAO*. Essential Air and Space Law Vol. 4, Series Editor Benkö, M.E., Utrecht: Eleven International Publishing, 2008, pp. 166-167. *See also* Abeyratne, R.I.R., *Strategic Issues in Air Transport, Legal, Economic and Technical Aspects*, Berlin, Heidelberg: Springer-Verlag, 2012, pp. 156-158.

Category 2 means that the air carriers of the audited State cannot initiate new services and are restricted to current levels of any existing service to the United States, while corrective actions are underway.

IASA ratings are released to the public, a method to inform travellers and to put serious pressure on the CAA concerned to take appropriate corrective measures. However, continuing non- or insufficient compliance by foreign air carriers or by the State assessed, could have an economic impact and possible humiliation of the State concerned. Nonetheless, the bottom line is and will be that minimum international aviation safety standards cannot be compromised.

Originally, the FAA established three categories of ratings for States to signify the status of a CAA's compliance with minimum international safety standards. There was a distinction between Category I (Acceptable), Category II (Conditional) and Category III (Unacceptable). On 25 May 2000, the categorization was changed to eliminate any confusion and misinterpretation that has resulted from having two different categories regarding non-compliance with ICAO Standards.[69]

The FAA does not support reciprocal code-share arrangements between air carriers from the assessed State and U.S. air carriers when the CAA has been rated Category 2. During this time, the foreign air carrier serving the United States is subject to additional inspections at U.S. airports. Until adequate improvements are identified, the burden of releasing an IASA rating to the public continues to have an undiminished effect.[70]

Category 2 operators from States that do not have air carriers with existing operations to the United States will not be permitted to commence service to the United States, which might be considered as partial blacklisting. However, the Category 2 air carriers could easily circumnavigate this barrier by conducting services if operated using aircraft wet-leased from an approved and reliable U.S. air carrier or a foreign air carrier from a Category 1 State that is authorized to serve the United States using its own aircraft.

The efforts of IASA to enhance foreign CAA performances and the attention of the European Union to its regional aviation safety issues prompted ICAO to launch USOAP in 1999, replacing the voluntary programme, to carry out regular, mandatory, systematic and harmonized safety audits on Contracting States in all regions of the world.

The intention of ICAO is to assist and advise the Contracting States to improve their capability of safety oversight by assessing whether the eight critical elements of a safety oversight system have been implemented effectively, so as to enable them to monitor their civil aviation sector in accordance with ICAO Standards.[71] Both IASA and USOAP

69 Federal Register Vol. 65, No. 102 (Thursday 25 May 2000), Categorization of Results of FAA Assessments.
70 www.faa.gov/travelers/international_travel/. *See also* Federal Register, Vol. 60, No. 210 of 31 October 1995.
71 The eight critical elements are specified in ICAO Doc 9734, Safety Oversight Manual. The initiative to establish USOAP has its origin in Assembly Resolution A29-13 (Improvement of Safety Oversight). In 1997, during the Conference on a Global Strategy for Aviation Oversight at Montreal, the need for safety oversight was reaffirmed. Assembly Resolution A32-11 (Establishment of an ICAO universal safety oversight audit programme) endorsed an enhanced USOAP to be launched in January 1999.

focus on the eight critical elements of an effective aviation safety oversight authority, as identified and defined by ICAO.

The eight critical elements of a State's safety oversight system are:

CE-1 Primary aviation legislation. The provision of a comprehensive and effective aviation law consistent with the environment and complexity of the State's aviation activity and compliant with the requirements contained in the Convention on International Civil Aviation.

CE-2 Specific operating regulations. The provision of adequate regulations to address, at a minimum, national requirements emanating from the primary aviation legislation and providing for standardized operational procedures, equipment and infrastructure, including safety management and training systems, in accordance with the SARPs, contained in the Annexes to the Convention on International Civil Aviation.

CE-3 State civil aviation system and safety oversight functions. The establishment of a CAA and or other relevant authorities or government agencies, headed by a CEO, supported by the appropriate and adequate technical and non-technical staff and provided with adequate financial resources. The State authority must have stated safety regulatory functions, objectives and safety policies.

CE-4 Technical personnel qualification and training. The establishment of minimum knowledge and experience requirements for the technical personnel performing safety oversight functions and the provision of appropriate training to maintain and enhance their competence at the desired level. The training should include initial and recurrent (periodic) training.

CE-5 Technical guidance tools and provisions of safety-critical information. The provision of technical guidance (including processes and procedures), tools (including facilities and equipment) and safety-critical information, as applicable, to the technical personnel to enable them to perform their safety oversight functions in accordance with established requirements and in a standard manner. In addition, this includes the provision of technical guidance by the oversight authority to the aviation industry on the implementation of applicable regulations and instructions.

CE-6 Licensing, certification, authorization and approval obligations. The implementation of processes and procedures to ensure that personnel and organizations performing an aviation activity meet the established requirements before they are allowed to exercise the privileges of license, certificate, authorization and/or approval to conduct the relevant aviation activity.

CE-7 Surveillance obligations. The implementation of processes, such as inspections and audits, to proactively ensure that aviation license, certificate, authorization and/or approval holders continue to meet the established requirements and function at the level of competency and safety required by the State to undertake an aviation-related activity for which they have been licensed, certified, authorized and/or approved to perform. This includes the surveillance of designated personnel who perform safety oversight functions on behalf of the CAA.

CE-8 Resolution of safety concerns. The implementation of processes and procedures to resolve identified deficiencies impacting aviation safety, which may have been residing in the aviation system and have been detected by the regulatory authority or other appropriate bodies.[72]

In order to assist States in forming an opinion on the status of the safety oversight capability of audited States, ICAO made available transparent summary reports to all Contracting States, although not without previous opposition (on 16 July 2008, all the audited States eventually consented to the release of the results). These reports included an abstract of the audit findings, the corrective actions proposed by the State concerned, the actual status of implementation of SARPs and comments by ICAO on the overall soundness of the safety oversight system in each audited State.

USOAP is in a real sense still a voluntary programme, because ICAO has no decisive legal power to oblige Contracting States to accept the necessary and valuable inspections and audits regarding the provisions of all safety-related Annexes (Comprehensive Systems Approach), while these States essentially are committed to apply all the ICAO Standards and collaborate in securing the highest practicable degree of uniformity in regulations, standards, procedures and organization (Chicago Convention, Art. 33, Recognition of certificates and licenses and Art. 37, Adoption of international standards and procedures). It is an accomplished fact that ICAO can only opt for a formal bilateral Memorandum of Understanding with Contracting States without creating any (international) right or obligation of a binding nature. Nevertheless, enforcement of ICAO Standards is essential for the safe operation of international air services.

Notwithstanding the voluntary nature of the programme, and thus being entirely dependent on consent and cooperation of the audited State, corresponding to (conditional) IASA airline safety audits, USOAP audits have demonstrated that transparent, accurate, factual and timely information will enable all Contracting States, and the aviation community in general, to develop a strategy to assist in the resolution of identified safety concerns. Contracting States have been unanimous in their recognition of the USOAP as an important and essential tool, which should continue to exist as one of the major activities of ICAO to contribute to the improvement of global civil aviation safety.

---

72 Note to CE-2: The term 'Regulations' is used in a generic sense to include but is not limited to instructions, rules, edicts, directives, sets of laws, requirements, policies and orders. Note to CE-3: The term 'State civil aviation system' is used in a generic sense to include all authorities with aviation safety oversight responsibility which may be established by the State as separate entities such as: CAA, Airport Authorities, Air Traffic Service Authorities, Accident Investigation Authority and Meteorological Authority. Note to CE-8: This would include the ability to analyze safety deficiencies, forward recommendations, support the resolution of identified deficiencies, as well as take enforcement action when appropriate. *See also* https://cfapp.icao.int/fsix/criticalelements.pdf.

Improvement of civil aviation safety could be considered as the result of constant and collective contributions of individuals and organizations in different aviation disciplines. However, in order to achieve the best constructive results, tremendous efforts, time and planning are required because there is simply no easy way or marked path to instantaneously make aviation globally safe. It is, rather, a step-by-step process. Establishing an outline for the practical global safety umbrella that should ensure safety, regularity and efficiency of civil aviation operations is one of the steps.

National, but above all, international, standardization is essential in all matters affecting operations of aircraft, airworthiness and the numerous facilities and services required in their support such as maintenance, telecommunications, aerodromes, navigation aids, meteorology, air traffic services, search and rescue, aeronautical information services and aeronautical charts. The next step is to achieve the highest practicable degree of uniformity worldwide whenever this will facilitate and improve civil aviation safety, efficiency and regularity, based on safety-relevant ICAO SARPs, associated procedures, guidance material and PANS.

Developing and harmonizing aviation safety oversight organizations and methods at the State and international level should be accomplished as a positive contribution. On the other hand, as a control method, counteracting complacency regarding safety in aviation is paramount. Further improvement of aviation safety will require constant investments by management in equipment, training, human resources, operational research and detailed analysis of aviation accidents and incidents to be able to learn lessons for the future.

While aviation safety improvements will assume a more extensive form, the civil aviation industry is split in different categories: those States "being compliant with the provisions of the ICAO Annexes," and those States "not or not fully being compliant."

To maintain confidence in the air transport system, and to protect the interest of European citizens who may be living in the vicinity of major airports or travelling on board a third-country aircraft, the European Community identified the need to effectively enforce international safety standards within the Community, where most States already have the status of being compliant with the provisions of the Annexes to the Chicago Convention.

Enforcement is done through the conduct of inspections, including random ramp inspections on foreign aircraft landing at airports located in EU Member States. Enforcement is legally recognized on the basis of the provisions in Directive 2004/36/EC (SAFA Directive), complemented by Regulation (EC) No. 2111/2005.[73]

---

73 Regulation (EC) No. 2111/2005 of the European Parliament and of the Council of 14 December 2005 on the establishment of a Community list of air carriers subject to an operating ban within the Community and on informing air transport passengers of the identity of the operating carrier, and repealing Art. 9 of Directive 2004/36/EC, *OJ EU* L 334/15, 27.12.2005.

The SAFA programme was initially launched by ECAC in 1996. SAFA was at that time not based upon a European legal binding basis, but merely upon a commitment of the Directors General of the participating ECAC Member States. The scope of the ramp inspections performed on foreign aircraft involved those aircraft which were not used or operated under the control of the inspecting competent authorities. As of 1 January 2007, following a decision by the Directors General of ECAC Member States, the SAFA programme was transferred under the European Community competence and the responsibility for the management and further development of the programme falls upon the European Commission assisted by EASA.

The SAFA programme is a mandatorily applied useful (bottom-up) instrument to gain insight into the safety condition and safety level of an aircraft, the air carrier concerned and subsequently the oversight capability of the relevant State. If this characteristic sequence is maintained, the SAFA programme could be considered as supplemental to more top-down oriented programmes, such as the ICAO USOAP and the FAA IASA program.

The SAFA programme comprises random ramp inspections or targeted inspections of third-country aircraft which aviation authorities of EU Member States suspect may not comply with ICAO Standards. As a reminder, third-country aircraft are, in this context, considered as aircraft that are not used or operated under the control of a competent authority of a Member State of the European Union.

A major and legitimate feature of the SAFA programme is its non-discriminatory nature. However, both the programme and the subsequent EU operating ban mechanism, in particular designed to protect European air travellers and citizens on the ground, and more generally to enhance global aviation safety, have triggered criticism as well. Safeguarding civil aviation through time-limited ramp inspections is assumed as an inexpedient method. Assessment of foreign aircraft in this manner will not reveal critical factors which only show up in flight conditions such as airmanship, pilot skills, situational awareness, distress handling, etc.. Other fundamental factors, such as the safety culture of the respective air operator and the extent of compliance with the established requirements, remain ostensibly hidden. Only pursuant to various sources of information, can a solid assessment be done.

There are concerns about the fact that serious political and economic interests are influencing the inclusion of air carriers in the EU blacklist because, for blacklisting, there are no defined global standards. In some cases, incumbent legacy air carriers would be favoured. International aviation bodies like IATA assume that such a list will not contribute to solving the fundamental safety problems associated with certain foreign aircraft operations. They have criticized the blacklist for being punitive rather than constructive in terms of improving safety procedures and oversight.

The EU blacklist is dominated by Asian and African air carriers. Most of these carriers are not even flying to Europe, but, in general, the list is intended more to inform European air travellers. Blacklisting is, in the opinion of many disadvantaged stakeholders, rather unfair, the reason why some of the banned air carriers find different ways (aircraft leasing) to operate to Europe. USOAP will be a more effective tool, as it has the potential to address core issues and global safety concerns. The downside is that this programme requires the consent of the Contracting State to be audited.

The EU blacklist is capable of identifying *ex ante* air safety deficiencies with potentially disastrous repercussions. Inclusion in the blacklist is prompted by criteria such as an inappropriate or insufficient corrective action plan applied by an operator, or by its deplorable safety record, as well as the repeated lack of ability to address safety deficiencies in a timely manner because of continued query by EU Member States. Ramp inspections and any subsequent operating bans are believed to be stringent measures, but provide irrefutably tangible results.

The EU blacklist and the SAFA programme have fostered a more close cooperation between the Community and non-EU States as well as international aviation-related organizations in order to improve international aviation safety oversight in general, and especially to verify compliance by air carriers with the relevant international aviation safety standards.

However, there are a number of restrictions: SAFA ramp inspections are only carried out within the Community, so far limiting the proposed global effect to improve civil aviation safety. Moreover, inclusion on the EU blacklist depends on available and verifiable information, while ailing and banned air carriers just as easily continue to fly to other regions in the world. In addition, during global or regional economic downturns, air carriers, being cyclical companies, have the tendency to cut back on aviation safety, the vital cornerstone of civil air transport.

Fortunately, the civil air transport system, being highly advanced and subject to strict supervision and international safety standards, has some safety redundancy, but there is a critical lower limit not to be exceeded downwards, in everyone's interest. The task of governments is to *a fortiori* strengthen their safety oversight capability, despite economic recession-related cutbacks in State expenditure, and the objective of aviation-related organizations is to join forces in finding the right tools to enhance global aviation safety today and in the foreseeable future.[74]

However, alleged disproportionate assessment and treatment by national aviation authorities regarding foreign air carriers using airports within the Community, resulting in suspension and revocation of air carrier operations by some Member States, prompted some of these carriers to file lawsuits, especially before 2006 when the European Union, through the careful assessment of the Aviation Safety Committee, adopted and published

---

74 Schnitker, R.M., van het Kaar, D., *Safety Assessment of Foreign Aircraft Programme, A European Approach to Enhance Global Aviation Safety*, Essential Air and Space Law, Vol. 11, Series Editor Benkö, M.E., The Hague: Eleven International Publishing, 2013, Conclusions (amended version of the text section pp. 219-225).

a Community-wide aviation blacklist of those air carriers banned from operating within the European Union. The list is based on the principle that air carriers which are banned in a Member State will be banned in all other Member States.

While the Contracting States, signatories to the Chicago Convention, recognize that every State has complete and exclusive sovereignty over the airspace above its territory, these States are unable to individually regulate the safety of international civil aviation without the cooperation of all other States. The EU Member States, although responsible for national aviation safety oversight, have developed a comprehensive mandatory Community air transport policy.

This process is unique and completely different from the ICAO approach in the sense that particular importance has been attached to the economic aspects of such a policy, and in that the rules are mandatory without the option for Member States to give notification of differences. The EU rules and regulations are there to be applied with the force of national law and European law as appropriate. Aviation safety is a vital element of this mandatory air transport policy. The first priority of the SAFA programme and the Community blacklist, which euphemistically has been renamed EU Air Safety list, is to maintain and enhance the already high level of aviation safety in Europe.

On 28 October 2012, the Implementing Rules on Air Operations entered into force as the new legal basis for the EU Ramp Inspection programme.

For various reasons, to think of avoiding different interpretations as to the nature and seriousness of inspections in different States, possible favouritism, disproportionate assessment and conflicts of political and economic interests, the new EU Ramp Inspection programme has replaced the original system established by the SAFA Directive and its implementing regulations, and has two major components:

1. SAFA ramp inspections (for third-country operators); and
2. SACA ramp inspections (for Community operators – checked against EU standards).

The EU Ramp Inspection programme is a European programme regarding the performance of ramp inspections on aircraft used by third-country operators or used by operators under the regulatory oversight of another EU Member State. The SACA ramp inspections are intended to cross-check the safety level of aircraft and oversight of another EU Member State in order to verify adherence to EU Standards and compliance with relevant EU regulations. The programme is regulated by the amended Commission Regulation (EU) No. 965/2012 and it provides for the inspection of aircraft suspected based on, for example, safety-relevant information collected by the 48 participating States (all ECAC States, EU Member States, non-EU ECAC States as well as non-EU States that have signed the EASA Working Arrangements), or on regular analysis of the centralized database performed by EASA) of non-compliance with the applicable requirements.[75]

---

75 *See supra* note 65, Commission Regulation (EU) No.965/2012.

Ramp inspections may also be carried out in the absence of any suspicion, in case a spot-check procedure is being used.

The applicable legal framework of the EU Ramp Inspection programme contains the following:

1. Commission Regulation (EU) No. 965/2012 of 5 October 2012;
2. Acceptable Means of Compliance and Guidance Material to Part-ARO, consolidated version, issue 3, 28 July 2014;
3. Inspection Instructions on the Categorization of Ramp Inspections (SAFA/SACA) Findings – INST.RI.01/002 approved on 18 November 2015.

In each participating State, aircraft of operators under the safety oversight of another Member State or of a third country can be subject to a ramp inspection, chiefly concerned with the aircraft documents and manuals, flight crew licenses, the apparent condition of the aircraft and the presence of mandatory cabin safety equipment.

The applicable requirements for those inspections are:

1. ICAO Standards for aircraft used by third-country operators, mainly Annexes 1, 6, and 8;
2. The relevant EU/EASA regulation for aircraft used by operators under the regulatory oversight of another Member State;
3. Standards of the manufacturers when checking the technical condition of the aircraft; and
4. Published national standards (e.g., Aeronautical Information Publications) that are declared applicable to all operators flying to that State.

EASA is responsible for coordinating the Ramp Inspection programme. The specific roles and responsibilities of EASA in this programme are to:

– collect by means of a centralized database the inspection reports of the participating States engaged in the EU Ramp Inspection programme;
– develop, maintain and continuously update the centralized database;
– provide necessary changes and enhancements to the database application;
– analyze all relevant information concerning the safety of aircraft and its operators;
– report potential aviation safety problems to the European Commission and all the participating States;
– advise the European Commission and all the participating States on the follow-up actions;
– propose coordinated actions to the European Commission and to the competent authorities when necessary on safety grounds, and ensure coordination at the technical level of such actions;
– liaise with other European institutions and bodies, international organizations and third-country competent authorities on information exchange.

The absolute number of inspection findings represents an important outcome of the inspection process, which provides valuable information on the aircraft concerned or its responsible operator. Three categories of findings have been defined: a Category 1 finding is called a minor finding, while a Category 2 finding is a significant finding and a Category 3 finding a major finding. The prime purpose of categorizing the findings is to clarify the compliance with a standard and the severity of non-compliance with the standard. Category 2 and Category 3 findings require the highest attention when it comes to the need for rectification. Based on the category, number and nature of the findings, several actions may be taken. If the findings indicate that the safety of the aircraft and its occupants is impaired, corrective actions will be required. If necessary measures are not taken by the aircraft commander on the reported deficiencies, the State of inspection will formally ground the aircraft. The formal act of grounding means that the aircraft is prohibited from resuming its flights until appropriate corrective measures are taken. Other actions are possible, like for example, departure only being allowed under operational restrictions. The inspections and the categories of findings are recorded in the centralized database.[76]

4.11 SESAR

Single European Sky ATM Research

The world of aviation is changing, starting with aircraft, which are set to become more autonomous, connected, intelligent and diverse. And then there is traffic, which is projected to grow significantly, from several thousand conventional aircraft in the sky every day to potentially hundreds of thousands of highly connected and automated air vehicles/devices operating in practically all airspace classes around the world, but in particular to and from any European airport, offering advanced data-driven services. Added to that, there are increasing demands from passengers for smart and personalized mobility options that allow them to travel seamlessly and without delay.

The SESAR (Single European Sky ATM Research) project aims for a comprehensive European ATM system capable of handling the growth and diversity of air traffic safely and efficiently, while improving environmental performance.

The smooth and safe handling of flights in Europe's airspace is guaranteed by ATM. This specific work is accomplished by ground-based controllers who direct aircraft on the ground and in the air. Their primary tasks are to prevent collisions and to organize and expedite the flow of air traffic uninterruptedly, 24 hours a day, 7 days a week. This system has worked very well in the last decades. However, aging technology together with significant increases in the volume of air traffic, higher environmental awareness and the

---

76　*See* www.easa.europe.eu/easa-and-you/air-operations/ramp-inspection-programmes-safa-saca.

need for cost efficiency are calling for a fundamental change to how aircraft, including drones or Remotely Piloted Aerial Systems, are directed in the future.

ATM technology is in dire need of major improvements to cope with these challenges. The answer to this substantial conversion is the SESAR. This project was launched in 2004 as the technological pillar of the Single European Sky initiative, originated with the European Commission following the severe delays to flights in Europe experienced in 1999.[77] An initial High Level Group (HLG) was established by the European Commission to investigate and report on the regulatory framework, civil and military airspace use, interoperability and air traffic management in the Member States.

At the time, the European Council and the Parliament issued a Regulation regarding the proposal of the Commission to reduce the fragmentation of the European airspace with respect to the organization, airspace use and air navigation services, whereas efficient airspace management is fundamental to increase the capacity of the air traffic system, to provide the optimum response to various user requirements and to achieve the most flexible use of airspace.[78]

Established in 2007, a public-private partnership, the SESAR Joint Undertaking (SJU) is responsible for the modernization of the European ATM system by coordinating and concentrating all ATM relevant research and innovation efforts in the European Union. The SJU was established under Council Regulation (EC) No. 219/2007, as modified by Council Regulation (EC) No. 1361/2008 (SJU Regulation) and last amended by Council Regulation (EU) No. 721/2014.[79]

The Single European Sky I is an ambitious initiative launched by the European Commission in 2004, following its adoption of the Single European Sky proposal in 2001 to

---

77 *See* COM (1999) 614 final/2, Brussels, 6.12.1999. Communication from the Commission to the Council and the European Parliament - The creation of the single European sky.

78 Regulation (EC) No. 551/2004 of the European Parliament and of the Council of 10 March 2004 on the organization and use of the airspace in the single European sky, *OJ EU* L 96/20, 31.3.2004. The SES legislative framework actually consists of four Basic Regulations: No. 549/2004 (framework Regulation), No. 550/2004 (service provision Regulation), No. 551/2004 (airspace Regulation) and No. 552/2004 (interoperability Regulation) covering the provision of Air Navigation Services (ANS), the organization and use of airspace and the interoperability of the European Air Traffic Management Network (EATMN). The four Regulations were revised and extended in 2009 with Regulation (EC) No. 1070/2009 of the European Parliament and of the Council of 21 October 2009 amending Regulations (EC) No. 549/2004, (EC) No. 550/2004, (EC) No. 551/2004 and (EC) No. 552/2004 in order to improve the performance and sustainability of the European aviation system, *OJ EU* L 300/34, 14.11.2009. *See also* Communication from the Commission on the creation of the single European sky of 30 November 2001.

79 Council Regulation (EC) No. 219/2007 of 27 February 2007 on the establishment of a Joint Undertaking to develop the new generation European air traffic management system (SESAR), *OJ EU* L 64/1, 2.3.2007, amended by Council Regulation (EC) No. 1361/2008 of 16 December 2008, *OJ EU* L 352/12, 31.12.2008. Council Regulation (EU) No. 721/2014 of 26 June 2014 of a Joint Undertaking to develop the new generation European air traffic management system (SESAR) as regards the extension of the Joint Undertaking until 2024, *OJ EU* L 191/1, 1.7.2014.

reform the architecture of European ATM.[80] It proposes a legislative approach to meet future capacity and safety needs at a European rather than local level. It includes the concept of Functional Airspace Blocks to reduce the European airspace fragmentation. The key objectives of the Single European Sky are:

- to restructure European airspace as a function of air traffic flows;
- to create additional capacity; and
- to increase the overall efficiency of the ATM system.

In order to fulfil these objectives, the European Commission has set the following high-level goals:

- Enable a threefold increase in capacity which will also reduce delays both on the ground and in the air.
- Improve safety by a factor of 10.
- Enable a 10% reduction in the effects flights have on the environment (ecological footprint and/or the aviation carbon footprint).
- Provide ATM services to the airspace users at a cost of at least 50% less.

SESAR's role is to define, develop and deploy what is needed to increase ATM performance and build Europe's intelligent air transport system. It aims to improve ATM performance by modernizing and harmonizing ATM systems through the definition, development, validation and deployment of innovative technological and operational ATM solutions. These innovative solutions constitute what is known as the SESAR concept of operations. This concept is defined in the European ATM Master Plan, which also defines as a main planning tool, the operational changes that needed a comprehensive roadmap for their deployment.

The operational changes are enabled through improvements to technical systems, procedures, human factors and institutional changes supported by standardization and regulation. SESAR will introduce a paradigm change in ATM, as its heart is a cooperative structure closing ranks between ground and air.[81]

In this light, the newest technology will enable a fast and easy information exchange, not only between air traffic controllers and pilots, but useful messages will in the future also come in real time from airline operation centres, meteorological services and airports. With more information on what is happening, for example, in the destination airspace, flights can be better planned and congestions can be avoided.

Predictability of departure and arrival times will increase, and unnecessary holding patterns will be a memory of the past. However, there are opposite or at least cautionary

---

80 SES I, the SES first package was published in 2004, delivering a new regulatory framework with the intention to lay the foundations of a transnational integrated network to cope with the expected growth in air traffic.
81 European ATM Master Plan: the Roadmap for Delivering High Performance Aviation for Europe, Edition 2015.

statements as well. In a recent report of EUROCONTROL, data-researcher David Marsh states that more delays are to be expected by 2040, due to the likely exponential growth of European air traffic and the capacity gap at European airports. Director General Eamonn Brennan of EUROCONTROL underlines the importance of the report for policy makers. He strongly urges Member States to address airspace constraints and airport infrastructural bottlenecks to prevent excessive delays. By 2040, there will be 1.5 million flights more in demand than can be accommodated. With this in mind, airport capacity expansion plans, even if they can be delivered in time, will prove to be insufficient.

Another worrying phenomenon will be frequently occurring extreme weather conditions, very well possible due to climate change, disrupting flight schedules and causing congestions especially at peak times associated with heavy delays.[82]

Mitigation options or methods for increasing airport capacity could be:

– Larger aircraft: Accelerates the introduction of larger aircraft on congested airport pairs.
– High-speed trains (HST): Accelerates investments in the high-speed train network, beyond existing plans.
– Alternative airports: Some excess traffic moves to secondary or regional airports from the main airports in Europe.
– Consensus benchmark throughput applied to smaller airports: Compensates for the fact that some smaller airports have a relatively short planning horizon and that their capacity may be greater in the future.
– SESAR improvements: Assumes that, where appropriate, airports can invest to benefit from SESAR technologies and improve their capacities to deliver more flights.
– Schedule smoothing: Moves flights to times of the day when more capacity is available.[83]

The SESAR project pools the knowledge and resources of the entire aviation community to develop the new generation of ATM. The SJU was set up in order to manage this considerably large-scale and truly international public-private partnership. The setting up of the SJU was planned before the end of the definition phase so that it could follow the work of the definition phase and prepare the development phase in order to ensure the rapid implementation of the European ATM Master Plan.

As the technological pillar of Europe's ambitious Single European Sky initiative, SESAR is the mechanism which coordinates and concentrates all EU research and devel-

---

82 Janboel dreigt in vol Europees luchtruim (Chaos threatens in overcrowded European airspace), *AD* Dutch daily newspaper, 2 January 2019. *See also* Eurocontrol cautious on 'serious capacity challenge', *ATW*, 20 June 2018.
83 EUROCONTROL European Aviation in 2040: Challenges of Growth Annex 3 Mitigation Measures, pp. 8-9.

opment (R&D) activities in ATM, pooling together experts from various relevant disciplines to develop the new generation of ATM.

The SESAR project aims to integrate and coordinate research and development activities which were previously undertaken in a dispersed and uncoordinated manner in the Community, including the most remote and outlying regions thereof.

ATM is an essential part of European air transport and aviation in general, connecting cities and citizens, as well as boosting jobs and growth. Although unseen and unnoticed by passengers, ATM plays several specific and important roles:

– It acts as a guardian of safety.
– It connects European cities and Europe with the rest of the world.
– It addresses climate change by enabling green and efficient route structures.
– It maximizes current infrastructure while delivering advanced information services.
– It acts as a catalyst for Europe's competitiveness and innovation capacity.

However, Europe's ATM system, based on late twentieth-century technology and procedures, needs updating particularly in light of the expected traffic growth between now and 2040. This is where SESAR comes in as one of the most innovative infrastructural projects ever launched by the European Union.

SESAR's vision aims to transform European ATM into a more modular, automated, interoperable, flight and flow-centric system that takes advantage of advances in digital and virtualization technologies. In other words, this vision relies on a concept of operations underpinned by technologies that enable improvements at every stage of the flight.

Furthermore, this vision sees the integration of all air vehicles with higher levels of autonomy and digital connectivity coupled with more automated support for the management of air traffic. In this new paradigm, the vehicles will fly their optimum trajectories, relying on improved data sharing between air vehicles and the ground infrastructure using mobile, terrestrial and satellite-based communication links. In this system, all categories of air vehicles from RPAS in whatever capacity, general aviation, and business aviation to commercial and military aircraft are safely integrated.

SESAR also addresses airport operational and technical systems capacity and efficiency, introducing technologies such as satellite-based tools for more accurate navigation and landing, and mobile communications to improve safety on the airport surface. Meanwhile, data analytics and better data sharing through system-wide information management (SWIM) are allowing for better flight planning, airport operations and their integration into the overall network.

SESAR's vision builds on the notion of tractor-based operations and relies on the provision of air navigation services in support of the execution of the business or mission trajectory, meaning that aircraft can fly their preferred trajectories without being constrained by airspace configurations.

The long-term vision of the SESAR project is enabled through the effective sharing of information between air and ground actors across the network from a gate-to-gate perspective, along with a progressive increase of the level of automation support facilities, the implementation of virtualization technologies as well as the greater use of standardized and interoperable systems. SESAR launched a knowledge transfer network, managed by a consortium of academia and ATM industry partners, including EUROCONTROL and EASA, with the aim to promote and facilitate the development of ATM research in Europe.[84]

The system infrastructure will gradually evolve with digitalization technology, allowing ANSPs, irrespective of national borders, to plug in their operations where needed, supported by a range of information services. Airports will be fully integrated into the ATM network level, which will facilitate and optimize airspace user operations.[85]

SESAR will definitely have an impact on the future of airline and airport operations. The future of airline operations is based on the results provided by the OCC (Operations Control Centre) project as part of the Single European Sky ATM Research (SESAR I) programme, through which SESAR aims to modernize the ATM system with a view to:
-   increase safety;
-   reduce environmental impact'
-   reduce ATM costs; and
-   increase airspace capacity.

The OCC project was managed by a consortium led by Airbus in which Lufthansa Systems, Sabre Airline Solutions and Airbus Defence and Space were involved in the following subjects:
-   Extended Flight Plan (EFPL)
-   Advanced Flexible Use of Airspace (AFUA)
-   User Driven Prioritization Process (UDPP)

The EFPL represents a new type of flight plan with extended data that will be aligned with upcoming international standards. It provides the following information: 4D trajectory including position, altitude, time at every waypoint and additional information such as aircraft mass and airspeed, outside air temperature, wind (direction and speed) at waypoints and flight-specific performance data to allow for unconstrained, optimum aircraft climb and descent profiles. The EFPL file will be in a new data format based on XML (Extensible Markup Language) and will align airline and ATM planned trajectories, enhance traffic predictions and improve traffic demand and capacity.[86]

---

84   www.sesarju.eu/news/sesar-lauches-atm-knowledge-transfer-network. 26 February 2018.
85   SESAR European ATM Master Plan Level 2017.
86   SESAR takes flight planning into the twenty-first century with the extended flight plan, 22 April 2016.

AFUA regulation consists of configuring modular airspace blocks to enable flexible airspace reservation. It aims to provide a more flexible management of airspace reservation (real-time airspace status data) in response to civil and military airspace user needs, meaning sharing of airspace in real time, which enables civil operators to get increasing opportunities to plan and execute more efficient trajectories.[87]

The UDDP aims to provide more flexibility to airlines in case of flight delays in capacity-constrained situations such as adverse weather conditions or industrial action.

After 2035, performance-based operations will be implemented across Europe, to be completed on schedule by 2050, with multiple options envisaged, such as seamless coordination between ANSPs or full end-to-end air navigation services provided at the network level. Furthermore, it is widely recognized that to increase performance, ATM modernization should look at the flight as a whole within a flow and network context, rather than segmented portions of its trajectory, as is the case today. With this in mind, the vision will be realized across the entire ATM system, offering improvements at every stage of the flight.

SESAR was set up to make a difference by developing solutions that will fundamentally change the way ATM is being handled in Europe today. Recognizing that this mission is too complex for one organization to accomplish alone, SESAR was created with the prospect of collaboration. SESAR unites the whole aviation community through its 19 Members and participating organizations. Due to the lengthy Brexit procedure and the final outcome, there might however be uncertainty about the continuing participation of the United Kingdom.

The first SESAR JU programme, known as SESAR I, ran from 2008 to 2016. In that period, SESAR Members ran over 400 projects, conducted some 350 validations, 30,000 flight trials and invested 20 million hours to ensure that the results of the programme would meet the operational needs of those who must implement them afterwards.

In the Single European Sky I timeframe, more than 60 SESAR solutions which reached maturity during the first R&D programme have been delivered. A number of these are mandated for synchronized deployment in Europe in the framework of the Pilot Common Project (PCP), which requires ANSPs and airspace users to roll out the solutions in a timely and coordinated way.[88] At the same time, local implementations have also started.

SESAR 2020 addresses demand and capacity balancing in a series of candidate solutions which focus on local hotspots and integrate these into the extended planning environment, while others address dynamic airspace configuration measures, flow management and shared trajectory planning to deliver more efficient resource management.

---

87 *See also* on this subject: Commission Regulation (EC) No. 2150/2005 of 23 December 2005 laying down common rules for the flexible use of airspace, *OJ EU* L 342/20, 24.12.2005.

88 *See* Commission Implementing Regulation (EU) No. 716/2014 of 27 June 2014 on the establishment of the Pilot Common Project supporting the implementation of the European Air Traffic Management Master Plan, *OJ EU* L 190/19, 28.6.2014.

The SESAR R&D solutions to some of the pressing challenges facing European aviation today, and which are in the process of deployment at local and European levels, are researched and developed in the following key areas:

– High-performing airport operations.

The future European ATM system relies on the full integration of airports as nodes into the network. This implies enhanced airport operations, ensuring a seamless process through collaborative decision-making (CDM), in both normal and adverse conditions. This feature addresses the enhancement of runway throughput, integrated surface management, airport safety nets and total airport management.

– Advanced air traffic services.

The future European ATM system will be characterized by advanced service provision, underpinned by the development of automation tools to support controllers in routine tasks. This feature reflects the move towards further automation with activities addressing enhanced arrivals and departures, separation management, enhanced air and ground safety nets and trajectory and performance-based free routing. The increased use of digital connectivity enables increased virtualization of service provision, opening up more options for ATM service delivery.

– Optimized ATM network services.

An optimized ATM network must be robust and resilient to a whole range of disruptions, including meteorological and unplanned events. An improved dynamic and collaborative mechanism will allow for a common, updated, consistent and accurate plan that provides reference information to all ATM actors involved in the planning and execution of flights. This feature includes activities in the areas of advanced airspace management, advanced dynamic capacity balancing (DCB) and optimized airspace user operations, as well as optimized ATM network management through a fully integrated network operations plan (NOP) and airport operations plans (AOPs), connected to the NOP via system-wide information management.

– Enabling aviation infrastructure.

The enhancement described in the first three key features will be underpinned by an advanced, integrated and rationalized aviation infrastructure, providing the required technical capabilities in a resource-efficient manner. This feature will rely on enhanced integration and interfacing between aircraft and ground systems, including ATC and other stakeholder systems, such as flight operations and military mission management systems. Communication, navigation and surveillance (CNS) systems, SWIM, trajectory management, common support services and the evolving role of the human will be considered in a coordinated way for application across the ATM system in a globally interoperable and harmonized manner.[89]

---

89   A list of all SESAR I delivered solutions, pipeline candidate solutions, new ideas, concepts and technologies to be investigated in the future can be found in SESAR Solutions Catalogue 2019, Third Edition (living document).

Within the framework of the Single European Sky, the European ATM Master Plan is the main planning tool or the collaboratively-agreed roadmap for defining ATM modernization priorities and ensuring that the SESAR target concept becomes a reality. The Master Plan is regularly updated to reflect the changing landscape in order to prioritize R&D activities and the solutions needed.

The components of this target concept are developed and validated by the SESAR JU. The validated essential operational changes are deployed through Common Projects supported by dedicated SESAR deployment governance and incentive mechanisms.[90]

All three of these processes, definition, development and deployment, are components of a virtual life cycle that actively involves the stakeholders and the European Commission in different forms of partnership. The definition phase of the project aimed to define the different technological actions to be taken, the priorities in the modernization programmes and the operational implementation and validation processes to be performed. It was co-financed by the Community and EUROCONTROL.

The definition phase was followed by the development phase. The scope of this phase is to develop new equipment, systems or standards, which will ensure a convergence towards a fully interoperable ATM in Europe. According to the planning, the development phase converted into the deployment phase (2014-2020) which will be a large-scale production and implementation of the new air traffic management infrastructure.

The initial version of the Master Plan, resulting from the first phase of the SESAR project's definition process, constituted the basis for the development and deployment activities of the SESAR project. The initial Master Plan was endorsed by the European Council on 30 March 2009. A first important update of the Master Plan, approved in 2012, identifies the Essential Operational Changes that need to be implemented for the full deployment of the new SESAR concept by 2030.

The recent 2015 Master Plan edition:
- introduces a vision for the future European ATM system;
- presents the wave of SESAR deployment, such as the Pilot Common Programme and details the key features of R&D activities (SESAR 2020). Each update of the ATM Master Plan reactivates the definition process, which adapts the requirements of the new ATM systems to the evolving Single European Sky performance objectives, and to the operational reality, and feeds these requirements into the subsequent SESAR processes (R&D and deployment).
- provides new deployment scenarios for elements that are sufficiently mature to be brought into the deployment pipeline;
- makes explicit reference to Remotely Piloted Aerial Systems and rotorcraft as airspace users, as well as to cyber security elements within ATM. The role of the human and the approach to change management are highlighted;

---

90 SESAR European ATM Master Plan, The roadmap for delivering high performing aviation for Europe, Executive View, Edition 2015.

– incorporates the results of a more comprehensive military involvement;
– reflects synergies and consistencies with the Deployment Program and the Network Strategy Plan.

Building on the 2012 edition of the Master Plan, the 2015 edition outlines the vision to achieve high-performing aviation for Europe by 2035. The vision reflects the goals captured in the Single European Sky II initiative (second package, launched in 2009 by the European Commission), which calls for more sustainable and better performing aviation, which states that in 2050, the European aviation community leads the world in sustainable aviation products and services, meeting the needs of EU citizens and society.[91]

In particular, the amendments to the Single European Sky I regulatory package introduced a comprehensive EU-wide Performance Scheme to refocus on the properties of the FABs and a Network Manager to coordinate certain actions at network level.[92] Up to 2019, EUROCONTROL has been entrusted with this centralized function at EU level. In addition, it extended the competences of EASA to ATM and thus shifted rulemaking support for technical implementing rules as well as oversight of Member States from EUROCONTROL to EASA.[93]

With the Implementing Regulation establishing the SESAR deployment framework (Commission Implementing Regulation (EU) No. 409/2013), the European Commission activated the deployment process that will close the loop of the SESAR life cycle and will allow SESAR to fully deliver its benefits from concept to implementation.[94] Through this binding framework, the Commission aims to ensure that the SESAR project evolves rapidly and seamlessly to its deployment phase by creating the right conditions for the timely and synchronized deployment of the essential functionalities of the SESAR concept of operations throughout the European ATM network.

---

91 *See* Regulation (EC) No. 1070/2009 of the European Parliament and of the Council of 21 October 2009 amending Regulations (EC) No. 549/2004, (EC) No. 550/2004, (EC) No. 551/2004 and (EC) No. 552/2004 in order to improve the performance and sustainability of the European aviation system, *OJ EU* L300/34, 14.11.2009.
Regulation (EC) No. 1108/2009 of the European parliament and of the Council of 21 October 2009 amending Regulation (EC) No. 216/2008 in the field of aerodromes, air traffic management and air navigation services and repealing Directive 2006/23/EC, *OJ EU* L309/51, 24.11.2009.
92 Commission Regulation (EU) No. 691/2010 of 29 July 2010 laying down a performance scheme for air navigation services and network functions and amending Regulation (EC) No. 2096/2005 laying down common requirements for the provision of air navigation services, *OJ EU* L 201/1, 3.8.2010.
93 Commission Regulation (EC) No. 677/2011 of 7 July 2011 laying down detailed rules for the implementation of Air Traffic Management (ATM) network functions and amending Regulation (EU) No. 691/2010, *OJ EU* L 185/1, 15.7.2011.
94 Commission Implementing Regulation (EU) No. 409/2013 of 3 May 2013 on the definition of common projects, the establishment of governance and the identification of incentives supporting the implementation of the European Air Traffic Management Master Plan, *OJ EU* L 123/1, 4.5.2013.

SESAR experts, air traffic controllers and RPAS or drone (the word drone is derived from the military aviation) specialists, completed in 2017 a workshop exploring how remotely-piloted aerial systems or large drones could be enabled to operate safely and efficiently on the airport surface, integrating with manned aircraft and operating in full compliance with ATC requirements. The use of commercial drones continues to accelerate.

Operators of drones, especially the larger types that can fly at higher altitudes and can remain airborne for many hours, are increasingly seeking access to airports to transport freight to places inaccessible, and mostly too dangerous for conventional fixed-wing aircraft or rotorcraft. These drones are subject to the same rules, procedures and appropriate performance requirements as any other airport user, so, in order to ensure safe airport surface operations, they must be shown to interface with ground-based airport systems and demonstrate their ability to act and respond to ATC and other airport users just like manned conventional aircraft, also in case of unexpected events.

Obviously, the next step will be the integration of commercial drones in non-segregated airspace, subjected to promulgated flight rules and applicable safety regulations.[95]

Current SESAR research projects are categorized into exploratory research, industrial research and validation and very large-scale demonstrations addressing four key areas, namely airport operations, network operations, air traffic services and technology enablers, which are defined as initiatives, such as advanced technologies, systems, operational procedures, and operational or socio-economic developments, which facilitate the implementation of operational improvements or of other enablers.

Implementation of FABs, Cross Border Areas (CBAs), operational synchronization, coordination at institutional level, strong industrial partnership and civil-military commitment and networks are of paramount importance to achieve all objectives of a Single European Sky. Nevertheless, it will be a tremendous challenge to achieve a single European air traffic system similar to the U.S. nationwide NextGen air transport system. The existing U.S.-EU Cooperation agreement on modernizing ATM will not only make it possible to put in place the mechanisms for coordinating the two programmes but also includes a reciprocity clause that will allow European industry to participate in the American program and American industry to participate in SESAR.[96]

Due to the fact that the Single European Sky II left overlaps in legislation, the European Commission launched an interim update of the Single European Sky rules, called

---

95 Demonstrating RPAS integration in the European aviation system, 28 September 2016. A summary of SESAR drone demonstration project results (RPAS-demo-final.pdf).

96 The EU-U.S. Memorandum of Cooperation (MoC) provides the framework for their respective programmes, SESAR and FAA's NextGen Air Transport System (NGATS) coordinated approach in particular with regard to ICAO's harmonization efforts. The European ATM Master Plan will serve to contribute to the update of ICAO's Global Air Navigation Plan (GANP) and the Aviation System Block Upgrades (ASBUS) in 2016. *See also* Signature of the Memorandum of Cooperation between the European Commission and the Federal Aviation Administration for the U.S. (FAA), 3 March 2011.

SES2+. This update focuses on independence and resources of the National Supervisory Authorities, where audits have shown deficiencies in the oversight of ANSPs. There will be more focus on cost-efficiency, transparency and on the strengthening of the Performance Scheme, on more flexibility of industry-led FABs and their performance, and to clarify the role of the Network Manager in opening the door to new centralized SESAR services. Finally, overlapping of responsibilities between EU-level organizations will be resolved, whereby EUROCONTROL, in the capacity of Network Manager, will focus on the operational side, EASA will concentrate on technical rule drafting and oversight authority tasks and the European Commission will work on economic regulation such as performance, charging, institutional issues, etc..

The Single European Sky initiative is a vital step forward to harmonize air traffic control operations and systems throughout Europe to improve efficiency and reduce delays due to air traffic control. The Single European Sky initiative provides for organizing airspace into FABs, according to traffic flows rather than national borders. Its primary aim is to meet future capacity and safety needs through legislation. Interoperability requirements provide one set of standards for air traffic control components and systems across Europe, ensuring full compatibility.

Outstanding R&D work by SESAR has already been started. Some technological and operational ATM solutions for the interoperable framework, the European Air Traffic Management Network (EATMN), have been developed and deployed, while others are in the pipeline. This significant process will also strengthen participation in the worldwide ATM research network.

However, the route to completion of the ambitious and comprehensive Single European Sky initiative, aided by the SESAR programme as the technological mechanism, coordinating and concentrating all R&D activities, will be lengthy, not least because of the lingering behaviour (e.g., Gibraltar dispute) of some Member States. Another setback is the struggle of the Single European Sky project in the past few years to achieve its targets. The results are lagging behind the significant traffic growth of today and the near future. That is exactly the reason why the European Commission is engaged in analyzing possible measures to relaunch the Single European Sky initiative in order to speed up its implementation process.

To reform the current European ATM system, a thorough digital transformation is needed to make the system more automated, innovative, efficient, safe and highly effective on data sharing.[97]

---

97   Single European Sky: can digitalisation improve air traffic in Europe? Analysis, 7 January 2019, www.air-port-technology.com/features/single-european-sky-latest-developments/.

Summary

The history of manned flight is rather short, but the idea that man can travel, bird-like, through the air is as old as history itself. In the nineteenth century, successful human flights were made using hot-air balloons and gliders. However, it took countless experiments with models, gliders and aircraft to successfully complete the first engine-powered, heavier-than-air, sustained flight.

On 17 December 1903, the great moment came at Kitty Hawk, North Carolina, when the Wright Flyer took to the air and remained airborne, under control, for 12 seconds. From its primitive beginnings in the early twentieth century, aviation advanced more rapidly than almost any other invention in the first decades of their existence.

This factuality prompted new discussions concerning the legal status of the airspace. The French academic lawyer Paul Fauchille suggested that a code of international air navigation be created by the *Institut de Droit International* , founded in 1873 at Ghent, Belgium. At subsequent sessions of the *Institut*, the legal status of the airspace was an opportunity for new discussions, in particular the right of innocent passage, in fact the freedom of flight, against the concept of absolute and exclusive sovereignty over national airspace. Especially the 1911 Madrid Session dealt with the report *Le régime juridique des aérostats* by Paul Fauchille and Ernest Nys.

While the first regulations for safety in air navigation were made at national level, it soon became evident that most of the legal problems could not be resolved on a purely national basis. International unification of law relating to civil aviation was deemed necessary.

Because of the emerging international character of civil aviation prior to, but especially following, World War I, international legal regulation has been developed in order to unify, harmonize and standardize the fundamental legal principles governing civil aviation. Apart from a few bilateral aviation agreements regarding the legal status of international flights, the international character was in fact much more widely expressed by the convening of the 1910 Paris International Air Navigation Conference, to deal with the first diplomatic effort to formulate the principles of international law relating to air navigation, in particular, but not exclusively, to the legal status of the airspace.

The decisive issue was whether the airspace was to be part of the sovereign territory of the subjacent State, or whether it was free to be used by any State without any restrictions. The Conference agreed on issues like registration and certification of aircraft, the privilege of subjacent States to set up prohibited zones above which no international flight was lawful and the recognition that cabotage (later, in 1944 described in the Convention on International Civil Aviation, Art. 7) could be reserved for national aircraft. However, most important is the now defined fact that the Conference first evidenced general international agreement that usable space above the lands and waters of a State is part of the territory of that State.

Unfortunately, due to political disagreement and rather diametrically opposed opinions, the Conference did not succeed in the effort to conclude an international convention. Nevertheless, the meaning of the clauses of a detailed draft convention has been of great value for subsequent treaties on civil aviation.

The Convention Relating to the Regulation of Aerial Navigation (1919 Paris Convention) was the first legal instrument to enter into force in the field of international air law, intended for the general regulation of post-war international aviation by using the relevant regulatory framework done at the earlier 1910 Paris Conference. The Convention established the principles of complete and exclusive sovereignty of the Contracting States over the airspace above their respective territories, but at the same time, recognized the right of innocent passage (freedom of the air) of aircraft of the other Contracting States, although under certain conditions.

In order to achieve a certain degree of uniformity, some technical annexes were added to the 1919 Paris Convention. Furthermore, it created the International Commission for Air Navigation (ICAN) to monitor the regulation of international civil aviation, to establish a uniform air code for all Contracting States, and specifically to amend the provisions of the Annexes A-G, the Convention's technical regulations which, remarkably, had the same legal status as the Convention itself.

In October 1926, the Spanish government decided, based on its irreconcilable political attitude towards the 1919 Paris Convention, to initiate a diplomatic counteraction and invited all Latin-American States and Portugal to a congress held in Madrid, in order to promulgate the 1926 Ibero-American Convention on Air Navigation (also called the Madrid Convention). Due to the restricted number of ratifications, this Convention had very limited impact. Moreover, there was no longer need for an alternative to the provisions of the 1919 Paris Convention.

A few years later, in 1928, the Latin American States were focusing on North America, away from Iberia. The isolationist but dominant United States strongly supported the project of a Pan-American Convention on Aerial Navigation. The result was the Pan-American (or Inter-American) Convention on Commercial Aviation (also called the 1928 Havana Convention).

It was the first attempt to construct an international aviation agreement completely in the Western Hemisphere. At the time, no international agreement applied, partly because the United States had never ratified the 1919 Paris Convention, which provided rudimentary governance over aviation for most of Europe.

Remarkably enough, the starting point in Havana was the 1919 Paris Convention, although a number of modifications were added. Regarding some provisions, there were fundamental differences. The Havana Convention focused on the purely commercial aspects of civil aviation such as traffic rights, different from the Madrid and Paris

Convention that emphasized the operational and technical aspects of civil aviation. In addition, the Havana Convention did not have any technical annexes, nor did it provide for the establishment of a permanent institution with capabilities similar to ICAN, reasons why the level of uniformity was not accomplished.

The Madrid Convention eventually did not enter into force, while the Paris Convention and the Havana Convention were superseded by the International Convention on Civil Aviation (also known as the Chicago Convention). During World War II, in 1943, at the Anglo-American Conference in Quebec City, Canada, the Allied political leaders Franklin Delano Roosevelt and Winston Leonard Spencer-Churchill discussed, in a highly remarkable anticipatory way, post-war aviation policy and were planning for a coordinating organization to handle the global aspects of international civil aviation.

The most ground-breaking and leading international treaty in the field of civil aviation is the Convention on International Civil Aviation. This document, in fact the constitution of world civil aviation, signed at the Chicago International Civil Aviation Conference on 7 December 1944, is a source of public international air law which sets out as its prime objective the development of international civil aviation in a safe and orderly manner, such that the international air transport services would be established on the basis of equality, of opportunity and operated soundly and economically.

The Chicago Conference produced the following main legal instruments contained in its Final Act: The Interim Agreement on International Civil Aviation, establishing the provisional coordinating body PICAO, pending the required number of ratifications for the official and permanent ICAO, the Convention on International Civil Aviation, extensive drafts of 12 Technical Annexes (in 2013 extended to 19 Annexes), a Standard Form of Bilateral Agreements and the International Air Services Transit Agreement (IASTA), guaranteeing two freedoms of the air as well as the International Air Transport Agreement (IATA) including, apart from the previous freedoms, three additional freedoms of the air. Both multilateral agreements have the status of being supplementary but are not part of the Convention on International Civil Aviation. They enable ICAO Member States which are also Parties to these multilateral agreements to grant each other greater freedom, however, without extensive application.

Instead, bilateral agreements are widely used in international air transport to regulate the operation of air services, in particular the exchange of traffic rights and certain provisions concerning tariffs and capacity between two States. The first bilateral agreement was signed in 1946 between the United States and the United Kingdom, known as Bermuda I, followed by Bermuda II. These classical air services agreements were largely amended due to upcoming liberalization, especially in the United States. The first liberalized agreement was signed in 1992 by the United States and the Netherlands. So-called Open Skies agreements provide for maximum operational flexibility for air carrier alliances throughout the world by allowing air carriers from a single State, or a group of

States in a region like the European Union, unlimited market access to partner markets and the right to fly to intermediate and beyond points.

The framework of the Chicago Convention is still without a doubt the main foundation for aviation rulemaking and the organic constitution of ICAO. It is apparent that the provisions of the 1919 Paris Convention formed the basis for the Chicago Convention. The doctrine of airspace sovereignty was the most elementary principle in both conventions.

In the *interbellum*, the unbridled development of commercial air transport gave rise to an oppressive awareness and concern regarding the lack of uniformly regulated liability. Unification of private international law with respect to the regulation of liability in the event of an aircraft accident or in case of death, injury or damage caused by foreign aircraft on the surface became a priority topic. At that time, liability was not covered by any international regulation to have formal assurance of any redress.

Response came through the adoption of the Warsaw Convention in 1929 and the Rome Convention in 1933. The Warsaw Convention was the first comprehensive legal framework governing international aviation, being extremely advanced at the time when it was concluded, and has been playing an essential role in regulating liability in the event of accidents.

Just as the Rome Convention, the Warsaw Convention was amended several times by subsequent legal instruments, due to changing insights and circumstances, technological progress and the advance of law. A number of supplementary instruments amended the Warsaw Convention, such as the 1955 The Hague Protocol, the 1961 Guadalajara Convention, the 1971 Guatemala City Protocol, four Montreal (Additional) Protocols amending all previous instruments as well as various Inter-carrier Agreements.

The 1999 Montreal Convention, the so-called new or modern Warsaw Convention, was intended to replace the antique Warsaw Convention and its various amending instruments (the Warsaw system). Increased mobility of passengers and the tremendous progress in globalization of the air transport industry had made this Warsaw system rather fragmented, incoherent and definitely obsolete. The Montreal Convention essentially consolidates the existing Warsaw system into a single treaty revising various articles and introduces contemporary principles in accordance with modern realities and concerns.

The first attempt to establish a worldwide uniform regime relating to liability for damage caused by foreign aircraft to third parties on the surface was the conclusion of the 1933 Rome Convention. The starting point of the liability regime, the burden of nearly absolute liability on the operator of the aircraft, was the protection of third parties, innocent non-participants and property on the surface. However, neither the 1933 Rome Convention nor the second attempt, the 1952 Rome Convention, were widely accepted or ratified, mainly due to the low interest of leading aviation States.

The 1933 Rome Convention should not be confused with the Convention for the Unification of Certain Rules Relating to the Precautionary Attachment of Aircraft, also adopted on 29 May 1933. This Convention exempts categories of aircraft, such as State aircraft, from precautionary arrest, while it safeguards or immunizes other aircraft susceptible for seizure by, among other things, pledging an adequate guarantee.

In the 1960s, in view of modernizing the 1952 Rome Convention, the ICAO Legal Committee and a subcommittee initiated a study into why States were opposed to ratification, and accordingly made proposals to overcome certain obstacles, resulting in the adoption of the Montreal Protocol in 1978. However, this Protocol did not receive wide acceptance due to inadequate liability limits. At the time, the Legal Committee started a revision cycle on outdated liability conventions, which was mainly accelerated by the impetus of the 9/11 terrorist attacks in the United States. On 2 May 2009, ICAO adopted the General Risk Convention and the Unlawful Interference Compensation Convention. However, neither instruments entered into force.

In the early days of civil aviation, no major incidents occurred as a result of criminal acts committed on board aircraft by individual or conspiracy terrorists. However, from 1948 onwards, this seemingly uncomplicated situation changed rapidly. The vulnerability of civil aviation became especially evident because of the increasing number of unlawful acts committed in flight, in particular hijackings. At the time of the Cold War, aircraft hijacking was practically commonplace.

The rise of extremely violent terrorism and the unlawful seizure of aircraft caused a definite and abrupt end to the fundamental openness of the international aviation industry. To curb this altered reality, legal instruments were deemed to be urgently needed. The first legal answer was the Tokyo Convention, concluded on 14 September 1963 under the auspices of ICAO. Since the 1950s, aviation security became a key element of ICAO's role in the world motivated by studies and drafts on the legal status of aircraft and the problem of crimes committed on board civil aircraft.

The objectives of the Tokyo Convention cover a variety of subjects with the intention of providing safety in aircraft, protecting life and property on board, providing the aircraft commander with the necessary authority to deal with offences and other acts committed on board and generally protecting the security of civil aviation. The Tokyo Convention is applicable to offences against penal law and any acts jeopardizing the safety on board civil aircraft while in flight and engaged in international air transportation.

The 1970 Hague Convention (Anti-hijacking Convention) made additions and amendments to the Tokyo Convention, while the 1971 Montreal Convention was more focused on the prevention and discouragement of sabotage and acts of violence against civil aviation in general, including airports and air navigation facilities used in international air navigation. In 2010, the Beijing Convention and its Protocol were concluded. The Convention is the result of collective efforts of the international community to modernize the legal framework for civil aviation security, mainly prompted by the 9/11 terrorist attacks. The Beijing Protocol supplements The Hague Convention by expanding its scope to cover different forms of aircraft hijacking and certain preparatory acts for the offence, including through modern technical means.

The most recent legal instrument within the Tokyo Convention regime is the 2014 Montreal Protocol, which focuses on unruly or disruptive passengers. The Tokyo Convention was considered outdated, ineffective and too easily avoided to empower air carriers to take remedial actions against unruly passengers. This Protocol provides for a more effective deterrent by making the consequences of unruly behaviour clear and enforceable.

A number of miscellaneous multilateral agreements pertaining to subjects on air transport operations such as commercial rights, airworthiness, tariffs and capacity, are concluded at Paris. A number of States Parties to the 1956 Paris Agreement on Commercial Rights of Non-scheduled Air Services in Europe, concluded within the framework of the European Civil Aviation Conference (ECAC), have agreed to admit non-scheduled commercial air services or certain categories thereof without prior permission. This Agreement generally provides for close cooperation and a more liberalized regime regarding the authorization of non-scheduled air services. Although the definition of non-scheduled air services is not very clear, the distinction between scheduled and non-scheduled is, to a large extent, fading away due to the global progress in liberalization of international air transport.

The 1960 Paris Agreement Relating to Certificates of Airworthiness for Imported Aircraft was ratified by almost all members of ECAC. Under this Paris Agreement, States are obliged to validate the certification of another Contracting State or issue a new certificate of civil aircraft imported from another Contracting State, provided that these aircraft have been constructed in accordance with the airworthiness requirements of the other Contracting State. In addition, these aircraft must meet the minimum standards of the Chicago Convention (Annex 8) and the operational requirements of the importing State, subject to additional specific conditions.

ECAC also paved the way for the 1967 Paris Multilateral Agreement (tariffs for scheduled air services). This Paris Agreement establishes tariff provisions between any two States who have no bilateral agreement in this field, or where an agreement exists, however, without a tariff clause. It also replaces the tariff clauses in any already concluded relevant bilateral agreement for the time the Paris Agreement remains in effect for the two States concerned. The Paris Multilateral Agreement is based on an existing system, which is reason why it is not really an innovative ratemaking mechanism but its provisions lead to harmonization and unification of tariff clauses in existing bilateral air services agreements.

The 1987 Paris Tariffs Agreement, replacing the 1967 Paris Tariffs Agreement, and the 1987 Paris Capacity Agreement, both concluded under the auspices of ECAC, constituted the first step of ECAC in the European air transport market to achieve liberalization. Eventually, both instruments were taken over by relevant regulations of the European Union.

Two important agreements were adopted by ICAO in 1948 and 1991, respectively, dealing with rights in aircraft and the detection of plastic explosives.

With the knowledge that financing aircraft would be crucial for the development and expansion of the post-war aviation industry, the manufacturers and air carriers agreed to work on the issues of rights in aircraft, mainly, rights of property in aircraft, international financing and leasing, ownership and the rights to possession of aircraft under certain leases, in accordance with national law. Therefore, ICAO adopted in 1948 the Convention on the International Recognition of Rights in Aircraft.

The 1988 Lockerbie air disaster drew urgent attention to the dangerously growing trend of acts of unlawful interference, in particular the use of plastic explosives aimed at the total destruction in flight of civil aircraft in commercial service and the death of as many people as possible on board and on the surface. The general belief was that the unprecedented potential threat of using devastating plastic explosives with regard to the aviation industry must by all means be halted.

Following a preparation phase with the highest and overriding priority, ICAO adopted in 1991 the International Convention on the Markings of Plastic Explosives for the Purpose of Detection, targeting possible terrorist acts of sabotage on the international air transportation system.

International civil aviation organizations, in particular the overarching world organization ICAO, all contribute to the safe, orderly and efficient operation of international civil aviation. Acts of these institutions such as agreements, regulations, international standards or norms, studies and research are of utmost importance, now and in the future. In addition, aviation safety assessment programmes are aiming at improving the safety level of air carriers and are auditing national aviation authorities to ensure that oversight and aviation activities are in compliance with the ICAO Standards for aviation safety.

Other aviation-related programmes focus on next generation air traffic flow management and airspace potential to cope with the tremendous increase in demand for air travel in various regions of the world according to the IATA prognoses.

ECAC, Europe's largest and longest-standing intergovernmental aviation organization, addresses issues like safety, security, environment, air navigation and economics affecting the European civil aviation sector. ECAC, as a think tank and a centre of expertise, works cooperatively and in close liaison with ICAO on these and other civil aviation issues, including individual ICAO Member States such as the United States, and regional institutions as EASA and the supranational European Union. ECAC introduced the voluntary SAFA programme to be able to build a European database of reports, incidents and findings, both technical and operational, of foreign aircraft using Community airports.

In 2001, the European Union recommended intensifying work to maintain and further improve the safety of aircraft operations within Europe, including the creation of EASA, and to verify that third countries actually apply internationally agreed aviation safety standards as well as, if applicable, to assist them in complying. The result was the adoption of the so-called SAFA Directive on the safety of foreign aircraft operating to and from Community airports. The ECAC SAFA programme initiative was eventually transferred to the European Union in 2012. The European Commission extended this Ramp Inspection programme to Community operators. These Safety Assessment of Community Aircraft (SACA) inspections are intended to cross-check the safety level of aircraft and the safety oversight capability of another EU Member State in order to verify adherence to EASA and ICAO Standards and compliance with relevant EU Regulations.

Back in time, in late 1944, the Chicago Convention formalized the expectation that a specialized international agency would be established, in order to organize and support the intensive international cooperation which the global air transportation network would require. The agency was first called Preliminary International Civil Aviation Organization, however, upon sufficient ratifications to the Chicago Convention, from 4 April 1947 officially, it was called ICAO.

ICAO is recognized as a governmental organization and a United Nations specialized agency. By the terms of its constitutive instrument, the Chicago Convention, it is empowered to obtain worldwide maximum technical standardization and to assist States to achieve the highest possible degree of uniformity in civil aviation regulations, standards, procedures and organization, and to improve international civil air navigation.

All States Parties to the Chicago Convention agree to conform to ICAO Standards to the greatest possible extent. Departure from international standards and procedures by a Contracting State must immediately be notified to ICAO stating the differences between its own practice and that established by the international standard. To monitor compliance, ICAO launched its own audit programme, the Universal Safety Oversight Audit Programme (USOAP). Both USOAP and IASA, the U.S. FAA audit program, focus on the eight critical elements of an effective aviation safety oversight authority, as identified and defined by ICAO.

USOAP is in a real sense a voluntary audit programme, carried out with the consent of the State concerned. ICAO has only modest enforcement powers to oblige Contracting States to comply with ICAO Standards and accept the necessary inspections and audits.

ICAO's forerunners, the International Commission for Air Navigation (ICAN) and the *Comité International Technique d'Experts Juridiques Aériens* (CITEJA) were created following World War I when the growth of civil aviation accelerated. In those days, aviation regulation was patchwork and required renewal and harmonization. Moreover, the aircraft accident rate, aircraft damage and loss of life increased proportionally with the growth in the number of emerging airlines.

Undeniably, these consequences of air operations gave rise to liability and claims, issues where private air law did not have an adequate answer. This rather chaotic situation needed the formulation of a uniform system of regulation regarding private international air law. A special body of legal experts (CITEJA) was appointed to develop a code of private international air law through the preparation of draft international conventions for final adoption.

ICAN, under the coordinating direction of the League of Nations, but practically operating autonomously, was to develop international regulations in the field of air navigation in line with the technical progress, and especially the safe transport by air of goods and persons over prolonged distances. ICAN dealt exclusively with the regulation of international air navigation and was particularly working in the field of public international air law.

The International Air Transport Association (IATA), founded in Havana, Cuba, on 19 April 1945, and headquartered in Montreal, is the trade association for the world's airlines, representing some 280 airlines from 120 States in every part of the globe. IATA is the prime institution for inter-airline cooperation in assisting the aviation industry to achieve adequate levels of profitability, to promote safe, reliable, secure and economical air services, in order to benefit consumers throughout the world.

IATA has its own safety audit mechanism, the IATA Operational Safety Audit (IOSA) programme.

It is an evaluation system designed to assess the operational management and control systems of an airline. All IATA Members are IOSA-registered, and must remain registered to maintain IATA membership. Where IATA's intention is to audit airlines, the U.S. FAA developed the International Aviation Safety Assessment (IASA) program focusing on a foreign State's ability to adhere to ICAO Standards in order to provide the safest, most efficient air transport system in the world. The present IATA was preceded by the International Air Traffic Association (IATA), formed at The Hague on 25 August 1919, the year of the world's first international scheduled air services.

This original IATA was formed by a small number of European airlines with a view to cooperate to mutual advantage in preparing and organizing international aerial traffic. With the outbreak of hostilities in 1939, civil air transport virtually came to a standstill until 1945 when the renamed IATA was founded.

Another organization in the field of aviation was the Joint Aviation Authorities (JAA), a European initiative, which was created by the aviation certification and regulatory agencies of the EU Member States. The objective was to cooperate in developing and implementing common aviation safety regulatory standards and procedures, called the Joint Airworthiness Requirements, adopted as guidelines.

The JAA became an associated body of ECAC and fully integrated over time. EASA, European's new agency with responsibilities for civil aviation safety, absorbed most functions of the JAA. What remained is the JAA Training Organization.

EASA's responsibilities include the analysis and research of safety parameters, authorizing foreign operators and advising the European Commission on the drafting of EU legislation. The agency was legally established in 2002 pursuant to the provisions of Regulation (EC) No. 1592/2002. Its mission is to ensure the highest common level of safety protection for EU citizens, environmental protection and provision for a single regulatory and certification process among its Member States.

Furthermore, it facilitates the internal aviation single market and creates a level playing field, and works with other international aviation organizations and regulators. The new Basic Regulation of 2018 expands EASA's mandate in several aviation areas, including cybersecurity, research and development, environmental protection and international cooperation, and it has been given additional tasks regarding the second regulatory package on the Single European Sky (SES II).

With respect to aviation rescue service, the international Cospas-Sarsat Programme Agreement was signed in 1984. This Agreement, established by four States, created a humanitarian endeavour that fosters international cooperation for search and rescue. Its purpose is to provide distress alert and location data derived from a worldwide operating system consisting of a space segment (satellites), a ground segment and radio beacons, to the international community in support of SAR operations on a non-discriminatory basis.

For the safety of air navigation, four European States agreed to set up a single international air traffic control centre to manage their upper airspace. This intergovernmental organization, the European Organization for the Safety of Air Navigation (known as EUROCONTROL) was established in 1960 by means of an international convention. As the European Union also became a participant, the European Commission made it possible to reflect the common objectives of the EU Member States within EUROCONTROL.

This kind of cooperation provides a platform for the contribution by EUROCONTROL to the Single European Sky initiative. On the other hand, the European Commission gained competences in ATM, in other words, the decision-making process moved away from an intergovernmental practice to the EU framework. The main objective of the European Commission, with its decision-making powers, is to reform ATM in Europe in order to cope with sustained air traffic growth and operations under the safest, most cost- and flight-efficient and environmentally friendly conditions.

EUROCONTROL assists Member States to effectuate safe, efficient and economic air traffic operations throughout the European region. It is also working on the ATM infrastructure of the future and contributing to the Single European Sky ATM Research Joint Undertaking (SJU), a public-private partnership responsible for the modernization of the European ATM system.

The Single European Sky initiative implies defragmenting the European airspace structure, reducing delays, enhancing safety standards and flight efficiency, mitigating the aviation environmental footprint and reducing costs related to services. However, with a EUROCONTROL expert prediction in mind that around the year 2040 the European airspace structure most probably will be completely congested, it is going to be an exceptional challenge to manage future air traffic flow.

International civil aviation is a global activity, largely regulated by a concurrence of public and private international air law. International air law covers a wide spectrum of issues and has its sources in both international multilateral conventions and customary law, bilateral and regional agreements, judicial decisions, national laws, norms, acts and resolutions issued and adopted by international aviation organizations, and inter-airline agreements, with greater or lesser significance for civil aviation.

International air law regulates literally every conceivable aspect related to international civil aviation. The increasing chances of perfecting universal compliance with international aviation standards, which means absolute harmonization within the aviation industry on a global scale, is due to the progress, versatility and legal binding nature of international air law, because its rules are accepted and function as law in international society.

REFERENCES

TEXTBOOKS AND SCIENTIFIC JOURNAL ARTICLES IN SPECIALIZED AREAS

Abeyratne, R.I.R., The Decision of the European Court of Justice on Open Skies – How Can We Take Liberalization to the Next Level, 68 *J. Air L. & Com.* (2003).

Abeyratne, R.I.R., *Aviation Security Law*, Berlin, Heidelberg: Springer Science & Business Media, 2010.

Abeyratne, R.I.R., *Aeronomics and Law: Fixing Anomalies*, Berlin, Heidelberg: Springer-Verlag, 2012.

Abeyratne, R.I.R., *Strategic Issues in Air Transport: Legal, Economic and Technical Aspects*, Berlin, Heidelberg: Springer-Verlag, 2012.

Abeyratne, R.I.R., *Convention on International Civil Aviation: A Commentary*, Cham: Springer International Publishing, 2014.

Abeyratne, R.I.R., *Megatrends and Air Transport, Legal, Ethical and Economic Issues*, Cham: Springer International Publishing, 2017.

Abeyratne, R.I.R., *Law and Regulation of Air Cargo*, Cham: Springer International Publishing, 2018.

Antwerpen, N. van, *Cross-Border Provision of Air Navigation Services with Specific Reference to Europe: Safeguarding Transparent Lines of Responsibility and Liability*, Aviation Law and Policy Series, Alphen aan den Rijn: Kluwer Law International, 2008.

Bantekas, I. & Nash, S., *International Criminal Law*, Third Edition, London: Routledge-Cavendish, 2007.

Bartsche, R.I.C., *International Aviation Law: A Practical Guide*, Milton Park, Abingdon, Oxon: Routledge, 2016.

Bergkamp, L., Faure, M., Hinteregger, M. & Philipsen, N., *Civil Liability in Europe for Terrorism-Related Risk*, Cambridge: Camebridge University Press, 2015.

Besson, S. & Aspremont, J. d'. (Eds.), Knuchel, S. (Assistant), *The Oxford Handbook of the Sources of International Law*, Oxford: Oxford University Press, 2017.

Boyle, R.P., *et al.*, The Tokyo Convention on Offences and Certain Other Acts Committed on Board Aircraft, 30 *J. Air L. & Com.* 305 (1964).

Brady, T. (Ed.), *The American Aviation Experience: A History*, Carbondale and Edwardsville, IL: Southern Illinois University Press, 2000.

Brisibe, T., *Aeronautical Public Correspondence by Satellite*, Essential Air and Space Law, Volume 3, Series Editor Benkö, M.E., Utrecht: Eleven International Publishing, 2006.

Brown, E.G., The Rome Conventions of 1933 and 1952: Do They Point a Moral, 28 *J. Air L. & Com.* 418 (1962).

Budd, L. & Ison, S. (Eds.), *Low Cost Carriers, Emergence, Expansion and Evolution*, Milton Park, Abingdon, Oxon: Routledge, 2016.

Budd, L. & Ison, S. (Eds.), *Air Transport Management: An International Perspective*, Milton Park, Abingdon, Oxon: Routledge, 2017.

Cento, A., *The Airline Industry: Challenges in the 21st Century*, Heidelberg: Physica-Verlag, 2009.

Cheng, C.-J., *The Use of Airspace and Outer Space for All Mankind in the 21st Century*, The Hague: Kluwer Law International, 1995.

Cheng, C.-J. & Kim, D.H. (Eds.), *The Utilization of the World's Air Space and Free Outer Space in the 21st Century*, The Hague: Kluwer Law International, 2000.

Clark Northrup, C. (Ed.), *Encyclopedia of World Trade: From Ancient Times to the Present*, Volumes 1-4. *Flight and Trade between the World Wars*, Milton Park, Abingdon, Oxon: Routledge 2015.

Cogen, M., *An Introduction to European Intergovernmental Organizations*, Milton Park, Abingdon, Oxon: Routledge, 2016.

Cooper, J.C., The International Air Navigation Conference, Paris 1910, 19 *J. Air L. & Com.*, 1952.

Czerny, A.I., Forsyth, P., Gillen, D. & Niemeier, H.-M. (Eds.), *Airport Slots: International Experiences and Options for Reform*, Milton Park, Abingdon, Oxon: Routledge, 2016.

Dagtoglou, P.D. & Ehlers, P.N. (Eds.), *Airline Liability: A Seminar on Liability and Claims Handling in the Airline and Aerospace Industries*, European Air Law Association Conference Papers 11, Athens: Ant.N. Sakkoulas Publishers, 1997.

Dam, R.D. van, Recent Developments at the European Organization for the Safety of Air Navigation (EUROCONTROL), (1997) 22 *AASL* – Part II 327.

Dempsey, P.S. & Jakhu, R.S. (Eds.), *Routledge Handbook of Public Aviation Law*, Milton Park, Abingdon, Oxon: Routledge, 2017.

Diederiks-Verschoor, I.H.Ph. & Butler, M.A. (Legal adviser), *An introduction to Air Law*, Eighth Revised Edition, Alphen aan den Rijn: Kluwer Law International, 2006.

Doganis, R., *Flying Off Course: The Economics of International Airlines*, Third Edition, London: Routledge, 2002.

Doganis, R., *The Airline Business*, Second Edition, Milton Park, Abingdon, Oxon: Routledge, 2006.

Dunk, von der, F.G. & Tronchetti, F. (Eds.), *Handbook of Space Law*, Cheltenham: Edward Elgar Publishing, 2015.

Elias, B., *Airport and Aviation Security: U.S. Policy and Strategy in the Age of Global Terrorism*, Boca Raton, FL: CRC Press, Taylor & Francis Group, 2009.

Folly, M. & Palmer, N., *The A to Z of U.S. Diplomacy from World War I through World War II*, Lanham, MD: Scarecrow Press, The Rowman & Littlefield Publishing Group, 2010.

Florio, F. de, *Airworthiness: An introduction to Aircraft Certification and Operations*, Third Edition, Kidlington, Oxford: Butterworth-Heinemann, 2016.

Forsyth, P., *et al.* (Eds.), *Liberalization in Aviation: Competition, Co-operation and Public Policy*, Milton Park, Abingdon, Oxon: Routledge, 2016.

Giemulla, E.M. & Weber, L. (Eds.), *International and EU Aviation Law: Selected Issues*, Alphen aan den Rijn: Kluwer Law International, 2011.

Goedhuis, D., *National Airlegislations and the Warsaw Convention*, Dordrecht: Copyright by Springer-Science and Business Media, 1937 (Originally published by Martinus Nijhoff, The Hague in 1937).

Goldhirsch, L.B. (Ed.), *The Warsaw Convention Annotated: A Legal Handbook*, The Hague: Kluwer Law International, 2000.

Haanappel, P.P.C., *The Law and Policy of Airspace and Outer Space: A Comparative Approach*, The Hague: Kluwer Law International, 2003.

Haberfeld, M.R. & Von Hassell, A. (Eds.), *A New Understanding of Terrorism: Case Studies, Trajectories and Lessons Learned*, New York: Springer, 2009 (Ebook).

Hanley, D.P., *Aircraft Operating Leasing: A Legal and Practical Analysis in the Context of Public and Private International Air Law*, Second Edition, Alphen aan den Rijn: Kluwer Law International, 2017.

Harrison, J., *International Aviation and Terrorism: Evolving Threats, Evolving Security*, Milton Park, Abingdon, Oxon: Routledge, 2009.

Havel, B.F. & Sanchez, G.S., The *Principles and Practice of International Aviation Law*, New York: Cambridge University Press, 2014.

Havel, B.F., *Beyond Open Skies: A New Regime for International Aviation*, Alphen aan den Rijn: Kluwer Law International, 2009.

Hodgkinson, D.I. & Johnston, R., *International Air Carrier Liability: Safety and Security*, Milton Park, Abingdon, Oxon: Routledge, 2017.

Honig, J.P., *The Legal Status of Aircraft*, The Hague: Martinus Nijhoff, 1956.

Honnebier, B.P., Collecting EUROCONTROL Air Navigation Charges by Precautionary Arresting the Aviation Fuel of Aircraft in the European Netherlands, *Journaal Luchtrecht*, Liber Amicorum in Honour of Roderick D. van Dam, Special Edition Nr. 2-3Juni 2013, The Hague: Sdu Uitgevers.

Huang, J., *Aviation Safety Through the Rule of Law, ICAO's Mechanisms and Practices*, Aviation Law and Policy Series, Alphen aan den Rijn: Kluwer Law International, 2009 (from: Aviation Safety and ICAO, Dissertation to obtain the degree of Doctor at the Leiden University).

Huang, J., *Aviation Safety and ICAO*, Alphen aan den Rijn: Kluwer Law International, 2009.

Ide, J.J., The History and Accomplishments of the International Technical Committee of Aerial Legal Experts (C.I.T.E.J.A.), 3 *J. Air L. & Com.* 27 (1932).

Johnson, D.H.N., *Rights in Airspace*, Manchester: Manchester University Press, 1965.

Joyner, C.C. (Ed.), *The United Nations and International Law*, Cambridge: Cambridge University Press, 1997.

Joyner, N.D., *Aerial Hijacking as an International Crime*, Dobbs Ferry, NY: Oceana Publications, 1974.

Kamminga, M.S., *The Aircraft Commander in Commercial Air Transportation*, The Hague: Martinus Nijhoff, 1953.

Kean, A. (Ed.), *Essays in Air Law*, The Hague: Martinus Nijhoff Publishers, 1982.

Kittichaisaree, K., *The Obligation to Extradite or Prosecute*, Oxford: Oxford University Press, 2018.

Kozuka, S. (Ed.), *Implementing the Cape Town Convention and the Domestic Laws on Secured Transactions*, Cham: Springer International Publishing, 2017.

Lawrence, R.Z., Drzeniek Hanouz, M. & Moavenzadeh, J. (Eds.), *The Global Enabling Trade Report 2009*, Geneva: World Economic Forum, 2009.

Leloudas, G., *Risk and Liability in Air Law*, London: Informa Law, 2009.

Leonard, T.M. (Ed.), *Encyclopedia of U.S.-Latin-American Relations*, Volume I, Los Angeles, CA: CQ Press, 2012.

Levesque, D. (Ed.), *The History and Experience of the International Cospas-Sarsat Programme for Search and Rescue*, Paris: International Austronautical Federation (IAF), 30 July 2016.

MacKenzie, D., *ICAO: A History of the International Civil Aviation Organization*, Toronto: University of Toronto Press, 2010.

Mankiewicz, R.H., The 1970 Hague Convention, 37 *J. Air L. & Com.* 195 (1971).

Manno, C., Liability Limitations of Warsaw Convention Applicable to the Carrier's Employees (Reed v. Wiser), 52 *St. John's L. Rev.* No. 2, Article 4 (1978).

Marquise, R.A., *Scotbomb: Evidence and the Lockerbie Investigation*, New York: Algora Publishing, 2006.

McWhinney, E., *Aerial Piracy and International Terrorism: The Illegal Diversion of Aircraft and International Law*, Second Revised Edition, Dordrecht: Martinus Nijhoff Publishers, 1987.

Melgar, B.H., *The Transit of Goods in Public International Law*, Leiden: Brill Nijhoff, 2015.

Mendes de Leon, P.M.J. (Ed.), *From Lowlands to High Skies: A Multilevel Jurisdictional Approach towards Air Law*, Essays in Honour of John Balfour, Leiden: Koninklijke Brill, 2013.

Mendes de Leon, P.M.J., *Handboek Internationaal Recht*, Hoofdstuk 22 Luchtrecht, Den Haag: T.M.C. Asser Press, 2014.

Mestral, A.L.C. de, Fitzgerald, P.P. & Ahmad, T.Md (Eds.), *Sustainable Development, International Aviation, and Treaty Implementation*, Cambridge: Cambridge University Press, 2018.

Milde M., *International Air Law and ICAO*, Essential Air and Space Law Volume 4, Series Editor Benkö, M.E., Utrecht: Eleven International Publishing, 2008.

Nasr, K.B., *Arab and Israeli Terrorism: The Causes and Effects of Political Violence, 1936-1993*, Jefferson, NC: McFarland & Company Publishers, 1997.

Nath, R. & Crans, B. (Eds.), *Aircraft Repossession and Enforcement: Practical Aspects*, Volume II, Alphen aan den Rijn: Kluwer Law International and International Bar Association, 2010.

Ndikum, P.F. & Ndikum, S.-D., *Liability Rules Developed by European Union, Australian, United Kingdom and United States of America Courts According to European Community Treaty-Warsaw 1929-Montreal 1999. Cases and Materials*, Volume 3, 2013 Edition, London: Ndikum Publications.

Northrup, C.C. (Ed.), *Encyclopedia of World Trade: From Ancient Times to the Present*, Volumes 1-4, Milton Park, Abingdon, Oxon: Routledge, 2015.

Notten, van, Ph., *Writing on the Wall: Scenario Development in Times of Discontinuity*, Boca Raton, FL: Dissertation.com, 2005.

Olla, Ph. (Ed.), *Commerce in Space: Infrastructures, Technologies, and Applications*, Hersley, PA: Information Science Reference, 2008.

Pelton, J.N., Jakhu, R.S. (Eds.), *Space Safety Regulations and Standards*, Kidlington, Oxford: Butterworth-Heinemann, 2010.

Piera, A. & Gill, M., Will the New ICAO-Beijing Instruments build a Chinese Wall for International Aviation Security?, *Vanderbilt Journal of Transnational Law*, Vol. 47:145 (January 2014).

Price, J.C. & Forrest, J.S., *Practical Aviation Security: Predicting and Preventing Future Threats*, Burlington, MA: Butterworth-Heinemann, 2009.

Rhoades, D.L., *Evolution of International Aviation: Phoenix Rising*, Third Edition, Milton Park, Abingdon, Oxon: Routledge, 2016.

Rinck, G., The International Factors in German Air Transport, 33 *J. Air L. & Com.* 102 (1967).

Rubin, B.M. & Rubin, J.C., *Chronologies of Modern Terrorism*, New York: M.E. Sharpe, 2008.

Saba, J., Worldwide Safe Flight: Will the International Financial Facility for Aviation Safety Help It Happen, 68 *J. Air L. & Com.* 537 (2003).

Sand, P.H., The International Unification of Air Law, 30 *Law Contemp. Prob.* No. 2, 400-424 (Spring 1965).

Schlumberger, C.E. & Weisskopf, N., *Ready for Take-off? The Potential for Low Cost Carriers in Developing Countries*, Washington, DC: The World Bank, 2014.

Schnitker, R.M. & Kaar, van het, D., *Safety Assessment of Foreign Aircraft Programme*, Essential Air and Space Law, Volume 11, Series Editor Benkö, M.E., The Hague: Eleven International Publishing, 2013.

Schwenk, W. & Schwenk, R., *Aspects of International Co-operation in Air and Space Law*, Utrecht Studies in Air and Space Law, Volume 17, The Hague: Martinus Nijhoff Publishers, 1998.

Shaw, M.N., *International Law*, Eighth Edition, Cambridge: Cambridge University Press, 2017.

Stadlmeier, S., *International Commercial Aviation: from Foreign Policy to Trade in Services*: Forum for Air and Space Law, Volume 5, Edited by Marietta Benkö in cooperation with Willem de Graaff, Paris: Editions Frontières, 1998.

Stolzer, A.J., Halford, C.D. & Goglia, J.J. (Eds.), *Implementing Safety Management Systems in Aviation*, Farnham, Surrey: Ashgate Publishing, 2013.

Stolzer, A.J. & Goglia, J.J., *Safety Management Systems in Aviation*, Second Edition, Milton Park, Abingdon, Oxon: Routledge, 2016.

Sweet, K.M., *Aviation and Airport Security: Terrorism and Safety Concerns*, Second Edition, Boca Raton, FL: CRC Press, Taylor & Francis Group, 2008.

Tobin, J., *First to Fly. The Unlikely Triumph of Wilbur and Orville Wright*, London: John Murray Publishers, 2003.

Thomas Jr. A.R., International Economic Regulation of Air Transport I, 1950 *Wash. U.L.Q. 324 (1950)*.

Thomas Jr. A.R. (Ed.), *Aviation Security Management: The Context of Aviation Security Management*, Volume 1, Westport, CT: Praeger Security International, 2008.

Tompkins Jr. G.N., *Liability Rules Applicable to International Air Transport as Developed by the Courts in the United States: From Warsaw 1929 to Montreal 1999*, Alphen aan den Rijn: Kluwer Law International, 2010.

Valdés, A.P., *Greenhouse Gas Emissions from International Aviation: Legal and Policy Challenges*, Essential Air and Space Law, Volume 14, Series Editor Benkö, M.E., The Hague: Eleven International Publishing, 2015.

Verzijl, J.H.W., *International Law in Historical Perspective*. Volume III, Part III State Territory, Leiden: Sijthoff, 1970.

Videla Escalada, F.N., *Aeronautical Law*, Alphen aan den Rijn: Sijthoff & Noordhoff International Publishers, 1979.

Wallace, R.M.M., *International Law*, Third Edition, London: Sweet & Maxwell, 1997.

Wallis, R., *Lockerbie: The Story and the Lessons*, Westport, CT: Praeger Publishers, 2001.

Westra, C., The April 2007 U.S.-EU 'Open Skies' Agreement: A Dream of Liberalization Deferred, 32 *B.C. Int'l & Comp. L. Rev.* 161 (2009).

Završnik, A. (Ed.), *Drones and Unmanned Aerial Systems. Legal and Social Implications for Security and Surveillance*, Cham: Springer International Publishing, 2016.

PUBLIC AND PRIVATE INTERNATIONAL AIR LAW INSTRUMENTS

Convention Relating to the Regulation of Aerial Navigation, signed at Paris on 13 October 1919 [Paris Convention 1919].

Ibero-American Convention on Air Navigation, signed at Madrid, on 1 November 1926 [Madrid Convention 1926].

Pan-American (or Inter-American) Convention on Commercial Aviation, signed at Havana, on 20 February 1928 [Havana Convention 1928].

Convention on International Civil Aviation, signed at Chicago, on 7 December 1944 [Chicago Convention 1944].

Protocol Relating to an Amendment to the Convention on International Civil Aviation, signed at Montreal, on 27 April 1947 [Article 93 *bis*].

Protocol Relating to an Amendment to the Convention on International Civil Aviation, signed at Montreal, on 14 June 1954 [Article 45].

Protocol Relating to an Amendment to the Convention on International Civil Aviation, signed at Montreal, on 14 June 1954 [Articles 48(a), 49(c) and 61].

Protocol Relating to an Amendment to the Convention on International Civil Aviation, signed at Montreal, on 21 June 1961 [Article 50(a)].

Protocol Relating to an Amendment to the Convention on International Civil Aviation, signed at Rome, on 15 September 1962 [Article 48(a)].

Protocol on the Authentic Trilingual Text of the Convention on International Civil Aviation, signed at Buenos Aires, on 24 September 1968 [Trilingual Text].

Protocol Relating to an Amendment to the Convention on International Civil Aviation, signed at New York, on 12 March 1971 [Article 50(a)].

Protocol Relating to an Amendment to the Convention on International Civil Aviation, signed at Vienna, on 7 July 1971 [Article 56].

Protocol Relating to an Amendment to the Convention on International Civil Aviation, signed at Montreal, on 16 October 1974 [Article 50(a)].

Protocol Relating to an Amendment to the Convention on International Civil Aviation, signed at Montreal, on 30 September 1977 [Final Paragraph, Russian Text].

Protocol on the Authentic Quadrilingual Text of the Convention on International Civil Aviation, signed at Montreal, on 30 September 1977 [Quadrilingual Text].

Protocol Relating to an Amendment to the Convention on International Civil Aviation, signed at Montreal, on 6 October 1980 [Article 83 *bis*].

Protocol Relating to an Amendment to the Convention on International Civil Aviation, signed at Montreal, on 10 May 1984 [Article 3 *bis*].

Protocol Relating to an Amendment to the Convention on International Civil Aviation, signed at Montreal, on 6 October 1989 [Article 56].

Protocol Relating to an Amendment to the Convention on International Civil Aviation, signed at Montreal, on 26 October 1990 [Article 50(a)].

Protocol on the Authentic Quinquelingual Text of the Convention on International Civil Aviation, signed at Montreal, on 29 September 1995 [Quinquelingual Text].

Protocol on the Authentic Six-Language Text of the Convention on International Civil Aviation, signed at Montreal, on 1 October 1998 [Six-Language Text].

Protocol Relating to an Amendment to the Convention on International Civil Aviation, signed at Montreal, on 29 October 1995 [Final Paragraph, Arabic Text].

Protocol Relating to an Amendment to the Convention on International Civil Aviation, signed at Montreal, on 1 October 1998 [Final Paragraph, Chinese Text].

Protocol on the Authentic Six-language Text of the Convention on International Civil Aviation, signed at Montreal, on 1 October 1998 [Six-language Text].

Protocol Relating to an Amendment to the Convention on International Civil Aviation, signed at Montreal, on 6 October 2016 [Article 50(a)].

Protocol Relating to an Amendment to the Convention on International Civil Aviation, signed at Montreal, on 6 October 2016 [Article 56].

International Air Services Transit Agreement, signed at Chicago, on 7 December 1944 [Transit Agreement].

International Air Transport Agreement, signed at Chicago, on 7 December 1944 [Transport Agreement].

Multilateral Agreement on Commercial Rights of Non-scheduled Air Services in Europe, signed at Paris, on 30 April 1956 [Paris Agreement 1956].

Multilateral Agreement Relating to Certificates of Airworthiness for Imported Aircraft, signed at Paris, on 22 April 1960 [Paris Agreement 1960].

International Agreement on the Procedure for the Establishment of Tariffs for Scheduled Air Services, signed at Paris, on 10 July 1967 [Paris Multilateral Agreement 1967].

International Agreement on the Procedure for the Establishment of Tariffs for Intra-European Scheduled Air Services, signed at Paris, on 16 June 1987 [Paris Tariff Agreement 1987, replacing Paris Multilateral Agreement 1967].

International Agreement on the Sharing of Capacity on Intra-European Scheduled Air Services, signed at Paris, on 16 June 1987 [Paris Capacity Agreement 1987].

Convention on Offences and Certain Other Acts Committed on Board Aircraft, signed at Tokyo, on 14 September 1963 [Tokyo Convention 1963].

Convention for the Suppression of Unlawful Seizure of Aircraft, signed at The Hague, on 16 December 1970 [The Hague Convention 1970].

Convention for the Suppression of Unlawful Acts Against the Safety of Civil Aviation, signed at Montreal, on 23 September 1971 [Montreal Convention 1971].

Protocol for the Suppression of Unlawful Acts of Violence at Airports Serving International Civil Aviation, Supplementary to the Convention for the Suppression of Unlawful Acts Against the Safety of Civil Aviation, done at Montreal, on 23 September 1971, signed at Montreal, on 24 February 1988 [Montreal Protocol 1988].

Convention on the Suppression of Unlawful Acts Relating to International Civil Aviation, signed at Beijing, on 10 September 2010 [Beijing Convention 2010].

Protocol Supplementary to the Convention for the Suppression of Unlawful Seizure of Aircraft, signed at Beijing, on 10 September 2010 [Beijing Protocol 2010].

Protocol to Amend the Convention on Offences and Certain Other Acts Committed on Board Aircraft [Montreal Protocol 2014].

Convention on the Marking of Plastic Explosives for the Purpose of Detection, signed at Montreal, done at Montreal, on 1 March 1991 (ICAO Doc 9571) [Montreal Convention 1991].

Convention for the Unification of Certain Rules Relating to International Carriage by Air, signed at Warsaw, on 12 October 1929 [Warsaw Convention 1929].

Protocol to Amend the Convention for the Unification of Certain Rules Relating to International Carriage by Air, signed at Warsaw, on 12 October 1929, done at The Hague, on 28 September 1955 [The Hague Protocol 1955].

Convention Supplementary to the Warsaw Convention for the Unification of Certain Rules Relating to International Carriage by Air Performed by a Person Other than the Contracting Carrier, signed at Guadalajara, on 18 September 1961 [Guadalajara Convention 1961].

Protocol to Amend the Convention for the Unification of Certain Rules Relating to International Carriage by Air, signed at Warsaw, on 12 October 1929, as Amended by the Protocol done at The Hague, signed at Guatemala City, on 8 March 1971 [Guatemala City Protocol 1971].

Additional Protocol No. 1 to Amend the Convention for the Unification of Certain Rules Relating to International Carriage by Air, signed at Warsaw, on 12 October 1929, signed at Montreal, on 25 September 1975 (ICAO Doc 9145) [Additional Protocol No. 1].

Additional Protocol No. 2 to Amend the Convention for the Unification of Certain Rules Relating to International Carriage by Air, signed at Warsaw, on 12 October 1929, as Amended by the Protocol done at The Hague on 28 September 1955, signed at Montreal, on 25 September 1975 (ICAO Doc 9146) [Additonal Protocol No. 2].

Additional Protocol No. 3 to Amend the Convention for the Unification of Certain Rules Relating to International Carriage by Air, signed at Warsaw, on 12 October 1929, as Amended by the Protocol done at The Hague on 28 September 1955 and at Guatemala City on 8 March 1971, signed at Montreal, on 25 September 1975 (ICAO Doc 9147) [Additional Protocol No. 3].

Montreal Protocol No. 4 to Amend the Convention for the Unification of Certain Rules Relating to International Carriage by Air, signed at Warsaw, on 12 October 1929, as Amended by the Protocol done at The Hague on 28 September 1955, signed at Montreal, on 25 September 1975 (ICAO Doc 9148) [Montreal Protocol No. 4].

Convention for the Unification of Certain Rules for the International Carriage by Air, signed at Montreal, on 28 May 1999 [Montreal Convention 1999].

Convention on the International Recognition of Rights in Aircraft, signed at Geneva, on 19 June 1948 [Geneva Convention 1948].

Convention for the Unification of Certain Rules Relating to Damage by Foreign Aircraft to Third Parties on the Surface, and Convention for the Unification of Certain Rules Relating to the Precautionary Attachment of Aircraft, signed at Rome, on 29 May 1933 [Rome Convention 1933].

Convention on Damage Caused by Foreign Aircraft to third Parties on the Surface, signed at Rome, on 7 October 1952 [Rome Convention 1952].

Protocol to Amend the Convention on Damage Caused by Foreign Aircraft to Third Parties on the Surface, signed at Rome, on 7 October 1952 [Montreal Protocol 1978].

Convention on Compensation for Damage Caused by Aircraft to Third Parties (General Risks Convention), and Convention on Compensation for Damage to Third Parties, Resulting from Acts of Unlawful Interference Involving Aircraft (Unlawful Interference Compensation Convention) [Montreal Convention 2009].

Convention on International Interests in Mobile Equipment, done at Cape Town, on 16 November 2001 [Cape Town Convention on Mobile Equipment 2001].

Protocol to the Convention on International Interests in Mobile Equipment on Matters Specific to Aircraft Equipment [Cape Town Protocol on Aircraft].

Agreement on the Joint Financing of Certain Air Navigation Services in Iceland (1956, as amended by the Montreal Protocol of 1982, signed at Geneva, on 25 September 1956 [Joint Financing Iceland].

Protocol for the Amendment of the 1956 Agreement of the Joint Financing of Certain Air Navigation Services in Greenland and the Faroe Islands, signed at Montreal, on 3 November 1982.

International Cospas-Sarsat Programme Agreement 1988.

Air Transport Agreement between the Government of the United States and the Government of the Kingdom of the Netherlands, signed at Washington, on 3 April 1957 as amended.

Multilateral Agreement on the Liberalization of International Air Transportation (MAL-IAT), done at Washington, on 1 May 2001 by the Asia-Pacific Economic Cooperation Members.

Montreal Intercarrier Agreement, 1966.

IATA Intercarrier Agreement on Passenger Liability [IIA].

Measures to Implement the IATA Intercarrier Agreement [MIA].

DOCUMENTS AND REGULATIONS

Review of Developments in Transport in Asia and the Pacific, 2007, *Data and Trends*, New York: United Nations Economic and Social Commission for Asia and the Pacific.

United Nations General Assembly Resolution 2645 (XXV) Aerial Hijacking or Interference with Civil Air Travel, Twenty-fifth Session, 1914th Plenary Meeting on 25 November 1970.

United Nations General Assembly Resolution 2551 (XXIV) Forcible Diversion of Civil Aircraft in Flight, Twenty-fourth Session, 1831st Plenary Meeting on 12 December 1969.

United Nations A/RES/60/288, Sixtieth Session, Resolution adopted by the General Assembly on 8 September 2006. The United Nations Global Counter-Terrorism Strategy.

Protocol to Amend the Convention for the Unification of Certain Rules Relating to International Carriage by Air, 107th Congress, Second Session, Senate, Treaty Doc 107-14. Message from the President of the United States Transmitting Protocol to Amend the Convention for the Unification of Certain Rules Relating to International Carriage by Air signed at Warsaw on 12 October 1929, done at The Hague, 28 September 1955 (The Hague Protocol), Washington, DC, 2002.

ICAO Aviation Security Manual (ICAO Doc 8973-Restricted).

ICAO Manual on the Regulation of International Air Transport (ICAO Doc 9626).

ICAO Safety Oversight Manual (ICAO Doc 9734 AN/959) Part A, The Establishment and Management of a State's Safety Oversight System.

ICAO Assembly Resolution A10-5: Relationship of ICAO with the European Civil Aviation Conference, superseded by A27-17 and A18-21: Air Transport Work in the Regions – General Policy, also superseded by A27-17.

ICAO Assembly Resolution A27-17: Relationship between ICAO and Regional Civil Aviation Bodies.

ICAO Assembly Resolution A29-13: Improvement of Safety Oversight.

ICAO Assembly Resolution A32-11: Establishment of an ICAO Universal Safety Oversight Audit Programme.

ICAO Assembly Resolution A33-1: Declaration on Misuse of Civil Aircraft as Weapons of Destruction and other Terrorist Acts Involving Civil Aviation.

ICAO Assembly Resolution A39-9: Promotion of the Montreal Convention of 1999.

ICAO Circular 288 LE/1 Guidance Material on the Legal Aspects of Unruly/Disruptive Passengers (June 2002).

ICAO DCCD Doc No. 42, 1/5/09, Convention on Compensation for Damage to Third Parties, Resulting from Acts of Unlawful Interference Involving Aircraft.

U.S. Department of Transportation (DOT) in the Matter of Defining 'Open Skies', Docket 48130, Final Order 92-8-13, issued on 5 August 1992.

Air Commerce Act of 1926. An Act to encourage and regulate the use of aircraft in commerce and for other purposes. It authorized the Secretary of Commerce to regulate the design of aircraft and materials used in their construction, as well as the safety and maintenance of airways, airports and air navigation facilities (Dempsey, 2013, McGill University).

Cape Town Treaty Implementation Act (Public Law No. 108-297, 08/09/2004).

Globalization, Transport and the Environment, Policy Instruments to Limit Negative Environmental Impacts: International Law, 10.2. International Air Transport, OECD 2000.

Convention on International Civil Aviation, done at Chicago on the 7th day of December 1944 (Authentic Text).

IATA Annual Review 2018, Industry Story in 2017. IATA – Future of the Airline Industry 2035.

EU Commission. Mobility and Transport. *Air Transport Agreement between the European Union and the United States of America*, 2007.

Regulation (EC) No. 2343/90 of 24 July 1990 on access for air carriers to scheduled intra-Community air service routes and on sharing of passenger capacity between air carriers on scheduled air services between Member States, *Official Journal of the European Communities* L 217/8, 11.8.90.

Council Regulation (EEC) No. 3922/91 of 16 December 1991 on the harmonization of technical requirements and administrative procedures in the field of civil aviation, *Official Journal of the European Communities* L 373/4, 31.12.91.

Council Regulation (EEC) No. 2407/92 of 23 July 1992 on licensing of air carriers, *Official Journal of the European Communities* L240/1, 24.8.92.

Council Regulation (EEC) No. 2408/92 of 23 July 1992 on access for Community air carriers to intra-Community air routes, *Official Journal of the European Communities* L 240/8, 24.8.92.

Council Regulation (EEC) No. 2409/92 of 23 July 1992 on fares and rates for air carriers, *Official Journal of the European Communities* L 240/15, 24.8.92.

Council Regulation (EEC) No. 95/93 of 18 January 1993 on common rules for the allocation of slots at Community airports, *Official Journal of the European Communities* L 14/1, 22.1.93.

Council Regulation (EC) No. 2027/97 of 9 October 1997 on air carrier liability in respect of the carriage of passengers and their baggage by air, *Official Journal of the European Communities* L 285/1, 17.10.97.

Regulation (EC) No. 889/2002 of the European Parliament and of the Council of 13 May 2002 amending Council Regulation (EC) No. 2027/97 on air carrier liability in the event of accidents, *Official Journal of the European Communities* L 140/2, 30.5.2002.

Regulation (EC) No. 1592/2002 of the European Parliament and of the Council of 15 July 2002 on common rules in the field of civil aviation and establishing a European Aviation Safety Agency, *Official Journal of the European Union* L 240/1, 7.9.2002.

Regulation (EC) No. 2320/2002 of the European Parliament and of the Council of 16 December 2002 establishing common rules in the field of civil aviation security, *Official Journal of the European Communities* L 355/1, 30.12.2002.

Regulation (EC) No. 549/2004 of the European Parliament and of the Council of 10 March 2004 laying down the framework for the creation of the single European sky, *Official Journal of the European Union* L 96/1, 31.3.2004.

Regulation (EC) No. 550/2004 of the European Parliament and of the Council of 10 March 2004 on the provision of air navigation services in the single European sky, *Official Journal of the European Union* L96/10, 31.3.2004.

Regulation (EC) No. 551/2004 of 10 March 2004 of the European Parliament and of the Council on the organization and use of the airspace in the single European sky (the airspace Regulation), *Official Journal of the European Union* L 096/20, 31.3.2004.

Regulation (EC) No. 552/2004 of the European Parliament and of the Council of 10 March 2004 on the interoperability of the European Air Traffic Management network (the interoperability Regulation), *Official Journal of the European Union* L 96/26, 31.3.2004.

Regulation (EC) No. 785/2004 of the European Parliament and of the Council of 21 April 2004 on insurance requirements for air carriers and aircraft operators, *Official Journal of the European Union* L 138/1, 30.4.2004.

Regulation (EC) No. 793/2004 of the European Parliament and of the Council of 21 April 2004 amending Council Regulation (EEC) No. 95/93 on common rules for the allocation of slots at Community airports, *Official Journal of the European Union* L 138/50, 30.4.2004.

Regulation (EC) No. 847/2004 of the European Parliament and of the Council of 29 April 2004 on the negotiation and implementation of air services agreements between Member States and third countries, *Official Journal of the European Union* L157/7, 30.4.2004.

Regulation (EC) No. 2111/2005 of the European Parliament and of the Council of 14 December 2005 on the establishment of a Community list of air carriers subject to an operating ban within the Community and informing air transport passengers of the identity of the operating air carrier, and repealing Article 9 of Directive 2004/36/EC, *Official Journal of the European Union* L 344/15, 27.12.2005.

Commission Regulation (EC) No. 2150/2005 of 23 December 2005 laying down common rules for the flexible use of airspace, *Official Journal of the European Union* L 342/20, 24.12.2005.

Council Regulation (EC) 219/2007 of 27 February 2007 on the establishment of a Joint Undertaking to develop the new generation European air traffic management system (SESAR), *Official Journal of the European Union* L 64/1, 2.3.2007.

Regulation (EC) No. 216/2008 of the European Parliament and of the Council of 20 February on common rules in the field of civil aviation and establishing a European Aviation Safety Agency, and repealing Council Directive 91/670/EEC, Regulation (EC) No. 1592/2002 and Directive 2004/36/EC, *Official Journal of theEuropean Union* L 79/1, 19.3.2008.

Regulation (EC) No. 300/2008 of the European Parliament and of the Council of 11 March 2008 on common rules in the field of civil aviation security and repealing Regulation (EC) No. 2320/2002, *Official Journal of the European Union* L 97/72, 9.4.2008.

Regulation (EC) No. 1008/2008 of 24 September 2008 on common rules for the operation of air services in the Community (Recast), *Official Journal of the European Union* L 293/3, 31.10.2008.

Regulation (EC) No. 1361/2008 of 16 December 2008 amending Regulation (EC) No. 219/2007 on the establishment of a Joint Undertaking to develop the new generation European air traffic management system (SESAR), *Official Journal of the European Union* L352/12, 31.12.2008.

Commission Regulation (EC) No. 272/2009 of 2 April 2009 supplementing the common basic standards on civil aviation security laid down in the Annex to Regulation (EC) No. 300/2008 of the European Parliament and of the Council, *Official Journal of the European Union* L 91/7, 3.4.2009.

Regulation (EC) No. 1070/2009 of the European Parliament and of the Council of 21 October 2009 amending Regulations (EC) No. 549/2004, (EC) No. 550/2004, (EC) No. 551/2004 and (EC) No. 552/2004 in order to improve the performance and sustainability of the European aviation system, *Official Journal of the European Union* L 300/34, 14.11.2009.

Regulation (EC) No. 1108/2009 of the European Parliament and of the Council of 21 October 2009 amending Regulation (EC) No. 216/2008 in the field of aerodromes, air traffic management and air navigation services and repealing Directive 2006/23/EC, *Official Journal of the European Union* L 309/51, 24.11.2009.

Commission Regulation (EU) No. 285/2010 of 6 April 2010 amending Regulation (EC) No. 785/2004 of the European Parliament and of the Council on insurance requirements for air carriers and aircraft operators, *Official Journal of the European Union* L 87/19, 7.4.2010.

Commission Regulation (EU) No. 691/2010 of 29 July 2010 laying down a performance scheme for air navigation services and network functions and amending Regulation (EC) No. 2096/2005 laying down common requirements for the provision of air navigation services, *Official Journal of the European Union* L 201/1, 3.8.2010.

Regulation (EU) No. 996/2010 of the European Parliament and of the Council of 20 October 2010 on the investigation and prevention of accidents and incidents in civil aviation and repealing Directive 94/56/EC, *Official Journal of the European Union* L 295/35, 12.11.2010.

Commission Regulation (EU) No. 677/2011 of 7 July 2011 laying down detailed rules for the implementation of air traffic management (ATM) network functions and amending Regulation (EU) No. 691/2010, *Official Journal of the European Union* L 185/1, 15.7.2011.

Commission Regulation (EU) No. 965/2012 of 5 October 2012 laying down technical requirements and administrative procedures related to Air Operations pursuant to Regulation (EC) No. 216/2008 of the European Parliament and of the Council, *Official Journal of the European Union* L 296/1, 25.10.2012.

Commission Implementing Regulation (EU) No. 409/2013 of 3 May 2013 on the definition of common projects, the establishment of governance and the identification of incentives supporting the implementation of the European Air Traffic Management Master Plan, *Official Journal of the European Union* L 123/1, 4.5.2013.

Commission Regulation (EU) No. 800/2013 of 14 August 2013 amending Regulation (EU) No. 965/2012 laying down technical requirements and adminstrative procedures related to Air Operations pursuant to Regulation (EC) No. 216/2008 of the European Parliament and of the Council, *Official Journal of the European Union* L 227/1, 24.8.2013.

Regulation (EC) No. 376/2014 of the European Parliament and of the Council of 3 April 2014 on the reporting, analysis and follow-up of occurrences in civil aviation, amending Regulation (EU) No. 996/2010 of the European Parliament and of the Council and Commission Regulations (EC) No. 1321/2007 and (EC) No. 1330/2007, *Official Journal of the European Union* L 122/18, 24.4.2014.

Council Regulation (EU) No. 721/2014 of 16 June 2014 amending Regulation (EC) No. 219/2007 on the establishment of a Joint Undertaking to develop the new generation European air traffic management system (SESAR) as regards the extension of the Joint Undertaking until 2024, *Official Journal of the European Union* L 192/1, 1.7.2014.

Commission Regulation (EU) No. 71/2014 of 27 January 2014 amending Regulation (EU) No. 965/2012 laying down technical requirements and administrative procedures related to Air Operations pursuant to Regulation (EC) No. 216/2008 of the European Parliament and of the Council, *Official Journal of the European Union* L 23/27, 28.1.2014.

Commission Implementing Regulation (EU) No. 716/2014 of 27 June 2014 on the establishment of the Pilot Common Project supporting the implementation of the European Air Traffic Management Master Plan, *Official Journal of the European Union* L 190/19, 28.6.2014.

Commission Implementation Regulation (EU) 2016/1185 of 20 July 2016 amending Implementing Regulation (EU) No. 923/2012 as regards the update and completion of the common rules of the air and operational provisions regarding services and procedures in air navigation (SERA Part C) and repealing Regulation (EC) No. 730/2006, *Official Journal of the European Union* L 196/3, 21.7.2016.

Regulation (EU) No. 2018/1139 of the European Parliament and of the Council of 4 July 2018 on common rules in the field of civil aviation and establishing a European Union Aviation Safety Agency, and amending Regulations (EC) No. 2111/2005, (EC) No. 1008/2008, (EU) No. 996/2010, (EU) No. 376/2014 and Directives 2014/30/EU and 2014/53/EU of the European Parliament and of the Council, and repealing Regulations (EC) No. 552/2004 and (EC) No. 216/2008 of the European Parliament and of the Council and Council Regulation (EEC) No. 3922/91, *Official Journal of the European Union* L 212/1, 22.8.2018.

Council Directive 85/374/EEC of 25 July 1985 on the approximation of the laws, regulations and administrative provisions of the Member States concerning liability for defective products, *Official Journal of the European Communities* L 210/29, 7.8.85.

Council Directive 87/601/EEC of 14 December 1987 on fares for scheduled air services between Member States, *Official Journal of the European Communities* No. L 374/12, 31.12.87.

Council Decision 87/602/EEC of 14 December 1987 on the sharing of passenger capacity between air carriers on scheduled air services between Member States and on access for air carriers to scheduled air-service routes between Member States, *Official Journal of the European Communities* No. L 374/19, 31.12.87.

Council Directive 91/670/EEC of 16 December 1991 on mutual acceptance of personnel licences for the exercise of functions in civil aviation, *Official Journal of the European Communities* No. L 373/21, 31.12.91.

Directive 2004/36/EC of the European Parliament and of the Council of 21 April 2004 on the safety of third-country aircraft using Community airports, *Official Journal of the European Union* L 143/76, 30.4.2004.

Directive 2008/101/EC of the European Parliament and of the Council of 19 November 2008 amending Directive 2003/87/EC so as to include aviation activities in the scheme for greenhouse gas emission allowance trading within the Community, *Official Journal of the European Union* L 8/3, 13.1.2009.

Directive 2014/30/EU of the European Parliament and of the Council of 26 February 2014 on the harmonization of the laws of the Member States relating to electromagnetic compatibility (Recast). *Official Journal of the European Union* L 96/79, 29.3.2014.

Directive 2014/53/EU on the harmonization of the laws of the Member States relating to the making available on the market of radio equipment and repealing Directive 1995/5/EC, *Official Journal of the European Union* L 153/62, 22.5.2014.

COM (1999) 614 final/2, Brussels, 6.12.1999. Communication from the Commission to the Council and the Parliament, the creation of the single European sky.

COM (2006) 169 final, 2006/0058, CNS Brussels, 21.4.2006. Proposal for a: Decision of the Council and the representatives of the governments of the Member States of the European Union, meeting within the Council on the signature and provisional application of the Air Transport Agreement between the European Community and its Member States, on the one hand, and the United States of America, on the other hand. Proposal for a: Decision of the Council and the representatives of the governments of the Member States of the European Union, meeting within the Council on the conclusion of the Air Transport Agreement between the European Community and its Member States, on the one hand, and the United States of America, on the other hand (presented by the Commission).

Air Transport Agreement (between the United States of America and the European Community and its Member States, signed on 25 and 30 April 2007), *Official Journal of the European Union* L 134/4. 25.5.2007.

Air Transport Agreement (between the United States of America, of the first part, and the Member States, being parties to the Treaty on European Union and the Treaty on the Functioning of the European Union and being Member States of the European Union, and the European Union, of the second part, Iceland, of the third part, and the Kingdom of Norway, of the fourth part, *Official Journal of the European Union* L 283/3, 29.10.2011.

Decisions Council. Decision of the Council and the representatives of the governments of the Member States of the European Union, meeting within the Council of 25 April 2007 on the signing and provisional application of the Air Transport Agreement between the European Community and its Member States, of the one hand, and the United States of America, on the other hand, 2007/339/EC, *Official Journal of the European Union* L 134/1, 25.5.2007.

International Agreements. Decision of the Council and the representatives of the governments of the Member States of the European Union, meeting within the Council of 24 June 2010 on the signing and provisional application of the Protocol to Amend the Air Transport Agreement between the United States of America, of the one part, and the European Community and its Member States, of the other part, 2010/465/EU, *Official Journal of the European Union* L 223/1, 25.8.2010.

International Agreements. Decision of the Council and of the representatives of the governments of the Member States of the European Union, meeting within the Council of 16 June 2011 on the signing, on behalf of the Union, and provisional application of the Air Transport Agreement between the United States of America, of the first part, the European Union and its Member States, of the second part, Iceland, of the third part, and the Kingdom of Norway, of the fourth part; and on the signing, on behalf of the Union, and provisional application of the Ancillary Agreement between the European Union and its Member States, of the first part, Iceland, of the second part, and the Kingdom of Norway, of the third part, on the application of the Air Transport Agreement between the United States of America, of the first part, the European Union and its Member States, of the second part, Iceland of the third part, and the Kingdom of Norway, of the fourth part, 2011/708/EU, *Official Journal of the European Union* L 283/1, 29.10.2011.

Ancillary Agreement between the European Union and its Member States, of the first part, Iceland, of the second part, and the Kingdom of Norway, of the third part, of the application of the Air Transport Agreement between the United States of America, of the first part, the European Union and its Member States, of the second part, Iceland, of the third part, and the Kingdom of Norway, of the fourth part (...), 2011/708/EU, *Official Journal of the European Union* L 283/16, 29.10.2011.

Protocol consolidating the EUROCONTROL International Convention relating to Co-operation for the Safety of Air Navigation of 13 December 1960 as variously amended, Brussels, 27 June 1997.

Final Act of the Diplomatic Conference on the Protocol on the accession of the European Community to the EUROCONTROL International Convention relating to Cooperation for the Safety of Air Navigation of 13 December 1960 as variously amended and as consolidated by the Protocol of 27 June 1997, Brussels, 8 October 2002.

Protocol on the accession of the European Community to the EUROCONTROL International Convention relating to Cooperation for the Safety of Air Navigation of 13 December 1960 as variously amended and as consolidated by the Protocol of 27 June 1997, *Official Journal of theEuropean Union* L 304/210, 30.9.2004.

Protocol to amend the Air Transport Agreement between the United States of America and the European Community and its Member States, signed on 25 and 30 April 2007, *Official Journal of the European Union* L 223/3. 25.8.2010.

Communication from the Commission. A European Community contribution to World Aviation Safety Improvement, COM (2001) 390 final, Brussels, 16.7.2001.

Communication from the Commission to the Council and the European Parliament. The creation of the single European sky, COM (2001) 123 final/2, 2001/0060 (COD), Brussels, 30.11.2001.

Communication from the Commission on relations between the Community and third countries in the field of air transport. Proposal for a European Parliament and Council Regulation on the negotiation and implementation of air service agreements between Member States and third countries, COM/2003/0094 final, 2003/0044 (COD), Brussels, 26.2.2003.

Communication from the Commission developing a Community civil aviation policy towards Canada, COM (2006) 871 final, Brussels, 9.1.2007.

SESAR European ATM Master Plan 2017.

ABOUT THE AUTHOR

Dick van het Kaar, LL.M, has been working in the aviation industry for more than 40 years. He started his flying career as a Royal Netherlands Air Force helicopter and jet fighter pilot and instructor. In 1977, he joined the world of commercial aviation and has logged over 23,000 flying hours. During his career as a Senior Captain B747 at KLM/ Martinair he studied international law at the Netherlands Open University, where he earned his degree of Masters of Laws.

He was a member of the Appeal Council of the Dutch Airline Pilots Association and is the author of a variety of aviation law-related essays, books and articles in a number of international air and space law journals. Following a term of six years as a board member at the Royal Netherlands Aeronautical Association, he now holds the positions of Chairman of the Legal Committee and Senior Advisor on Rules of the Air, Airspace Infrastructure and Environmental Affairs within the same organization. In addition, he is an external examiner associated with the Aviation Academy of the Amsterdam University of Applied Sciences.

Dick van het Kaar was born on 30 January 1948, coincidently the day Orville Wright died and Mahatma Gandhi was assassinated.

Essential Air and Space Law (Series Editor: Marietta Benkö)

Volume 1: Natalino Ronzitti & Gabriella Venturini (eds.), The Law of Air Warfare – Contemporary Issues, ISBN 978-90-77596-14-2

Volume 2: Marietta Benkö & Kai-Uwe Schrogl (eds.), Space Law: Current Problems and Perspectives for Future Regulations, ISBN 978-90-77596-11-1

Volume 3: Tare Brisibe, Aeronautical Public Correspondence by Satellite, ISBN 978-90-77596-10-4

Volume 4: Michael Milde, International Air Law and ICAO, ISBN 978-90-77596-54-8

Volume 5: Markus Geisler & Marius Boewe, The German Civil Aviation Act, ISBN 978-90-77596-72-2

Volume 6: Ulrich Steppler & Angela Klingmüller, EU Emissions Trading Scheme and Aviation, ISBN 978-90-77596-79-1

Volume 7: Heiko van Schyndel (ed.), Aviation Code of the Russian Federation, ISBN 978-90-77596-80-7

Volume 8: Zang Hongliang & Meng Qingfen, Civil Aviation Law in the People's Republic of China, ISBN 978-90-77596-91-3

Volume 9: Ronald M. Schnitker & Dick van het Kaar, Aviation Accident and Incident Investigation. Concurrence of Technical, ISBN 978-94-90947-01-9

Volume 10: Michael Milde, International Air Law and ICAO, second edition, ISBN 978-90-90947-35-4

Volume 11: Ronald Schnitker & Dick van het Kaar, Safety Assessment of Foreign Aircraft Programme. A European Approach to Enhance Global Aviation Safety, ISBN 978-94-9094-793-4

Volume 12: Marietta Benkö & Engelbert Plescher, Space Law: Reconsidering the Definition/Delimitation Question and the Passage of Spacecraft through Foreign Airspace, ISBN 978-94-6236-076-1

Volume 13: Heiko van Schyndel (ed.), Aviation Code of the Russian Federation, second edition, ISBN 978-94-6236-433-2

Volume 14: Alejandro Piera Valdés, Greenhouse Gas Emissions from International Aviation: Legal and Policy Challenges, ISBN 978-94-6236-467-7

Volume 15: Peter Paul Fitzgerald, A Level Playing Field for "Open Skies': The Need for Consistent Aviation Regulation, ISBN 978-94-6236-625-1

Volume 16: Jae Woon Lee, Regional Liberalization in International Air Transport: Towards Northeast Asian Open Skies, ISBN 978-94-6236-688-6

Volume 17: Tanveer Ahmad, Climate Change Governance in International Civil Aviation: Toward Regulating Emissions Relevant to Climate Change and Global Warming, ISBN 978-94-6236-692-3

Volume 18: Michael Milde, International Air Law and ICAO, third edition, ISBN 978-94-6236-619-0

Volume 19: Nataliia Malysheva, Space Law and Policy in the Post-Soviet States, ISBN 978-94-6236-847-7

Volume 20: Philippe Clerc, Space Law in the European Context, ISBN 978-94-6236-797-5

Volume 21: Benjamyn Scott, Aviation Cybersecurity: Regulatory Approach in the European Union, ISBN 978-94-6236-961-0

Volume 22: Dick van het Kaar, International Civil Aviation: Treaties, Institutions and Programmes, ISBN 978-94-6236-972-6